AF521973

NY IN THE SNOW

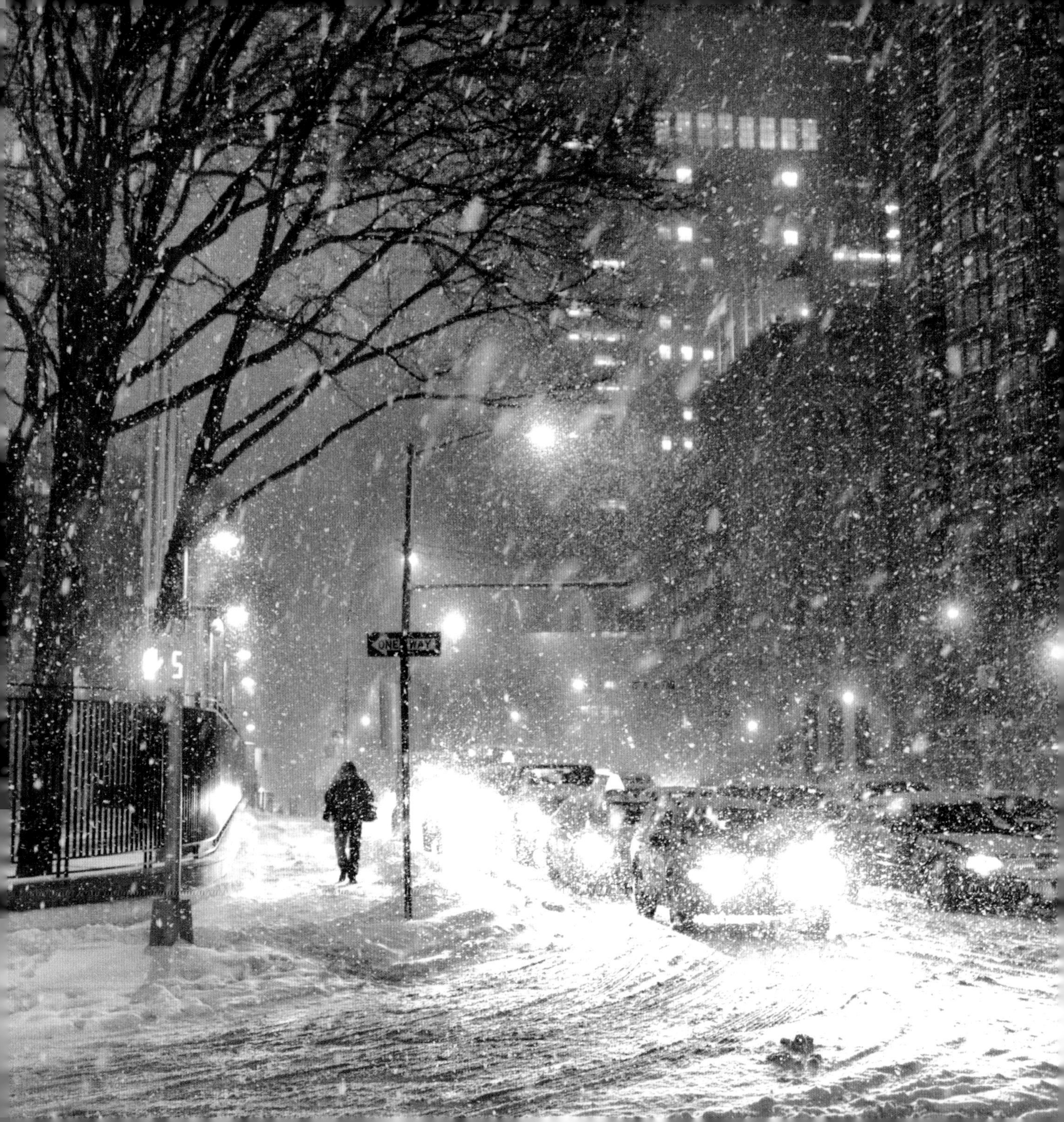
ONE WAY
5

VIVIENNE GUCWA THE HIT PHOTOBLOGGER OF NY THROUGH THE LENS

ilex

NY IN THE SNOW

A MAGICAL VISION OF NEW YORK CITY

An Hachette UK Company
www.hachette.co.uk

First published in Great Britain in 2017 by
ILEX, an imprint of Octopus Publishing Group Ltd
Octopus Publishing Group
Carmelite House
50 Victoria Embankment
London, EC4Y 0DZ
www.octopusbooks.co.uk
www.octopusbooksusa.com

Distributed in the US by Hachette Book Group
1290 Avenue of the Americas, 4th and 5th Floors
New York, NY 10104

Distributed in Canada by Canadian Manda Group
664 Annette St. Toronto, Ontario, Canada M6S 2C8

Publisher, photography: Adam Juniper
Publisher: Roly Allen
Specialist Managing Editor: Frank Gallaugher
Editor: Rachel Silverlight
Art Director: Julie Weir
Design: JC Lanaway
Assistant Production Manager: Lucy Carter

ISBN 978-1-78157-876-6

A CIP catalogue record for this book is available from the British Library

Printed and bound in China

10 9 8 7 6 5 4 3 2 1

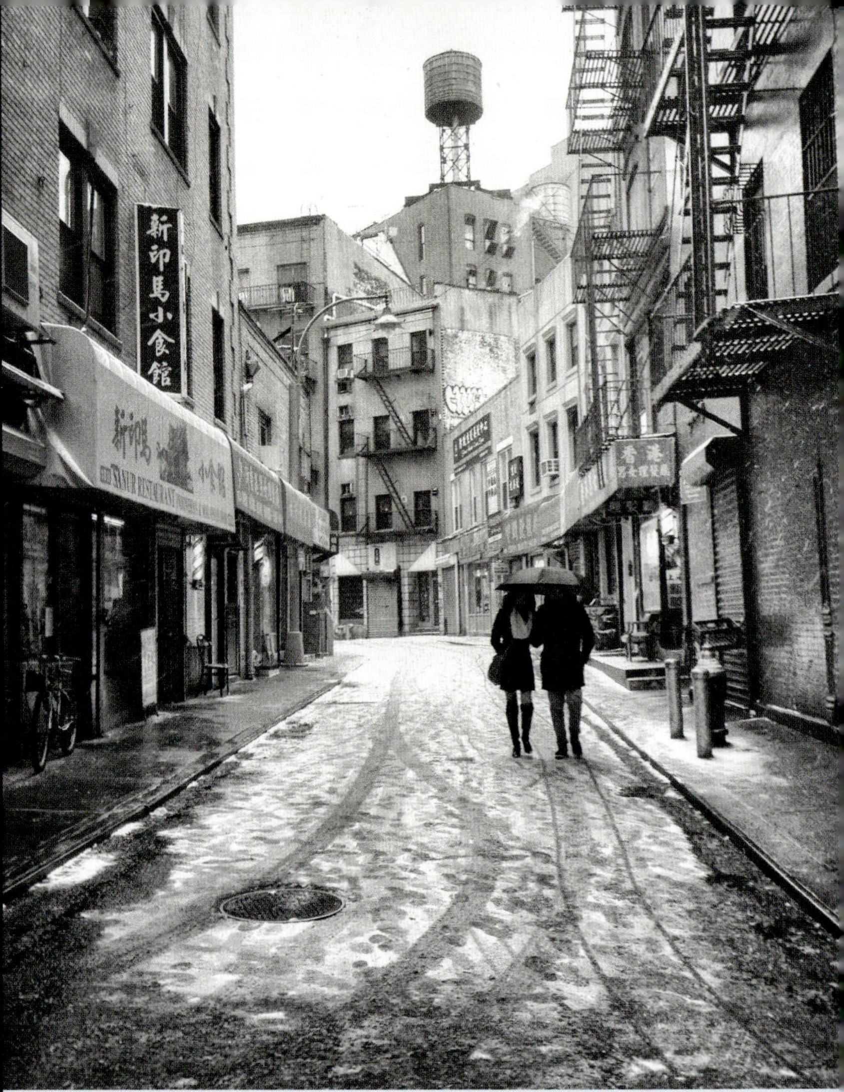

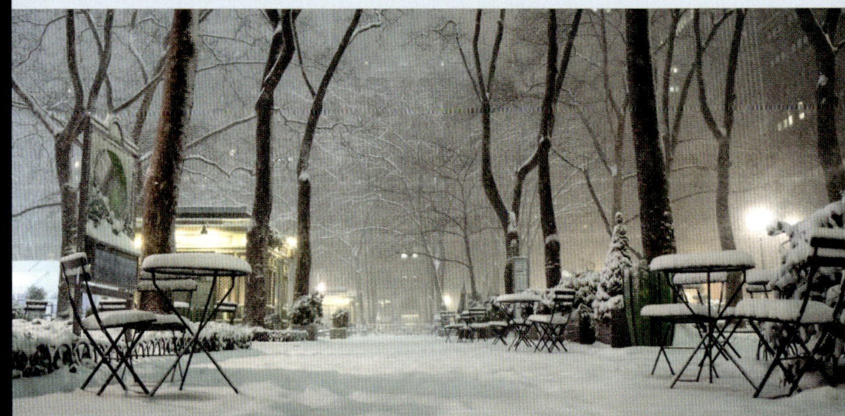

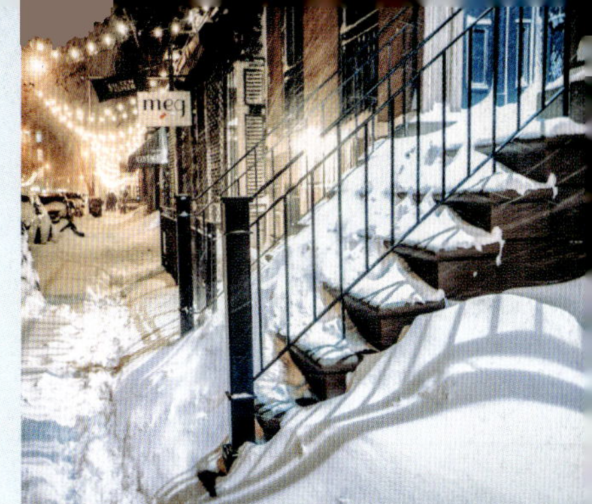
meg

CONTENTS

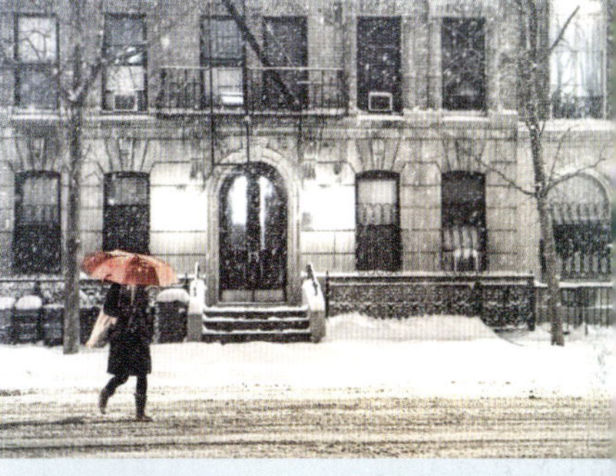

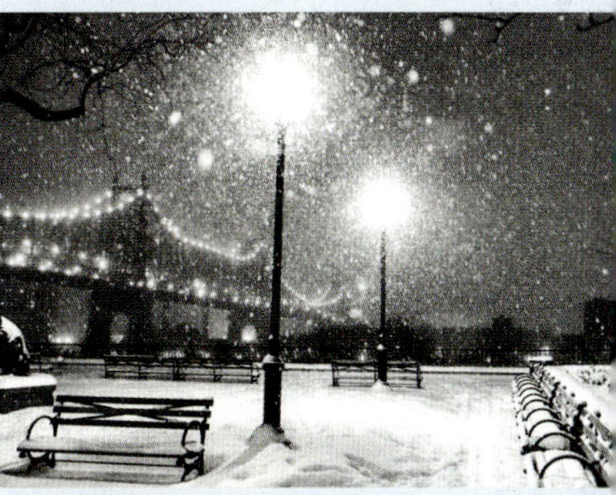

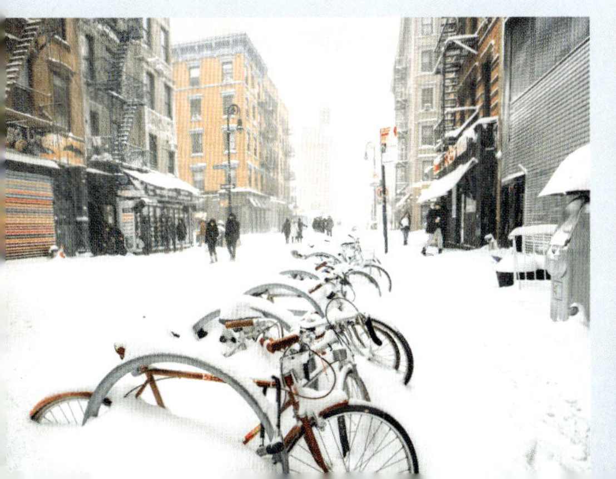

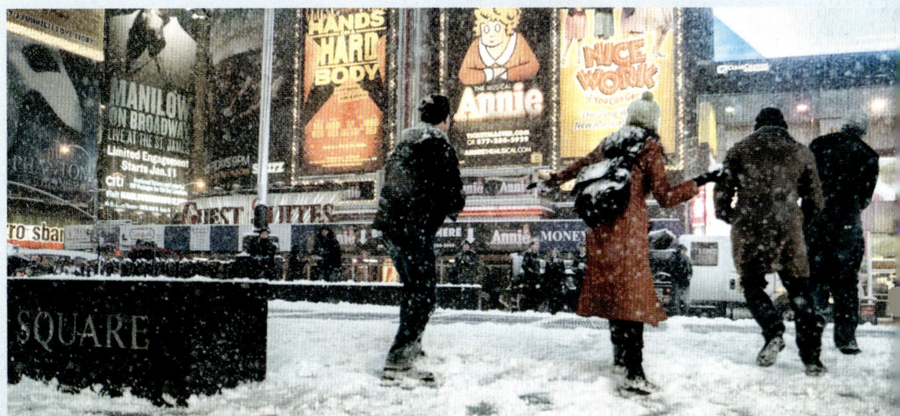
HANDS ON A HARD BODY
MANILOW ON BROADWAY
Annie
NICE WORK
SQUARE

INTRODUCTION

Central Park, Manhattan
Sony SLT-A99V | *f*/5 | 1/60 second | ISO 400

I wish I could say that there was one photo that started it all. It would be the one photo that somehow ignited my passion for snow photography in New York City. The one that people could look at to understand why I might walk up to eight miles through snowstorms at night. But there isn't. That's because my passion for New York in the snow began at a very early age.

I grew up in a financially challenged household in a tumultuous set of circumstances in Queens, New York City. I spent an inordinate amount of my childhood daydreaming and wishing myself into the other lives I either read about in literature or saw in the vast number of movies I watched.

A few memories from that time period stand out as brilliant beacons of light in an otherwise stark and bleak memoryscape. One such memory was getting pulled on a neighbor's sled through the streets of Flushing late at night during a blizzard. I remember looking up at the streetlights through the large fluffy flakes as they cast the most beautiful warm glow over the empty streets. We may not have had a lot in the way of material possessions but in that moment it felt like the city was ours. And there was a gorgeous silence that rooted itself deep inside of me until all of life seemed muffled, silenced into an eerie submission, and all that was left was the purest feeling of peace.

That particular silence resonated so loud that it became the moment I would replay over and over again at night as I drifted off to sleep. It wasn't until I discovered photography accidentally in 2010 and decided to trek through Central Park in a blizzard with camera in hand that I even thought I could attempt to convey how that childhood memory had made such an indelible impression on my soul.

My photography has been an exploration of both isolation and nostalgia, and I have found that my snow photography in New York City has often unconsciously tackled both themes, sometimes at the same time. In a city of millions, isolation is something I have grappled with personally, especially since it seems to go hand in hand with anxiety. Loneliness is one of the most visceral states of being when surrounded by millions of people, and that sense of isolation becomes super apparent on nights when the snow blankets the streets and only a few people walk the streets.

At the same time, snow is also the embodiment of different forms of nostalgia. It's the nostalgia for what once was, but also the nostalgia for what could be. It's the warm cocoon that transports us into an ethereal in-between realm where cities can suddenly become silent and empty. It's longing and fairytales wrapped up in a beautiful fleeting package. It's the embodiment of metaphorical ephemerality.

When I return back to my apartment after walking seven or eight miles through the snow, it's as if I have walked through dreams all night, sleepwalking through an almost empty city. And it's one of the most incredible feelings I have ever experienced.

My greatest wish with these images is to share that feeling with all of you. May you enjoy dreamwalking with me through this book.

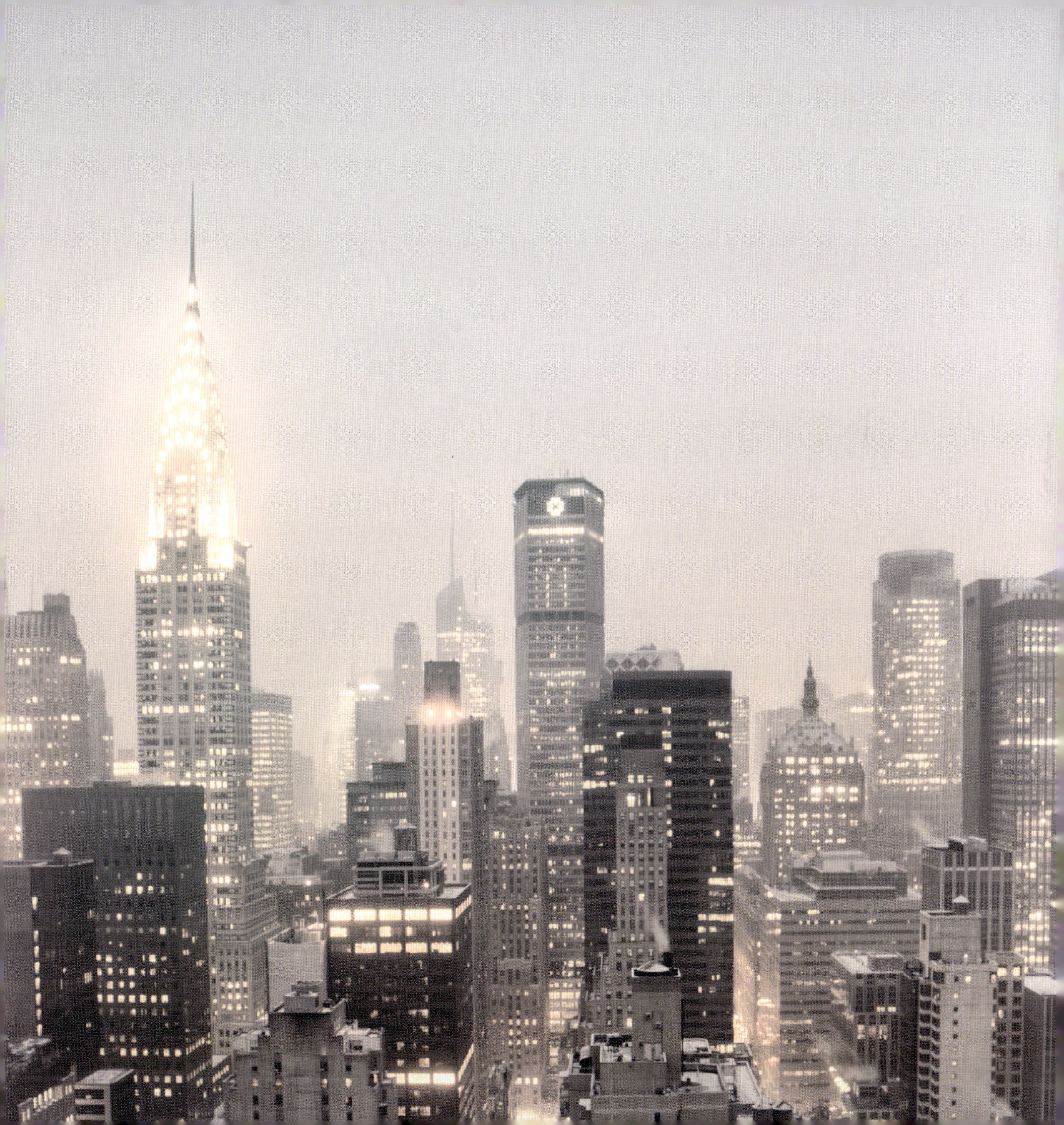

CHAPTER #1 | # SILENCE

"I love the surreality of snowstorms in NYC. Familiar neighborhood places take on an otherworldly feel. The snow adds a dimension of serene strangeness to a city that is defined by its capacity to change instantaneously.

Central Park, Manhattan
Sony SLT-A99V | *f*/7 | 1/160 second | ISO 200

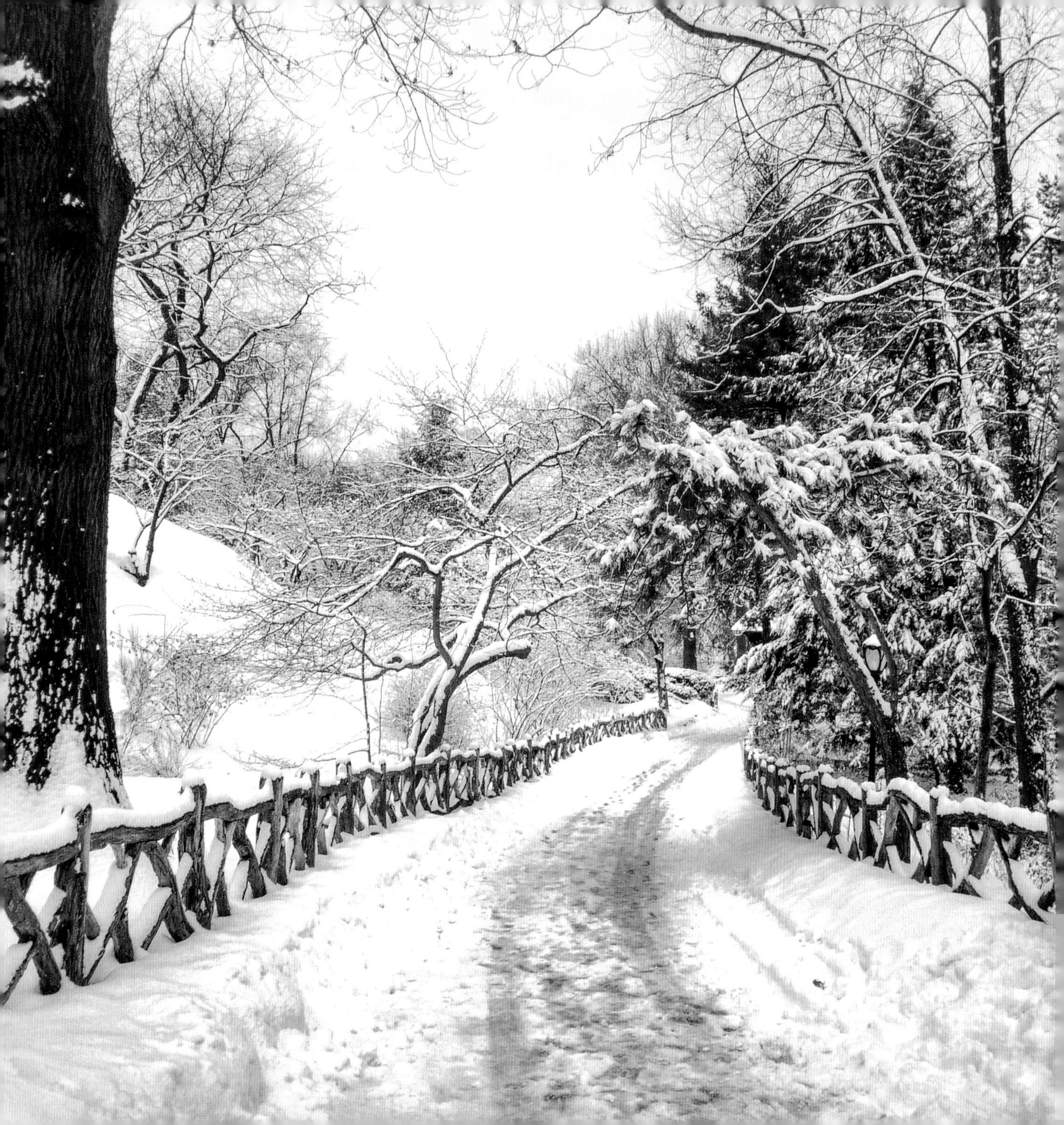

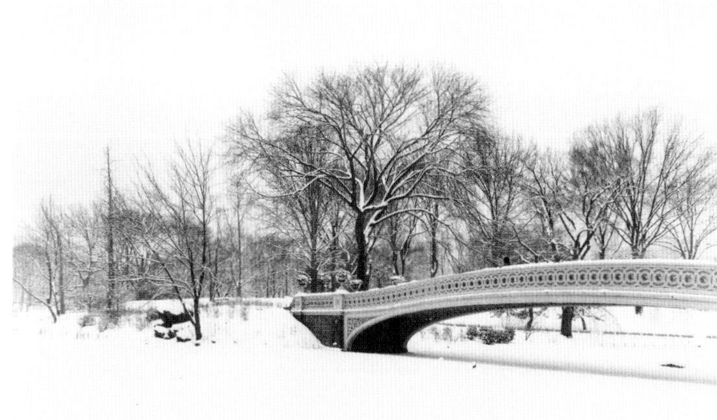

Bow Bridge—Central Park, Manhattan
Sony SLT-A55V | f/5.6 | 1/200 second | ISO 200

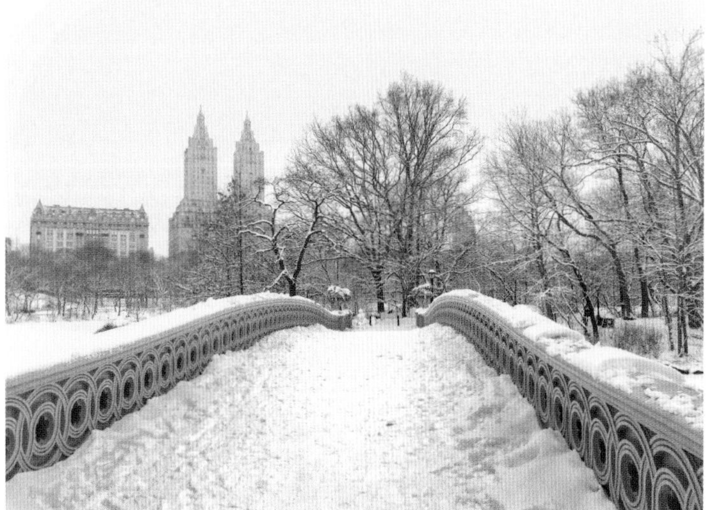

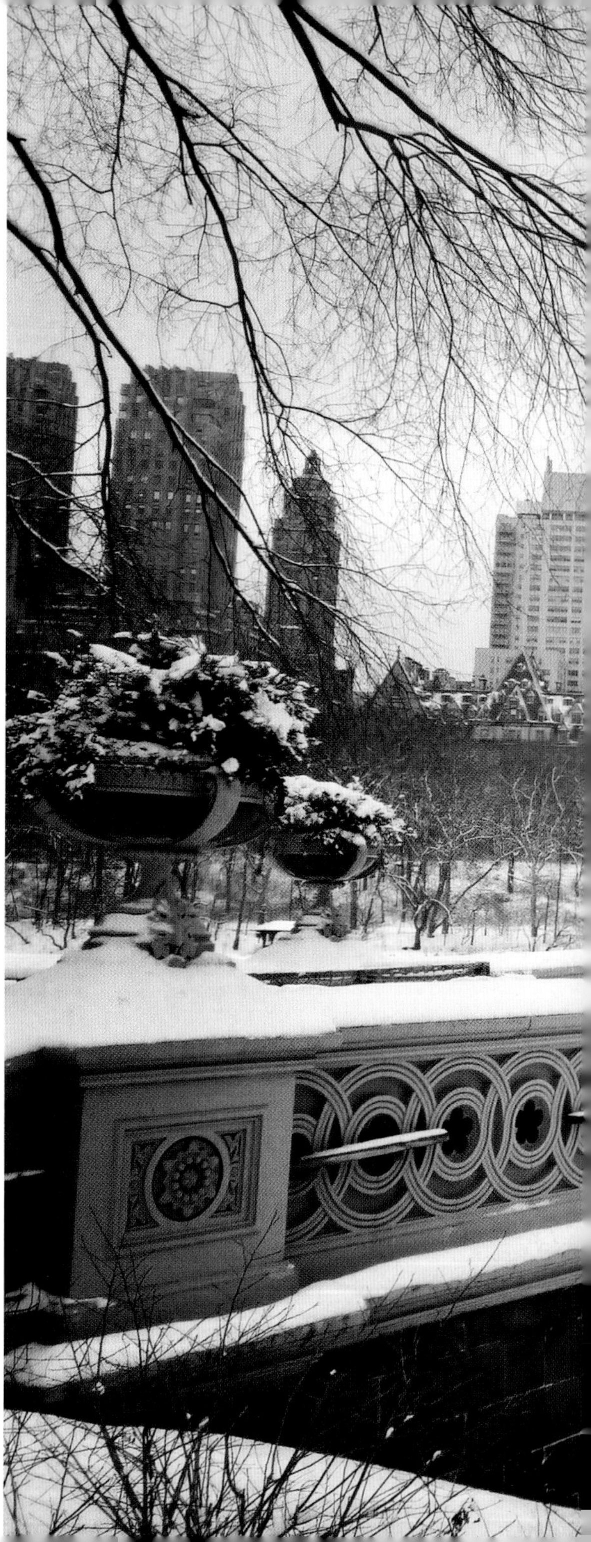

Bow Bridge—Central Park, Manhattan
Panasonic DMC-FZ35 | f/5.6 | 1/200 second | ISO 200

Bow Bridge—Central Park, Manhattan
Sony SLT-A55V | f/4 | 1/200 second | ISO 200

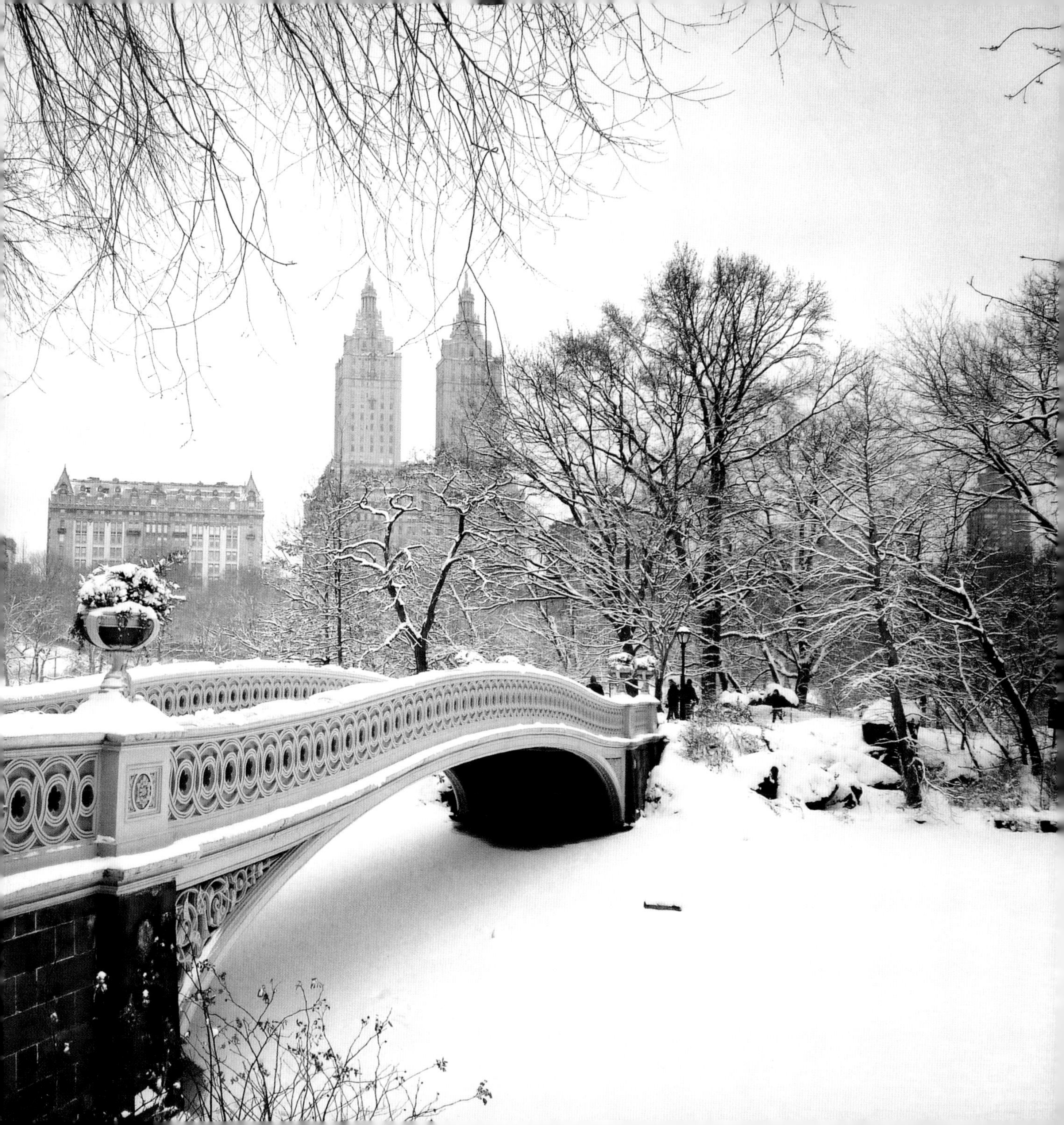

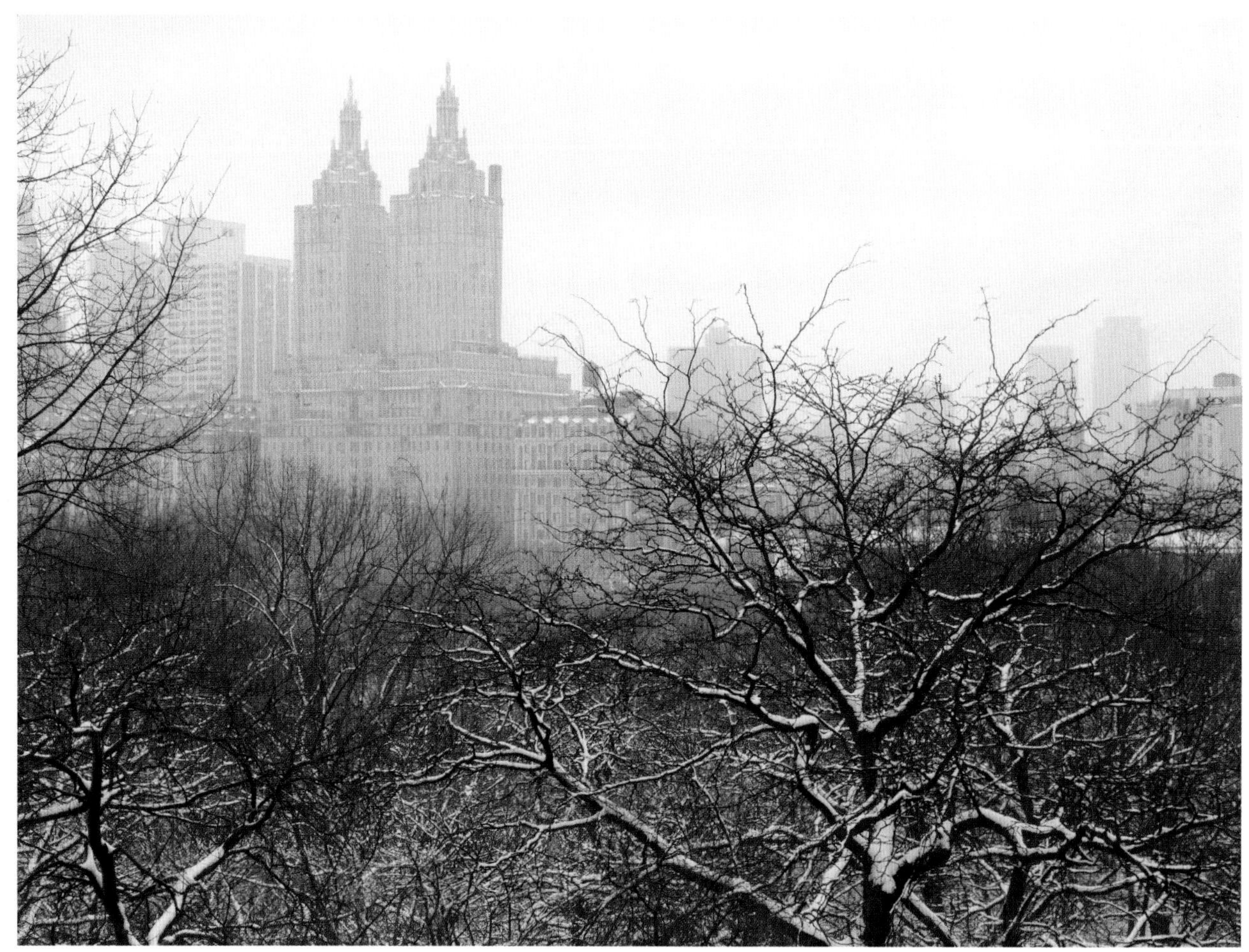

▲ Central Park, Manhattan
Sony SLT-A55V | *f*/7 | 1/160 second | ISO 200

▶ Central Park, Manhattan
Sony SLT-A55V | *f*/7 | 1/160 second | ISO 200

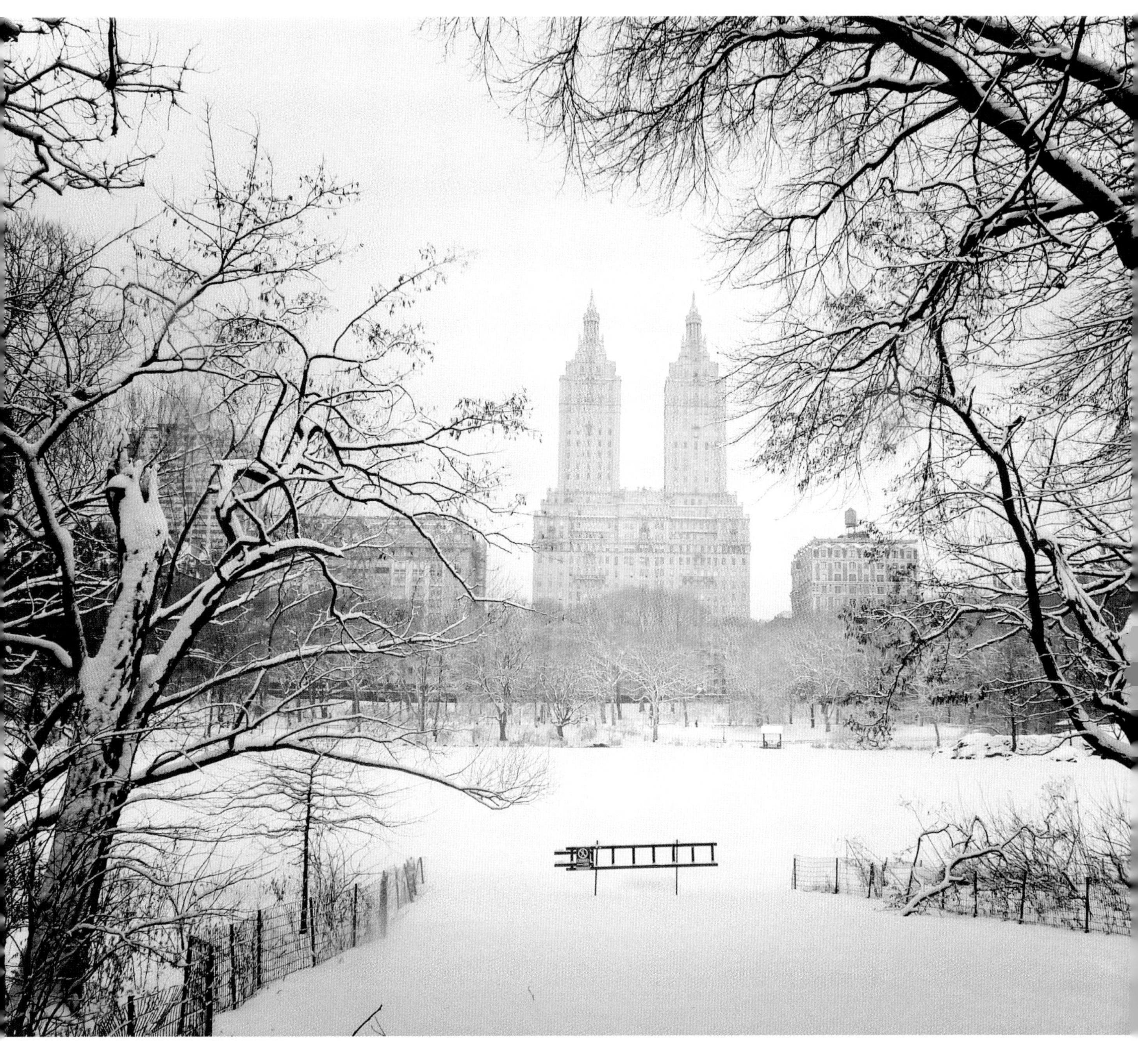

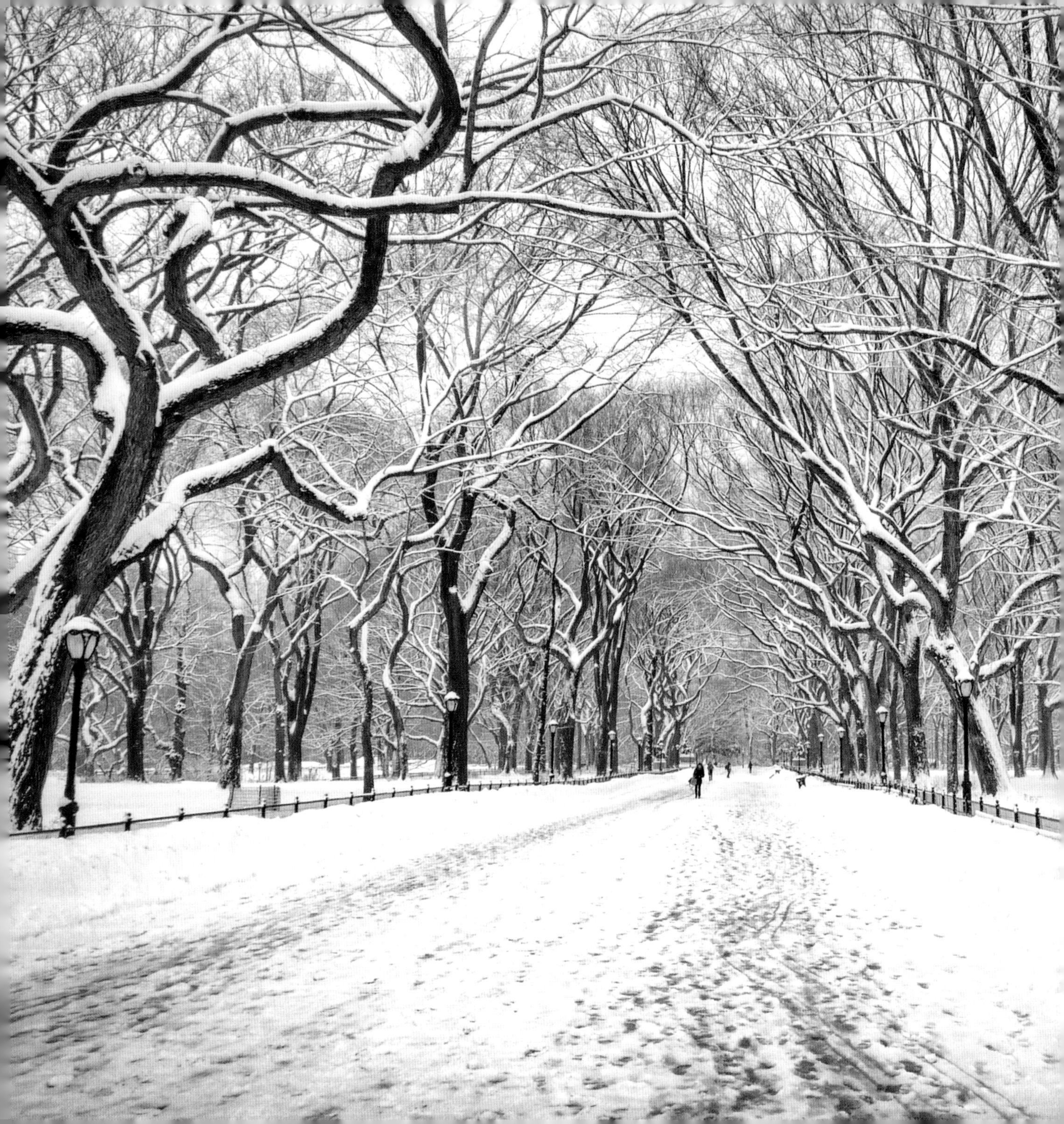

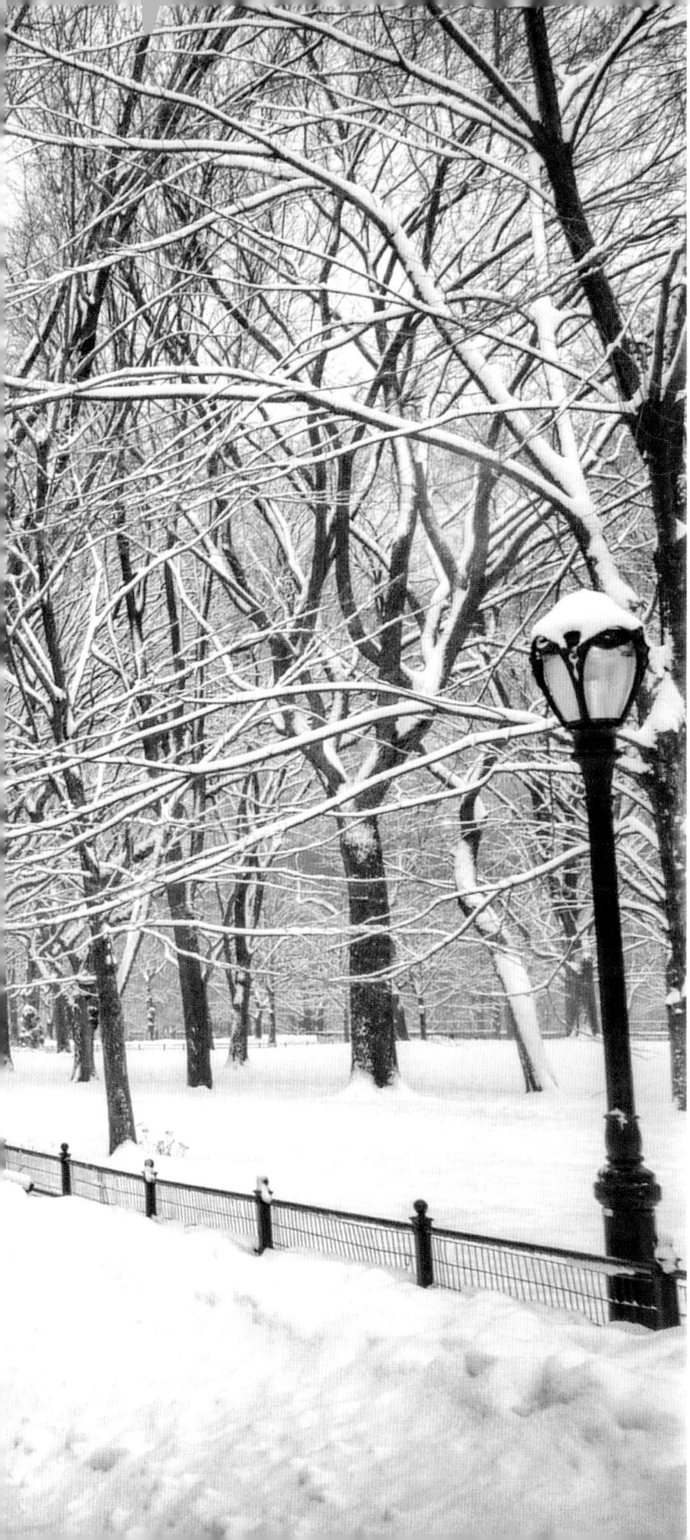

Central Park, Manhattan
Sony SLT-A99V | *f*/4.5 | 1/80 second | ISO 400

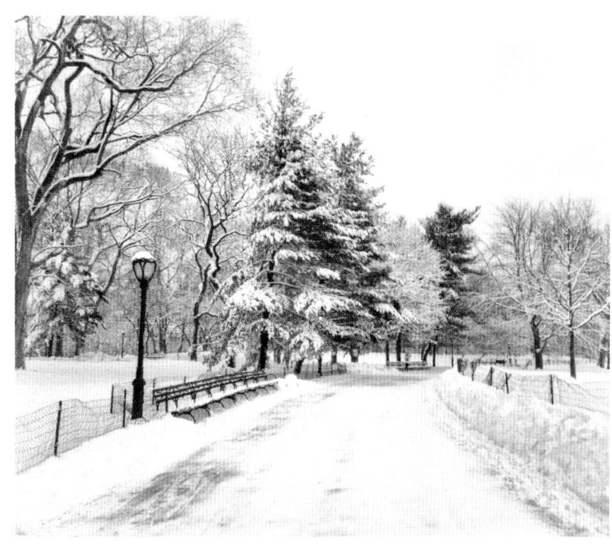

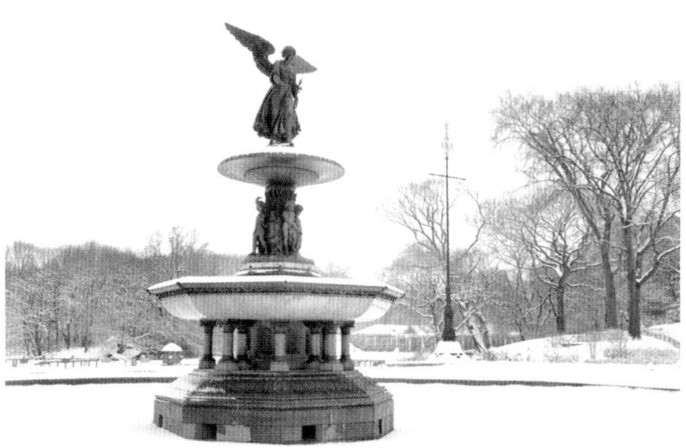

Angel of the Waters—Central Park, Manhattan
Panasonic DMC-FZ35 | *f*/5.6 | 1/200 second | ISO 200

The Mall—Central Park, Manhattan
Sony SLT-A55V | *f*/5 | 1/100 second | ISO 200

Winter's silence is deafening
as the earth pauses,
swallowed by the engulfing
embrace of serenity.

Memories sit suspended like
words caught momentarily
in the throat of winter: stifled
tales of yesteryear wrapped
in a blanket of alabaster.

And dreams sputter, breaking
through shards of branches,
conjuring up the outline of
buildings and cityscapes.

Trees stretch their fragile limbs
as winter muffles the earth,
silencing its yearnings, until
all at once there is peace.

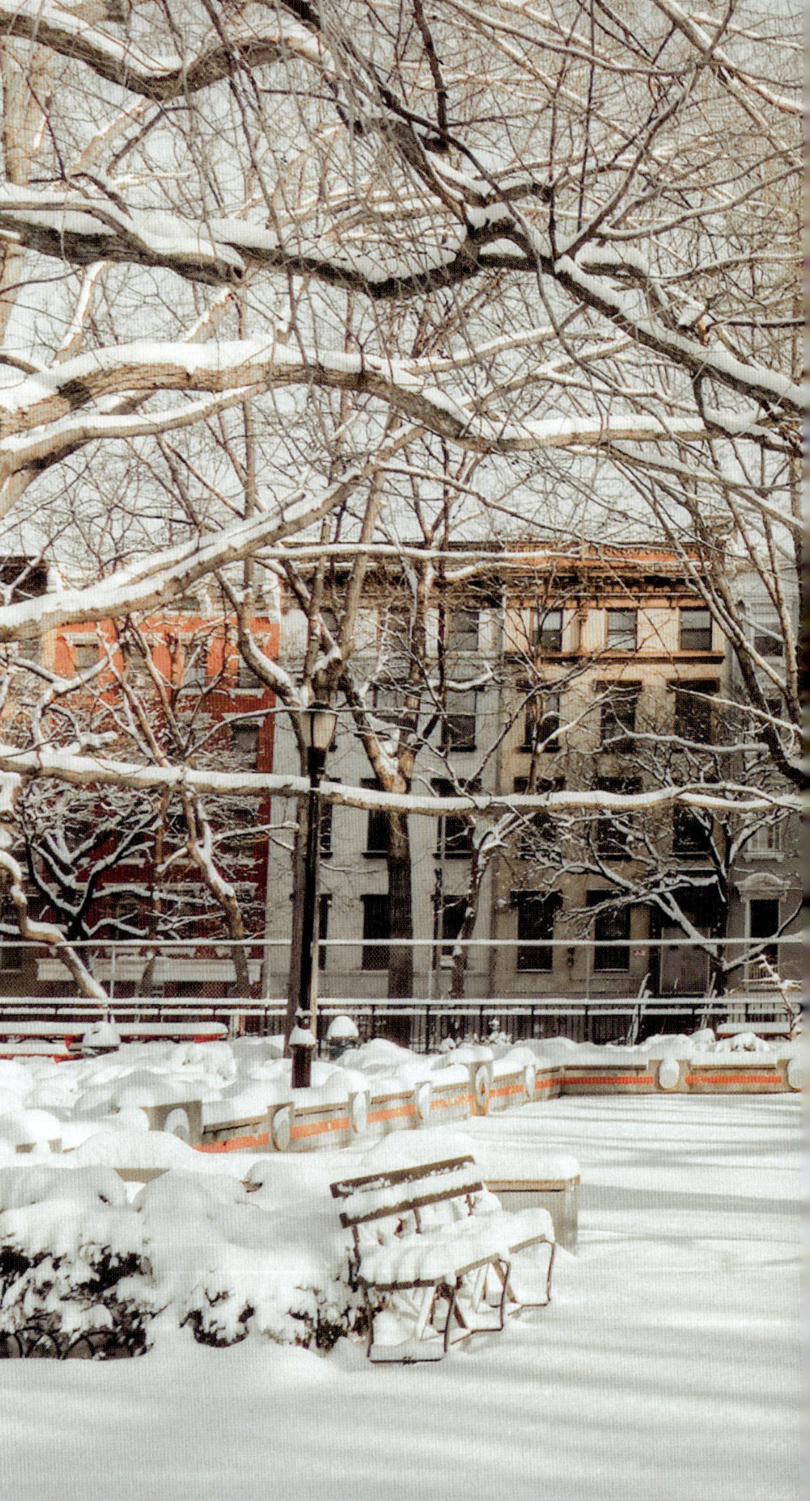

Central Park, Manhattan
Sony SLT-A55V | *f*/5 | 1/60 second | ISO 400

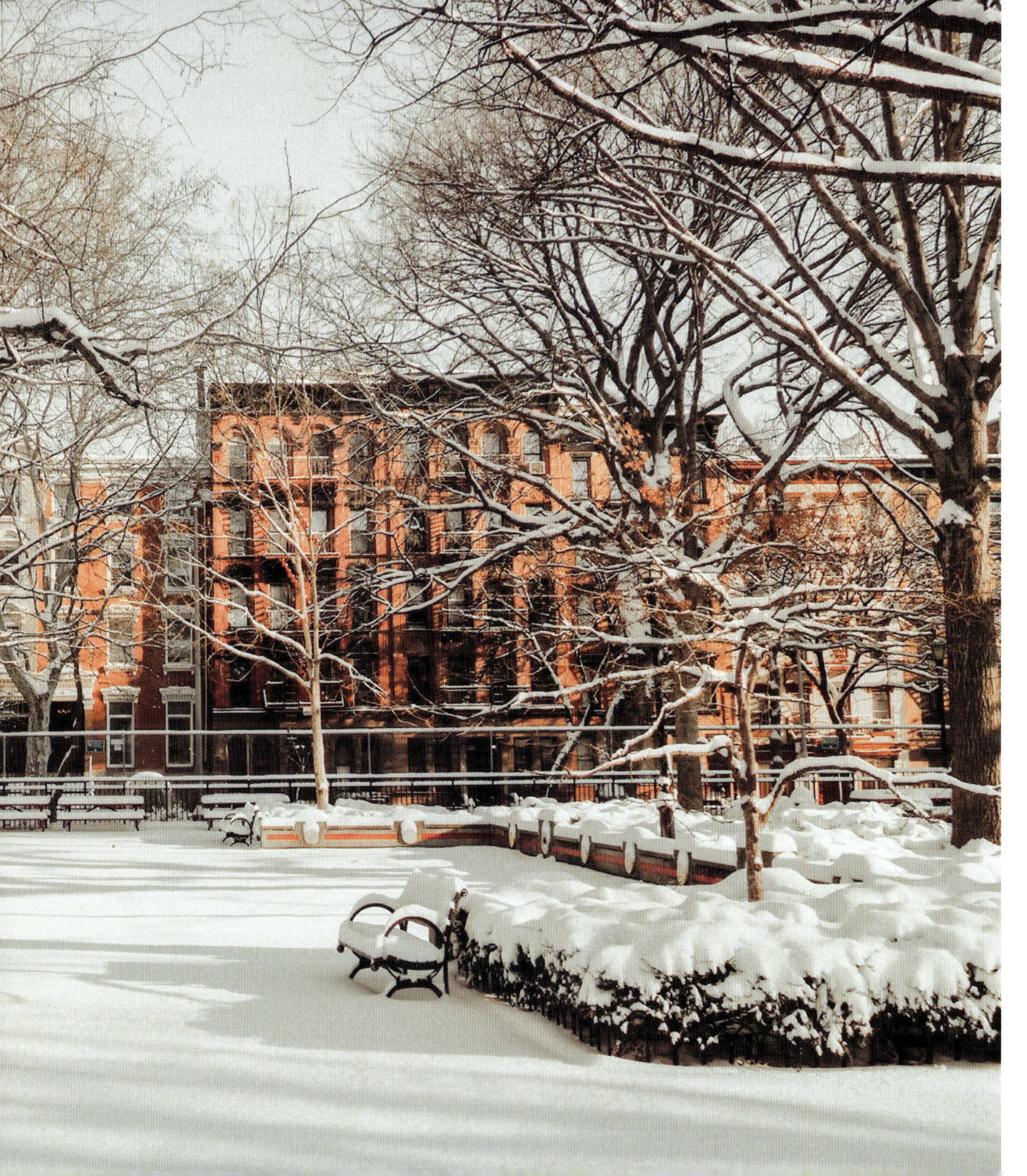

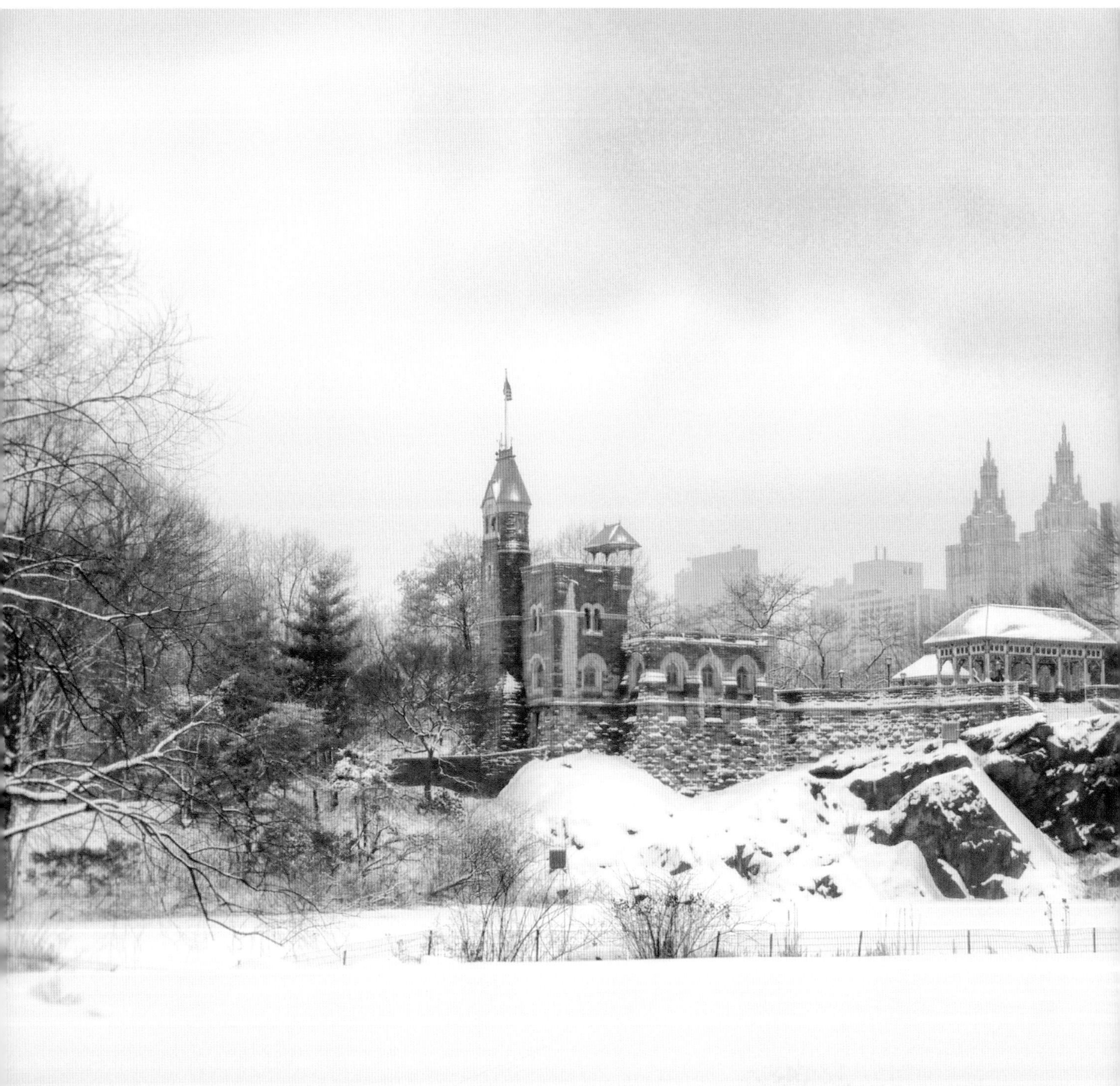

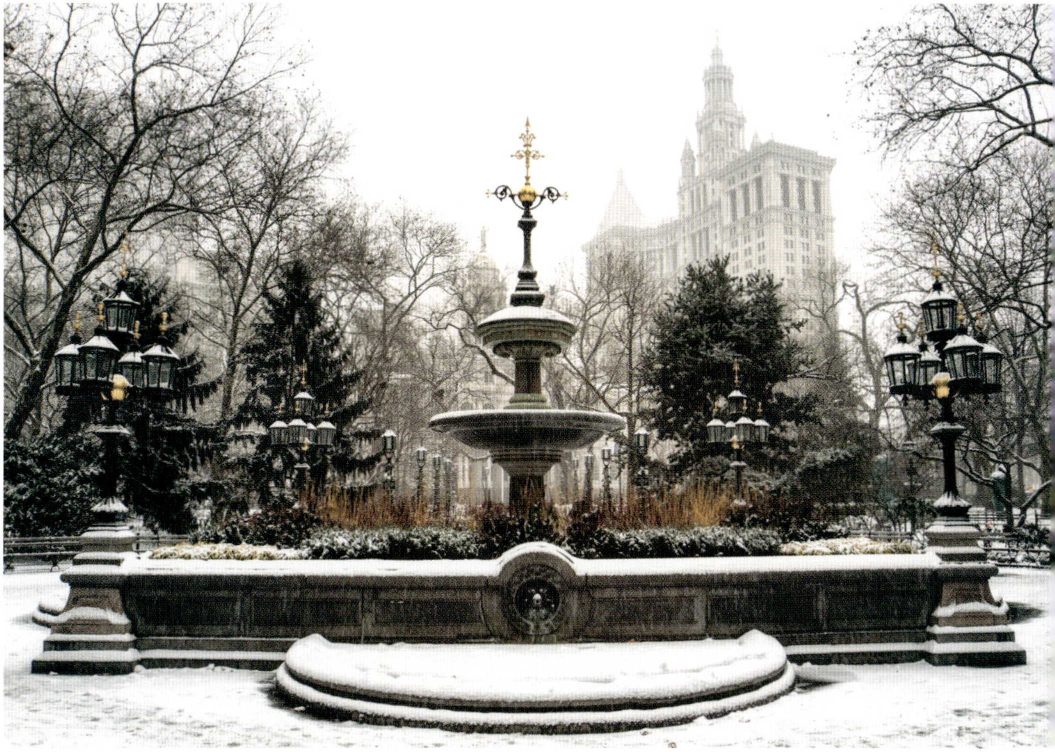

City Hall Park, Lower Manhattan
Sony NEX-6 | *f*/5 | 1/60 second | ISO 100

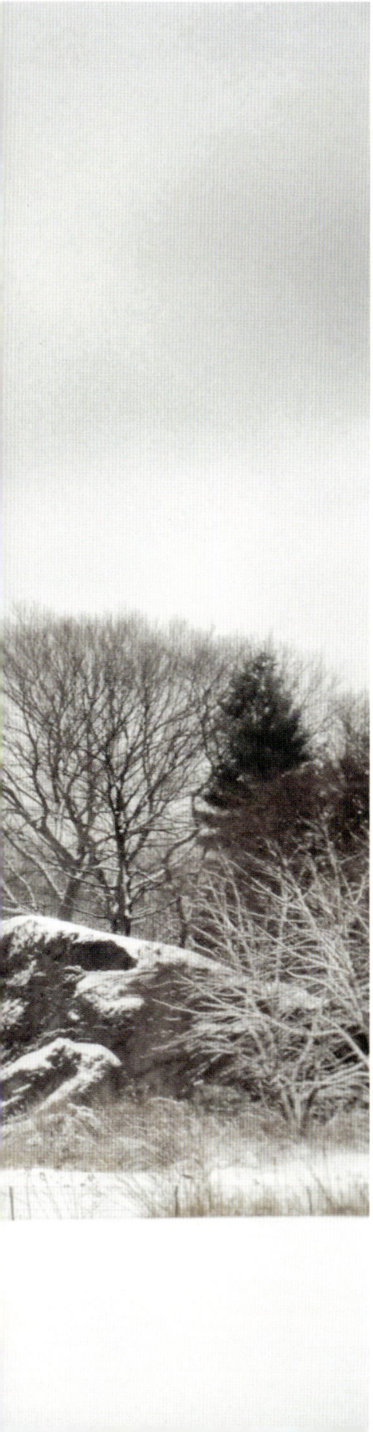

Belvedere Castle—Central Park, Manhattan
Sony SLT-A99V | *f*/5 | 1/200 second | ISO 400

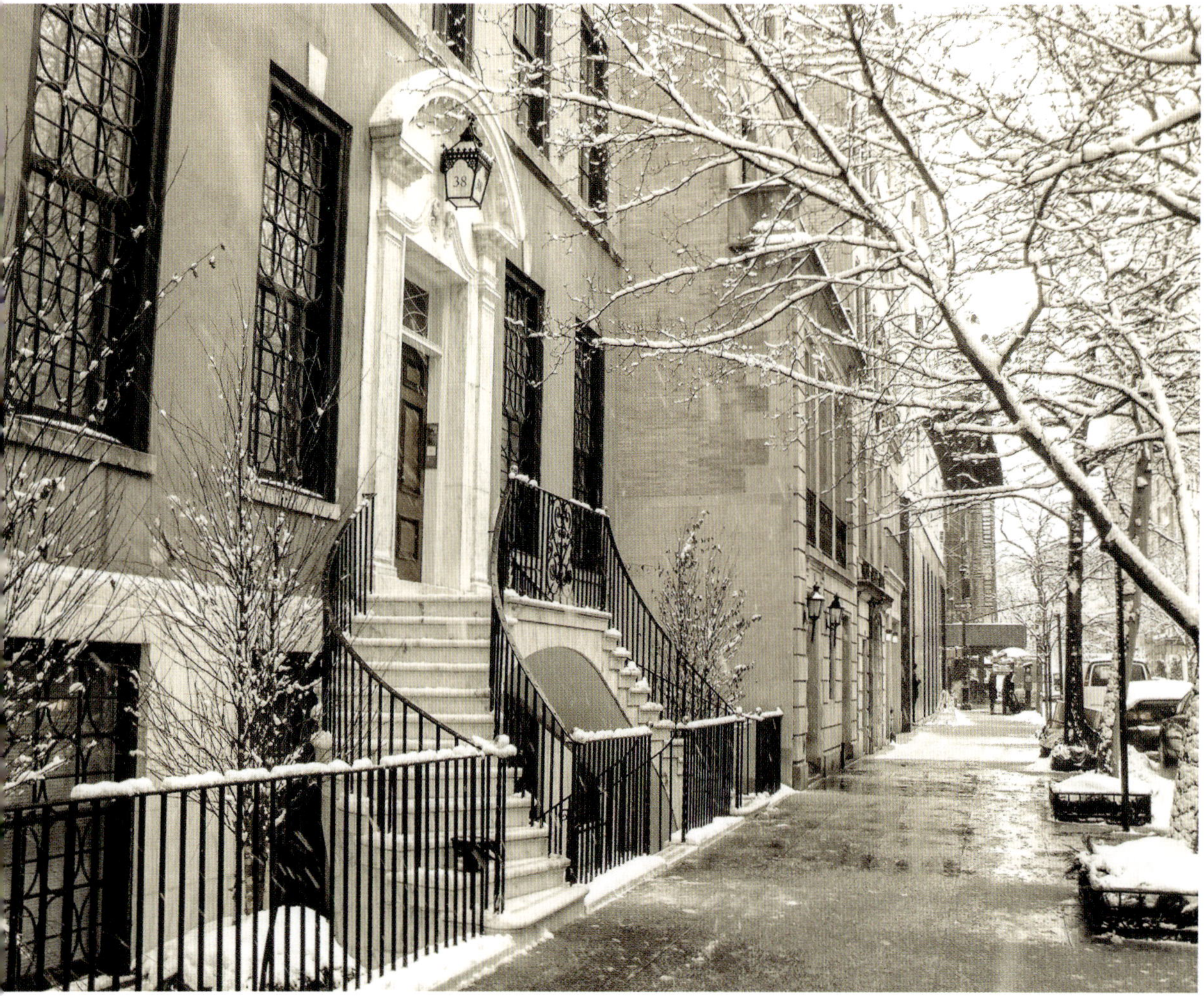

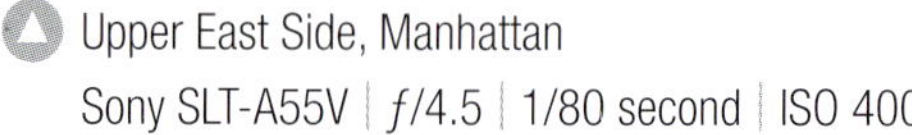

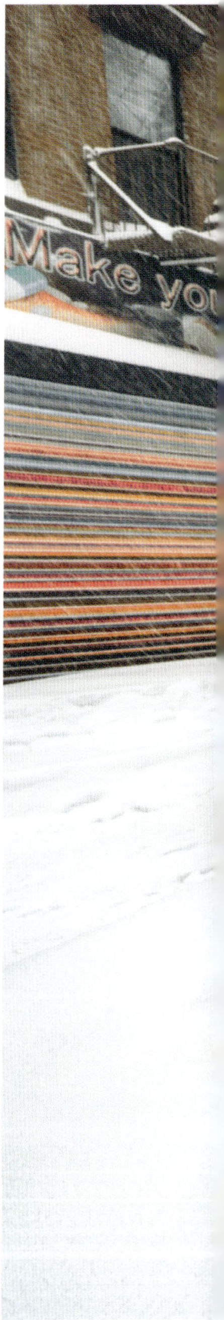

Upper East Side, Manhattan
Sony SLT-A55V | ƒ/4.5 | 1/80 second | ISO 400

Lower East Side, Manhattan
Sony ILCE-7RM2 | ƒ/7 | 1/60 second | ISO 200

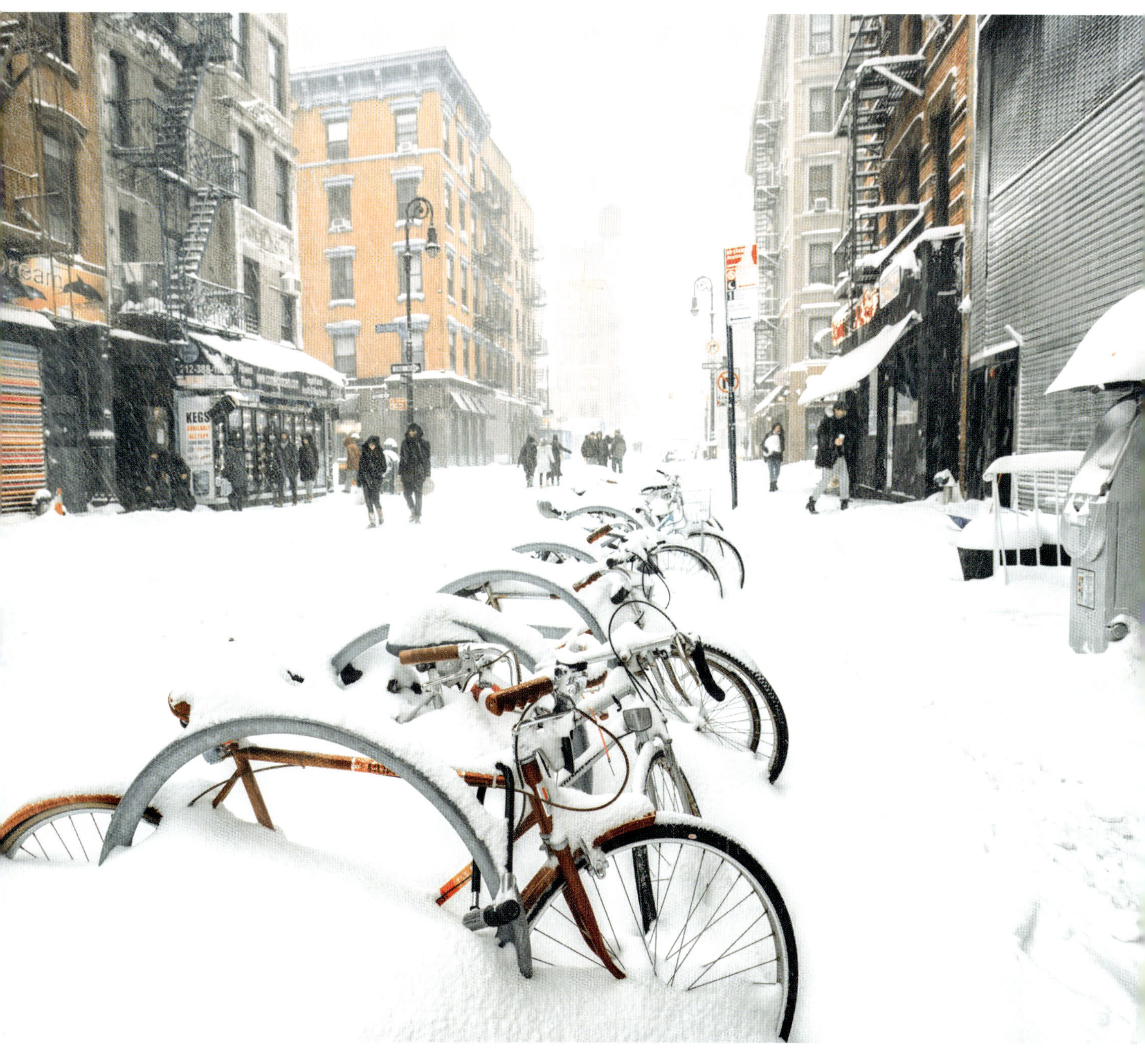
KEGS

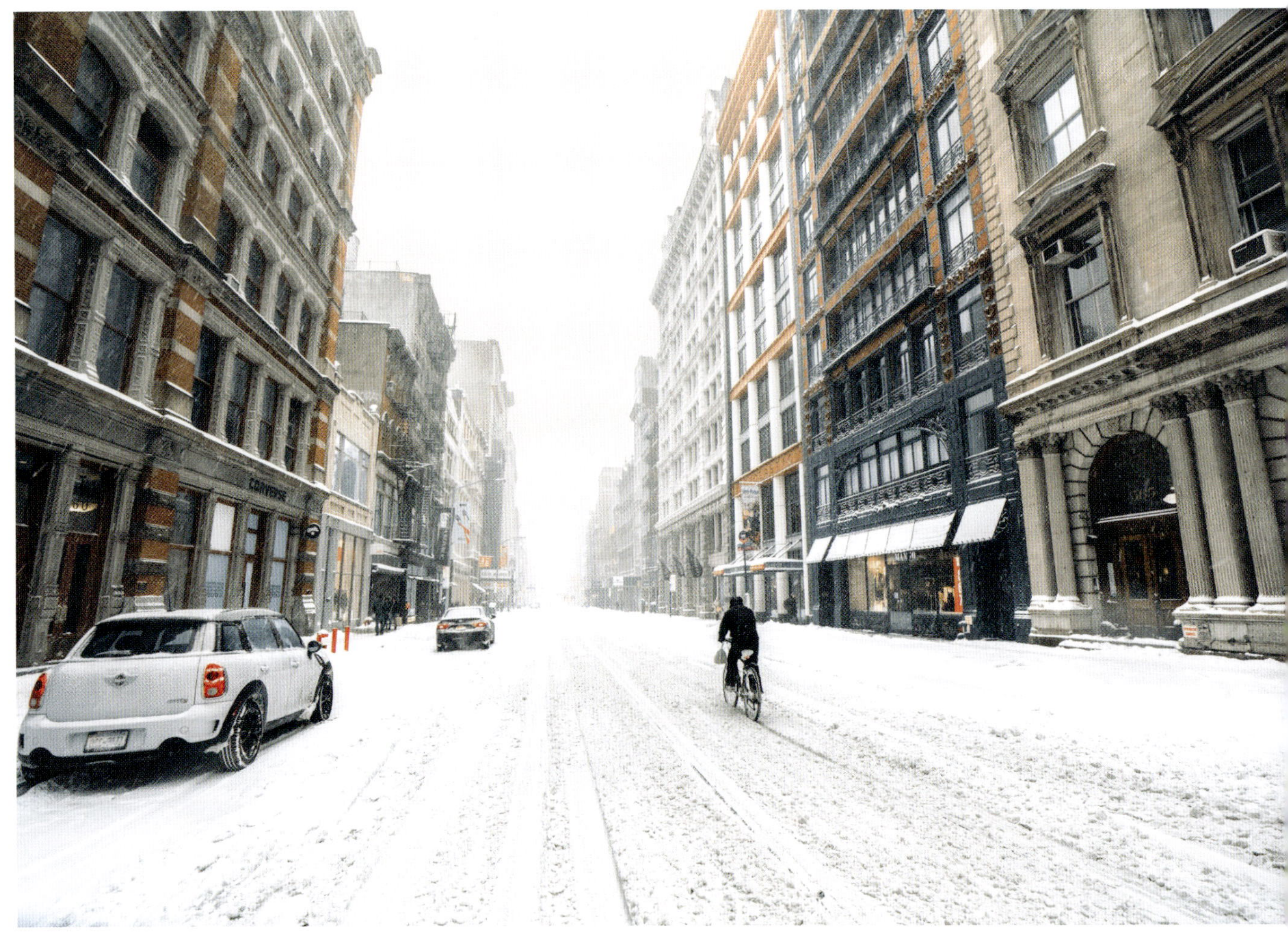

Soho, Lower Manhattan
Sony NEX-6 | f/5 | 1/60 second | ISO 100

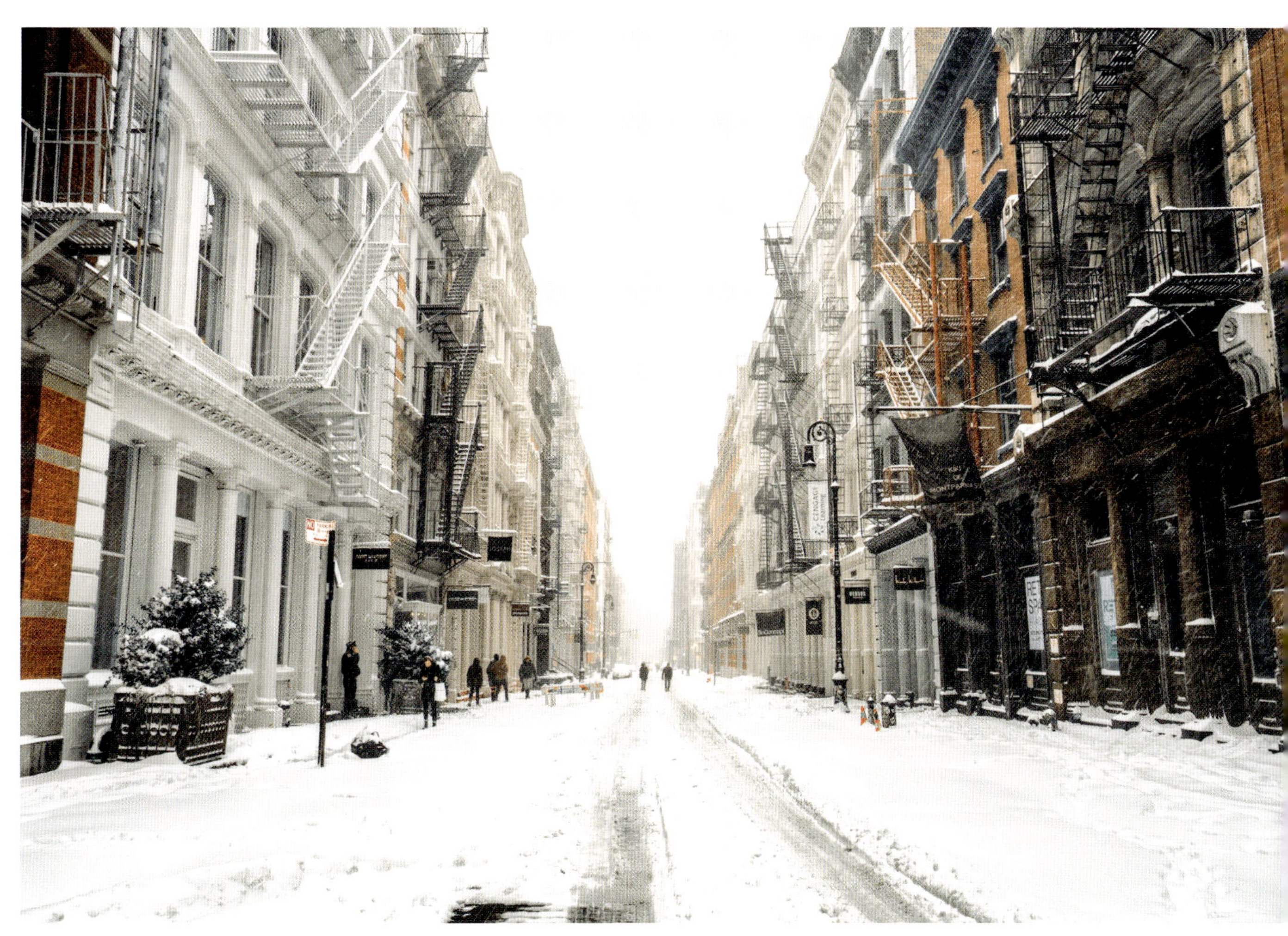

Soho, Lower Manhattan
Sony ILCE-7RM2 | $f/5$ | 1/60 second | ISO 400

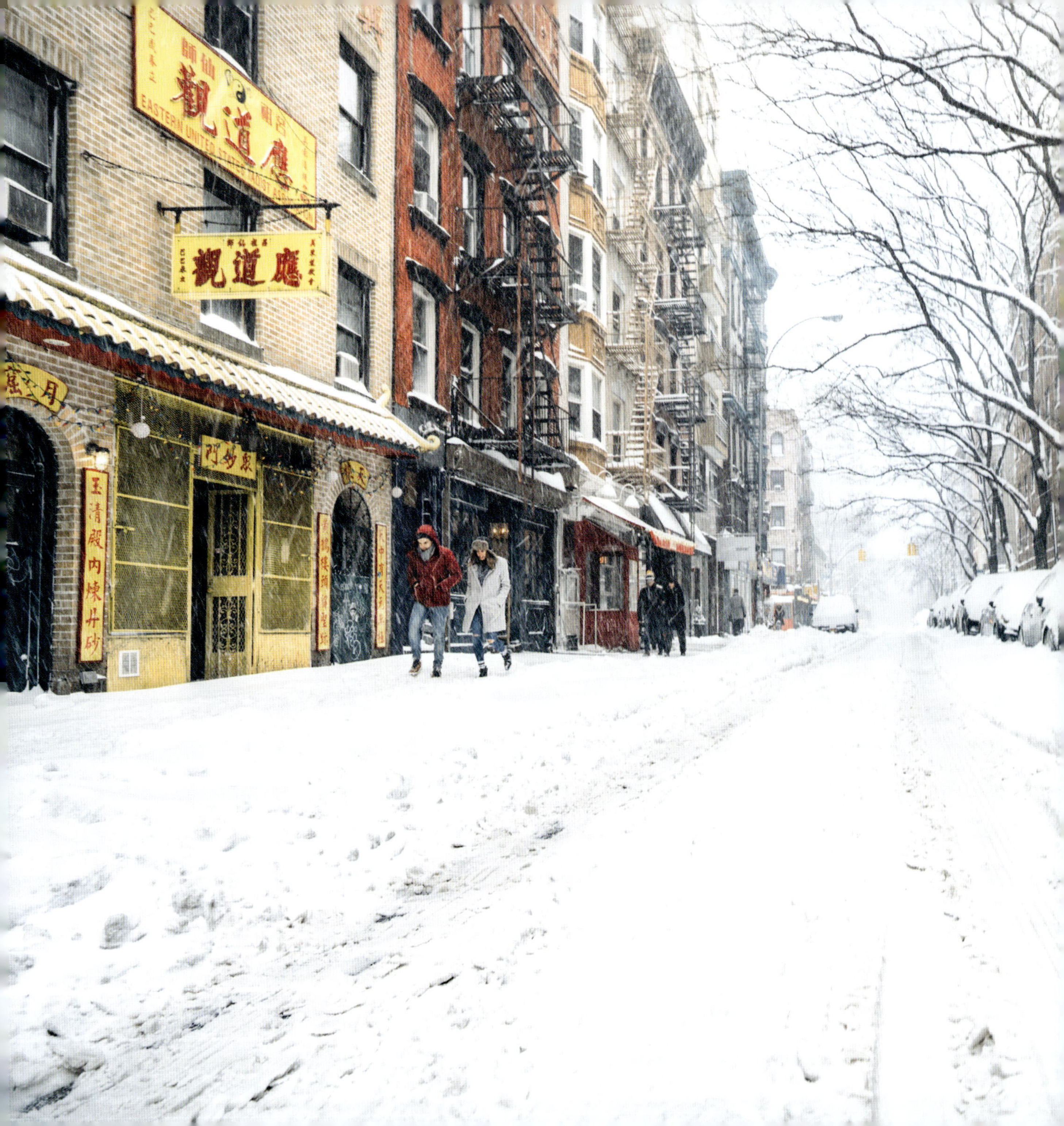

應道觀
應道觀
玉清殿内煉丹砂

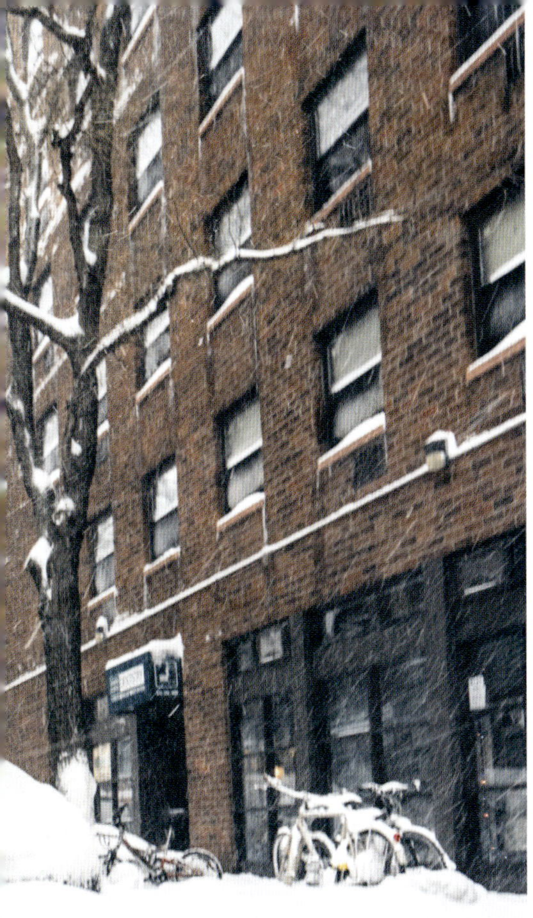

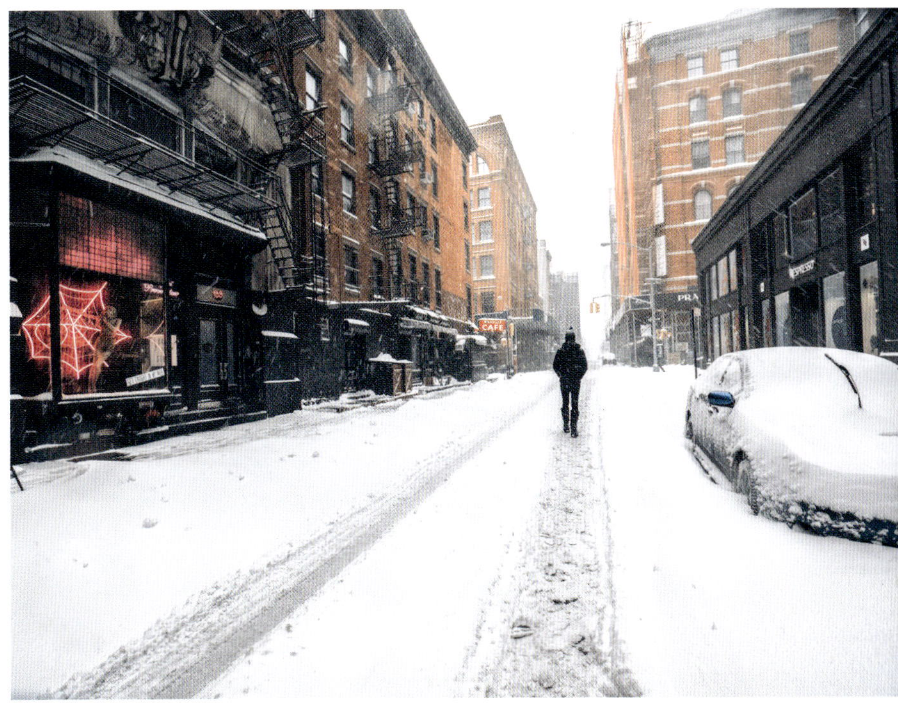

Soho, Lower Manhattan
Sony ILCE-7RM2 | ƒ/5 | 1/100 second | ISO 200

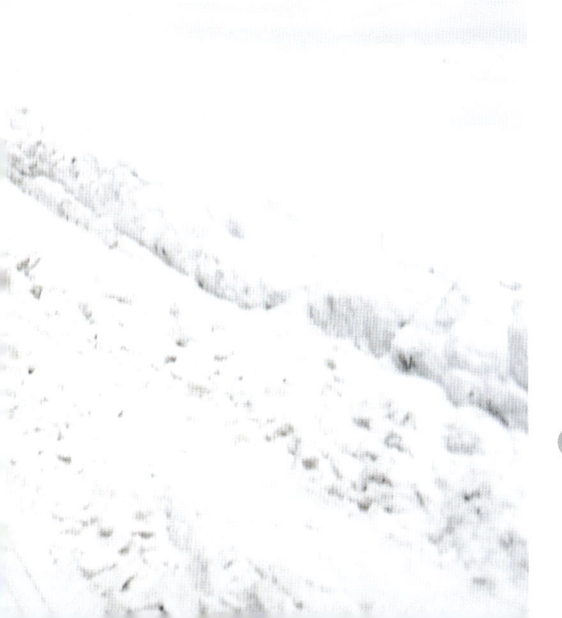

Chelsea, Manhattan
Sony ILCE-7RM2 | ƒ/7 | 1/80 second | ISO 200

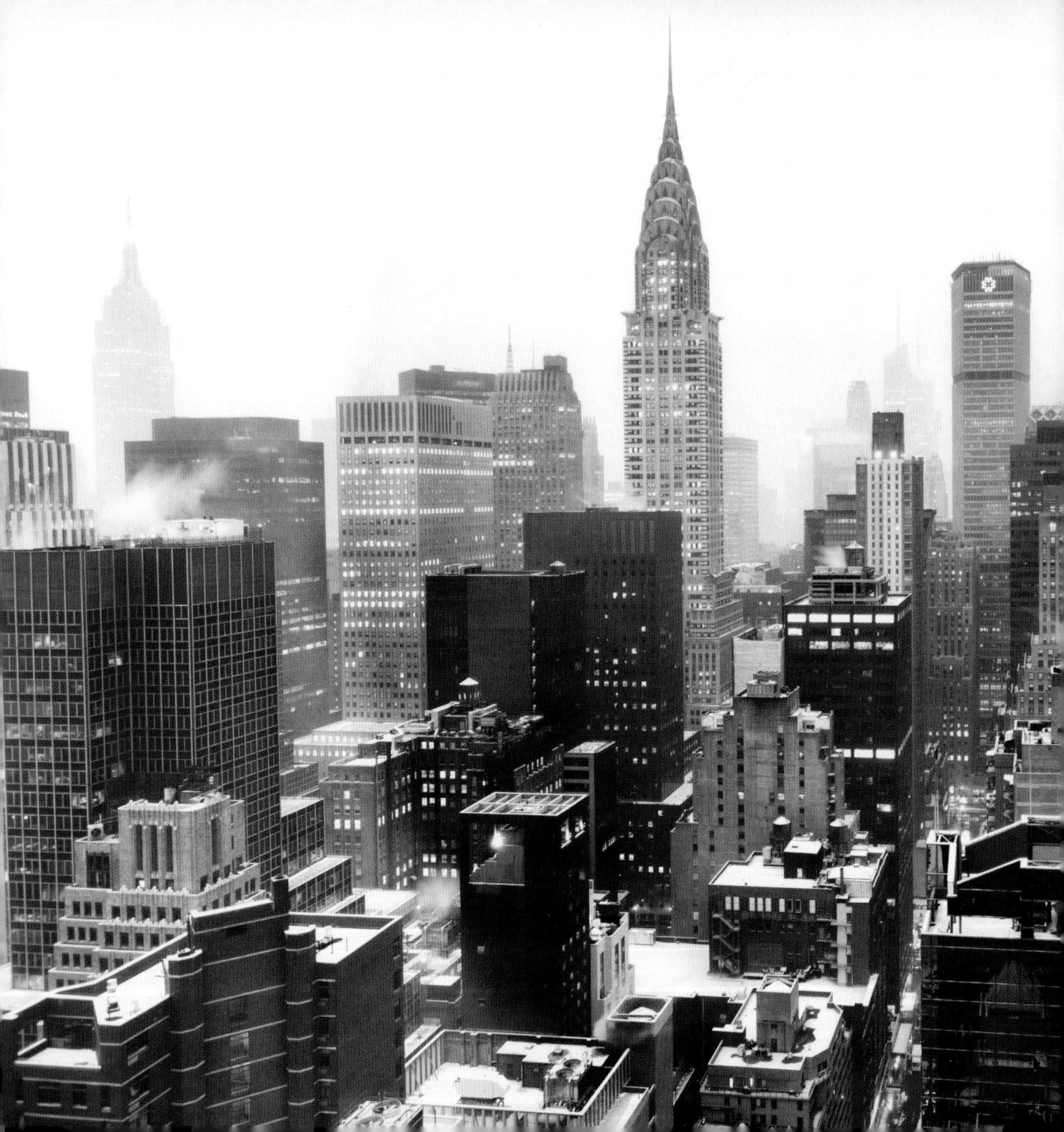

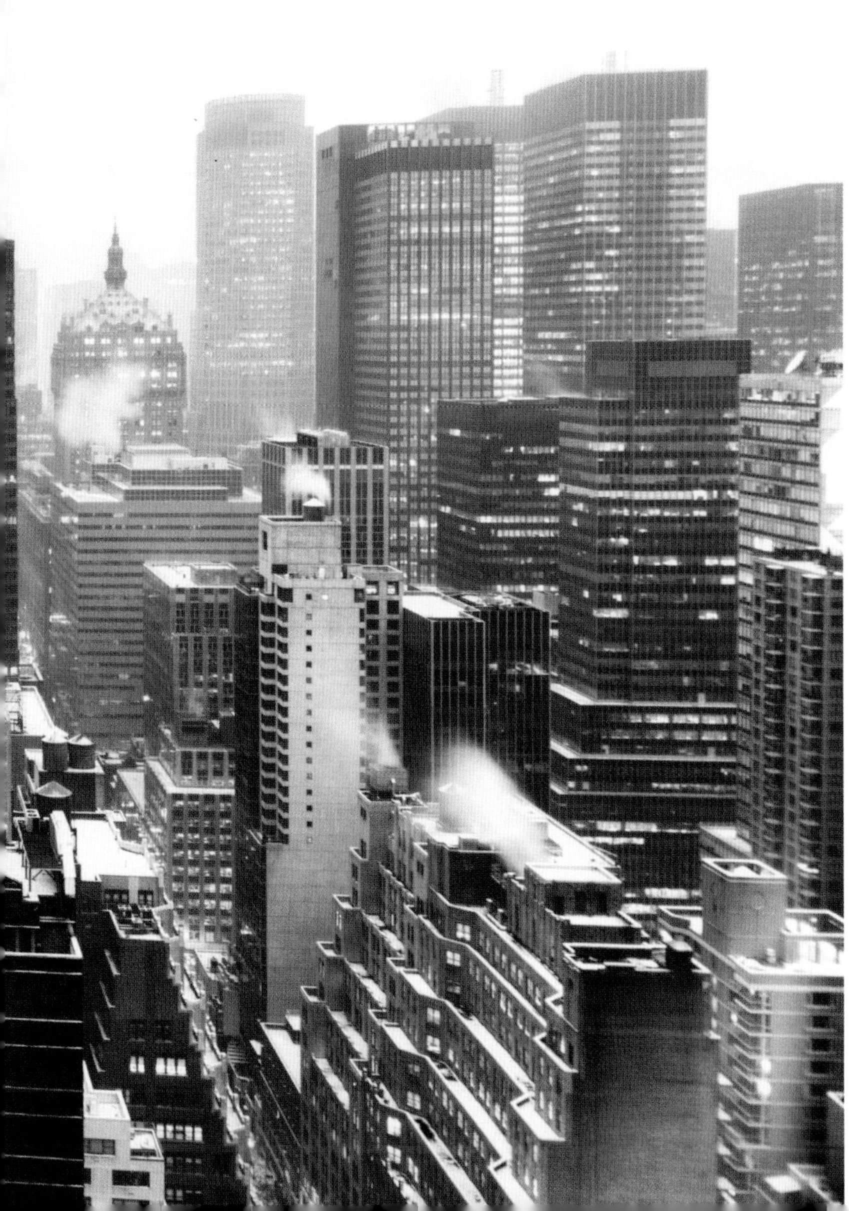

Midtown Manhattan
Sony NEX-7 | $f/5$ | 1/80 second | ISO 200

In the silent stillness of winter
the world stops rotating
temporarily.

All sound, speech, and
thought is muffled as the
earth slumbers briefly under
a blanket of freshly fallen
snow.

In each snowflake rest
the hopes of all who have
ever felt the warmth of an
anticipatory heart-flutter:

dream-sputters that wrap
the earth in the weight of
their desires.

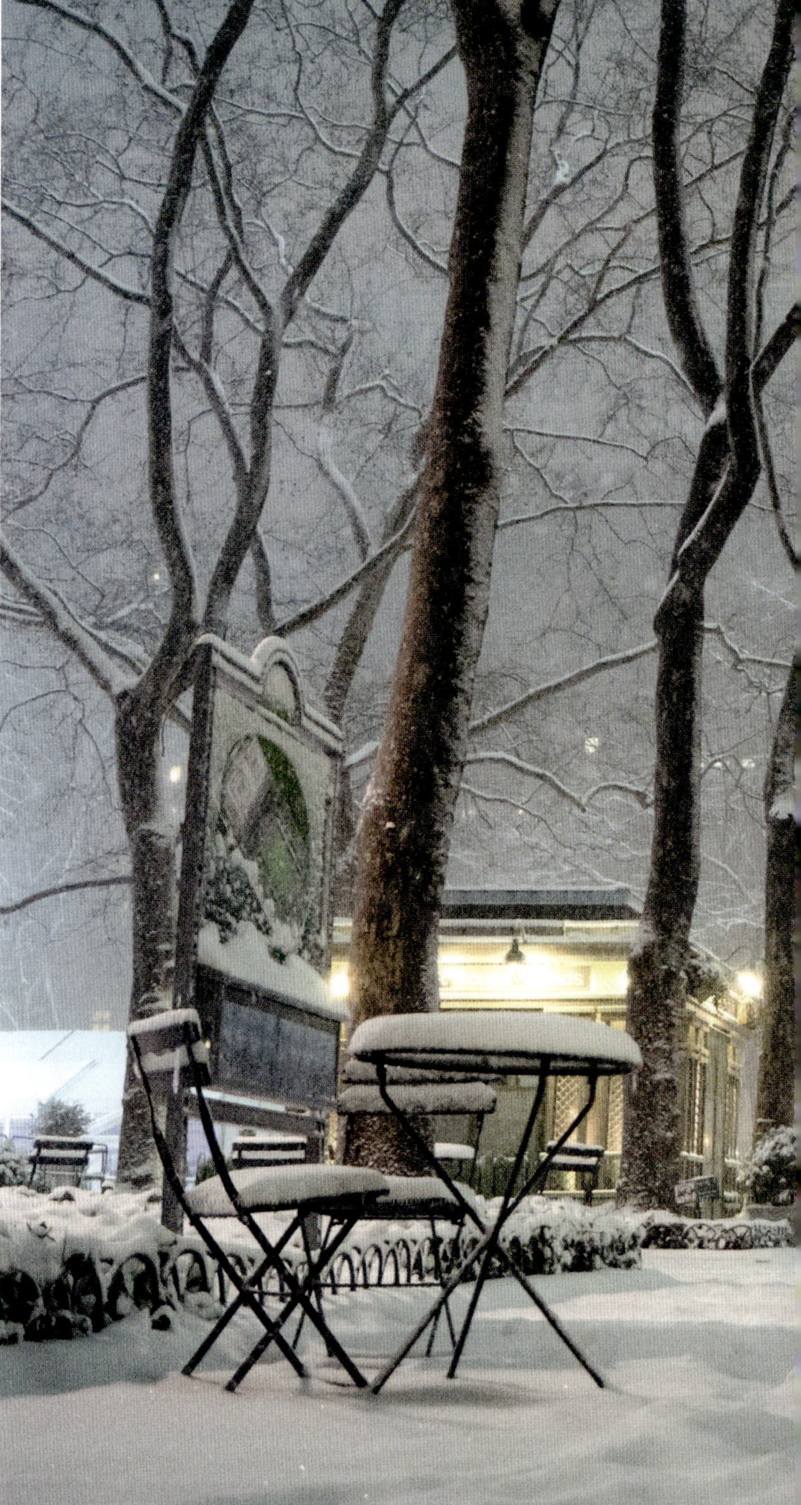

Bryant Park, Midtown Manhattan
Sony SLT-A99V | *f*/3.2 | 1/125 second | ISO 4000

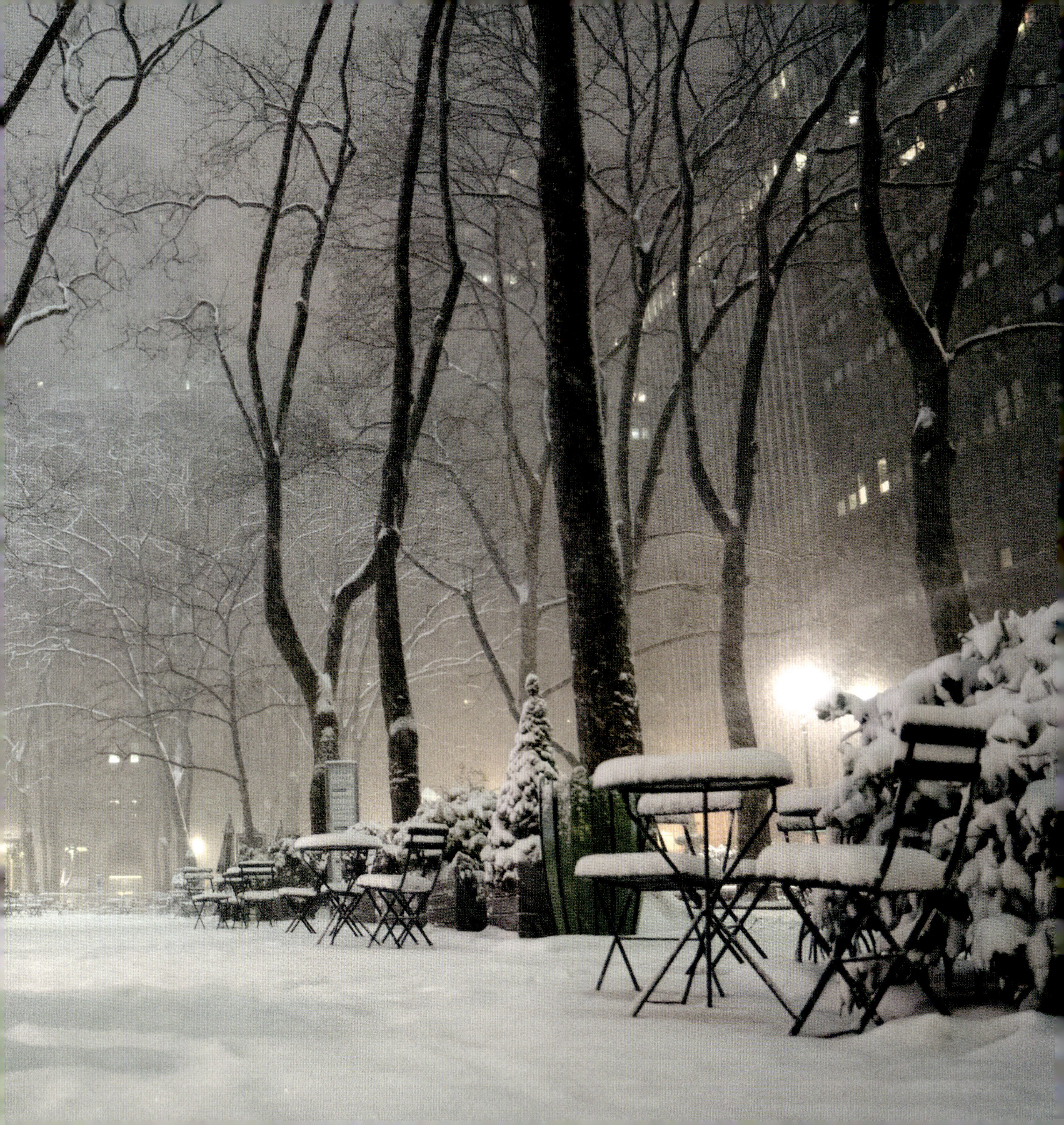

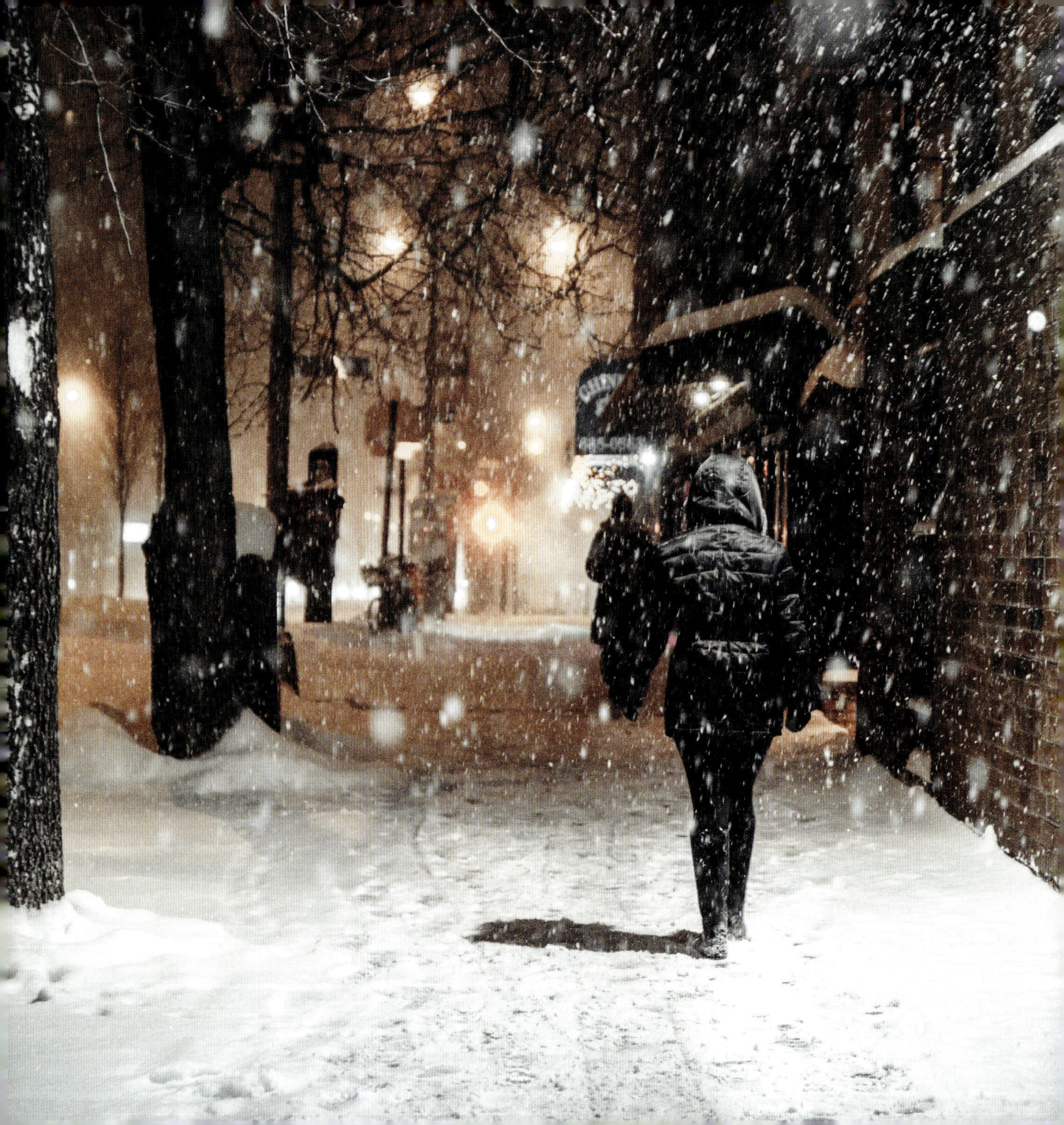

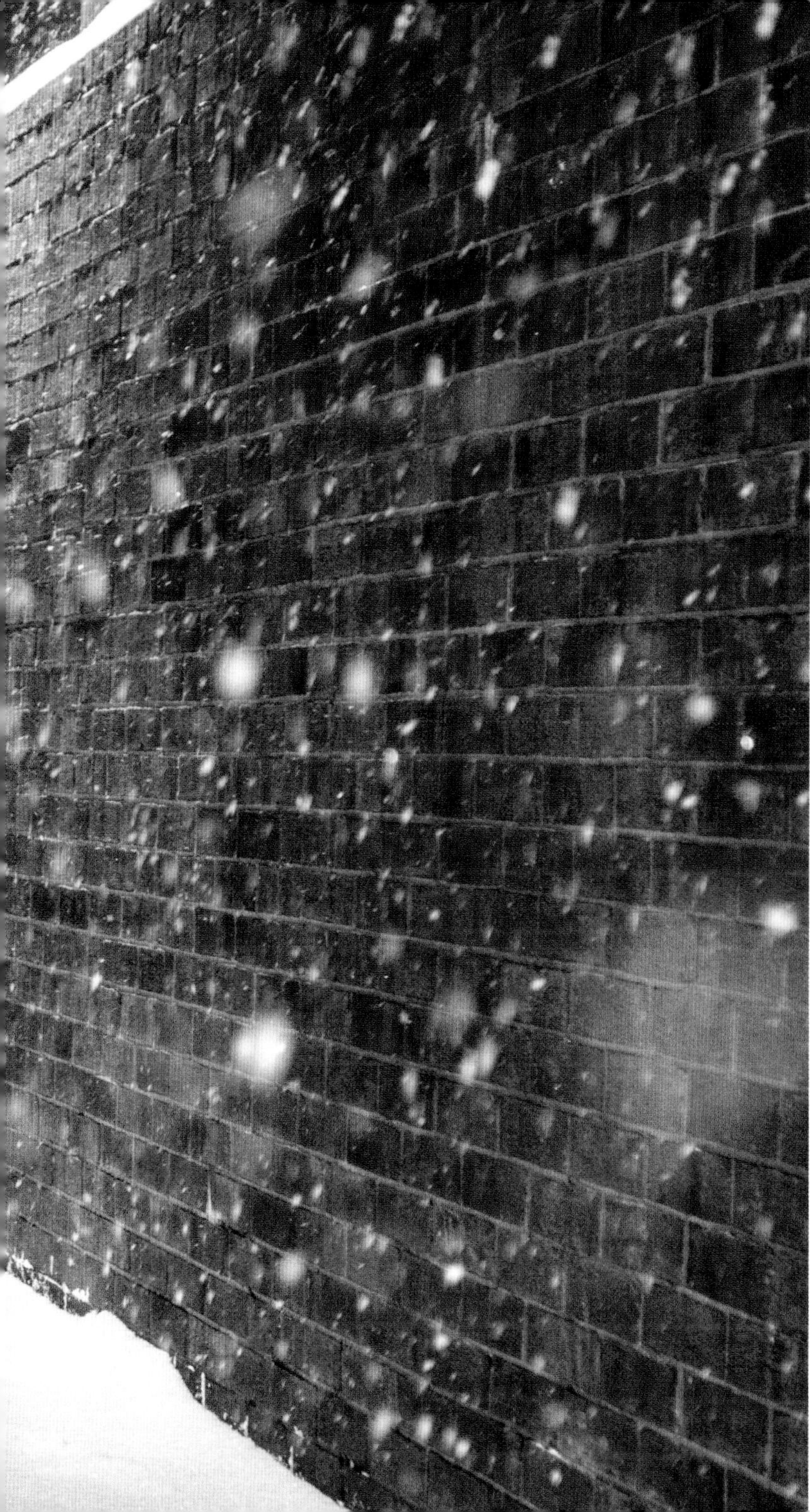

East Village, Lower Manhattan
Sony ILCE-7RM2 | $f/4$ | 1/30 second | ISO 4000

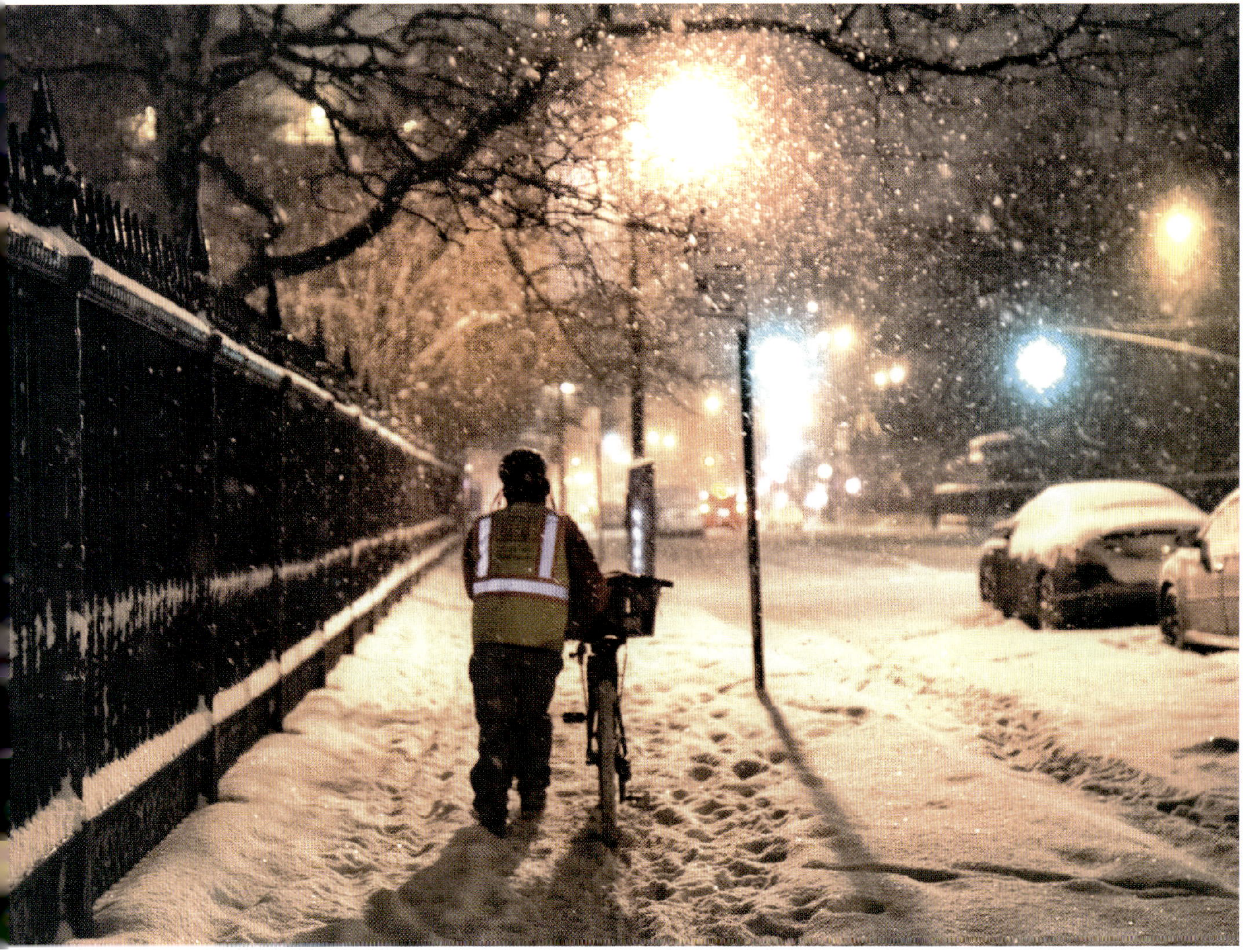

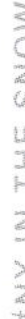

Union Square, Manhattan
Sony SLT-A99V | $f/4$ | 1/80 second | ISO 4000

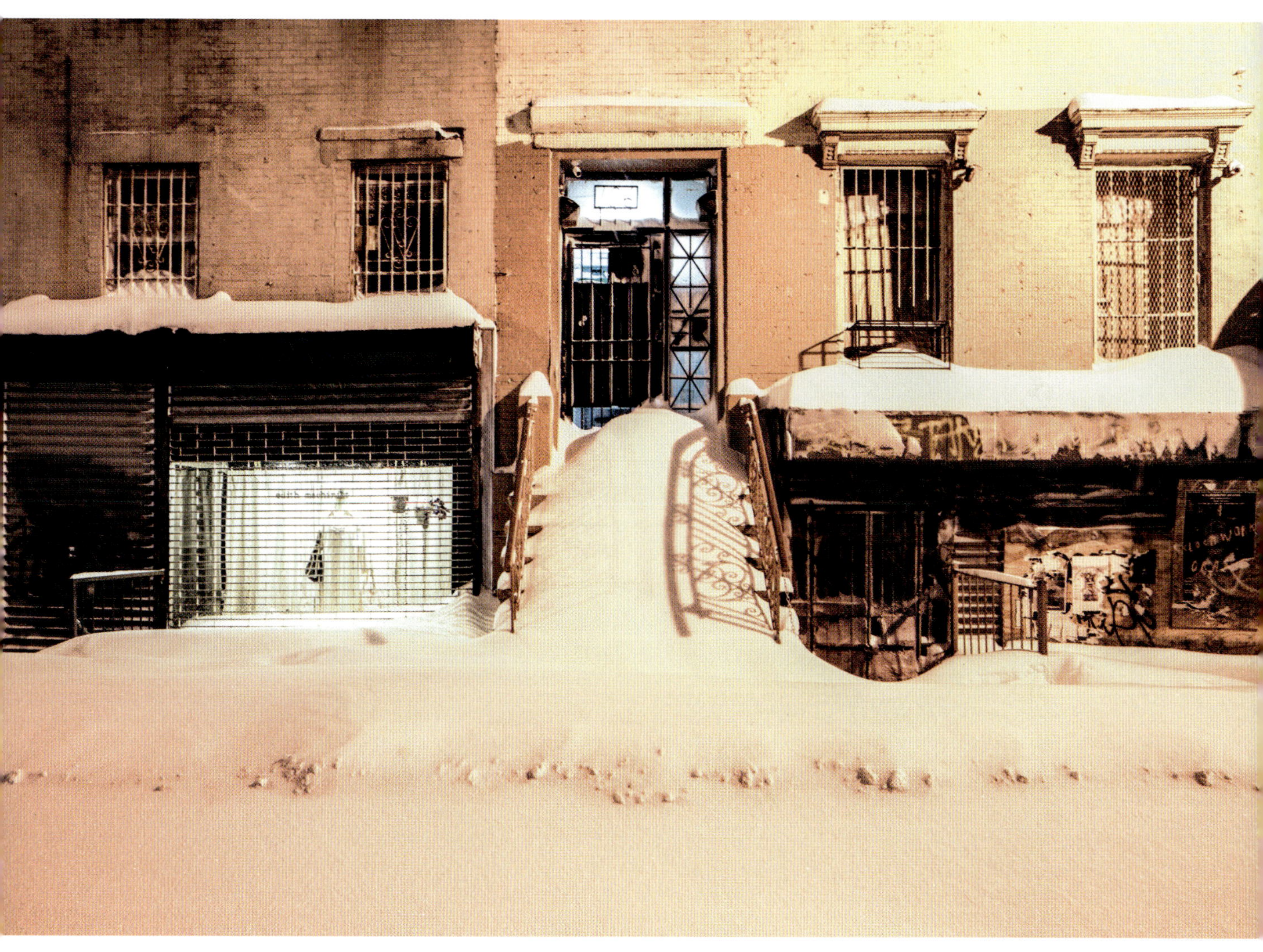

Lower East Side, Manhattan

Sony ILCE-7RM2 | f/5 | 1/60 second | ISO 2000

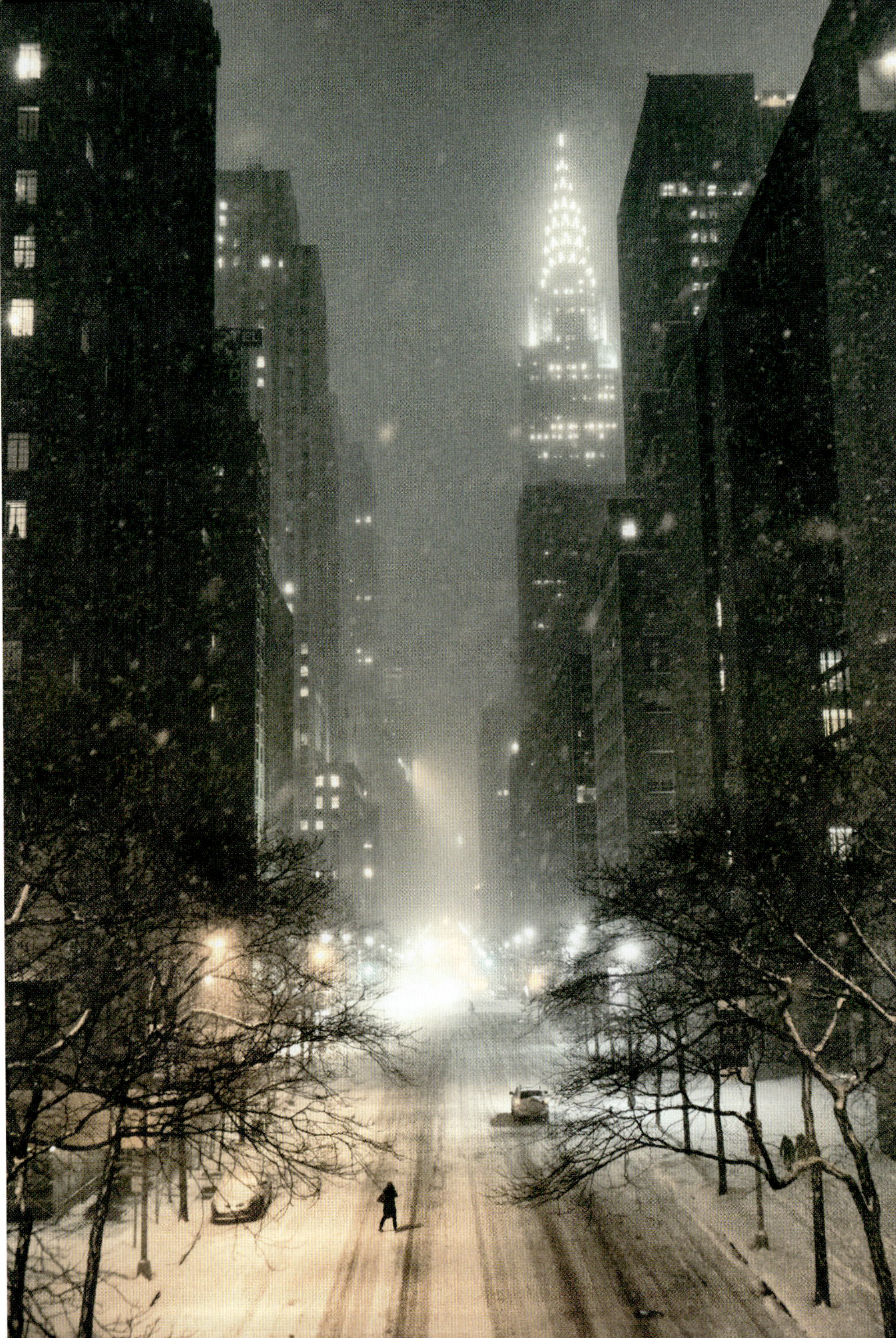

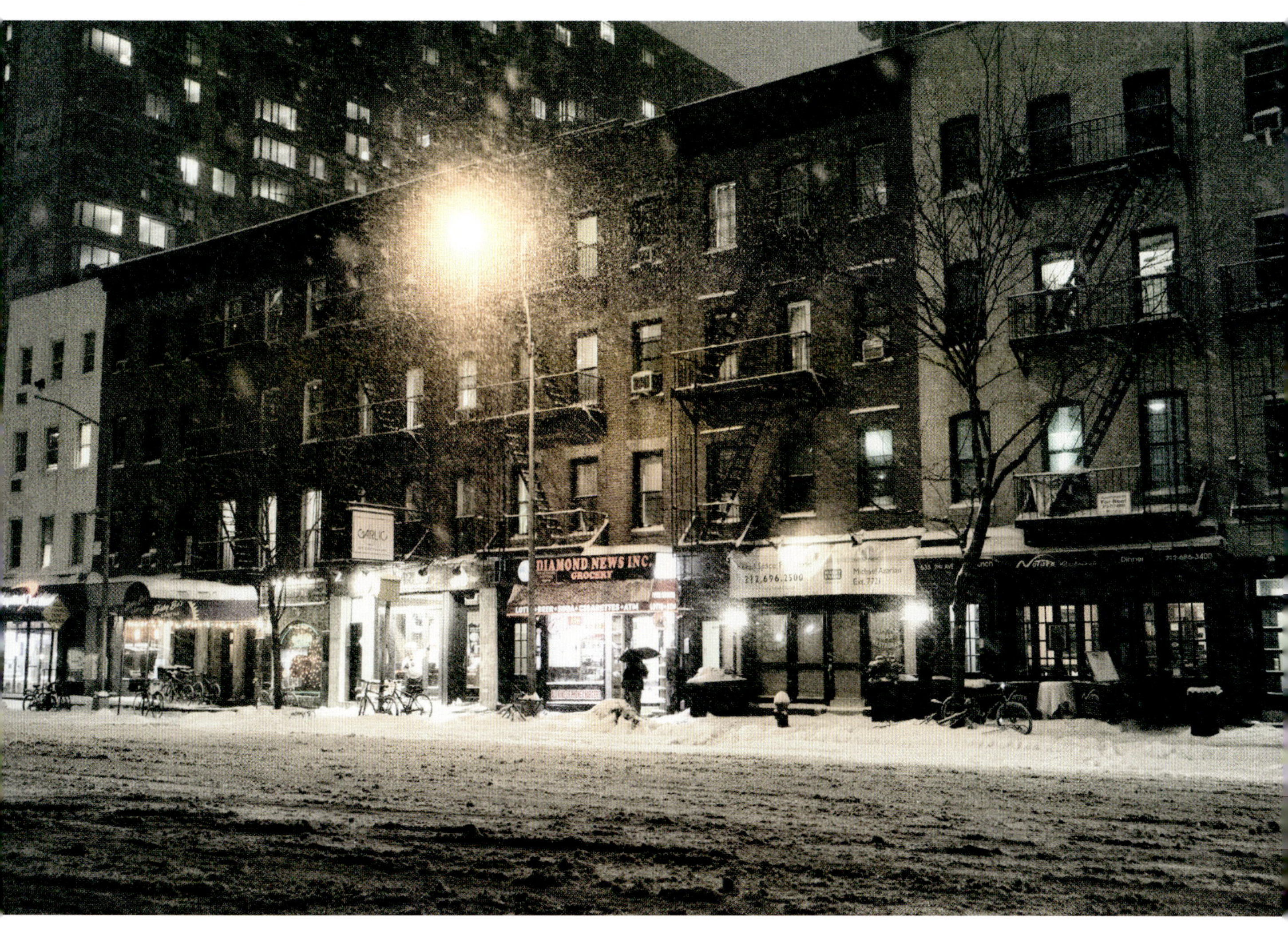

Chelsea, Manhattan
Sony NEX-6 | ƒ/5 | 1/40 second | ISO 2000

Tudor City Place, Midtown Manhattan
Sony SLT-A99V | ƒ/5.6 | 1/80 second | ISO 4000

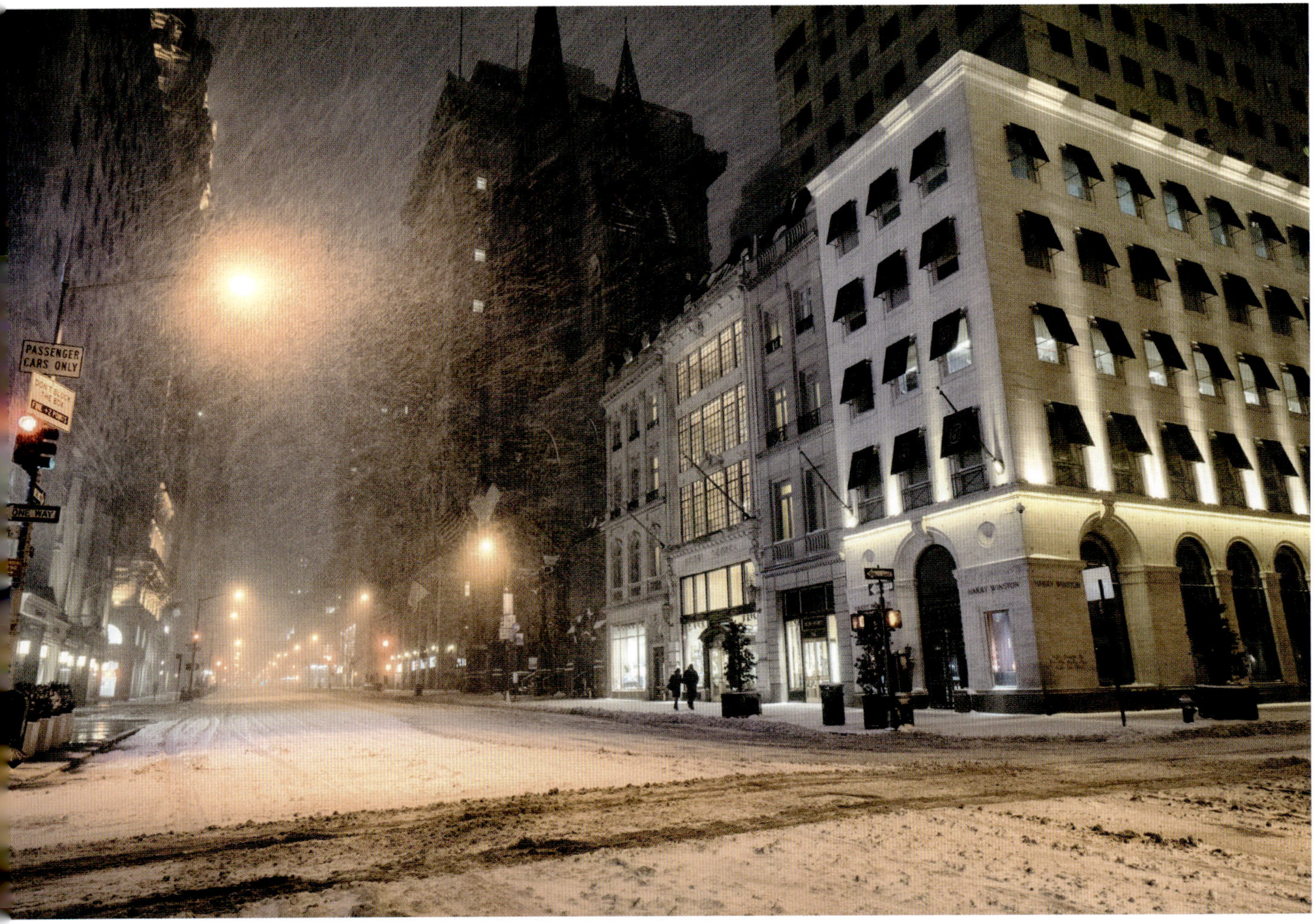

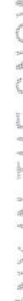

Midtown Manhattan

Sony SLT-A99V | *ƒ*/4 | 1/80 second | ISO 4000

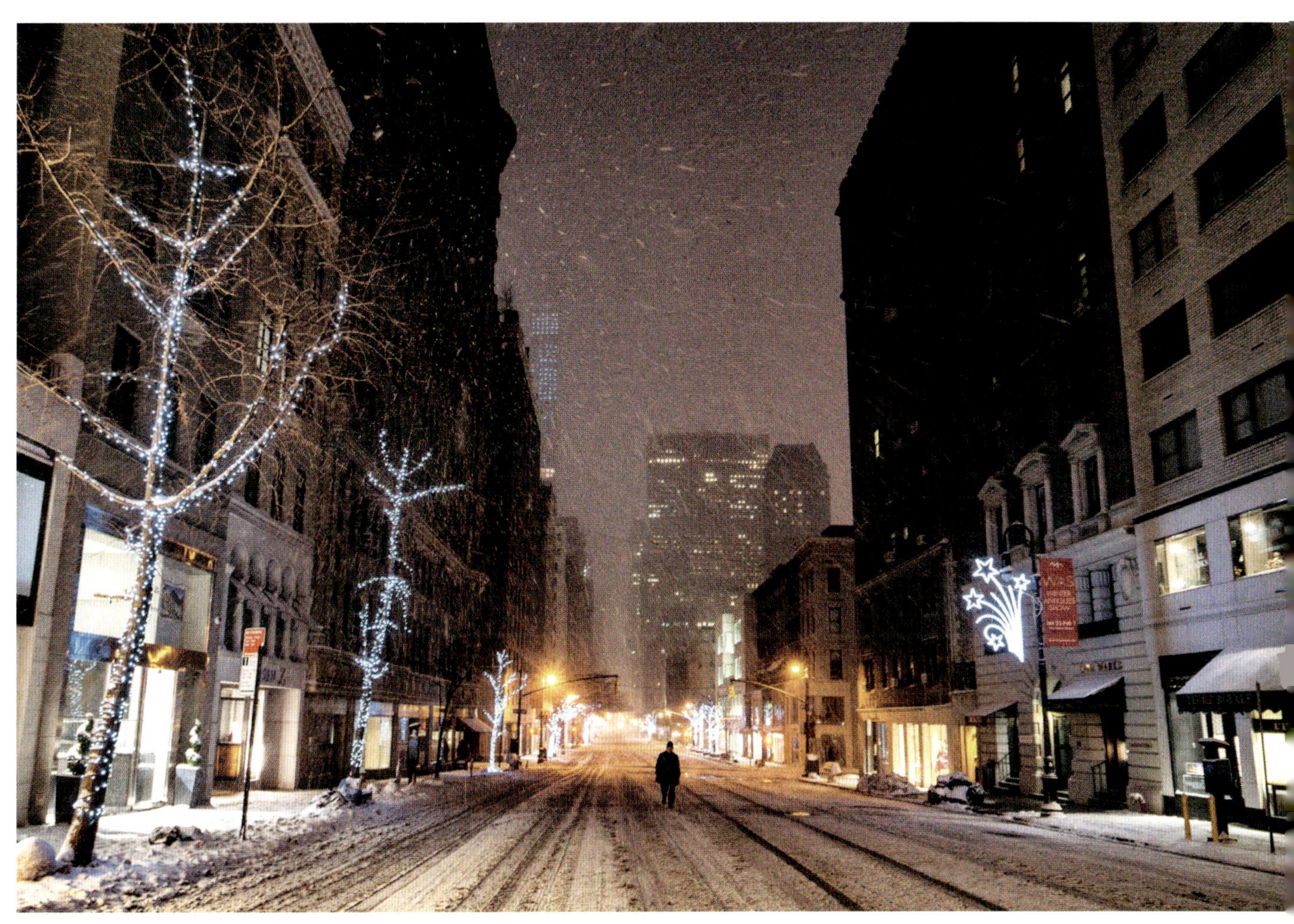

Greenwich Village, Lower West Side, Manhattan
Sony SLT-A99V | *f*/4 | 1/80 second | ISO 4000

Living in a city as populated as New York City can be wonderful but also overwhelming. The feeling of being isolated in a city of millions is one that many people grapple with on a regular basis.

Having dealt with depression and anxiety for most of my life, it has been therapeutic to explore the depths of both in my art, particularly with my photography of New York in the snow.

When it snows at night, the city has a tendency to empty out, especially when cars and transportation are banned from the streets. And so, the streets become an almost perfect representation of what it feels like to live here with sometimes crippling anxiety.

The emptiness and loneliness of urban living is magnified during snowstorms as the city transforms into an endless series of muffled ice-halls. The beauty of it all is intense, of course, but there is a deep sadness too that coats the streets. It's the perfect metaphor for life in New York City.

Lower East Side, Manhattan
Sony SLT-A99V | *f*/3.2 | 1/80 second | ISO 4000

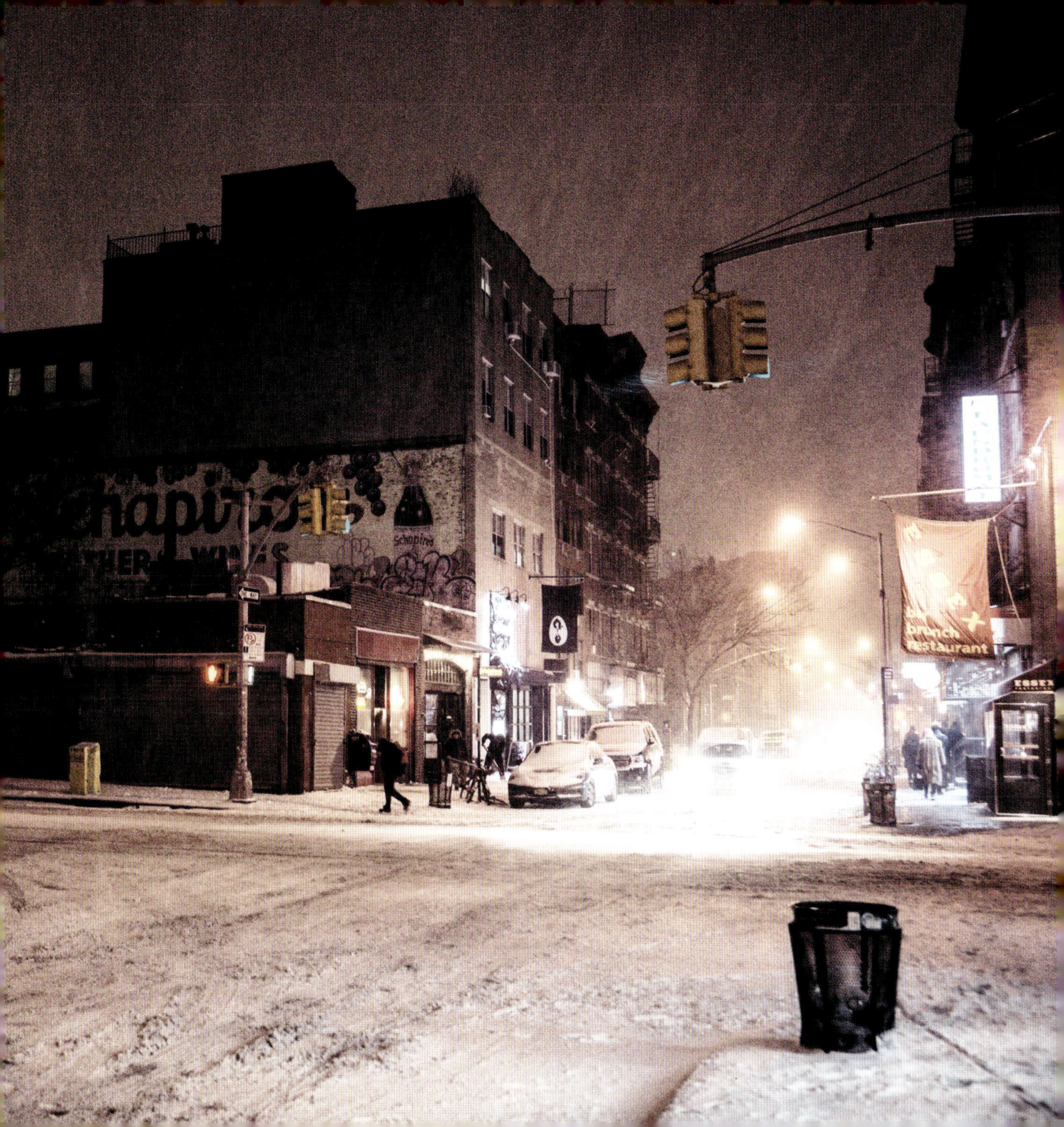
Schapiro's
brunch
restaurant

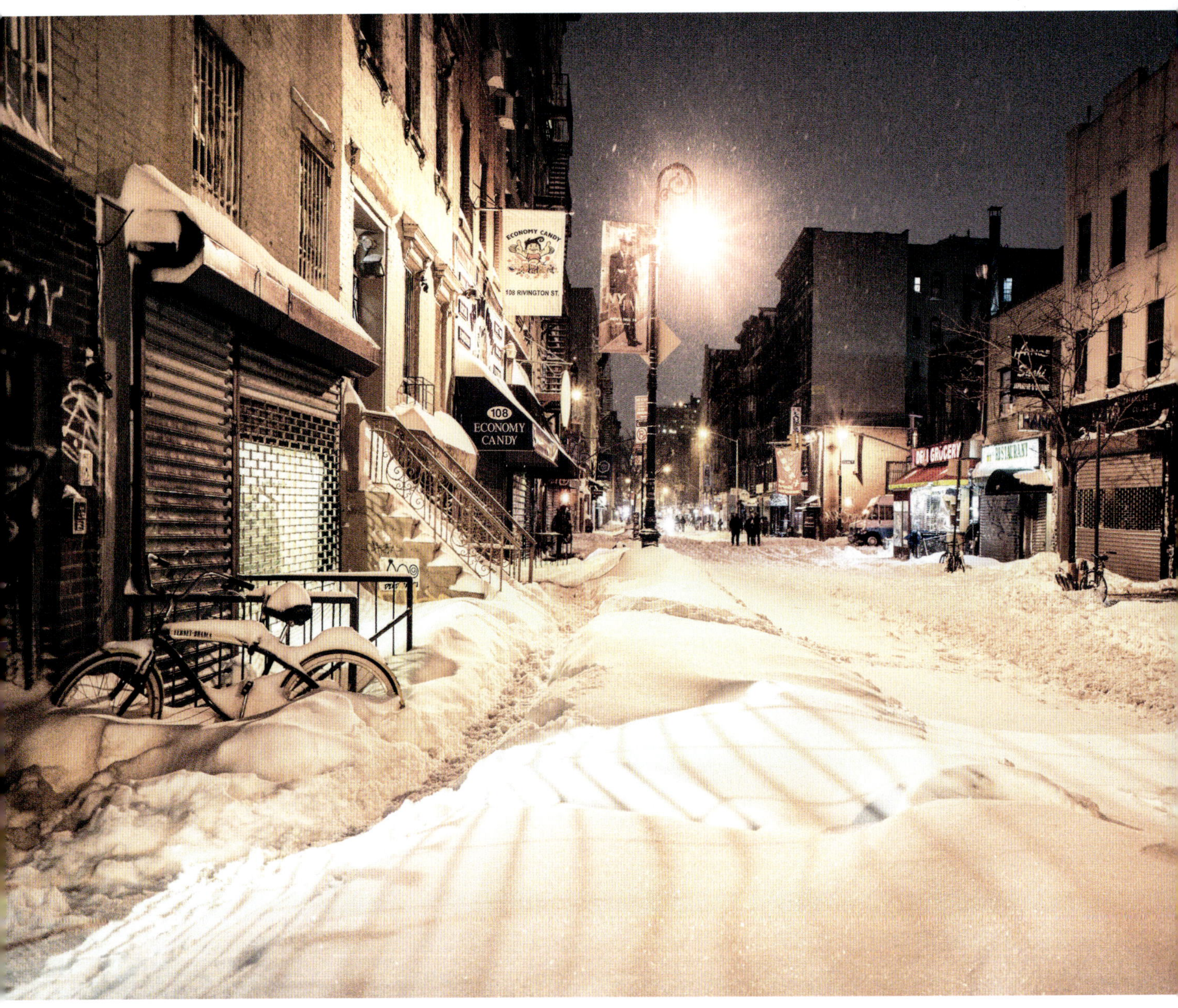

East Village, Manhattan
Sony SLT-A99V | ƒ/4 | 1/60 second | ISO 4000

Lower East Side, Manhattan
Sony SLT-A99V | ƒ/3.2 | 1/80 second | ISO 4000

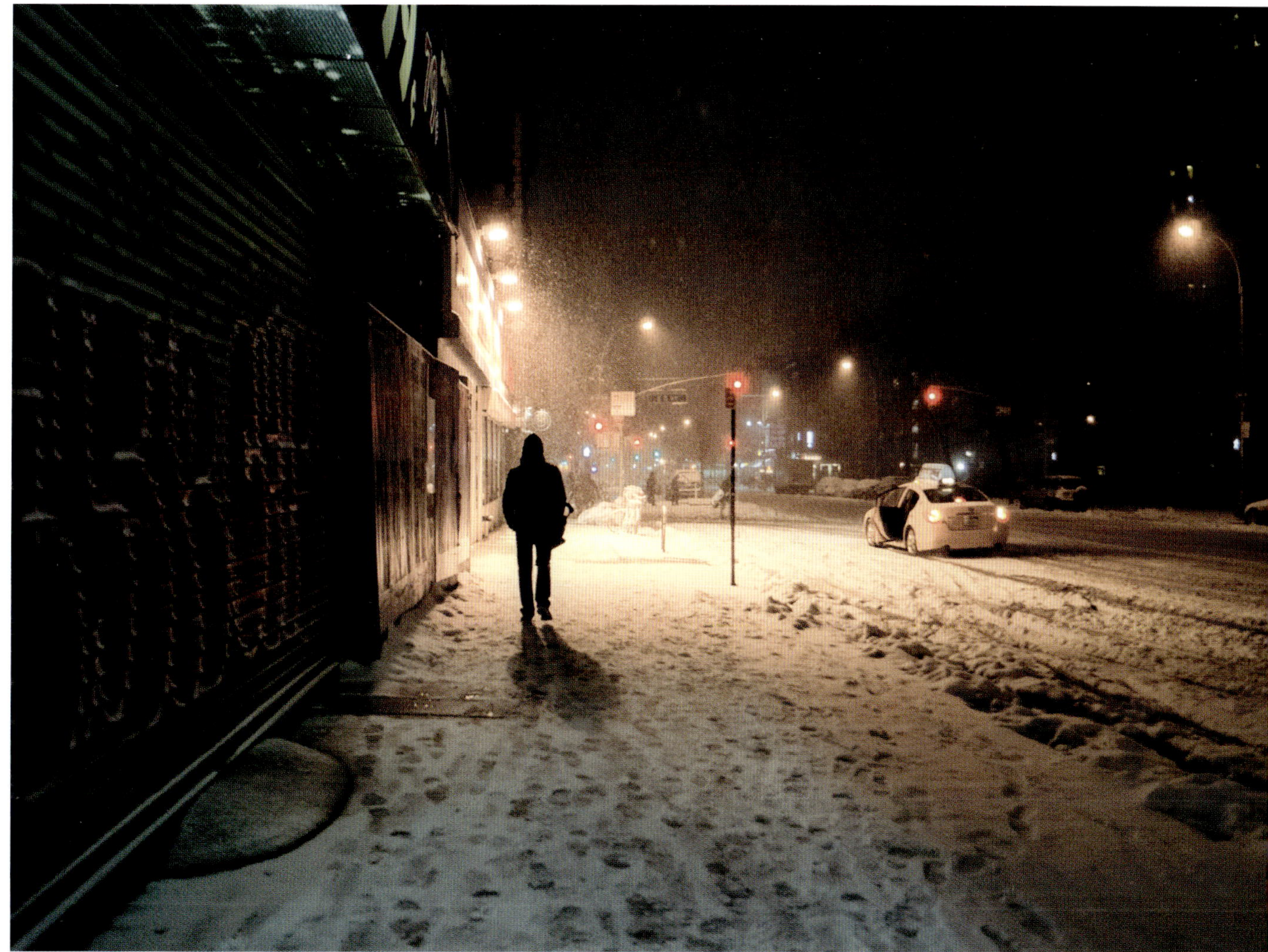

I miss the snow.

I miss the silence: deafening silence punctuated by small breaths signifying flutters of life in a world swallowed by the sinking, seductive embrace of serenity.

That type of serenity isn't easy to come by in a city that moves faster than the speed of hope: it's frenetic core blinked into existence by anxious dreamers.

If I hold still, very still, for just a moment and close my eyes, I can paint my serenity memory on the backs of my eyelids.

In this moment the world stops rotating long enough and my breath reverberates alongside the earth's heartbeat.

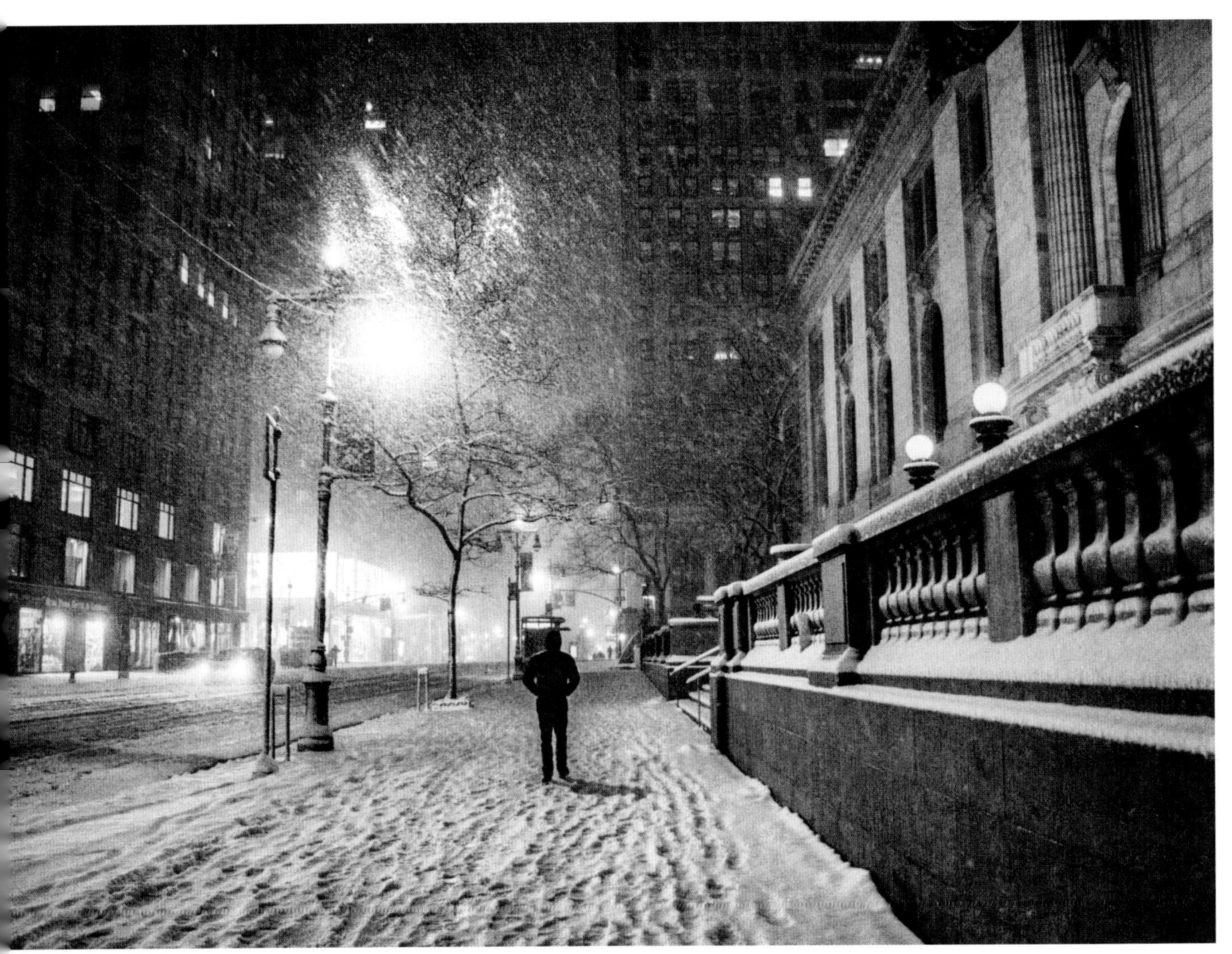

Bryant Park, Midtown Manhattan

Sony SLT-A99V | *f*/4 | 1/100 second | ISO 2500

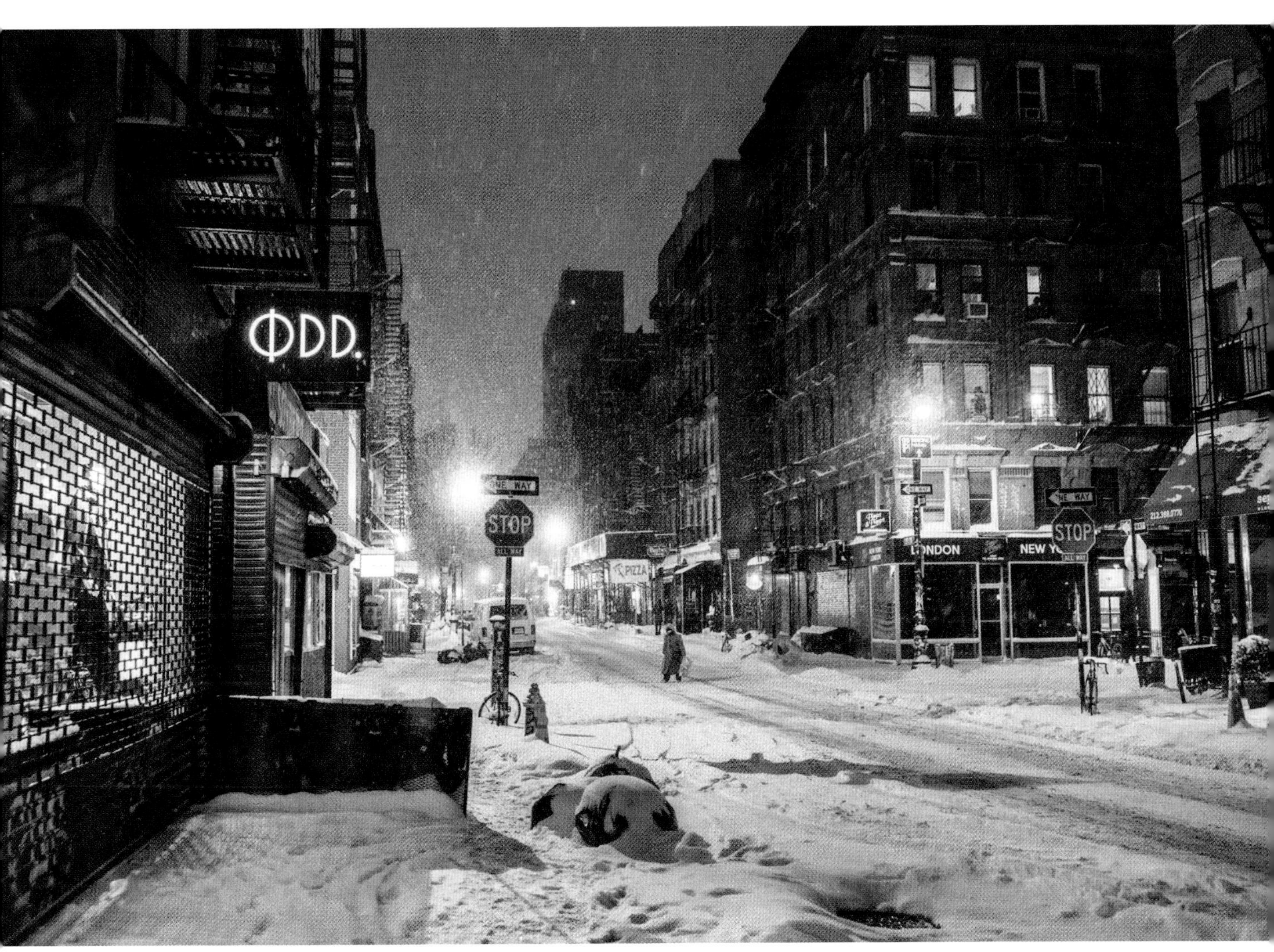

Lower East Side, Manhattan
Sony SLT-A99V | $f/4$ | 1/80 second | ISO 4000

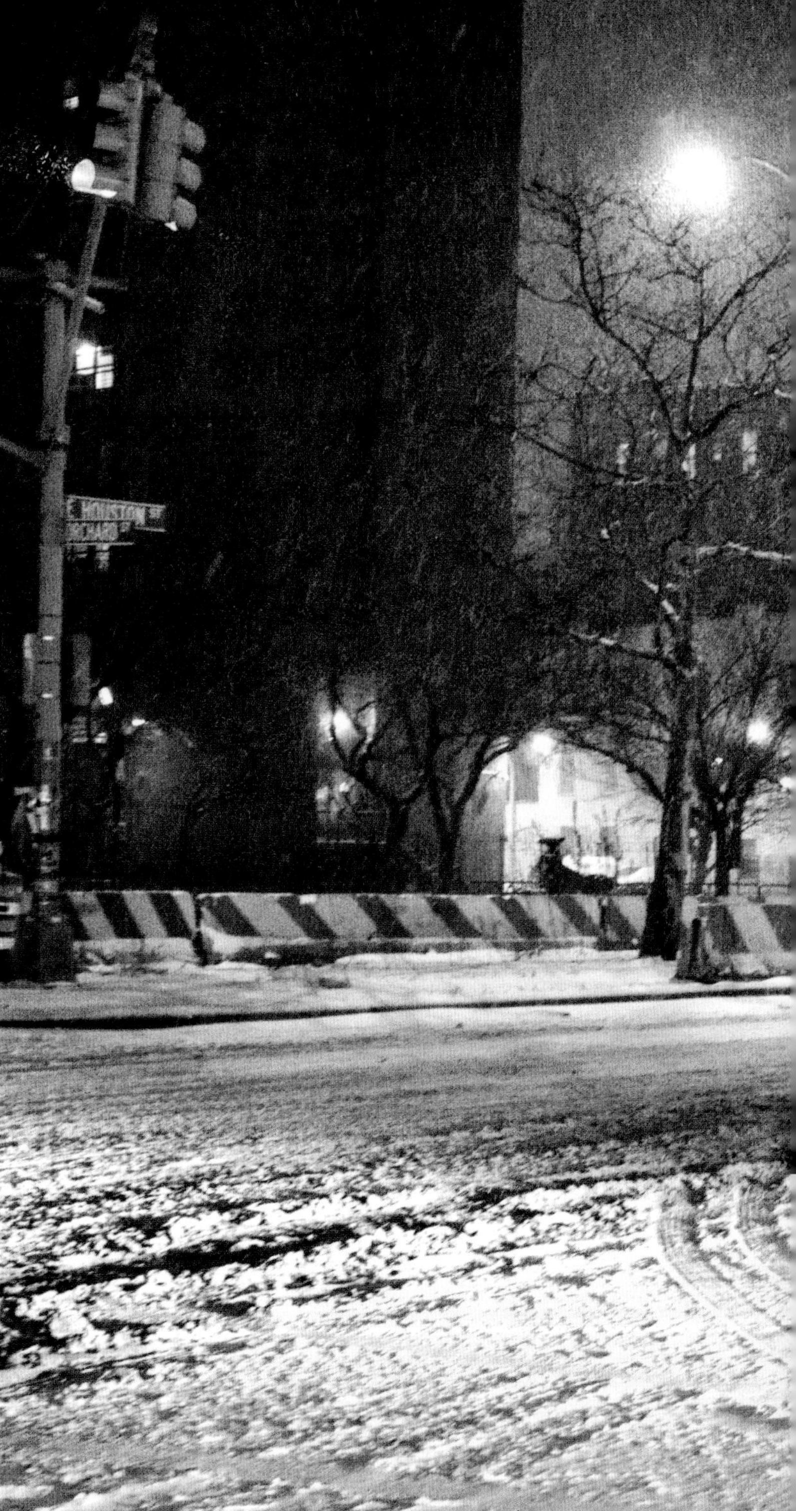

Lower East Side, Manhattan
Sony SLT-A99V | *f*/3.2 | 1/80 second | ISO 4000

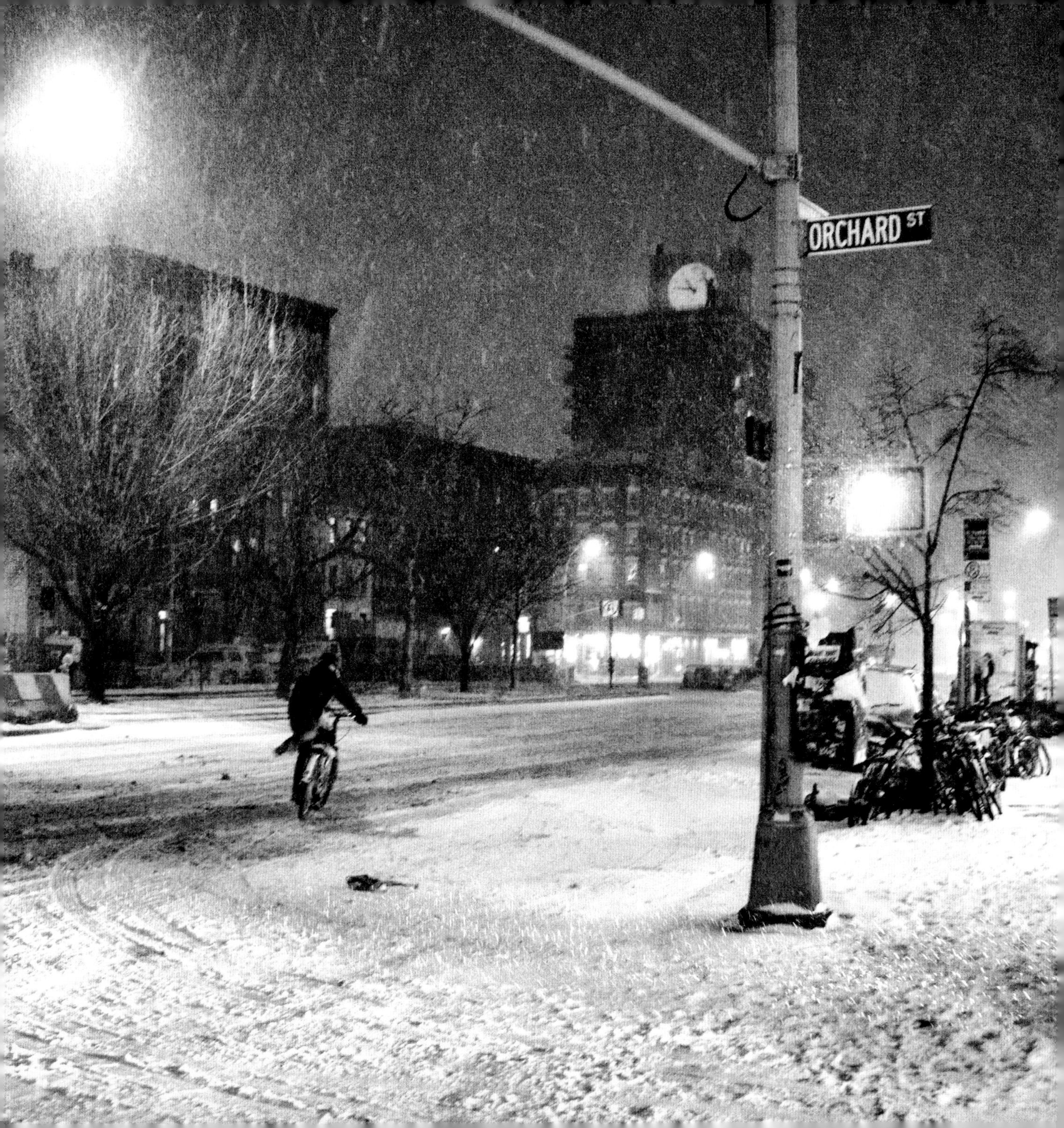
ORCHARD ST

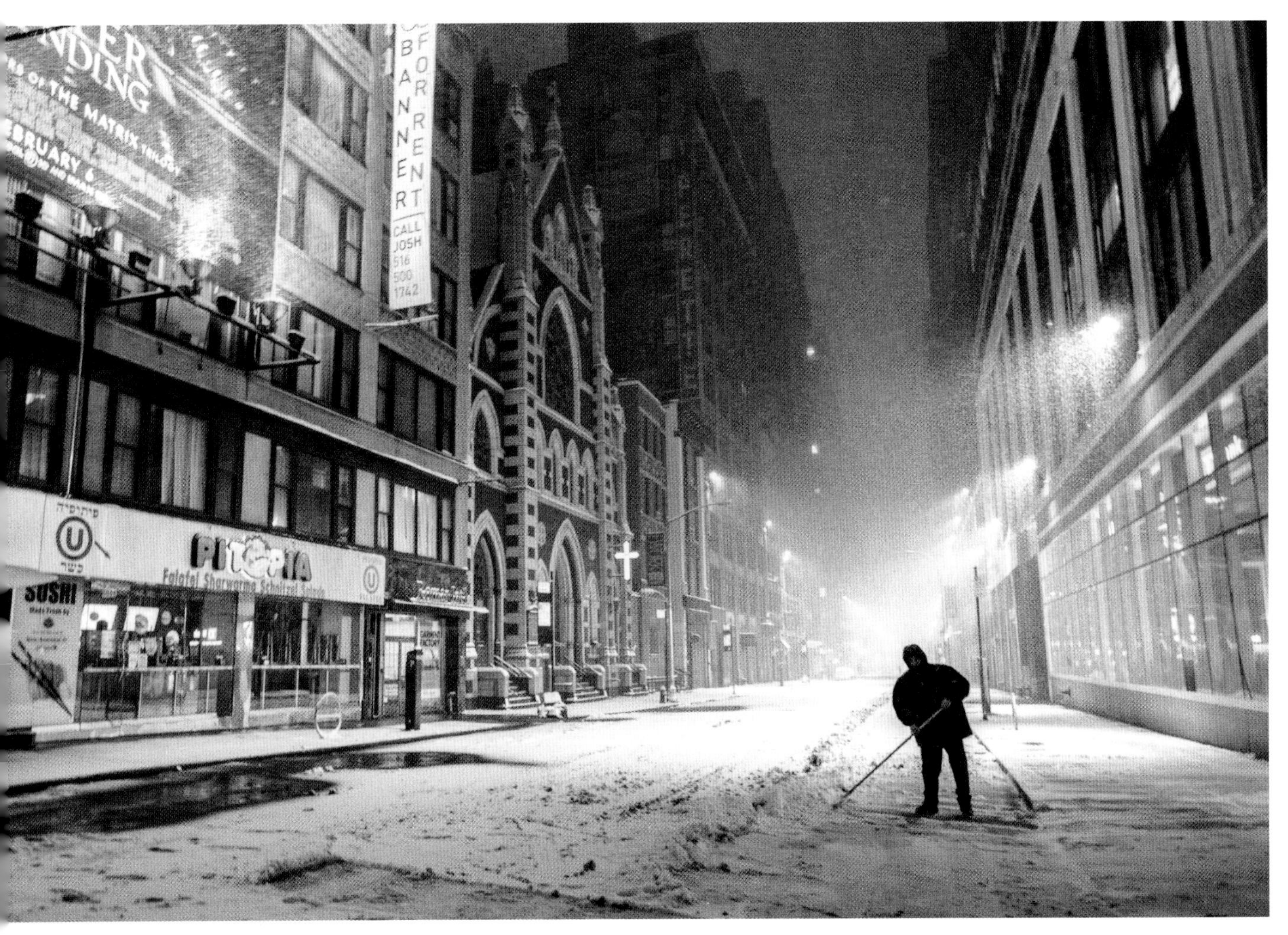

Midtown Manhattan
Sony SLT-A99V | *f*/4 | 1/80 second | ISO 4000

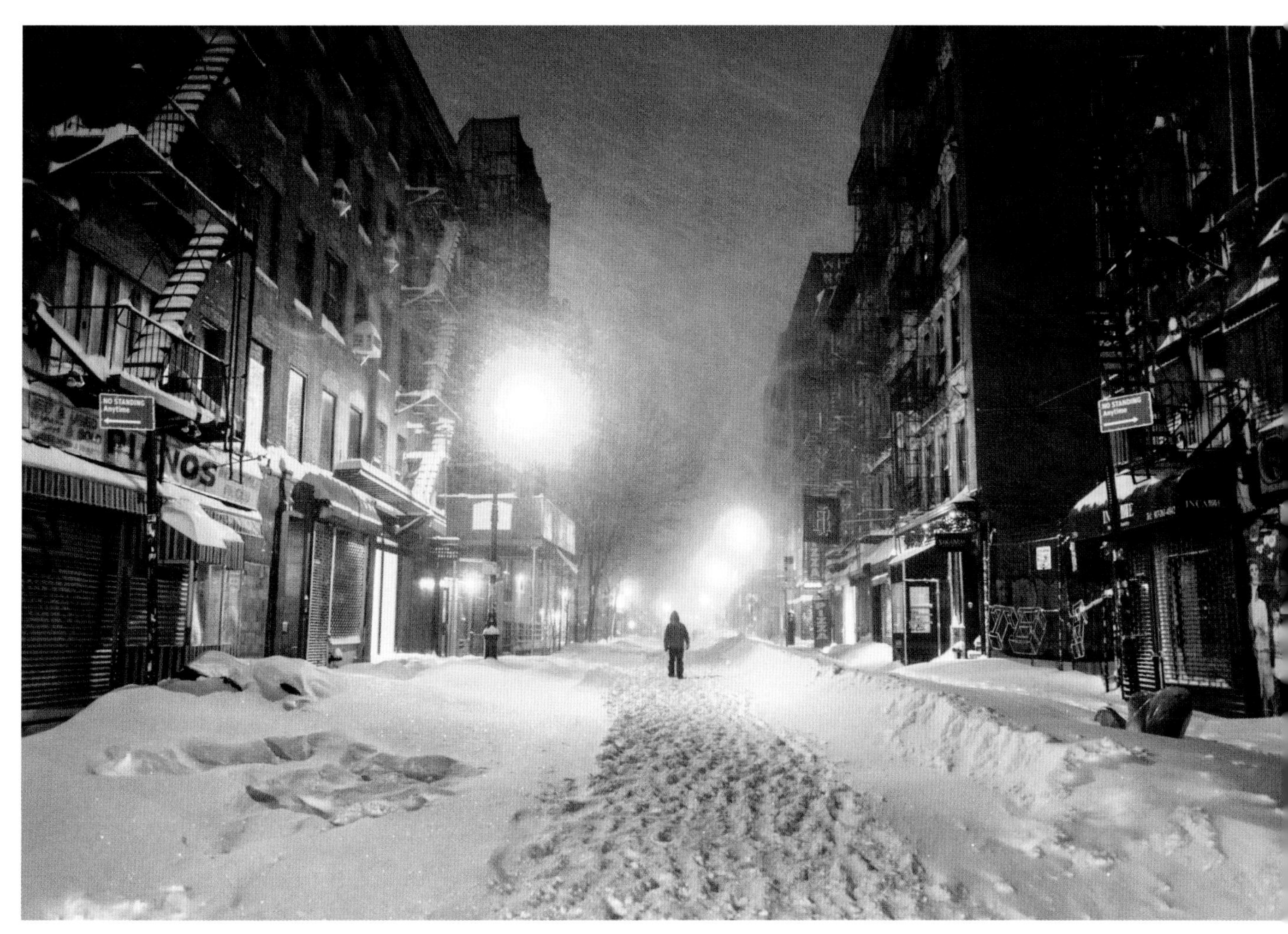

Lower East Side, Manhattan
Sony ILCE-7RM2 II | *f*/4 | 1/80 second | ISO 4000

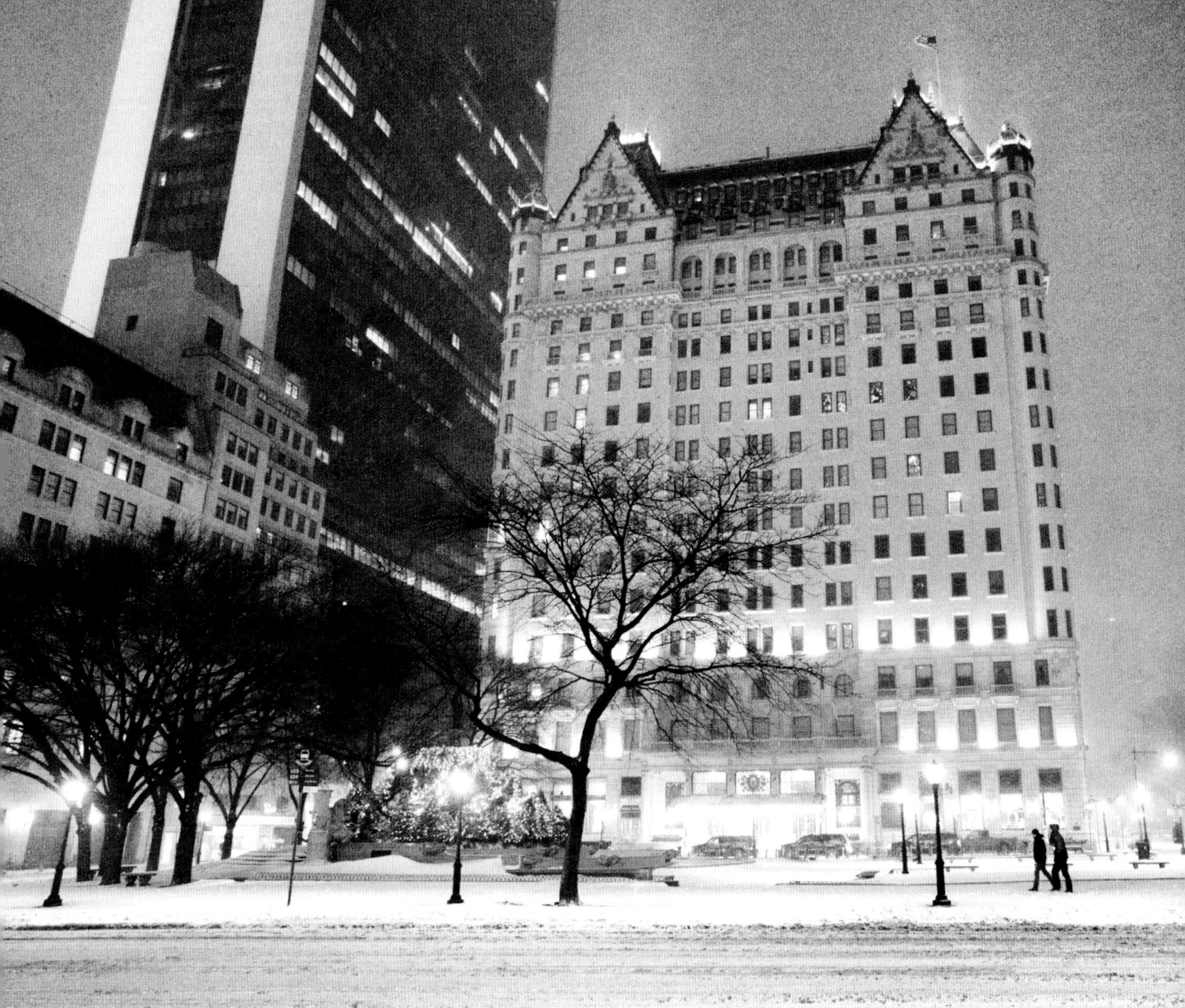

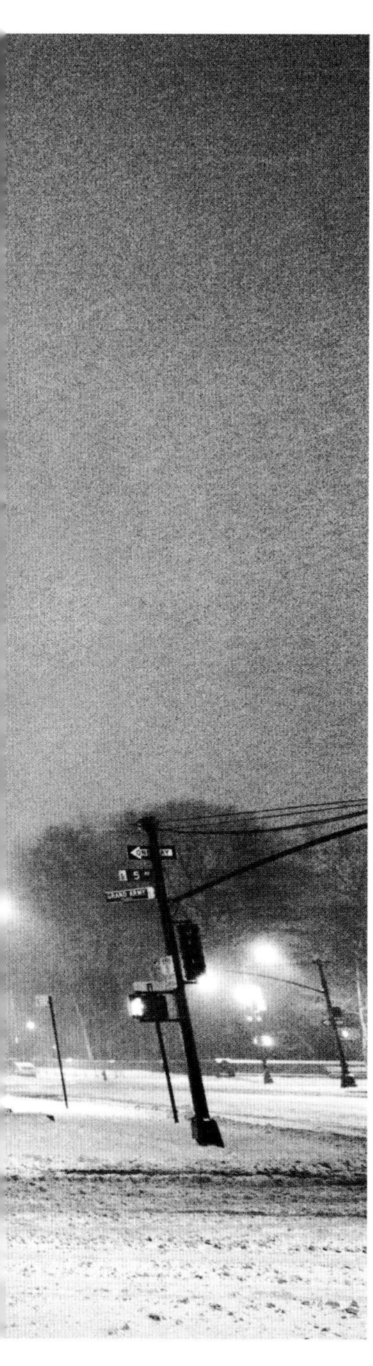

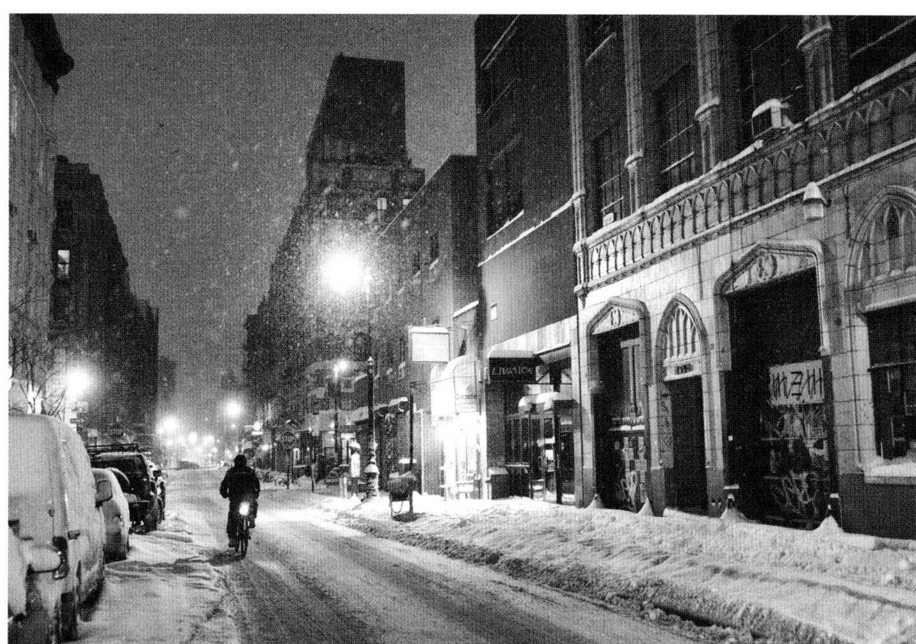

Lower East Side, Manhattan
Sony SLT-A99V | ƒ/3.2 | 1/125 second | ISO 4000

Plaza Hotel, Midtown Manhattan
Sony A7II | ƒ/5 | 1/20 second | ISO 4000

There are nights when dreams illuminate the city streets like stars.

Memories dance with steam ghosts exhaling into the night air.

And the city streets lie dormant under winter's heavy thoughts as the sky kisses the air and tree branches reach for the night sky while we make our way home stopping for brief moments to relish the silence.

Upper East Side, Manhattan
Sony A7II | *f*/5 | 1/30 second | ISO 4000

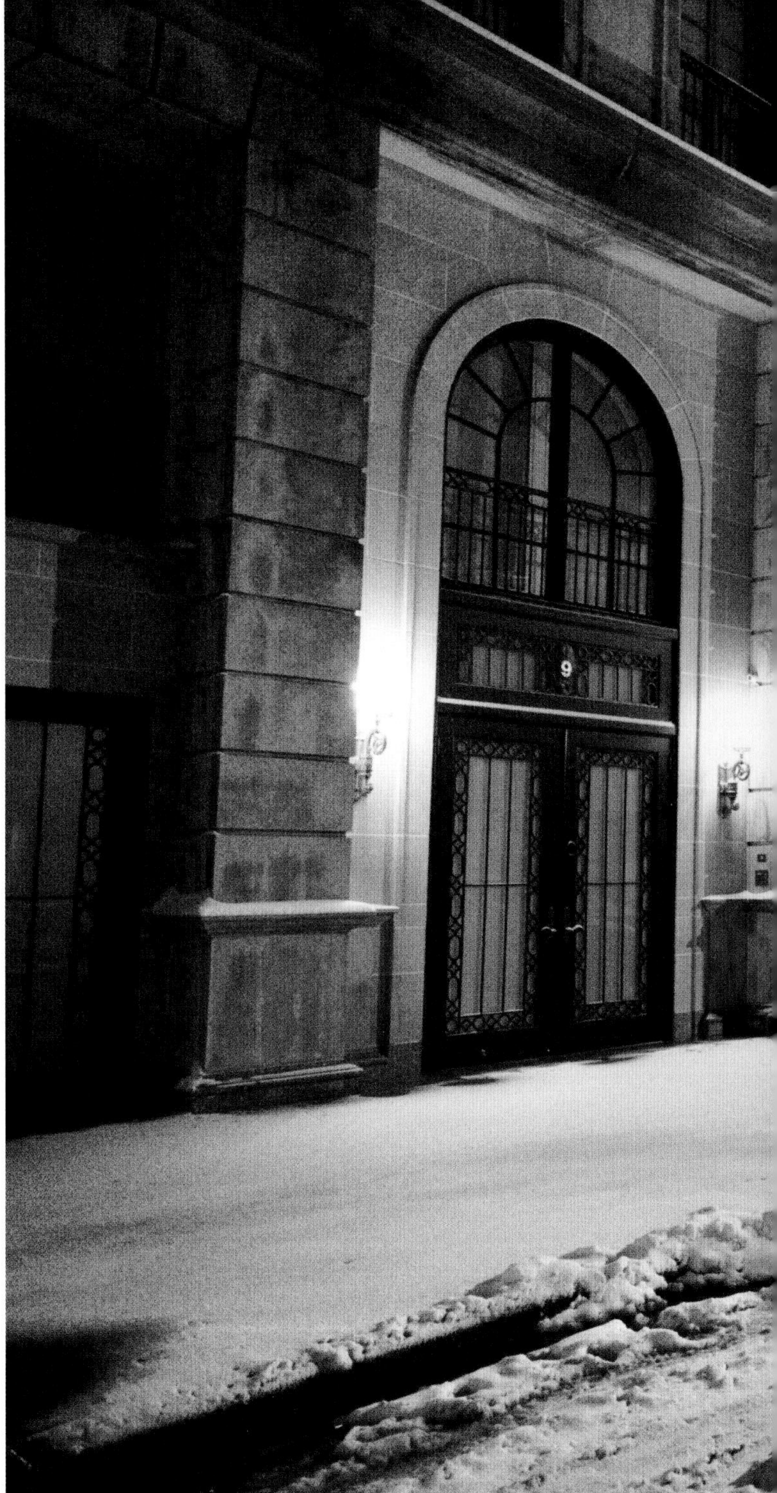

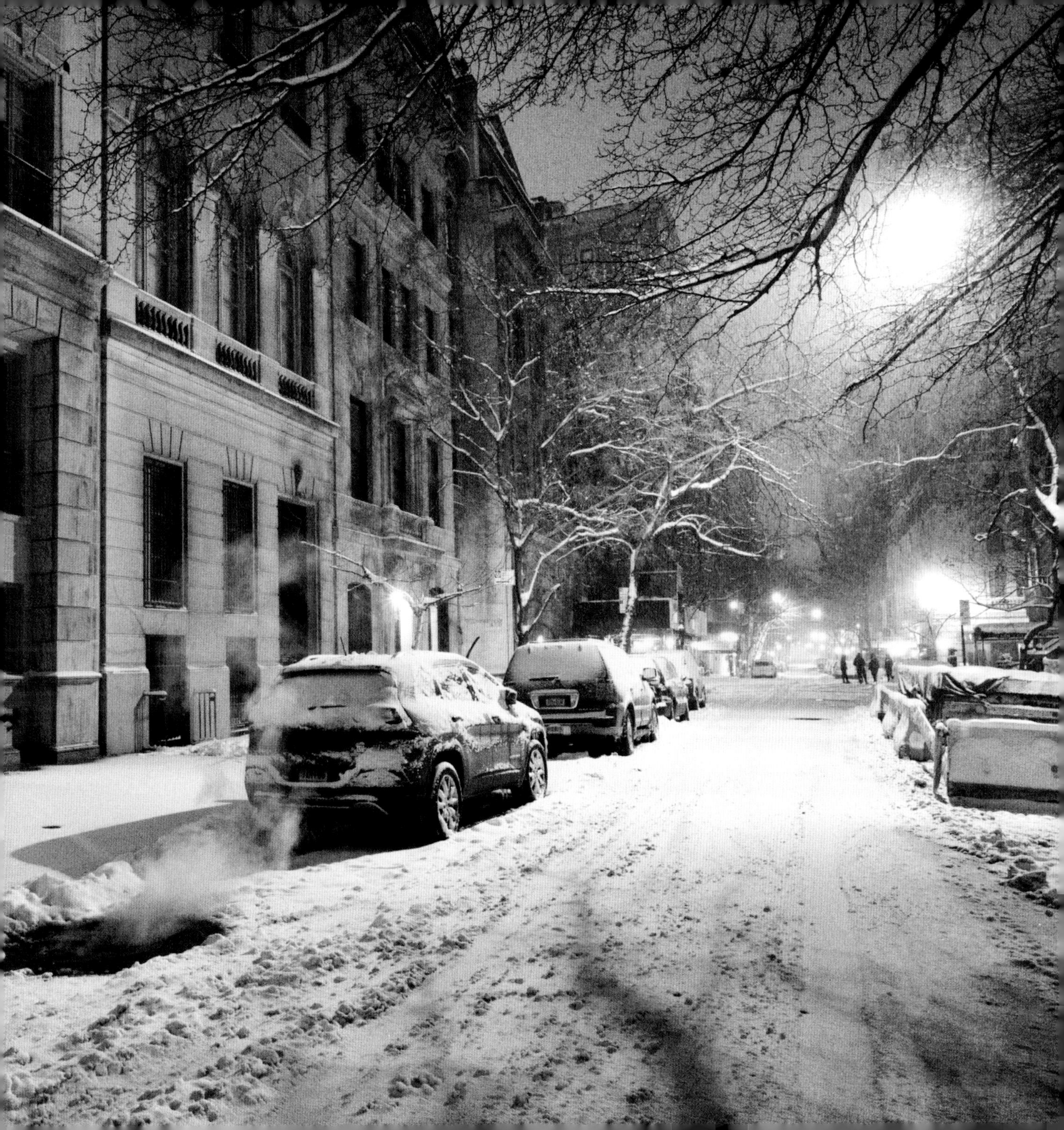

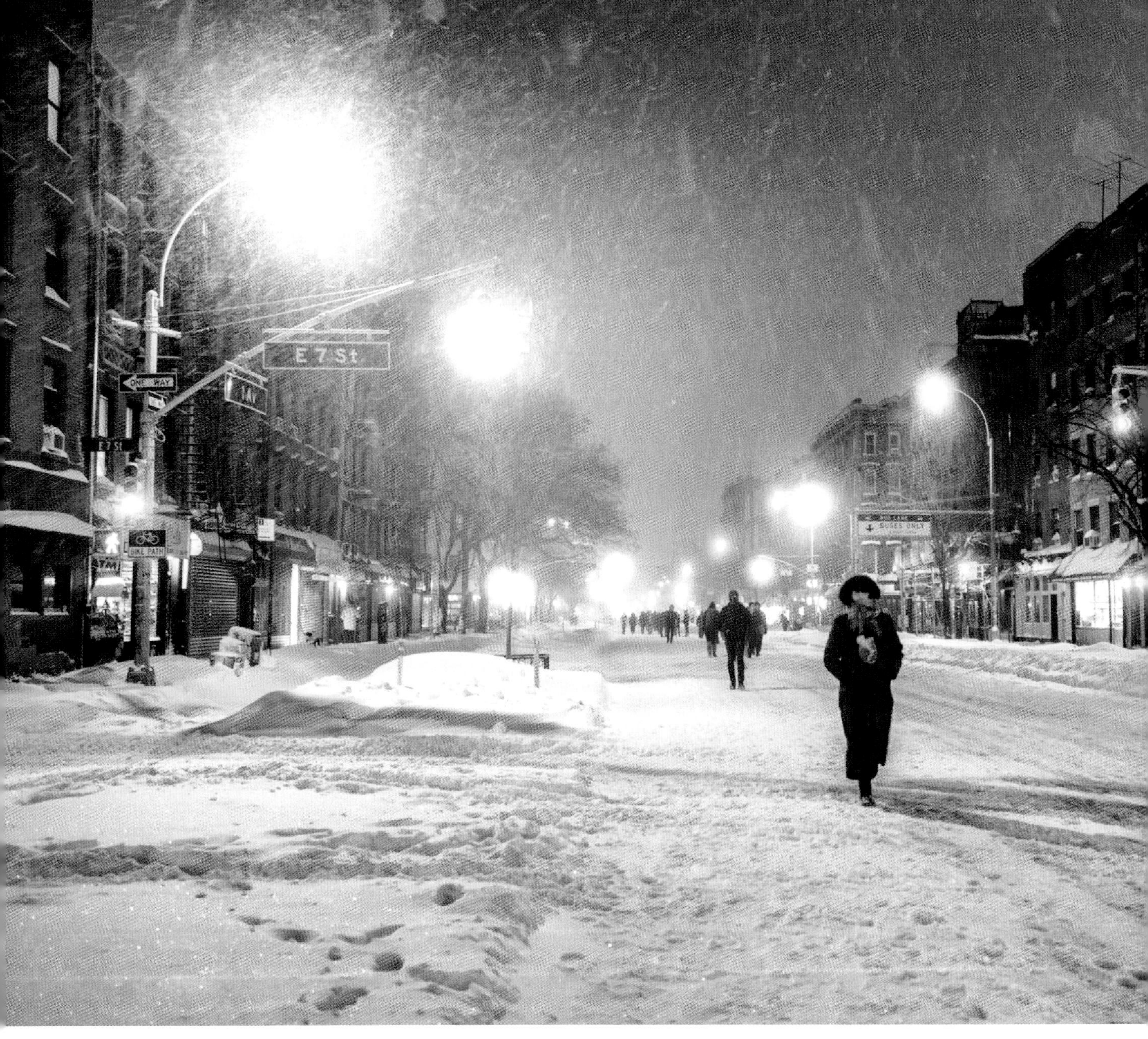
E 7 St
ONE WAY
1 Av
E 7 St
BIKE PATH
ATM
BUSES ONLY

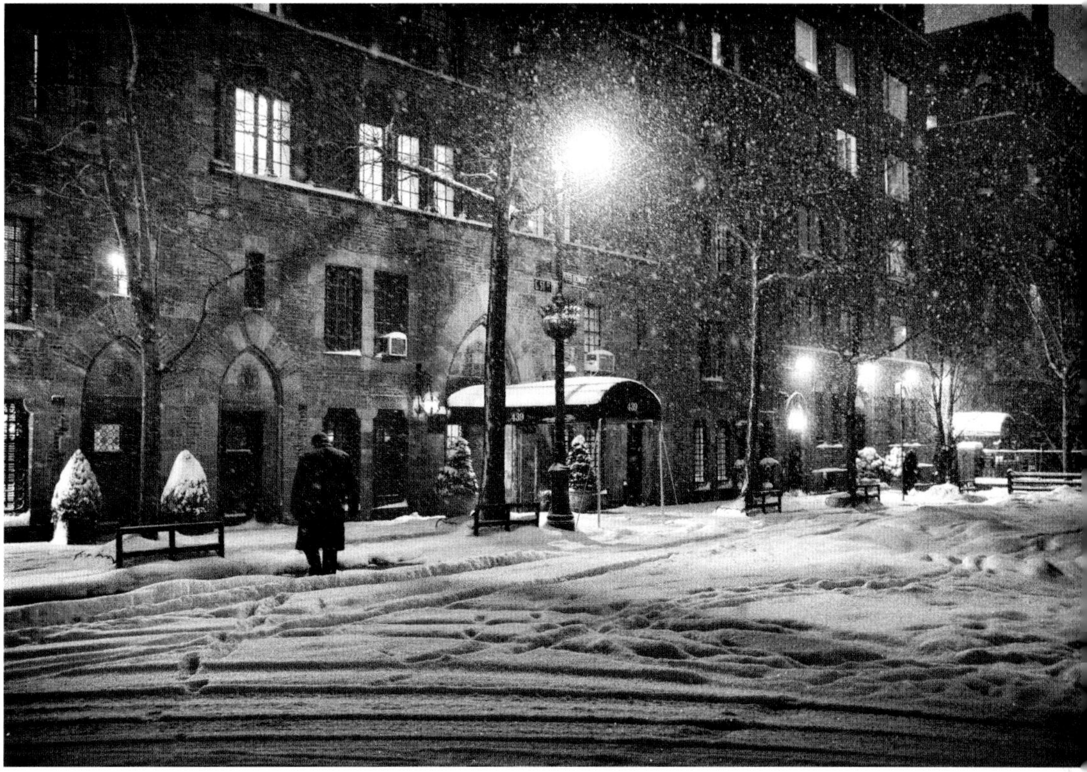

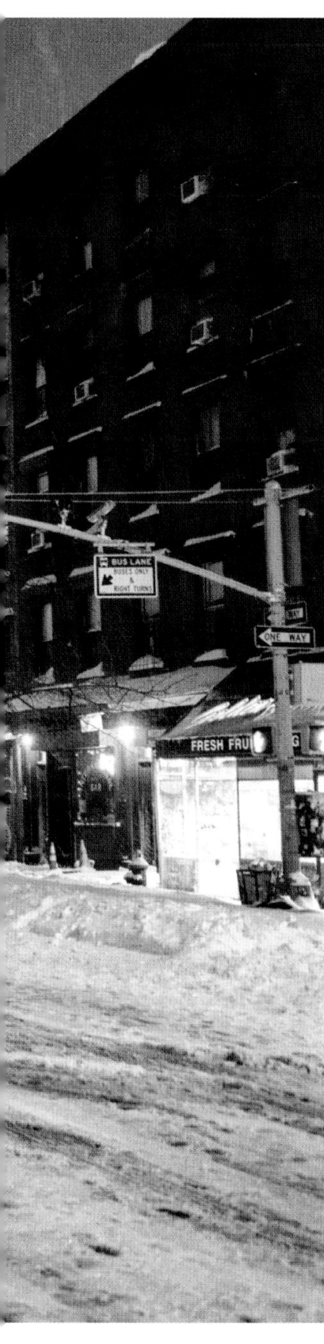

Sutton Place, Midtown Manhattan
Sony SLT-A99V | *f*/3.5 | 1/100 second | ISO 4000

Lower East Side, Manhattan
Sony ILCE-7RM2 II | *f*/4 | 1/20 second | ISO 3200

CHAPTER #2 | STORMS

“Dreams linger in the warm embrace of storms conjuring up the outline of buildings and cityscapes on winter’s frozen breath.

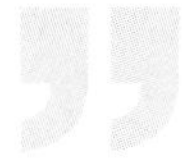

Midtown Manhattan
Sony SLT-A99V | f/3.2 | 1/80 second | ISO 4000

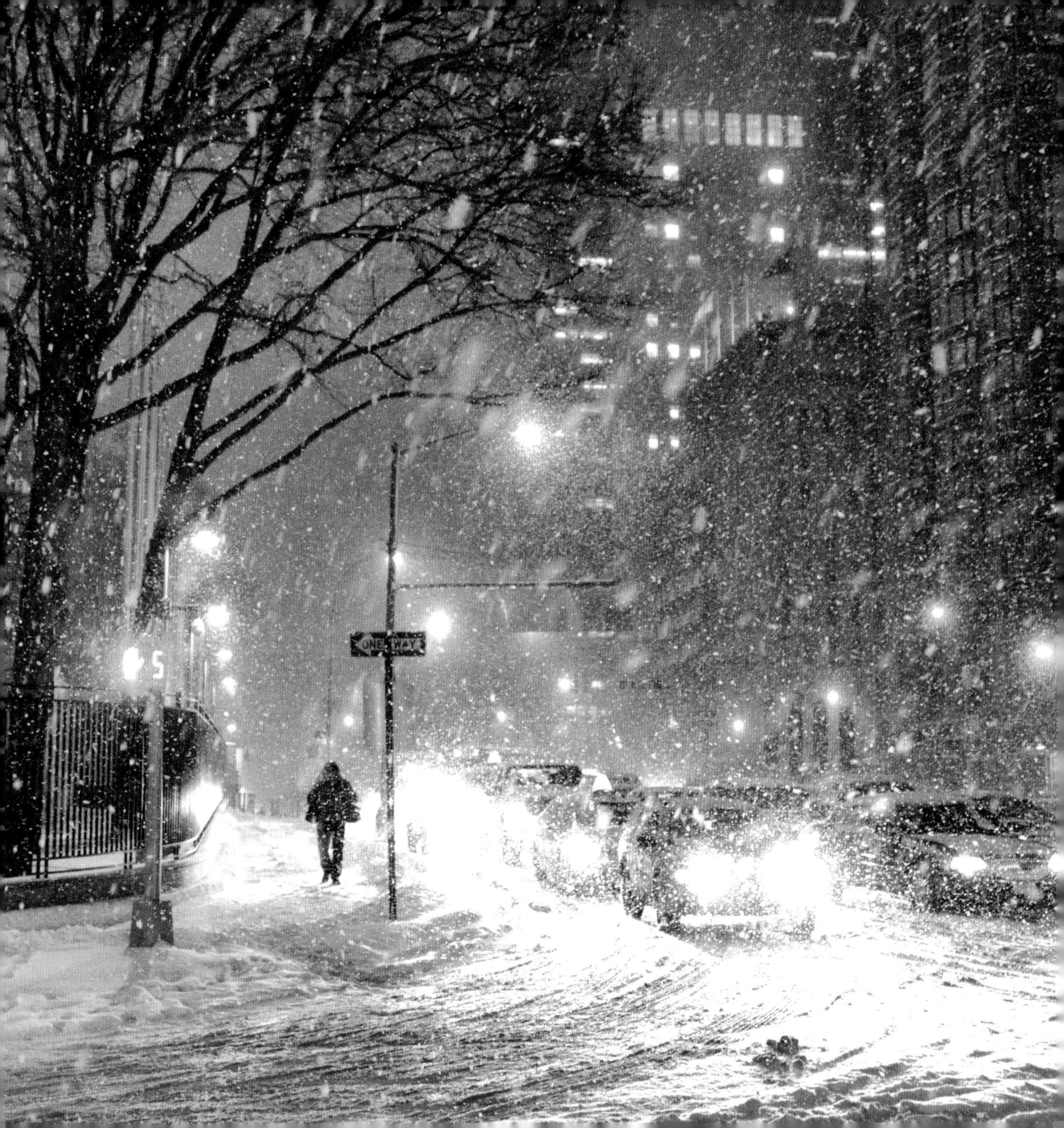
ONE WAY

A lot of people have asked me about how I protect myself and my camera when I take my snow photos. I have photographed every single snowstorm in NYC for the last five years. It's my passion project and what I love the most. During the first storm I ever photographed, I nearly got frostbite. I was shooting with a broken point-and-shoot camera, covering it between shots with my useless gloves.

Thankfully, I have come quite a long way since then! My camera bodies (all Sony) do really well in snow and rain, but my lenses are not weather-sealed and I am paranoid about ruining them. So to protect them I use . . . drum-roll . . . a plastic bag! To be precise, a trash bag—the thickest I can find. I take the bag and snip one of the corners with scissors. I then put the bag over my lens with the snipped corner in the center of the lens. Then I stretch the bag over my lens with only the glass of the lens exposed.

> “(Bonus: I put my face into the rest of the bag when shooting. It looks pretty funny actually.)”

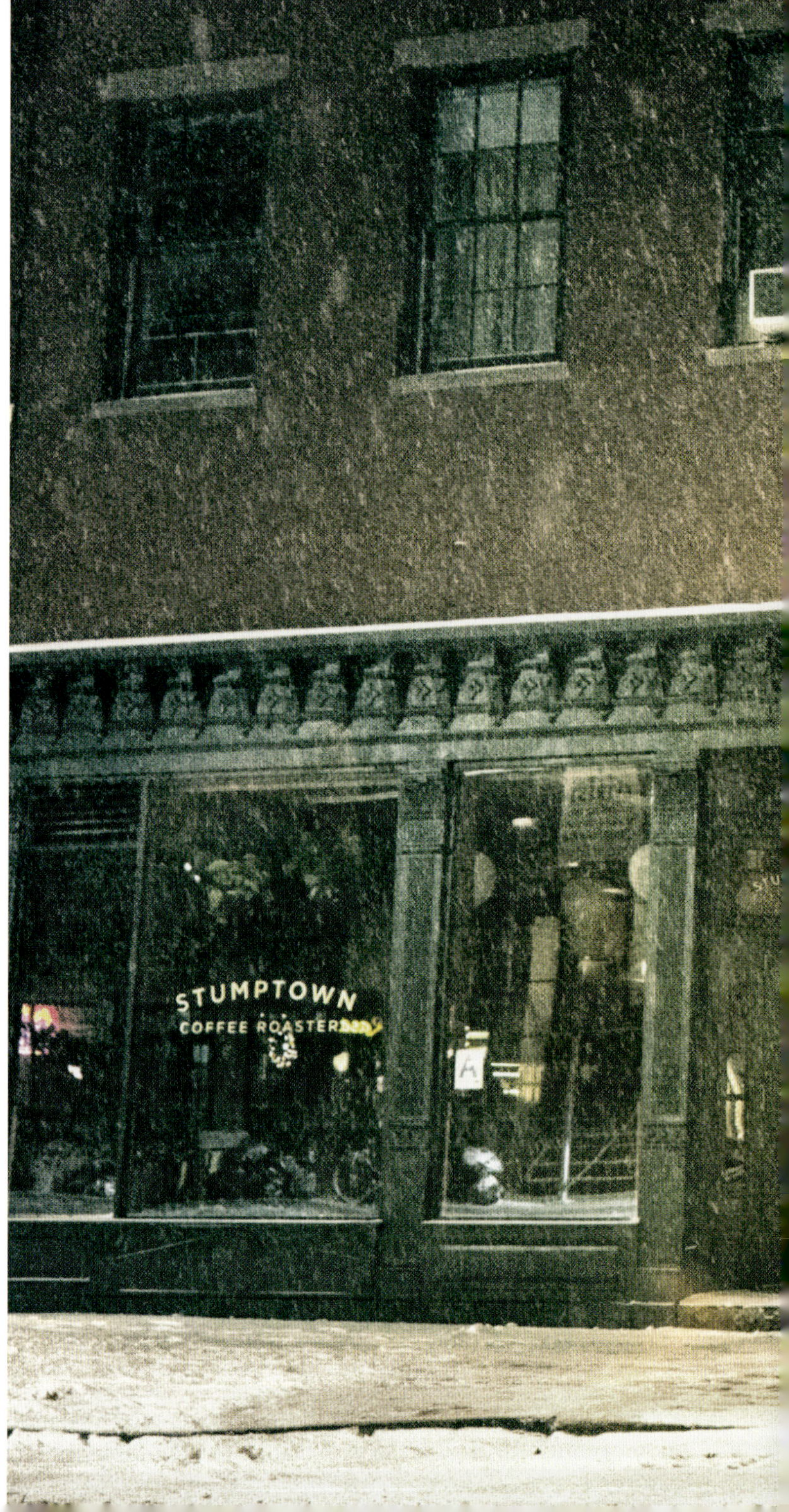

Greenwich Village, Lower West Side, Manhattan
Sony SLT-A99V | *f*/3.2 | 1/20 second | ISO 4000

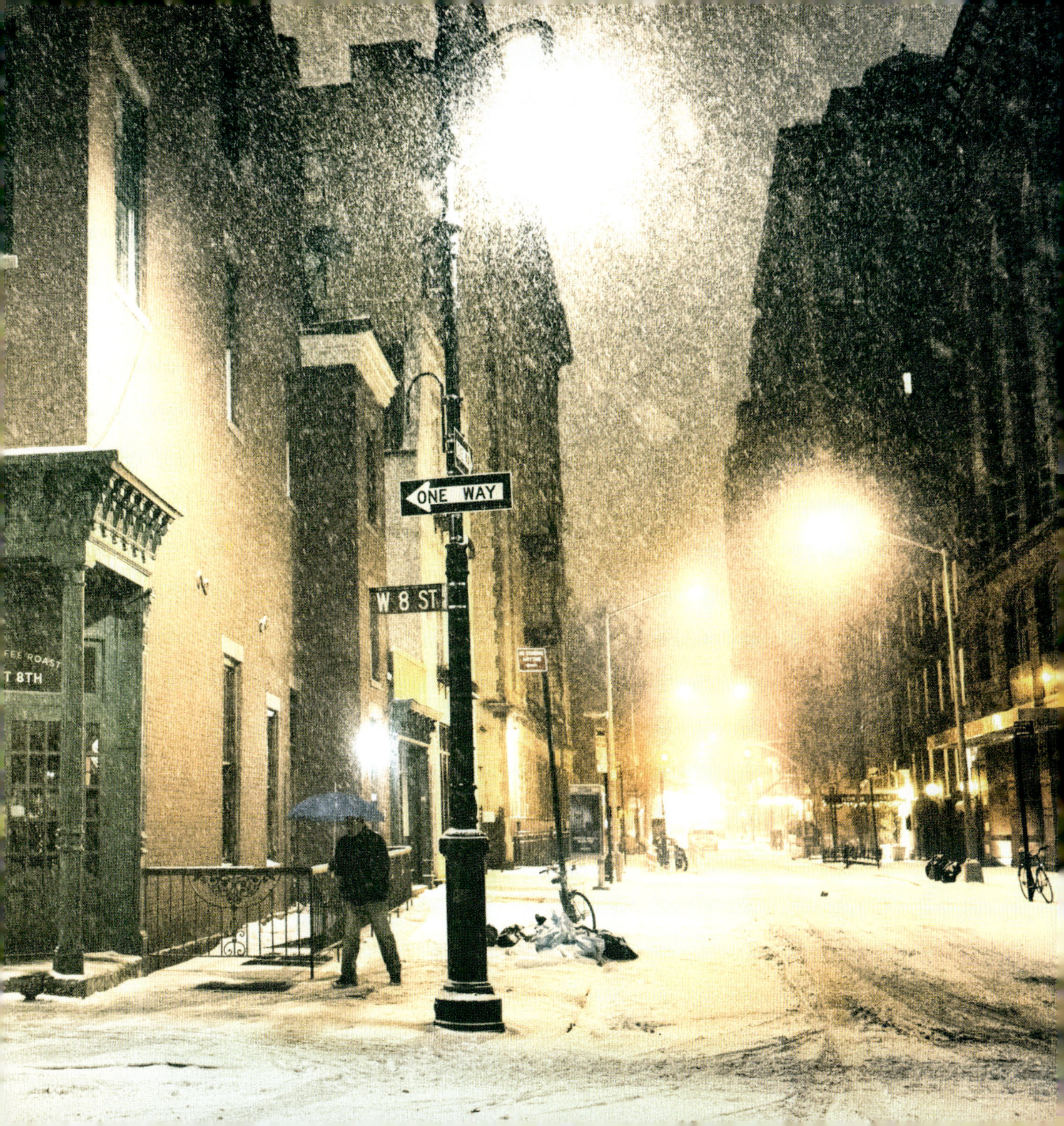
ONE WAY
W 8 ST
FEE ROAST
T 8TH

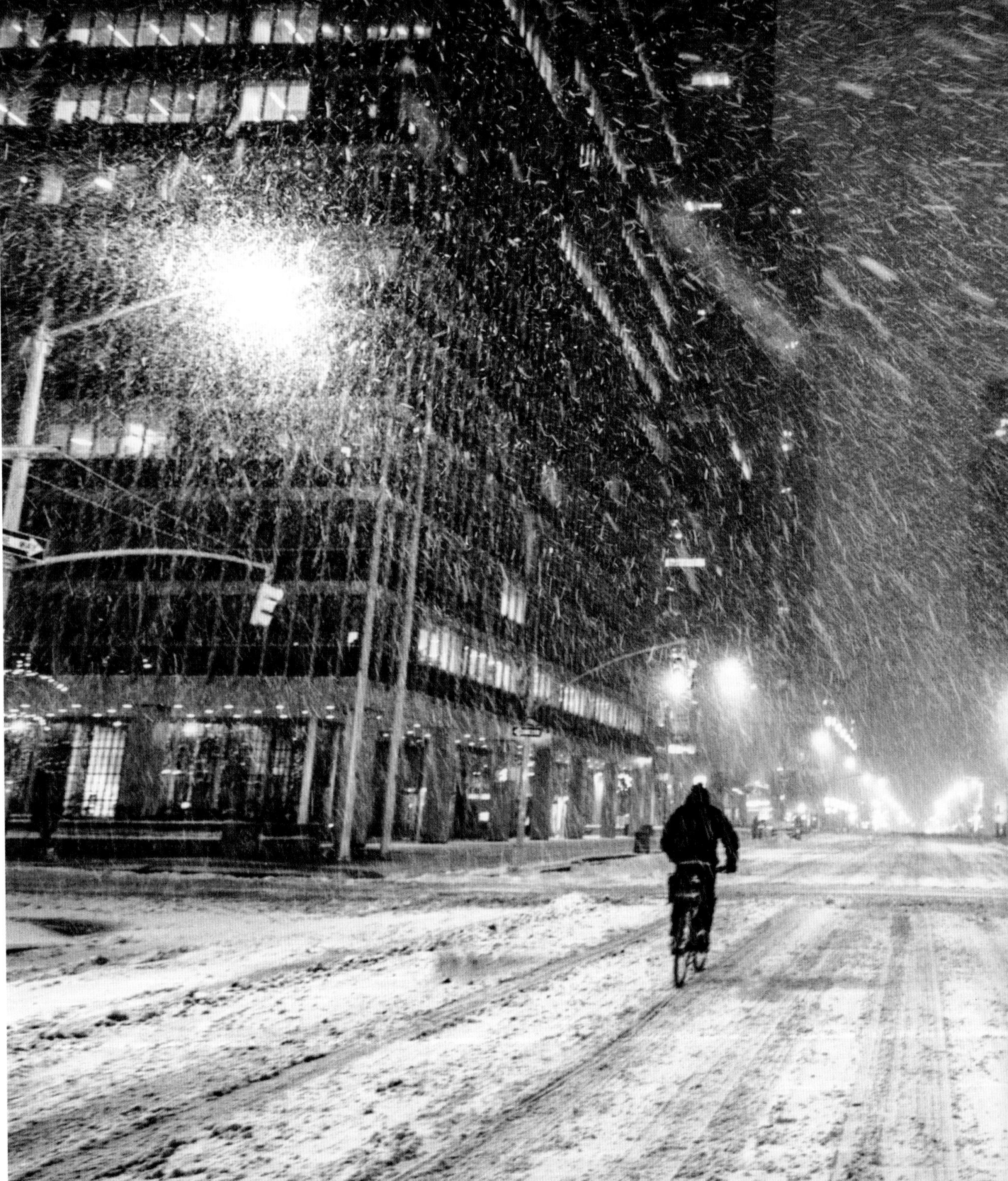

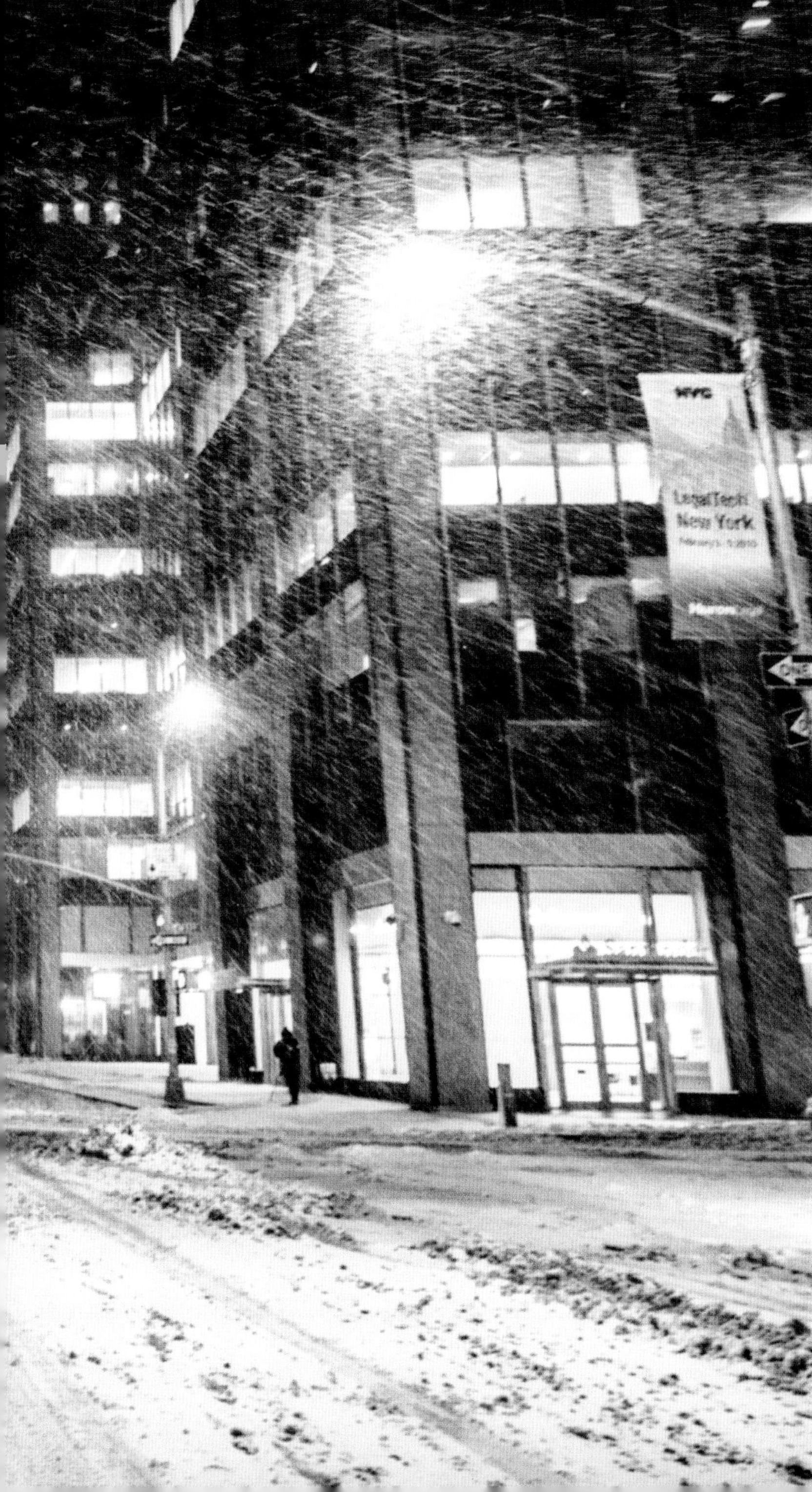

When the lens is covered (this bit is important!), I take the lens hood and put it on the lens with the bag stretched as already detailed. Sometimes I take a hair-tie or rubber band and put it around the lens near the body. The hood is useful protection when walking around for miles. I point the camera down between shots and blowing snow collects on the outside of the lens hood, where it can easily be brushed off.

Since I always shoot in manual mode, and because I'm mainly shooting these photos at night, I check and adjust my settings every single block so that I don't miss a shot. I have to shoot very, very, very quickly due to the conditions.

Midtown Manhattan
Sony SLT-A99V | *f*/4 | 1/80 second | ISO 4000

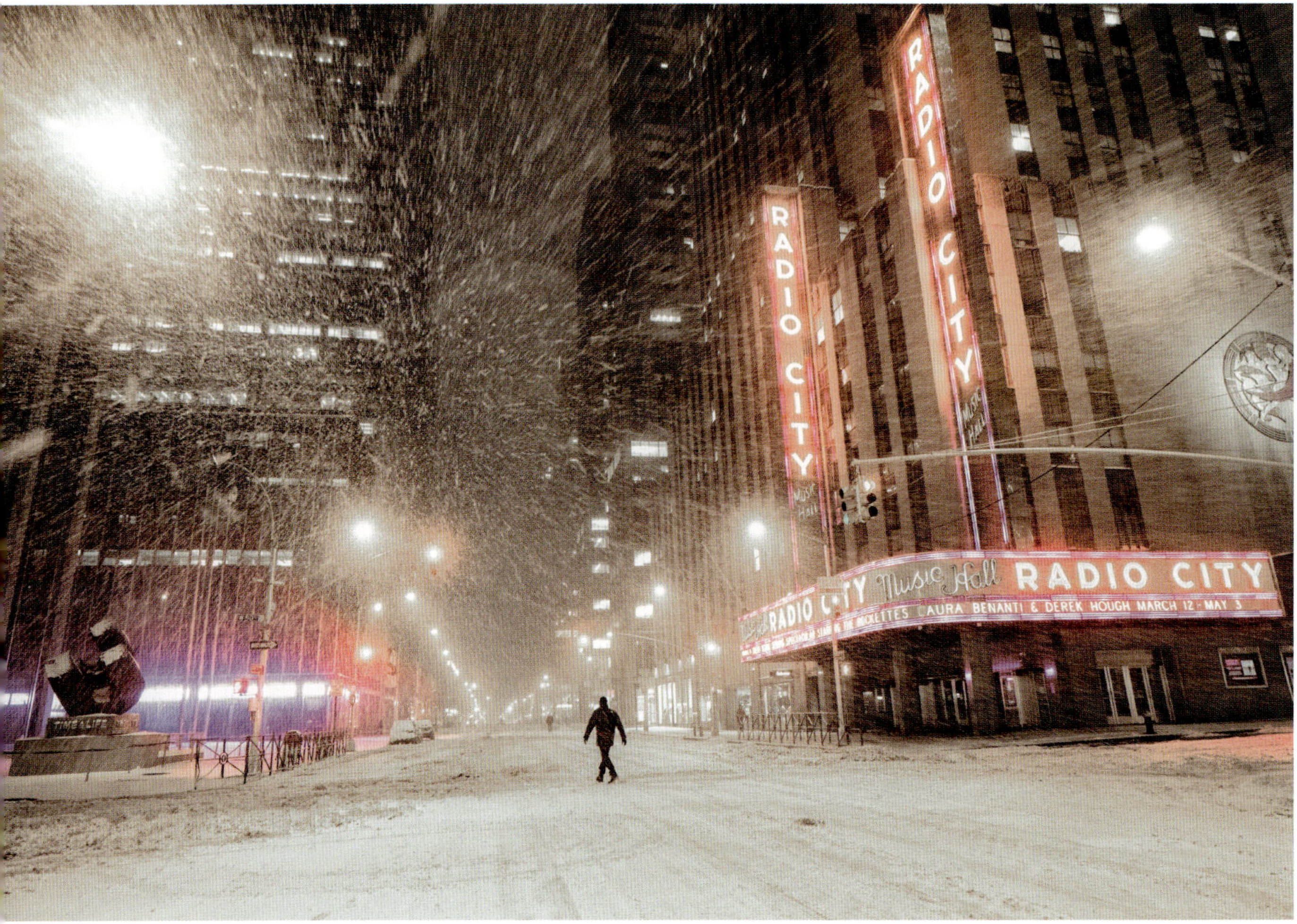

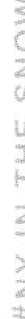

Midtown Manhattan

Sony ILCE-7M2 | *f*/5 | 1/30 second | ISO 4000

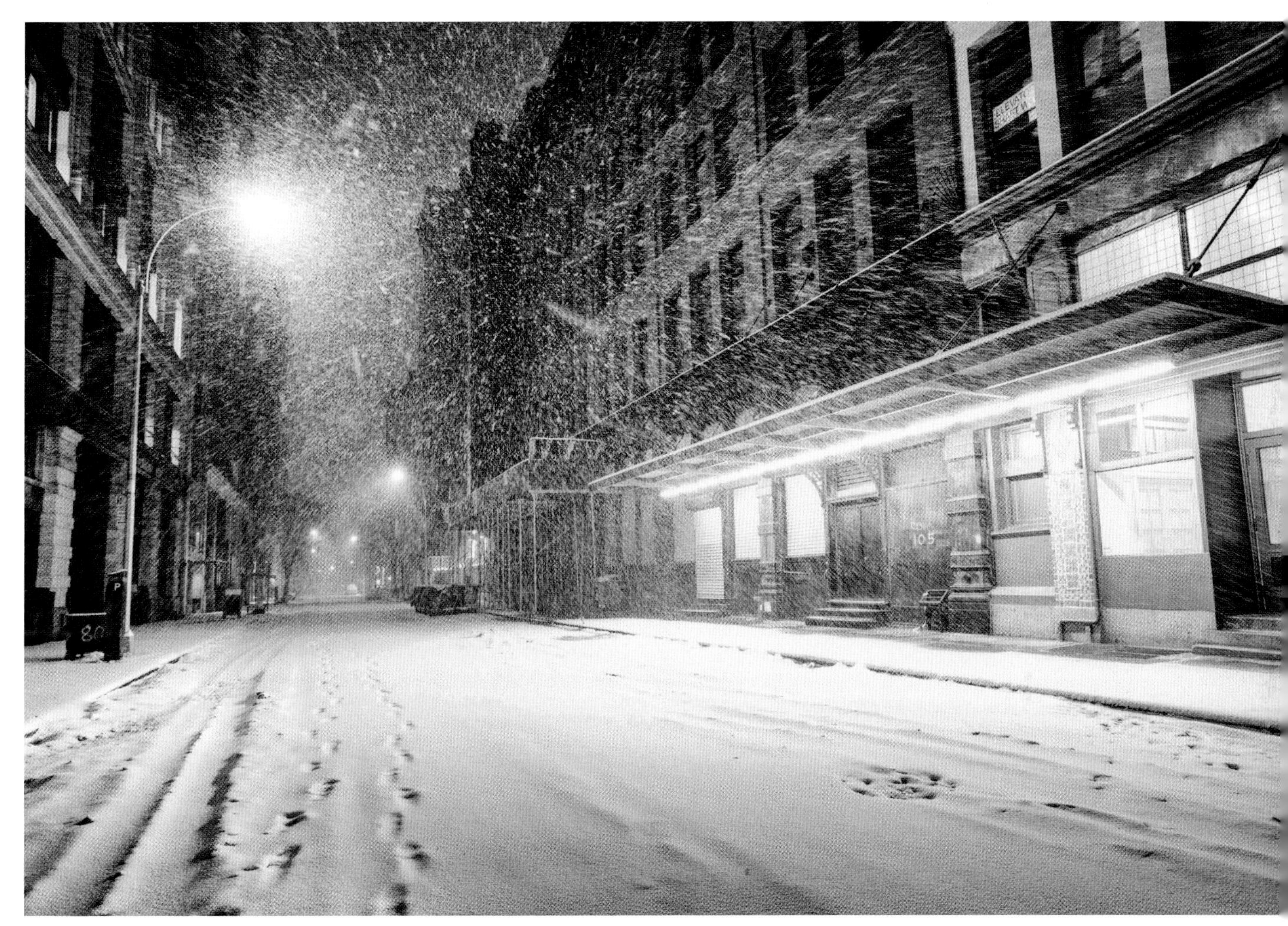

Upper East Side, Manhattan
Sony ILCE-7M2 | f/5 | 1/10 second | ISO 4000

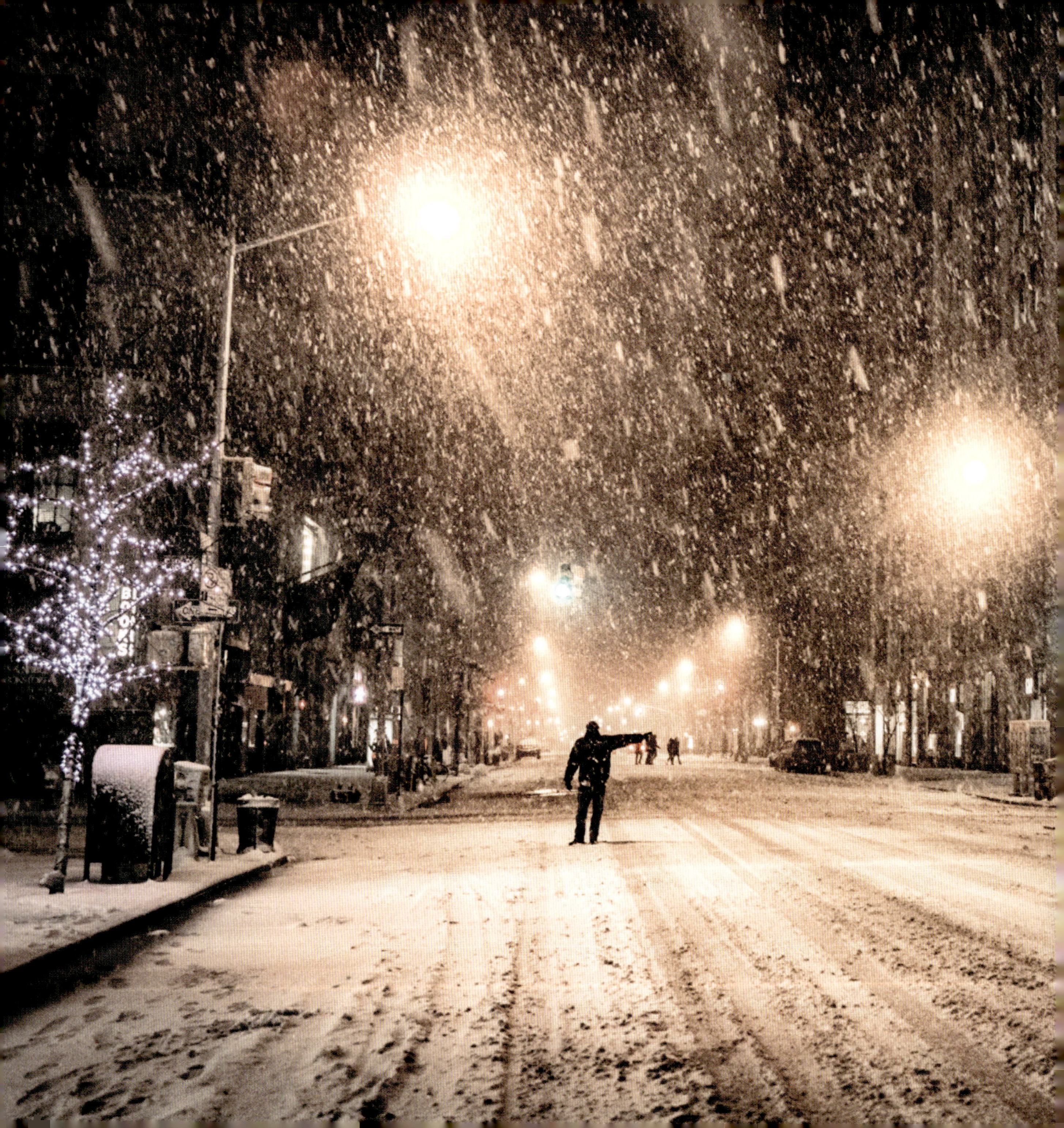

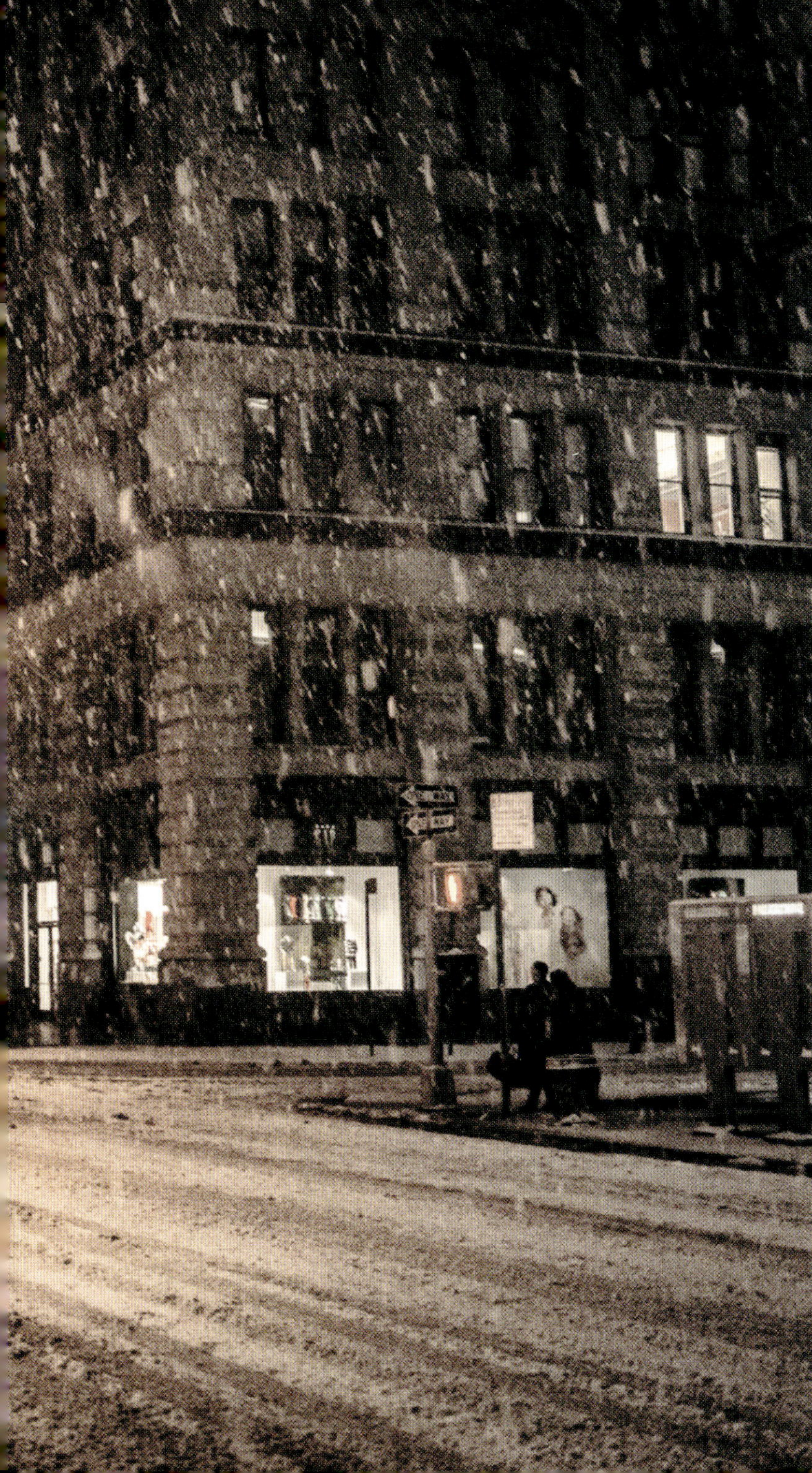

Outer clothing: I wear a waterproof, insulated, down-filled, knee-length parka, and insulated, waterproof snowboard/ski pants with waterproof snow boots (great grip, and grip is a must—I learned my lesson the hard way two years back). I wear a balaclava, ski goggles (eyes are important and only one of mine works), and a beanie hat. I have to have my hood up and drawn to my face to keep the blowing snow away from my head area. I have giant Thinsulate gloves that I wear with thin gloves underneath so that my skin is never exposed when I mess with my manual settings every block.

Inner clothing: thermal leggings, shirt, and socks, a breathable light layer over the thermal shirt, and breathable thermals over the leggings. Something I have learned is that breathable fabrics are essential. When you're walking several miles, even in below zero windchills, you can get hot. If you are too hot in your gear you can become dehydrated from sweating too much, and in extreme conditions this can contribute to hypothermia.

◀ Chelsea, Manhattan
Sony SLT-A99V | ƒ/3.2 | 1/100 second | ISO 2500

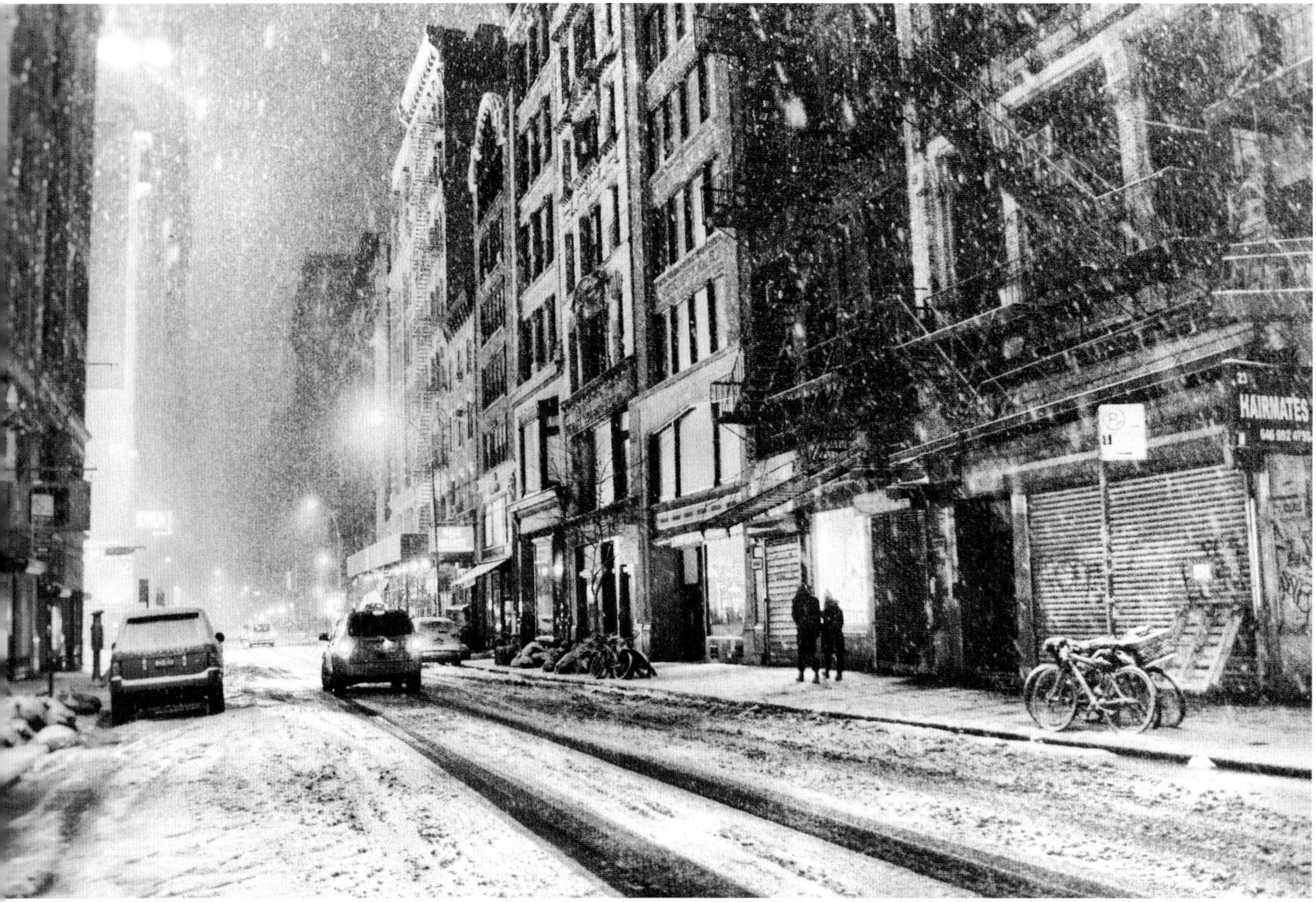

Greenwich Village, Lower Manhattan
Sony SLT-A99V | *f*/3.2 | 1/125 second | ISO 4000

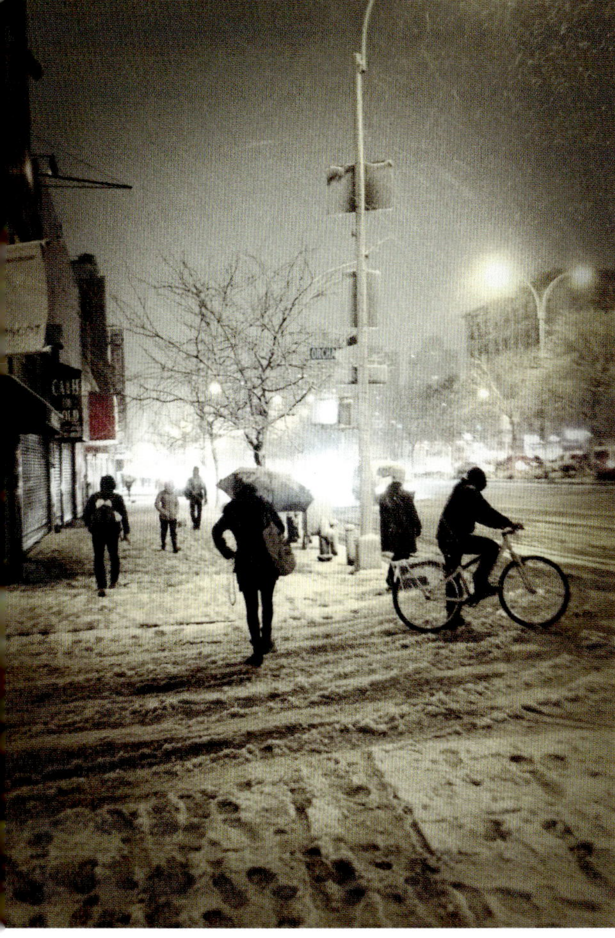

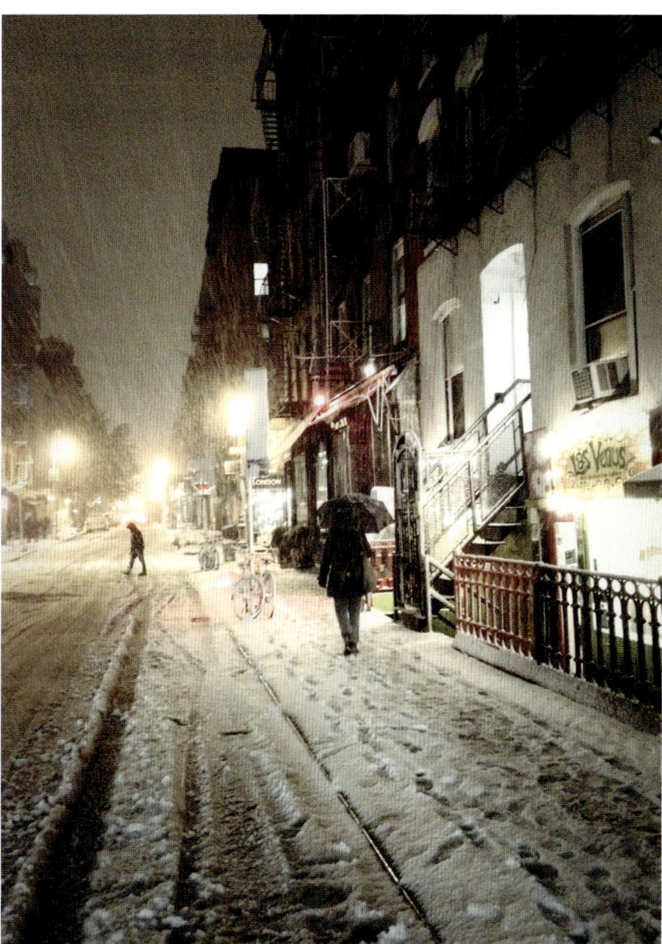

Lower East Side, Manhattan
iPhone 5S

Lower East Side, Manhattan
iPhone 5S

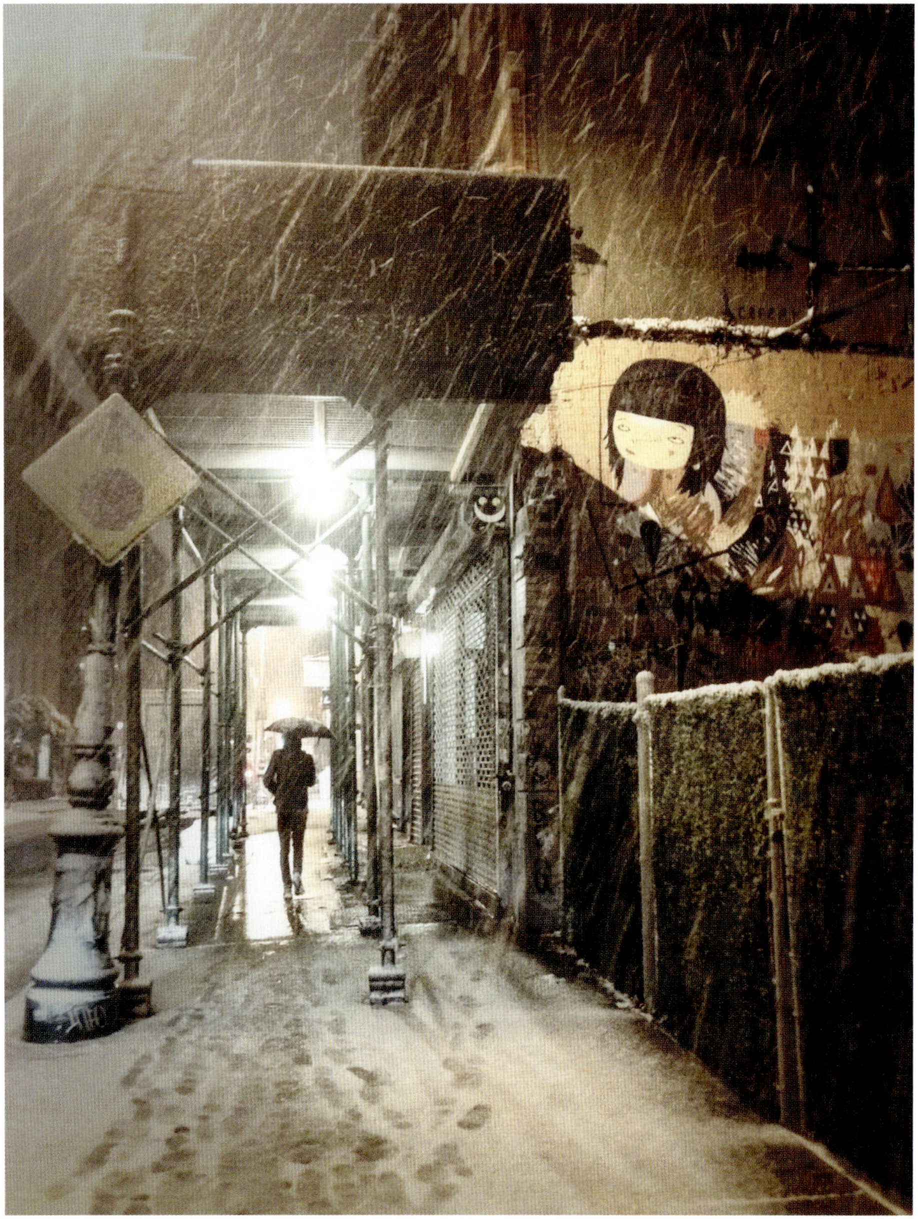

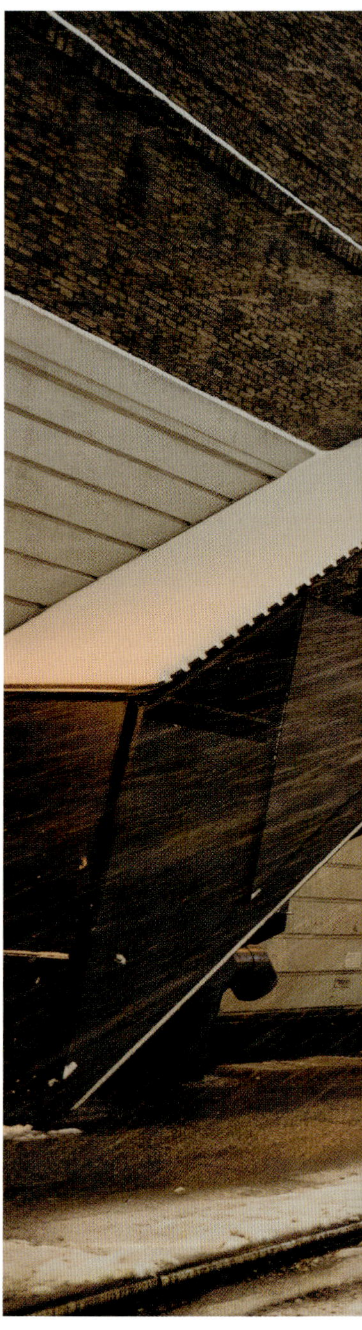

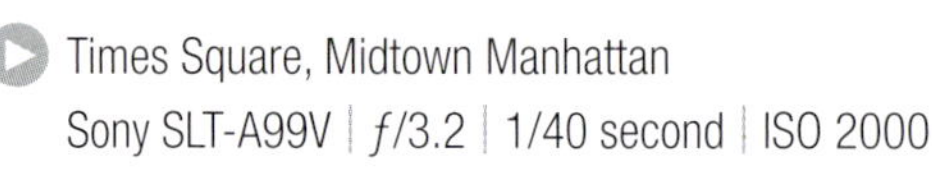

▲ Lower East Side, Manhattan
iPhone 5S

▶ Times Square, Midtown Manhattan
Sony SLT-A99V | ƒ/3.2 | 1/40 second | ISO 2000

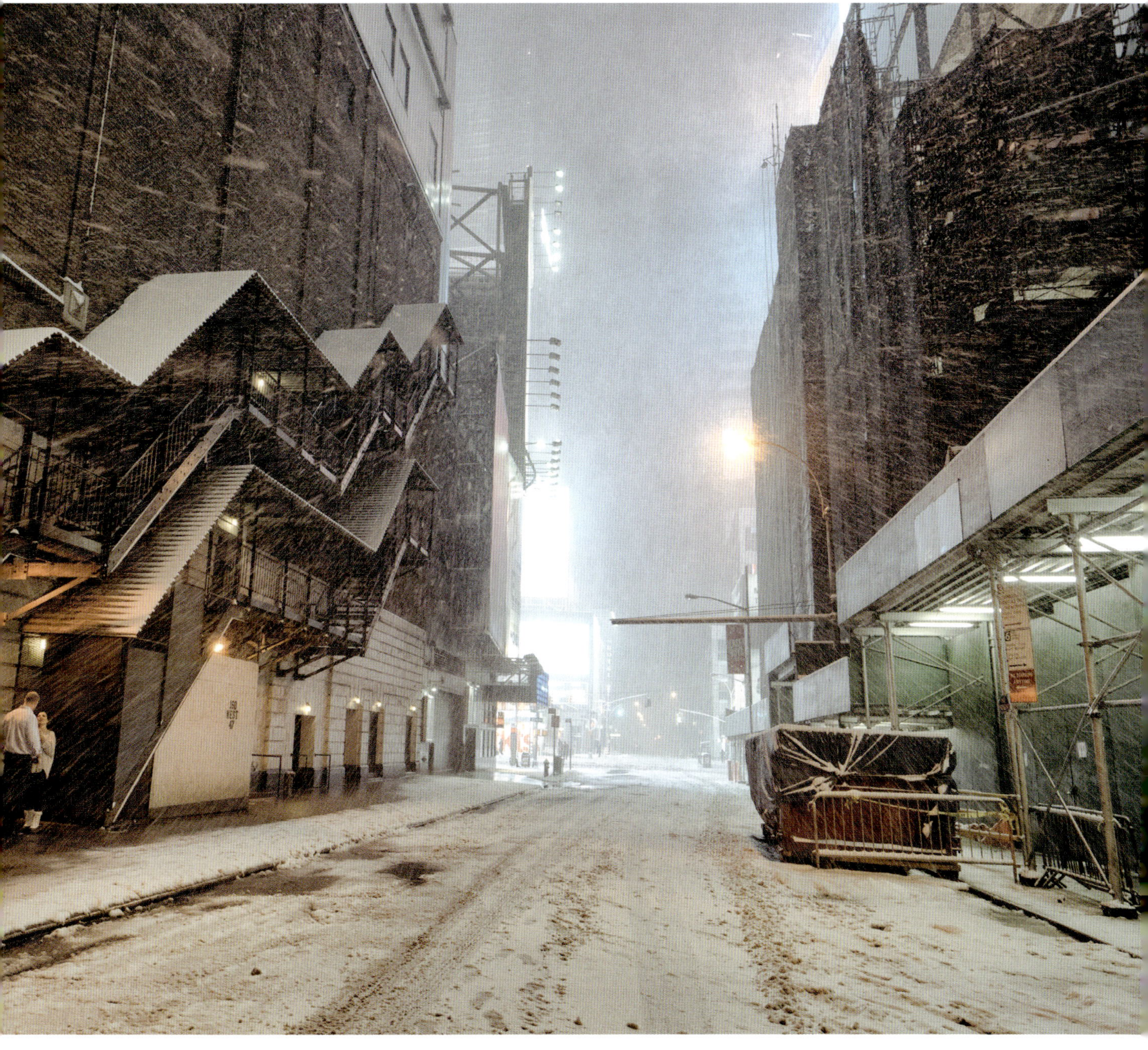

Having grown up the daughter of a parent who worked nights (my father was a pressman for the *Daily News*), I have always been drawn to those whose lives revolve around keeping the city running late at night. Working nights isn't easy, and in my father's case it was back-breaking manual labor that he engaged in while everyone else slept.

In snowstorms especially, those who shovel the city sidewalks and streets are the hidden heroes of New York City. It's an often lonely and painful task but there is some beauty in being surrounded by a nearly empty city while working.

My father didn't particularly love his job but I remember once when I was quite young that he took me with him via the subway to see the large machines he worked on at night. We both marveled at the peacefulness of the city late at night in Midtown.

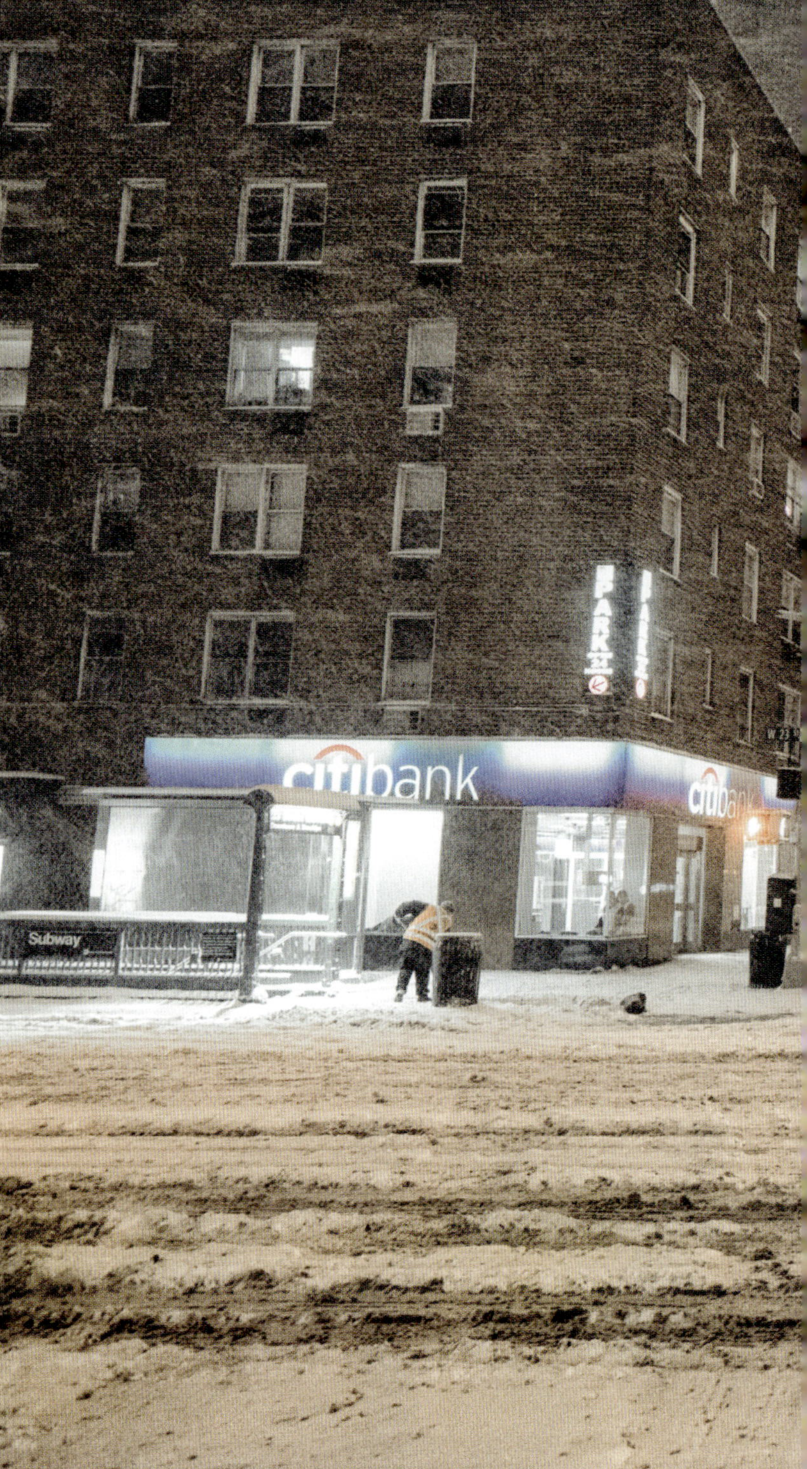

Greenwich Village, Lower West Side, Manhattan
Sony ILCE-7M2 | *f*/3.2 | 1/20 second | ISO 2000

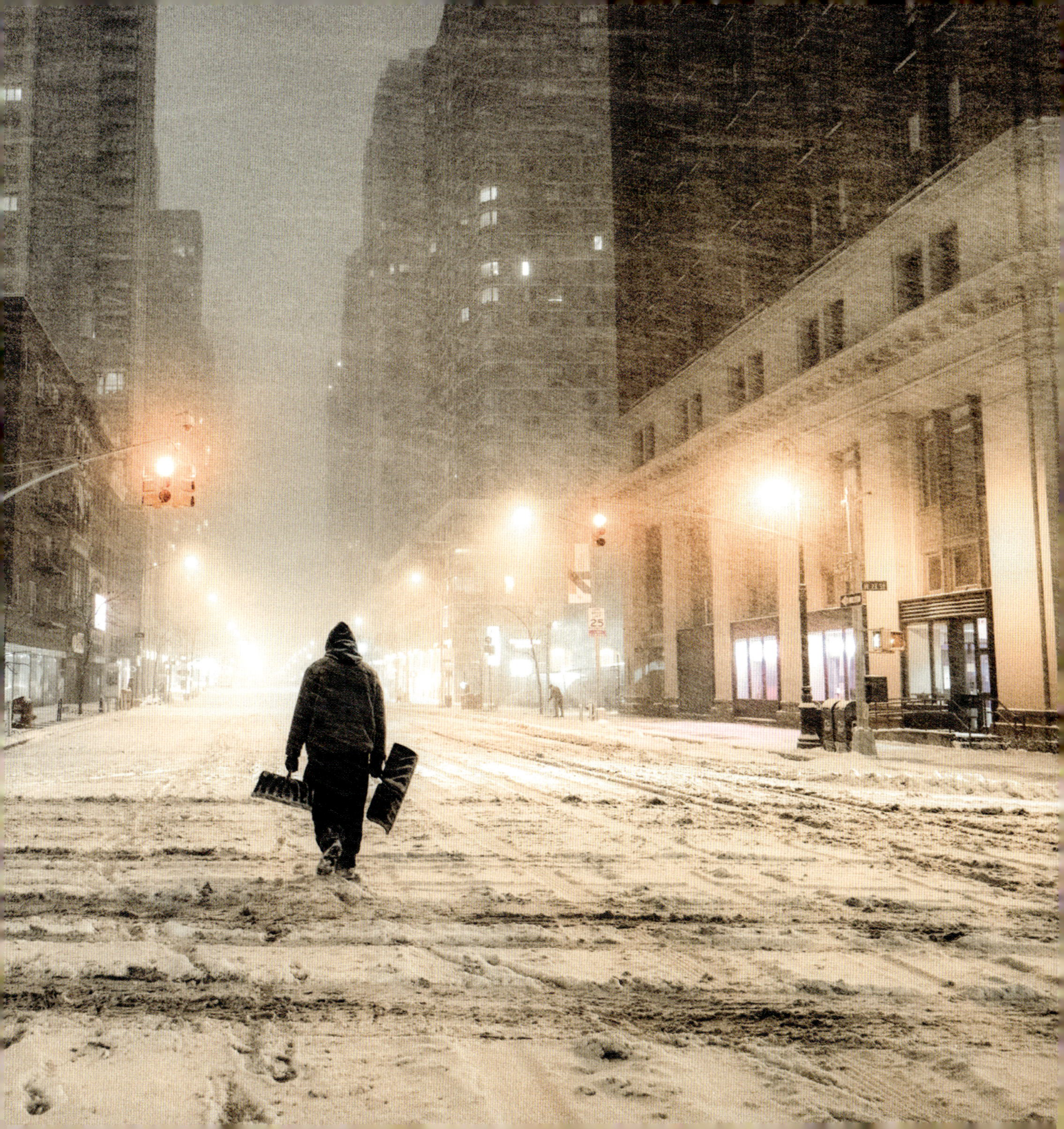
25

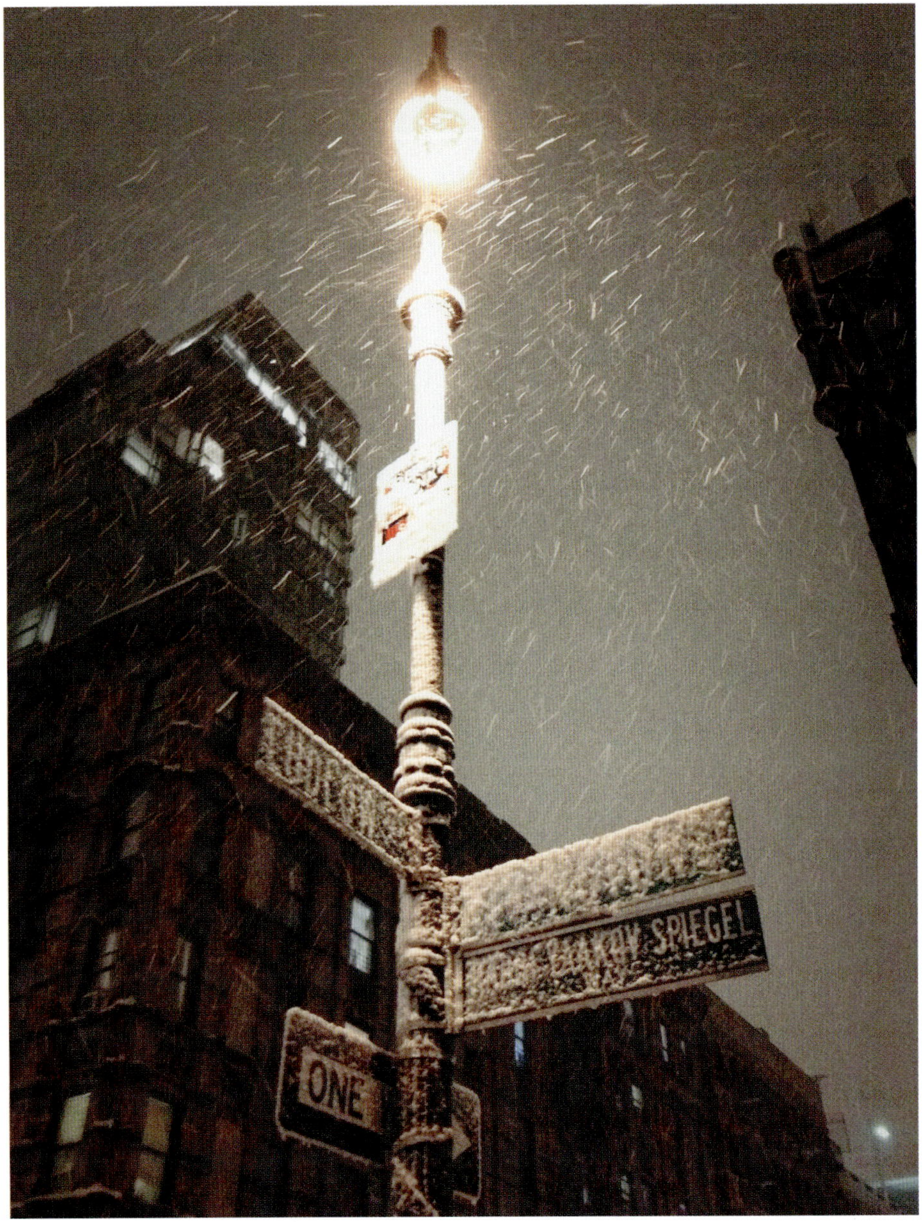

East Village, Lower Manhattan
Sony ILCE-7RM2 | ƒ/5 | 1/80 second | ISO 2000

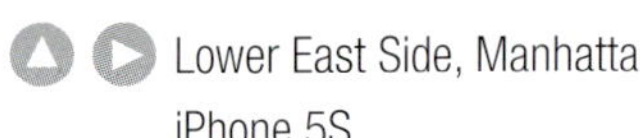

Lower East Side, Manhattan
iPhone 5S

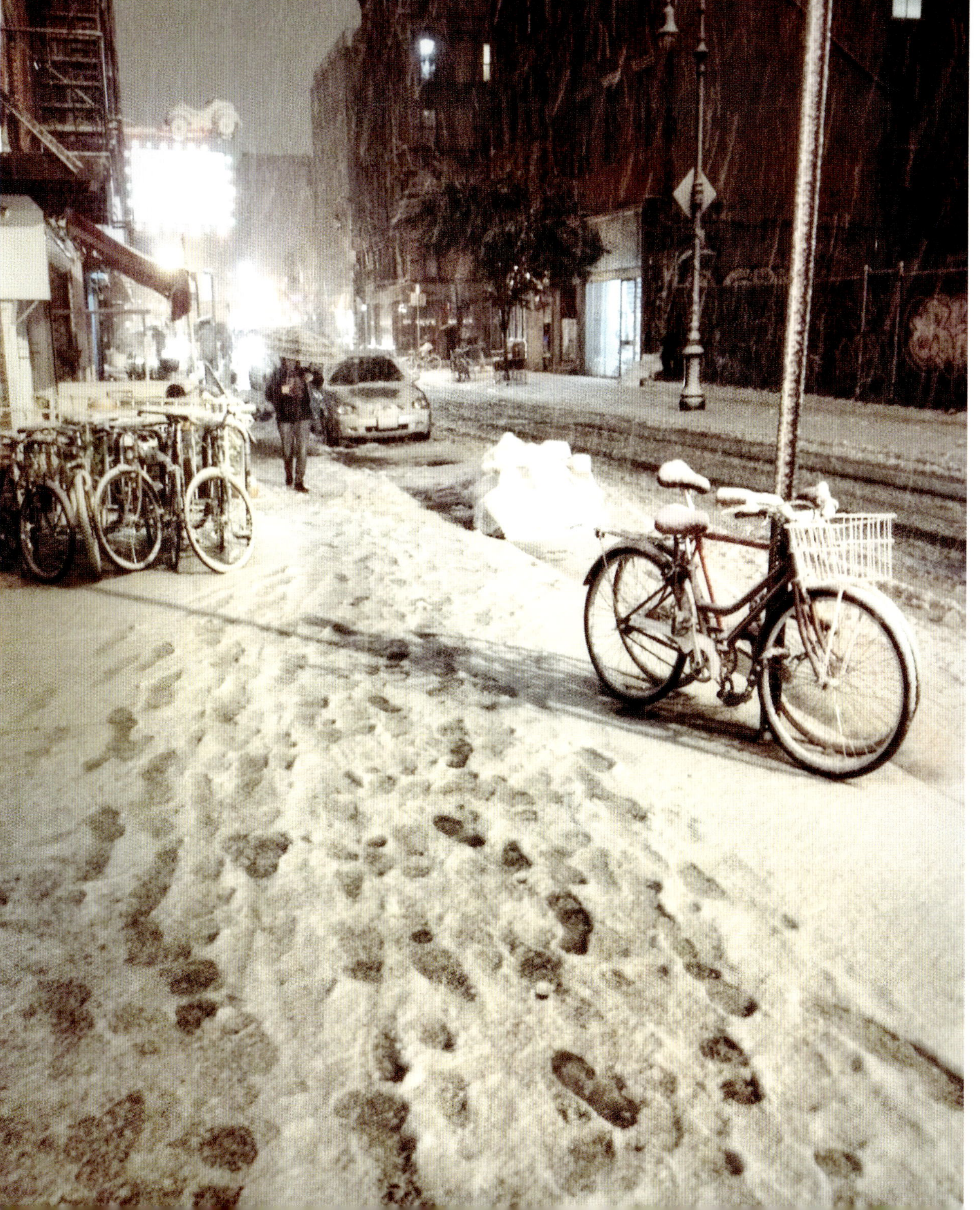

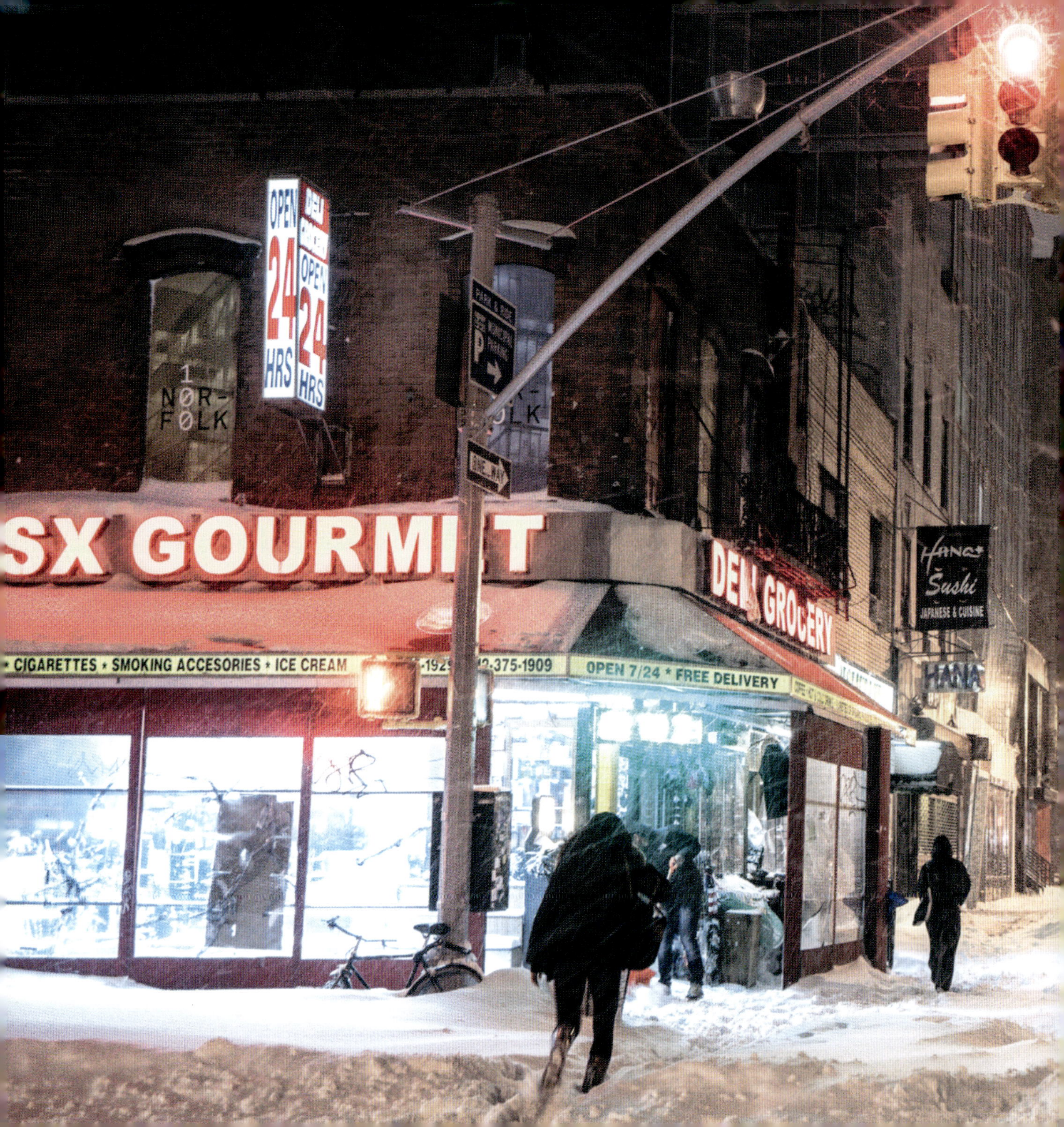

OPEN 24 HRS
OPEN 24 HRS
1 N0R-F0LK
SX GOURMET
DELI GROCERY
CIGARETTES * SMOKING ACCESORIES * ICE CREAM
OPEN 7/24 * FREE DELIVERY
ONE WAY
Hana Sushi
JAPANESE & CUISINE
HANA

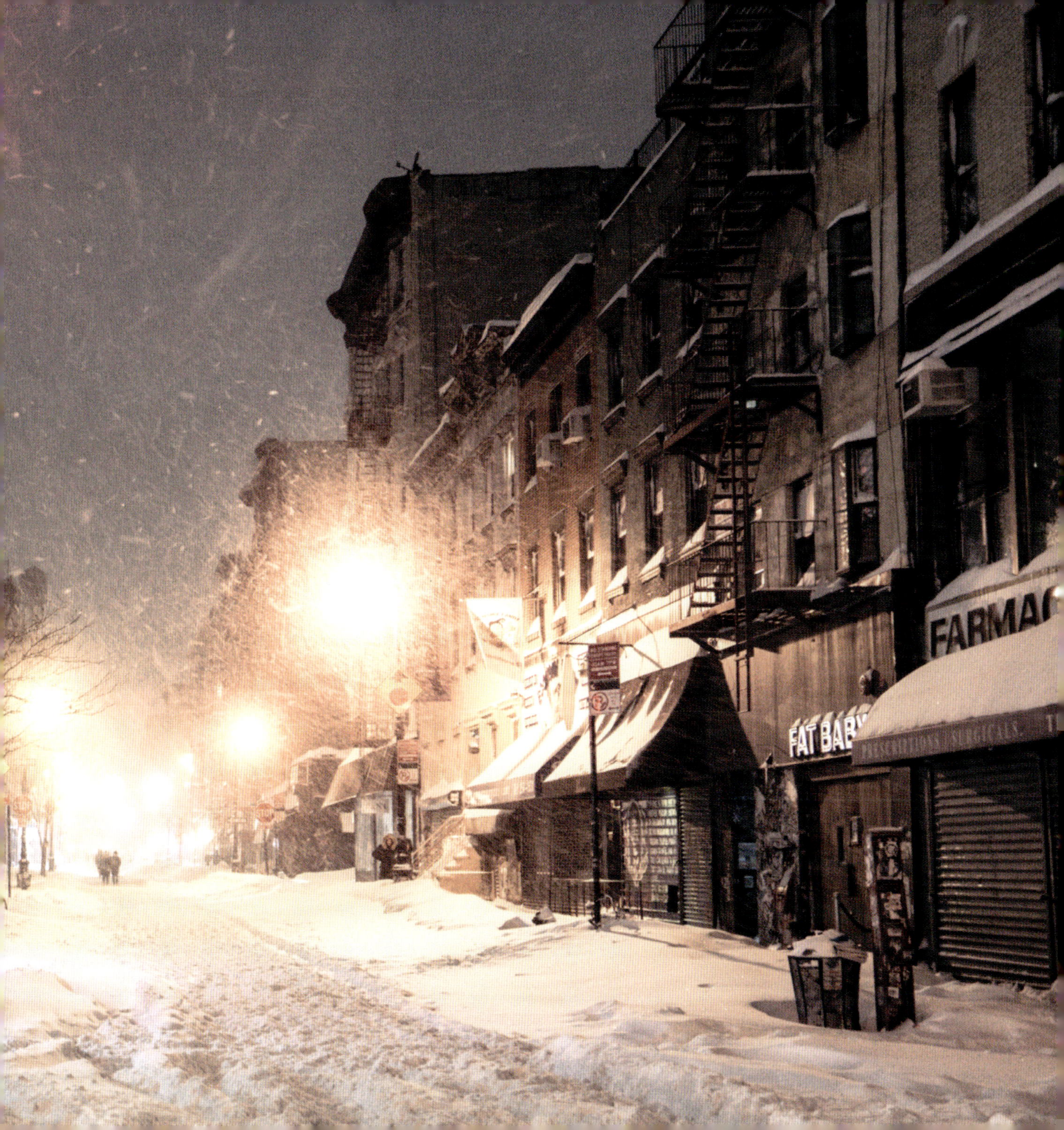
FARMAC
FAT BAB

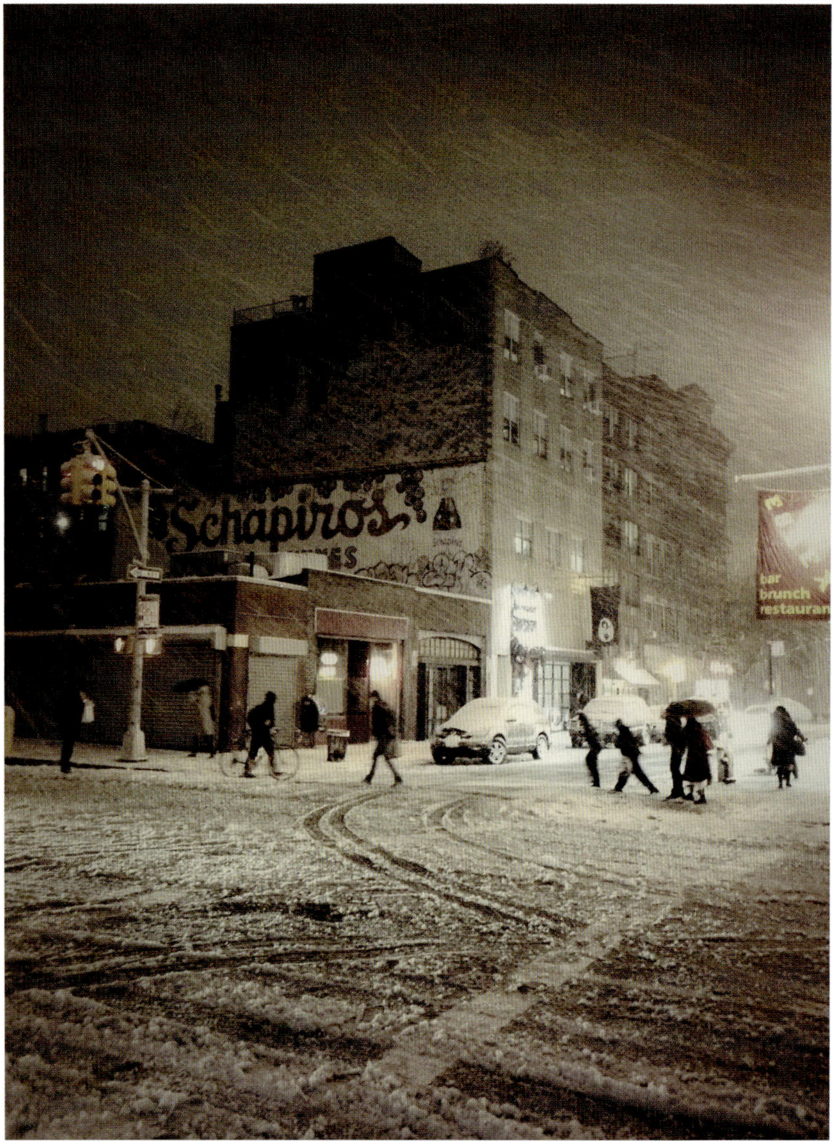

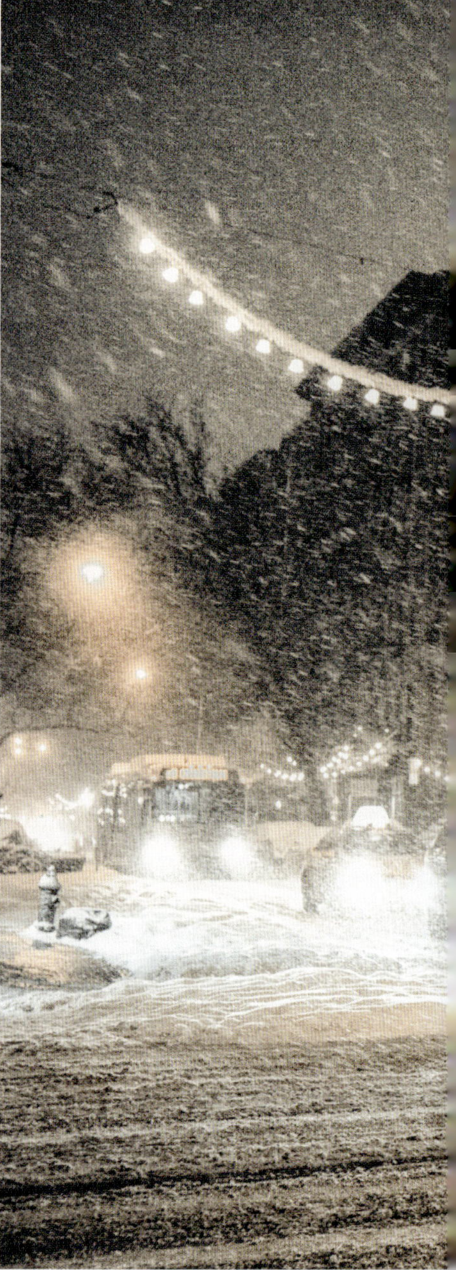

Lower East Side, Manhattan
iPhone 5S

East Village, Lower Manhattan
Sony SLT-A99V | ƒ/5 | 1/30 second | ISO 2000

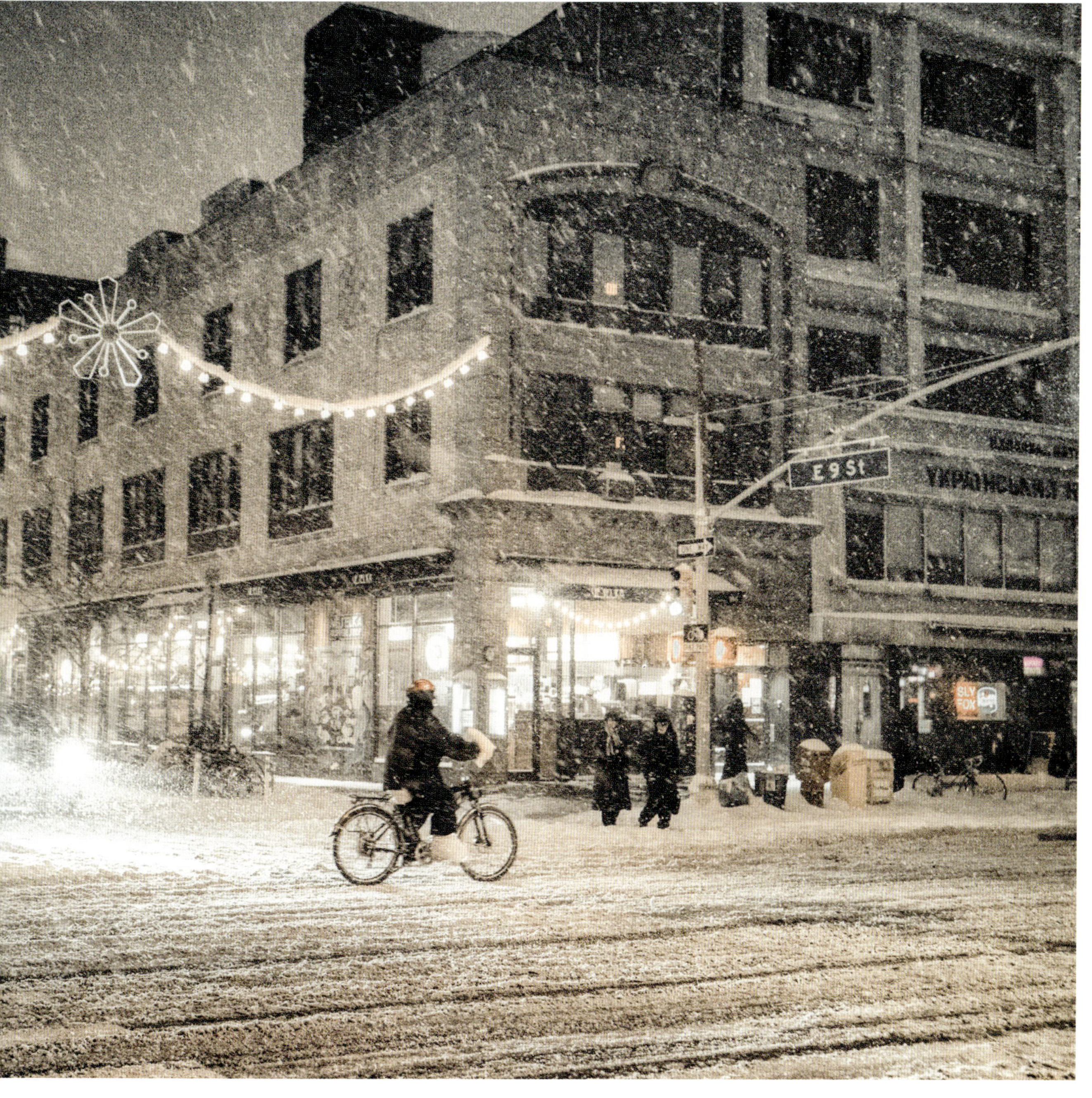
E 9 St
SLY FOX

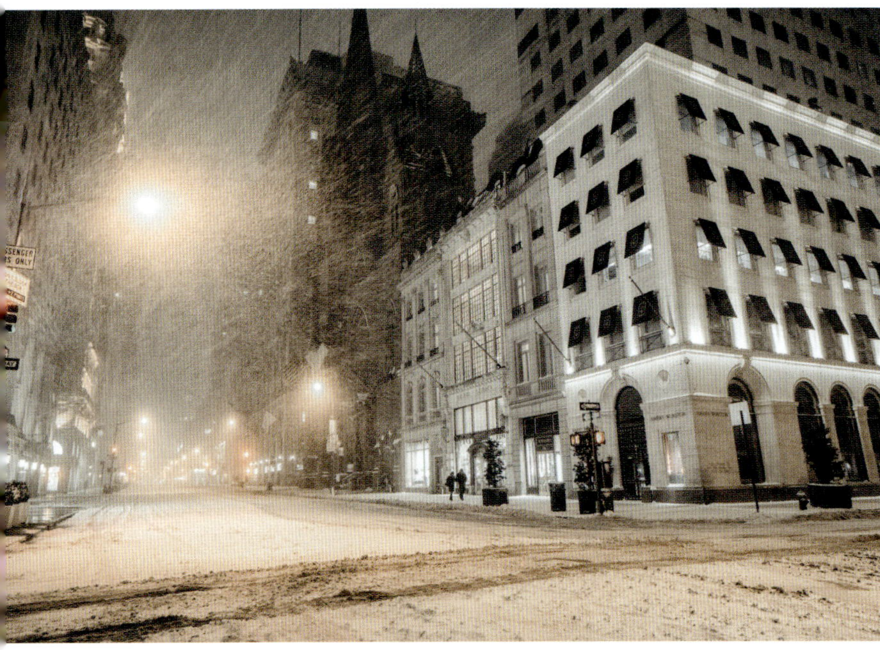

Upper East Side, Manhattan
Sony ILCE-7M2 | *f*/3.2 | 1/40 second | ISO 2000

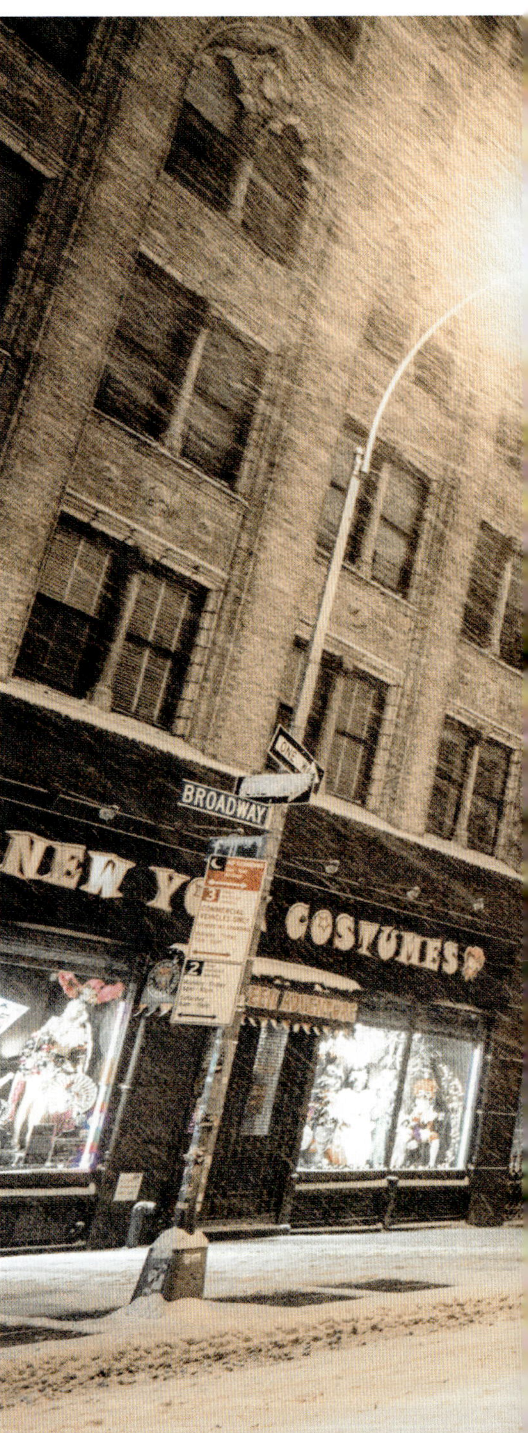

Greenwich Village, Lower Manhattan
Sony ILCE-7M2 | *f*/3.2 | 1/40 second | ISO 2000

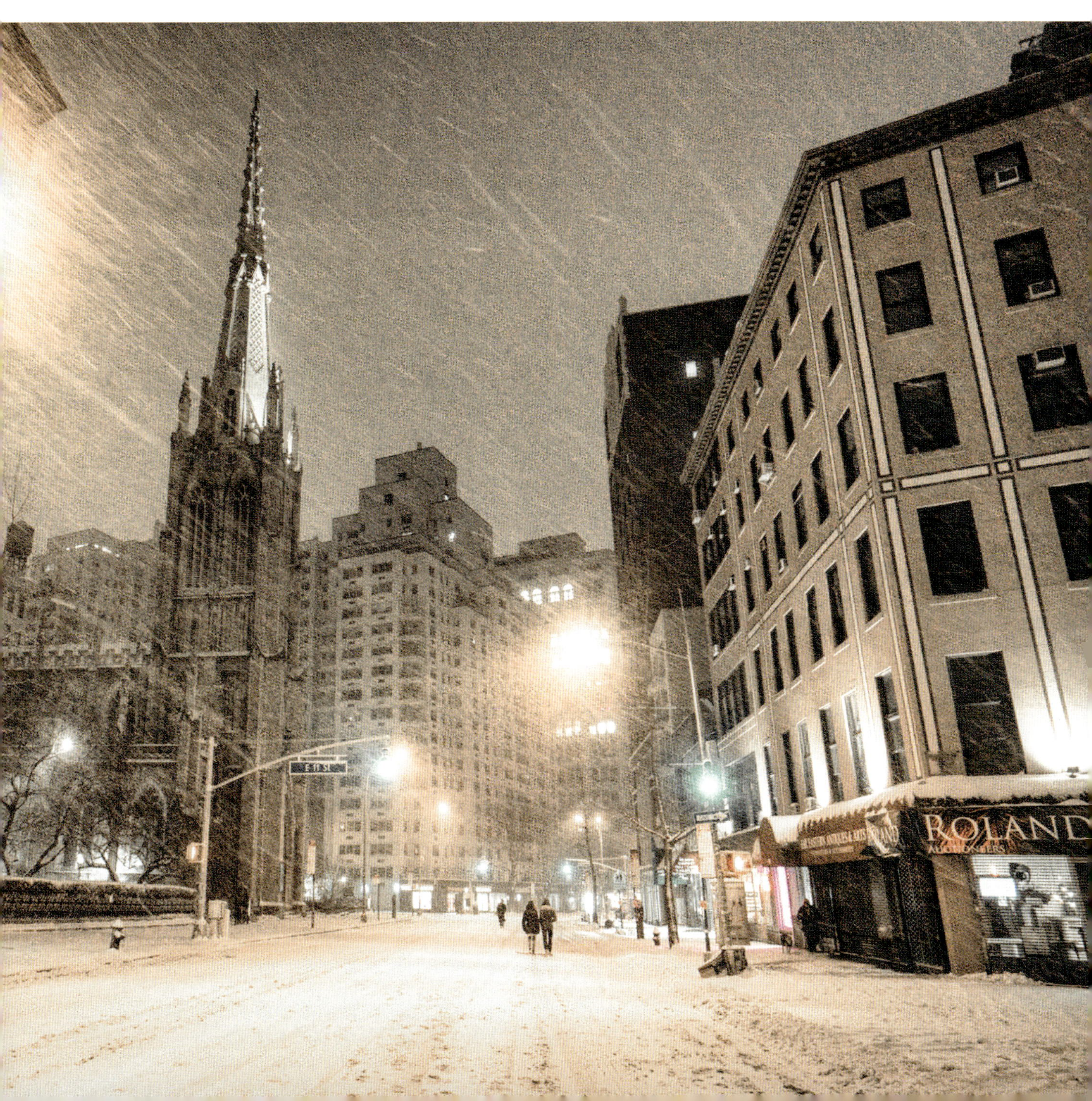
ROLAND

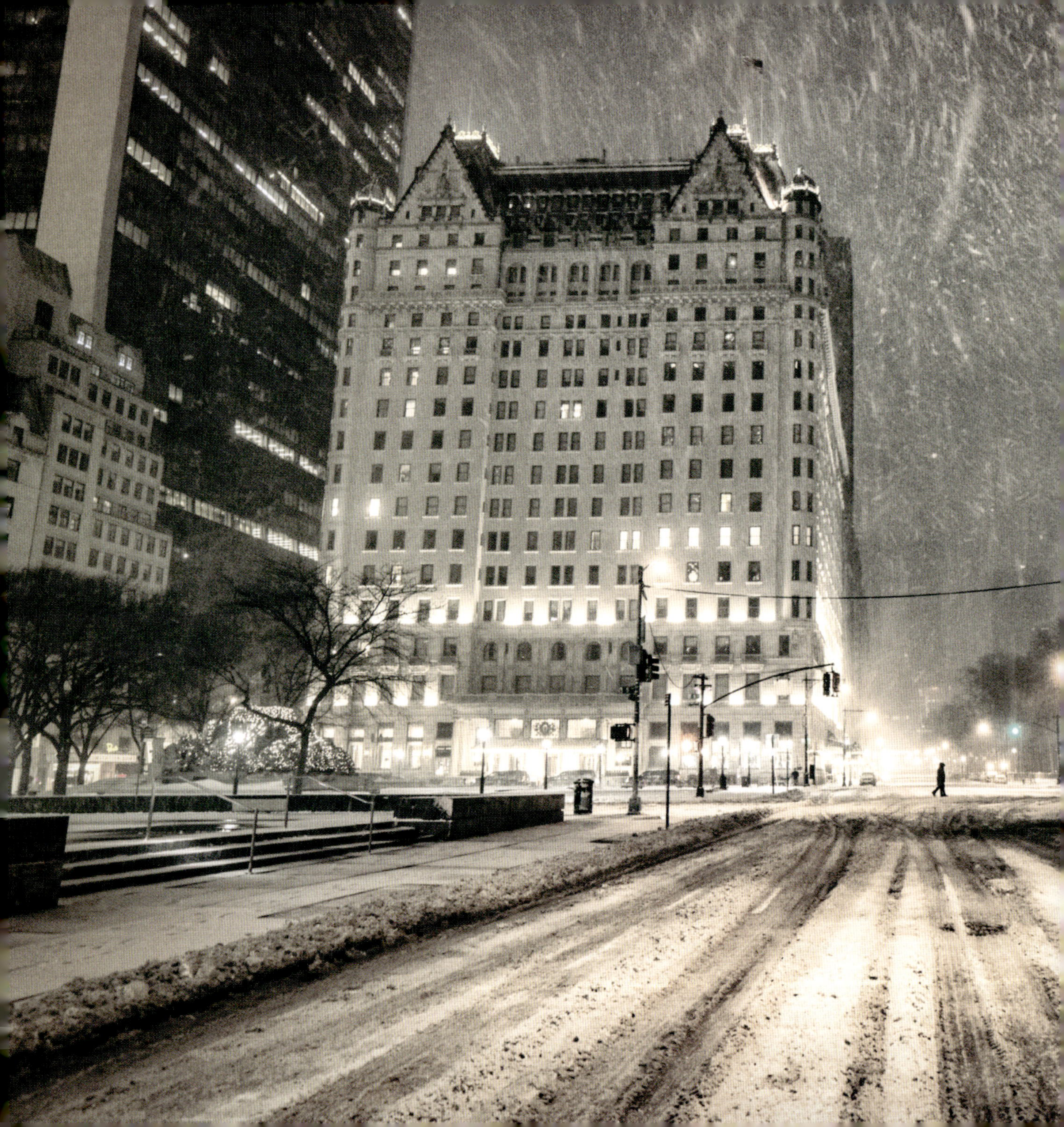

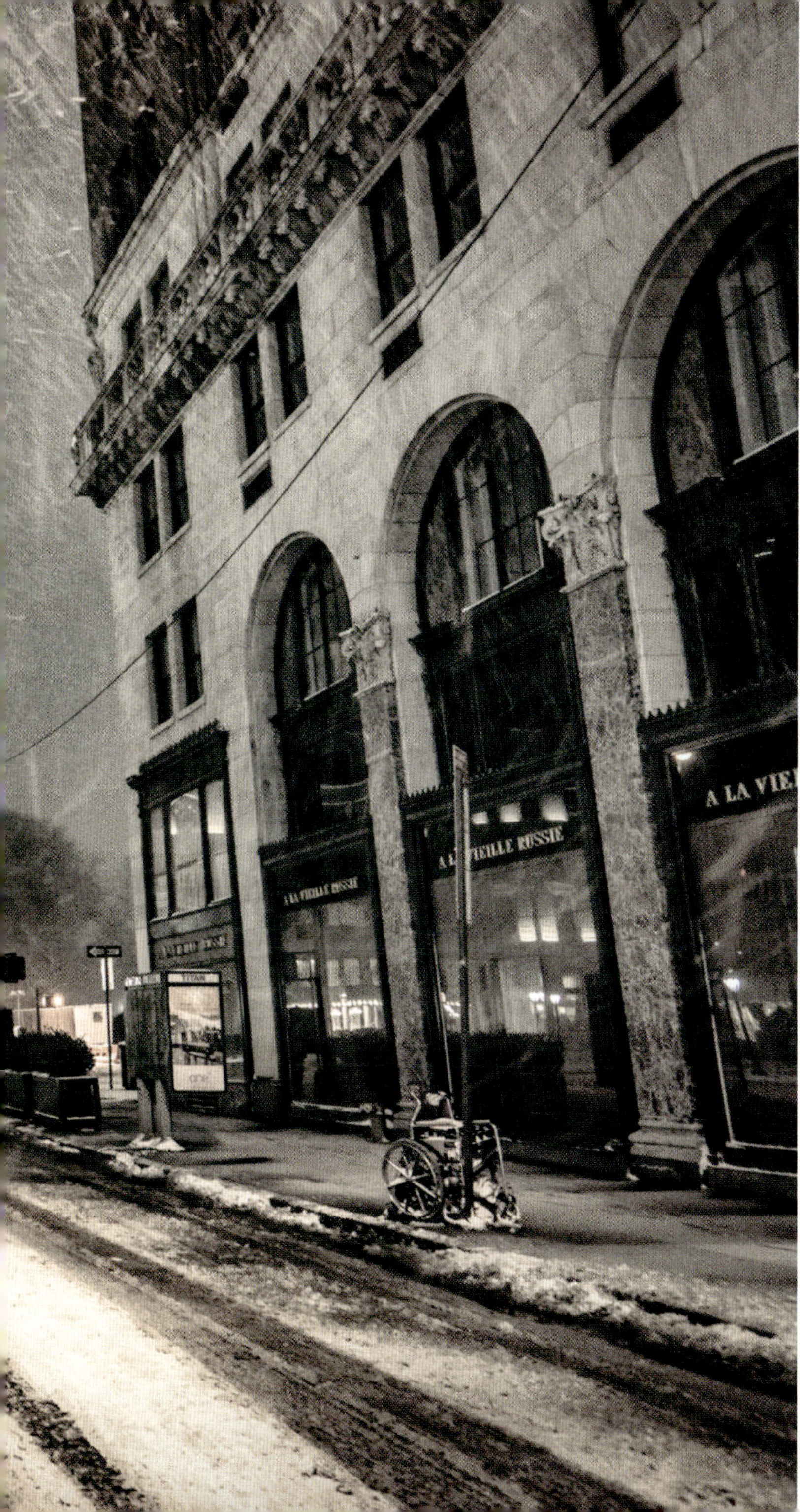

Midtown Manhattan
Sony SLT-A99V | $f/4$ | 1/80 second | ISO 4000

Midtown Manhattan
Sony SLT-A99V | ƒ/3.2 | 1/80 second | ISO 4000

Times Square, Midtown Manhattan
Sony SLT-A99V | ƒ/3.2 | 1/40 second | ISO 2000

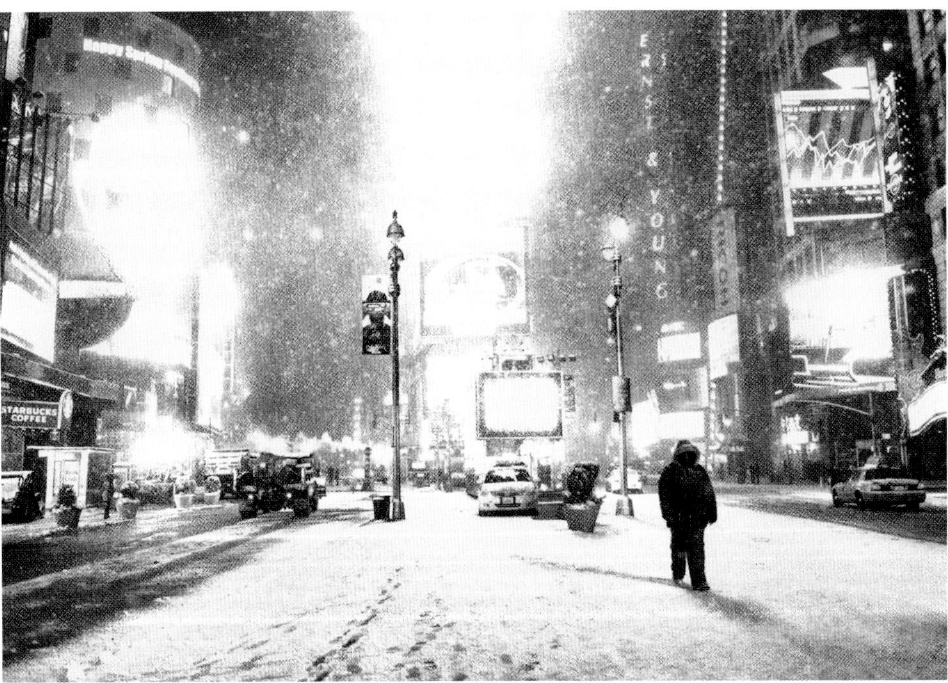

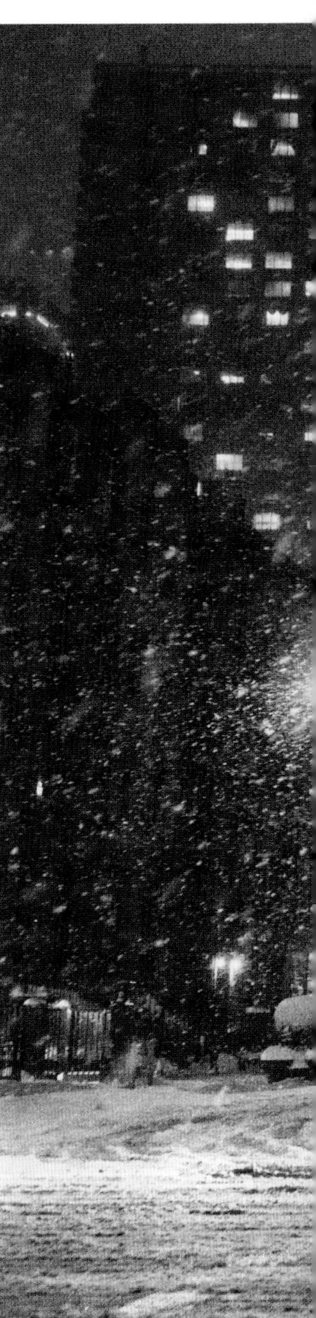

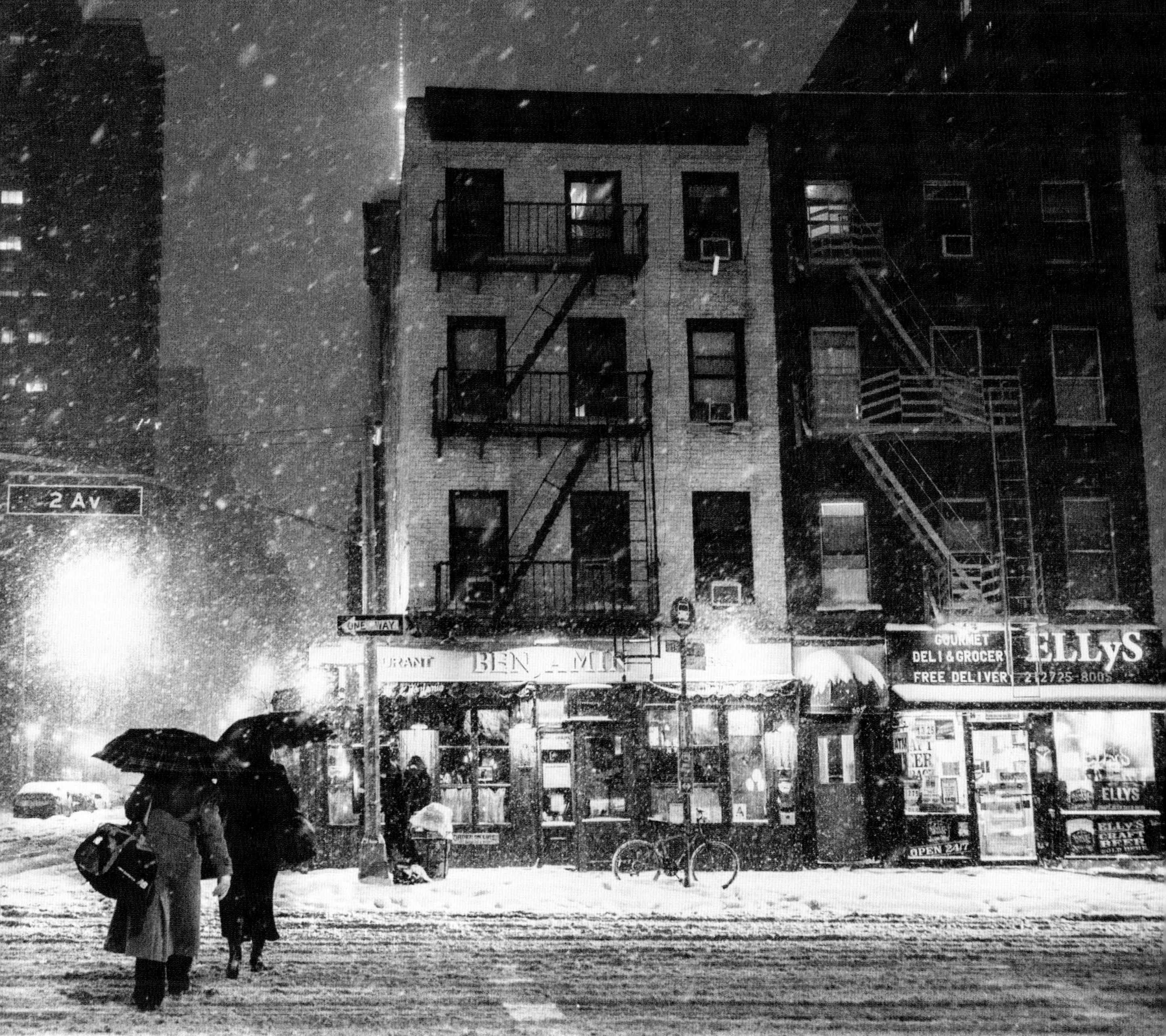
2 Av
ONE WAY
GOURMET
DELI & GROCER
FREE DELIVER
ELLyS
OPEN 24/7

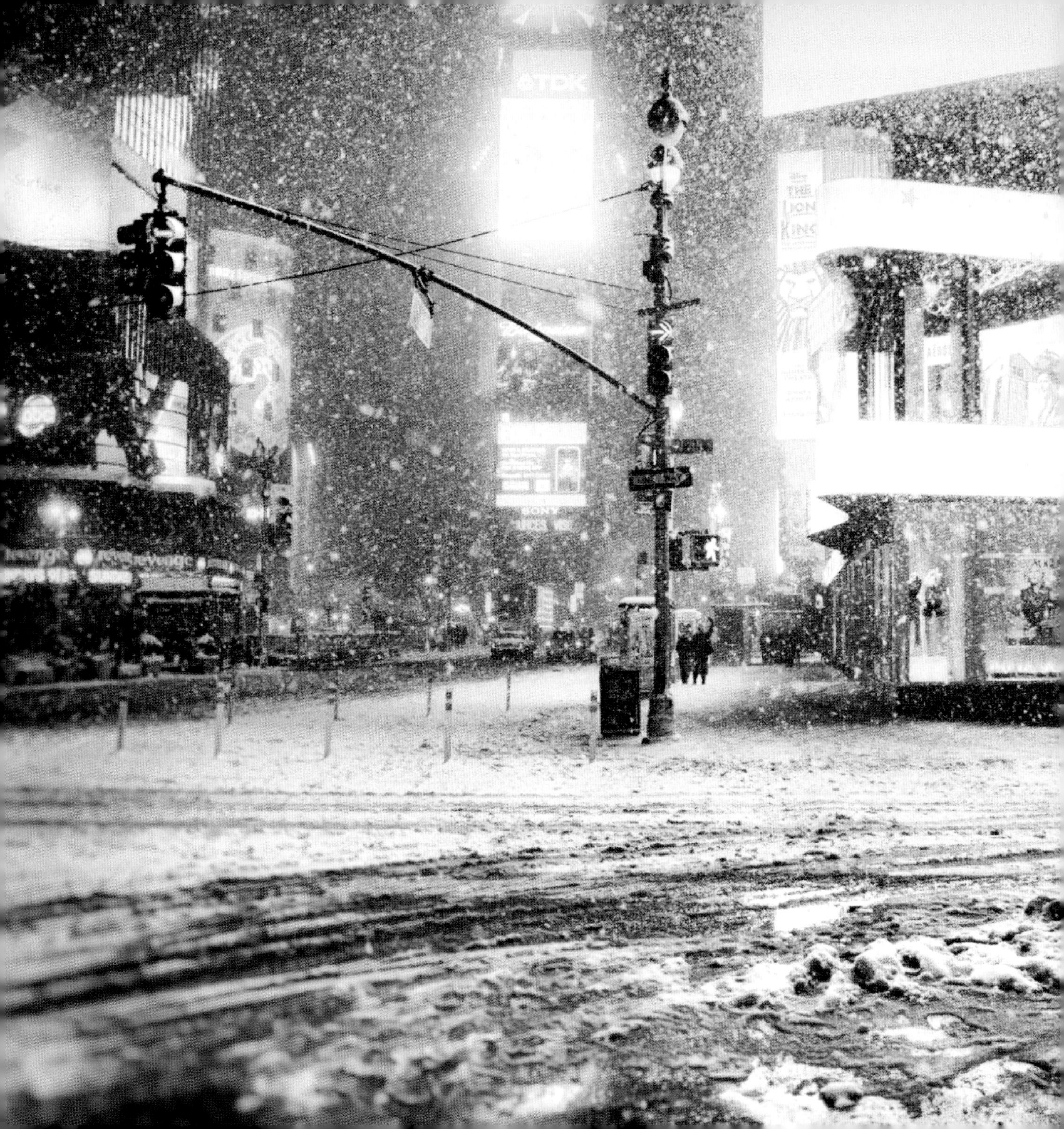
TDK
THE LION KING
SONY

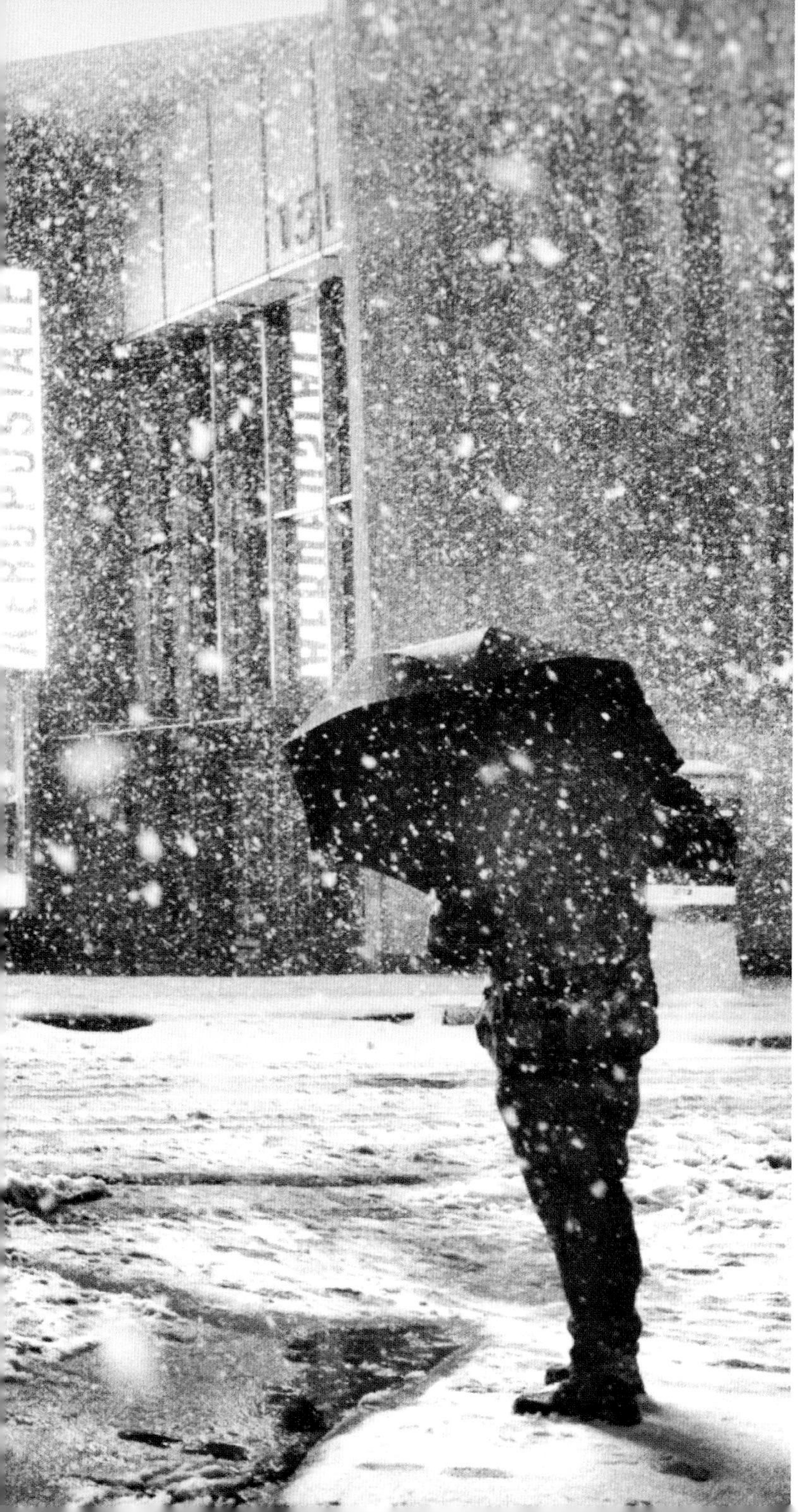

Times Square, Midtown Manhattan
Sony SLT-A99V | *f*/3.2 | 1/60 second | ISO 2000

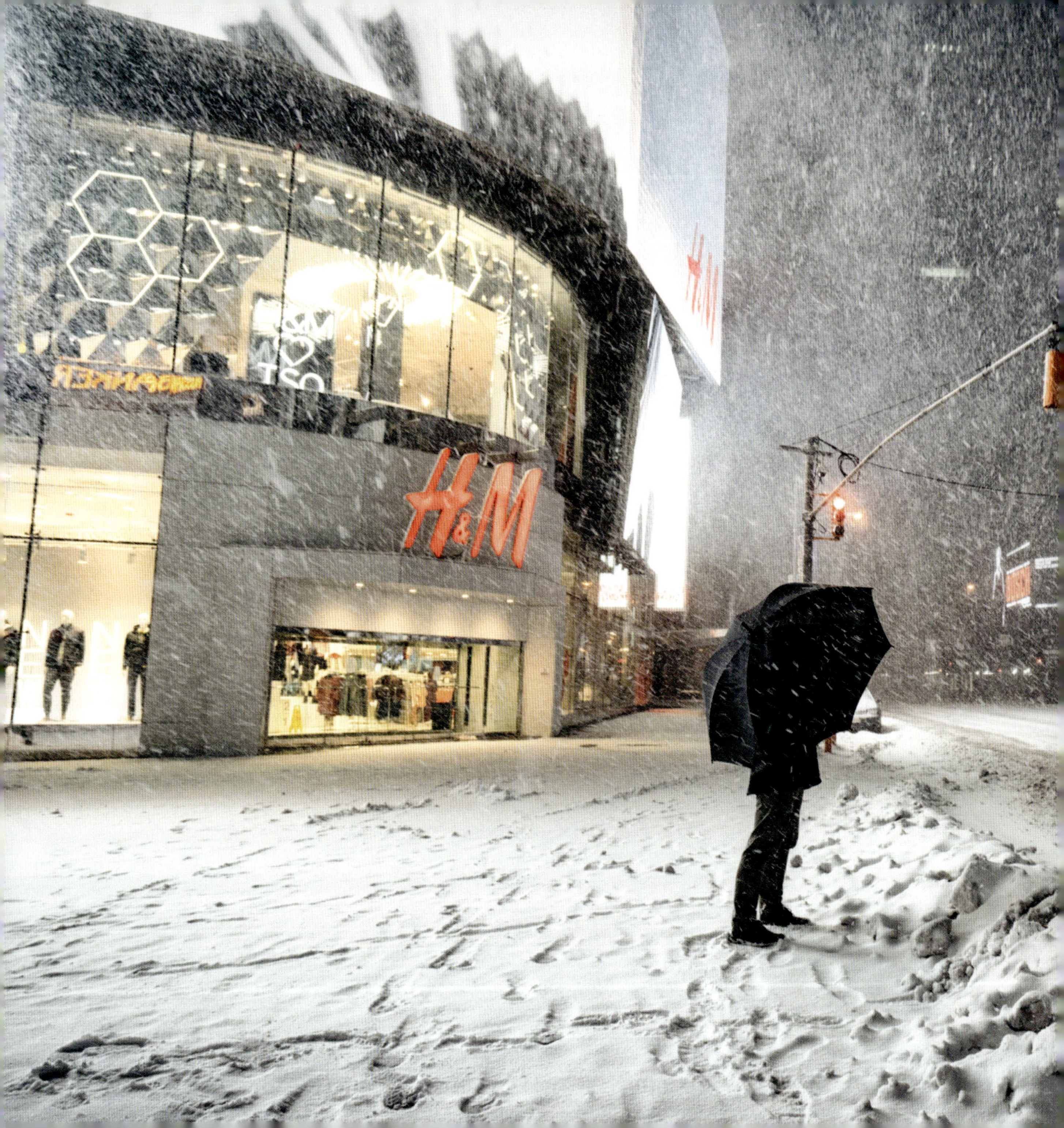
H&M
H&M

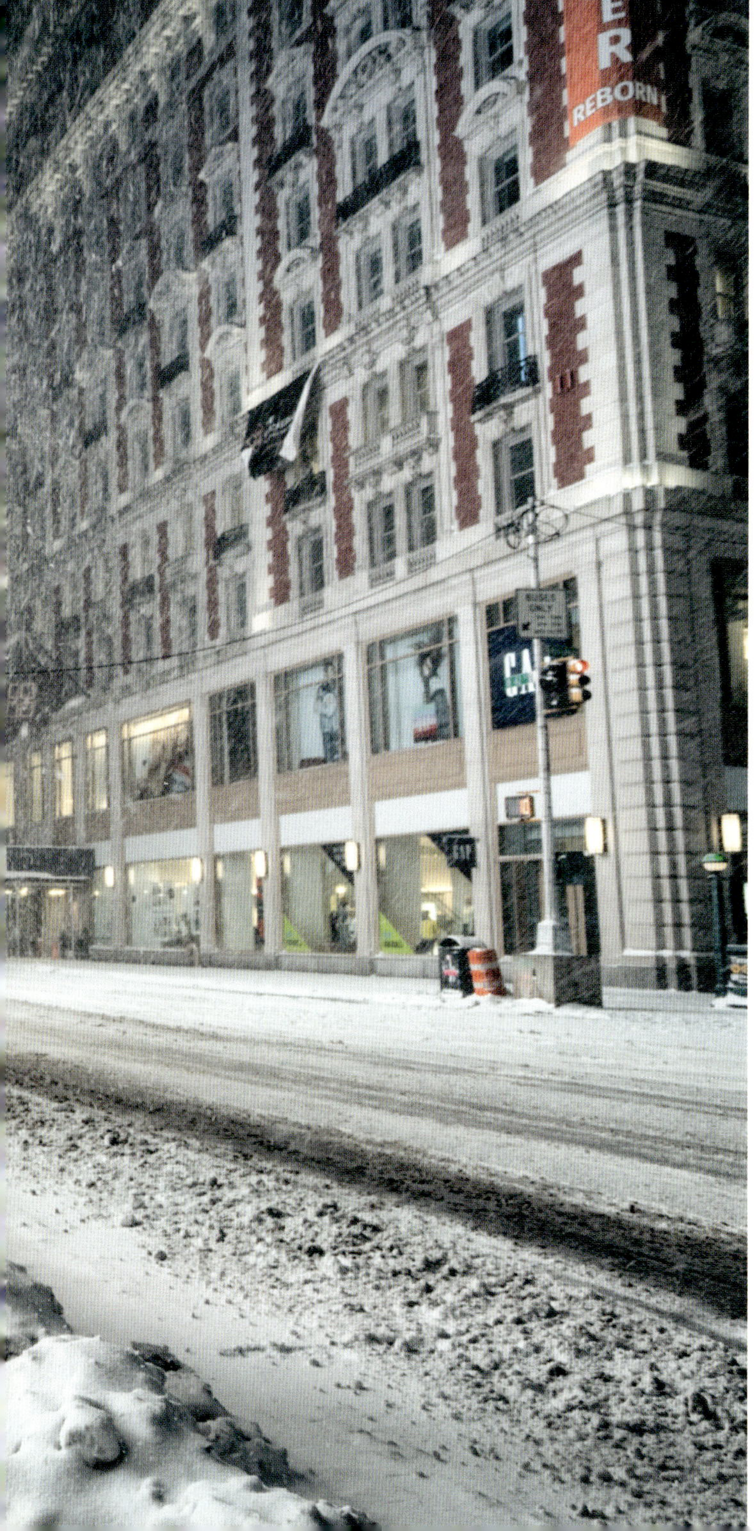

Times Square, Midtown Manhattan
Sony ILCE-7M2 | $f/3.2$ | 1/40 second | ISO 2000

Colorful cityscapes are not what one usually thinks of when thinking about snowstorms in New York City, and yet snowstorms are when the colors of the lights at night become the most intense. I have always been partial to impressions of lights at night in the city: the way lights blend with movement particularly.

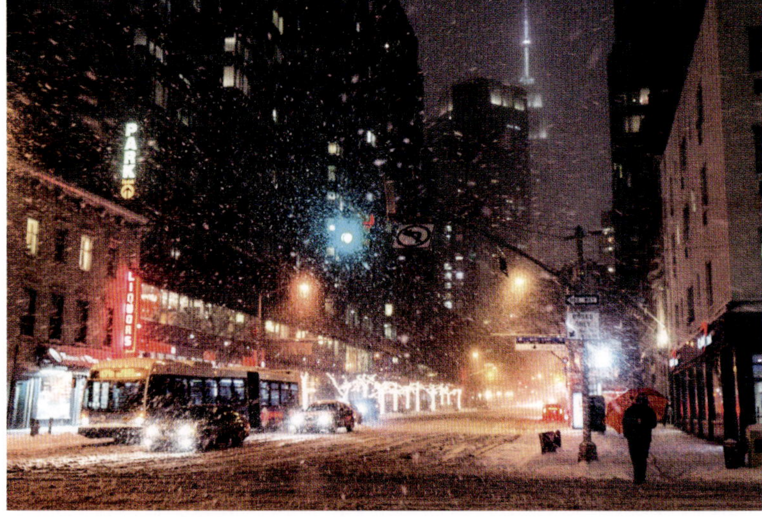

Midtown Manhattan
Sony ILCE-7M2 | *f*/4 | 1/30 second | ISO 4000

Tudor City Place, Manhattan
Sony ILCE-7M2 | *f*/4 | 1/30 second | ISO 4000

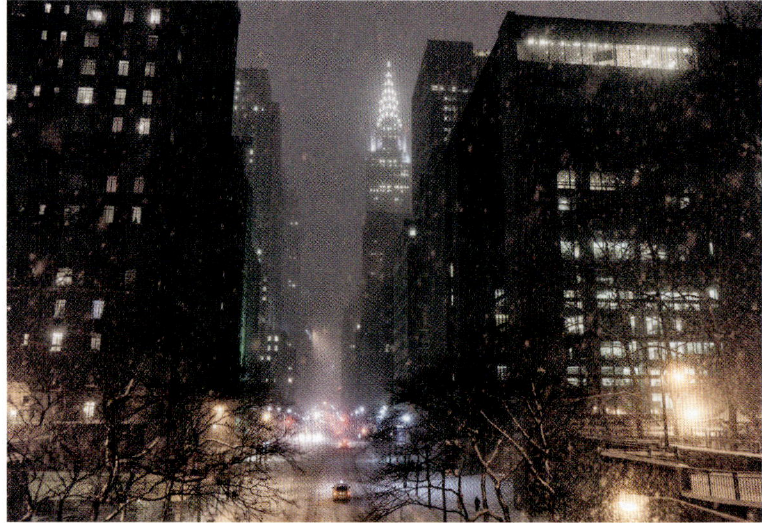

East Village, Manhattan
Sony ILCE-7M2 | *f*/4 | 1/30 second | ISO 4000

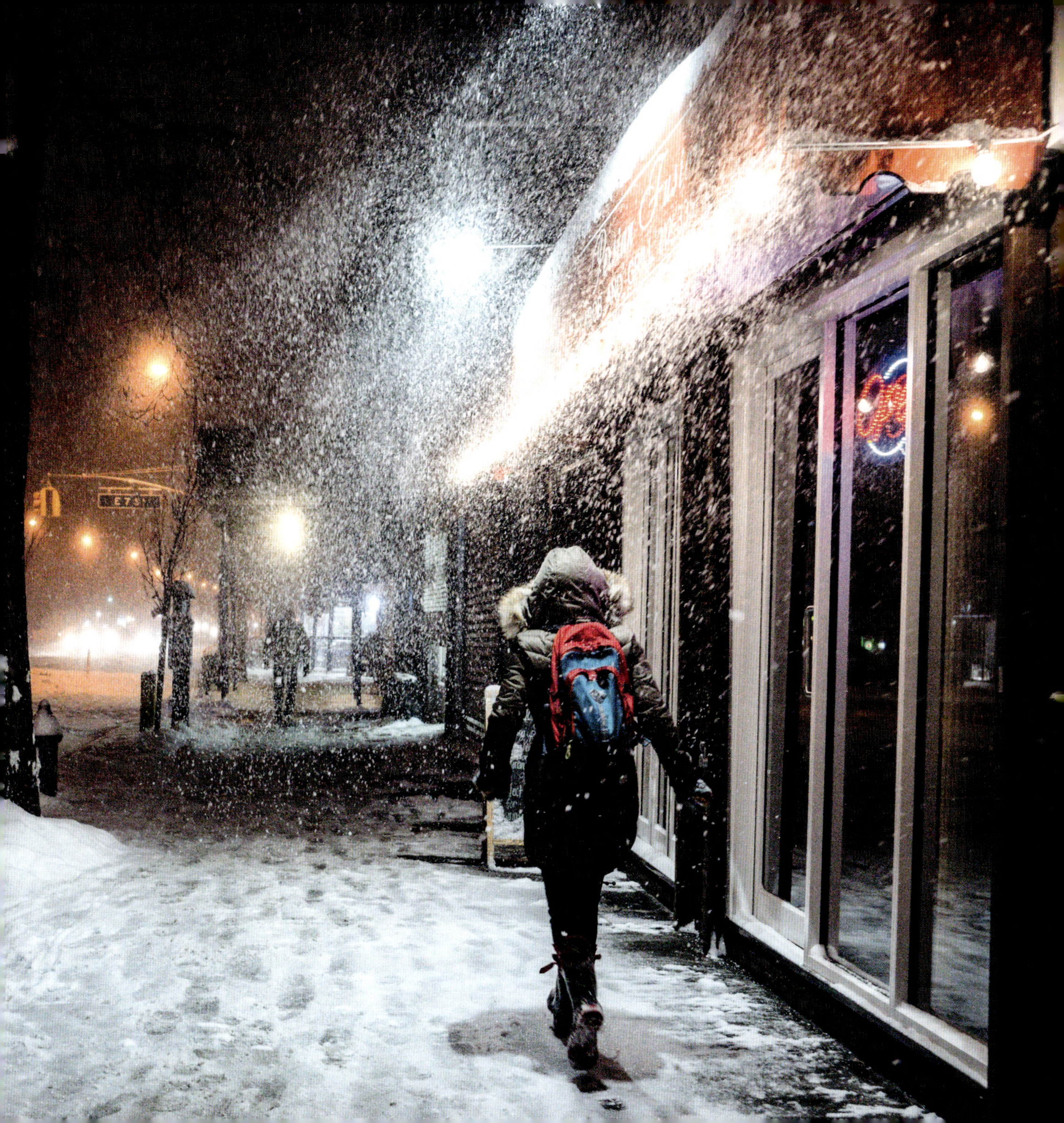

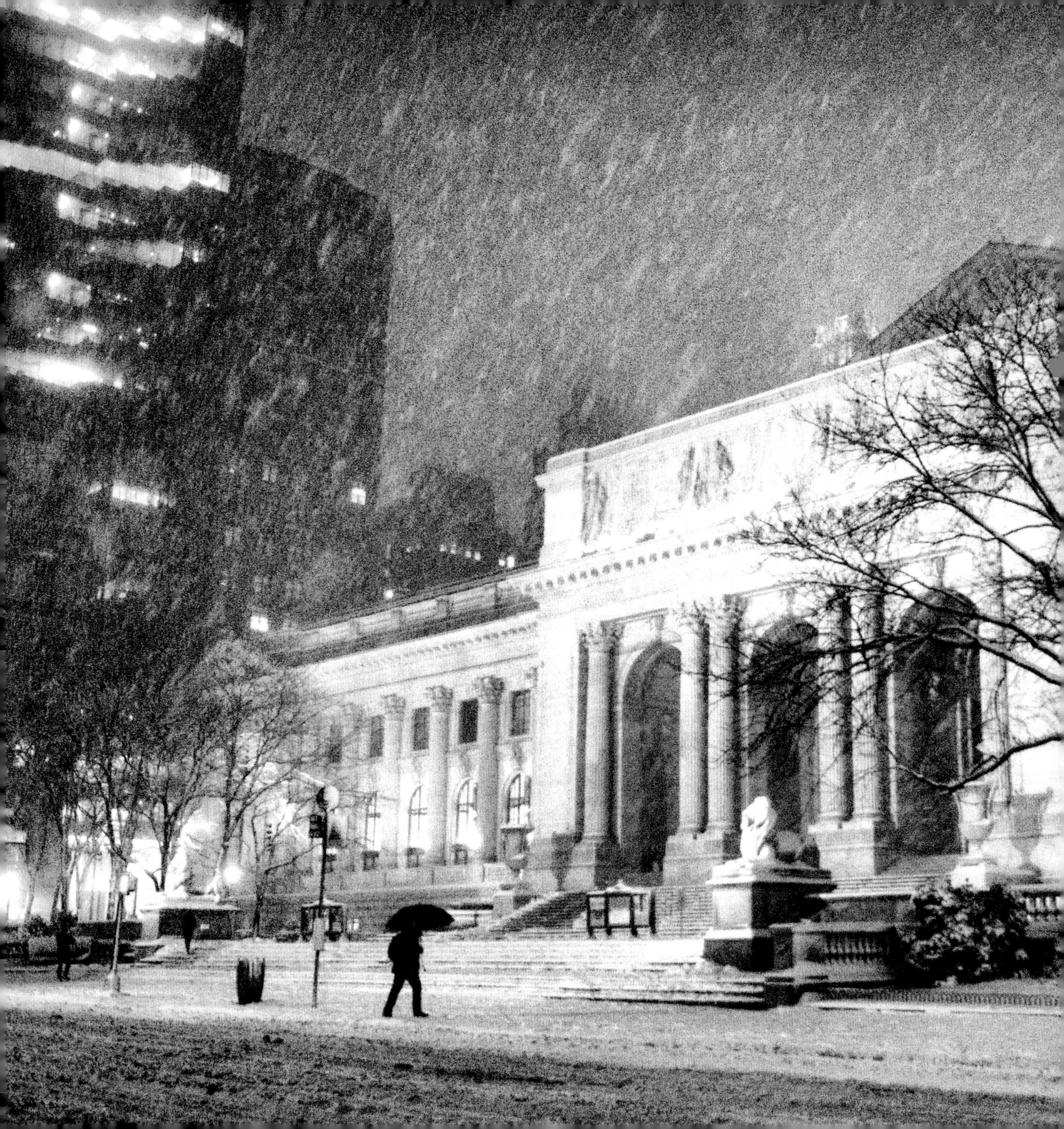

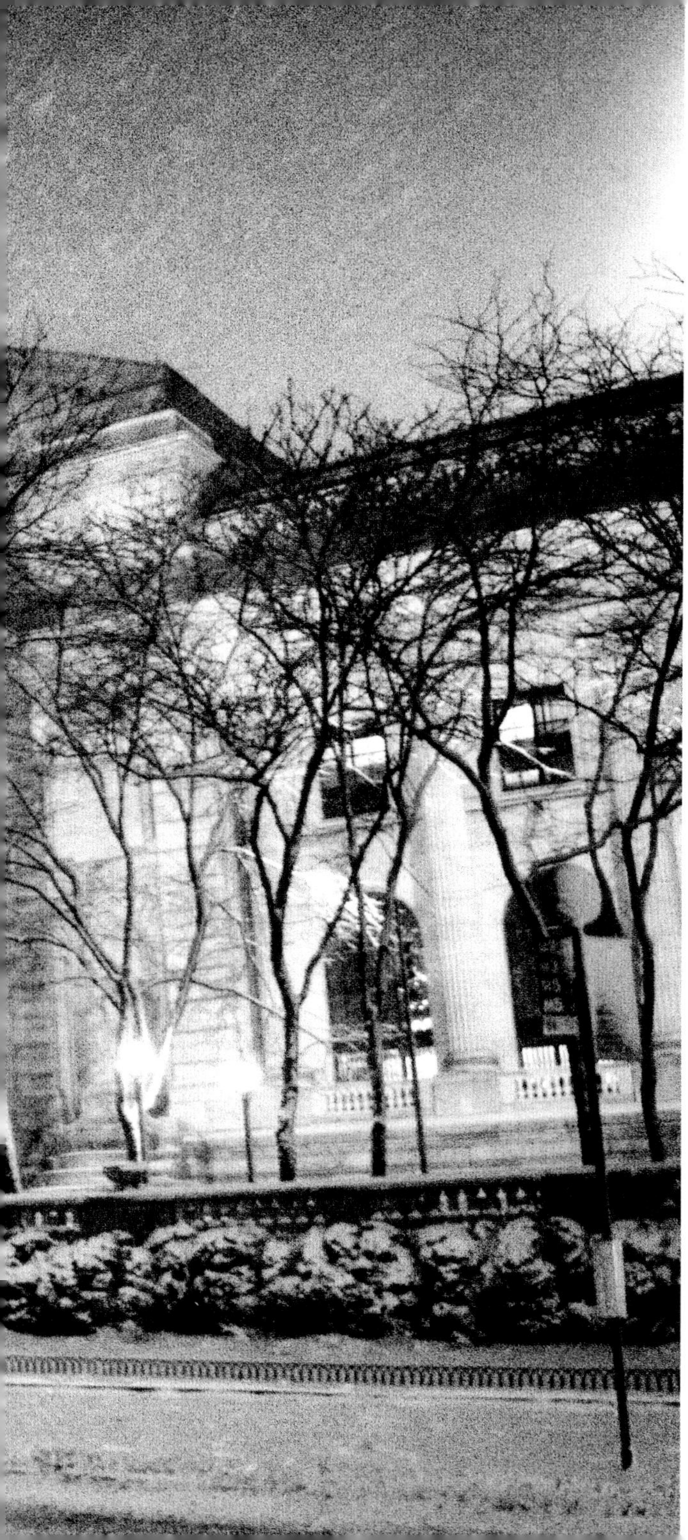

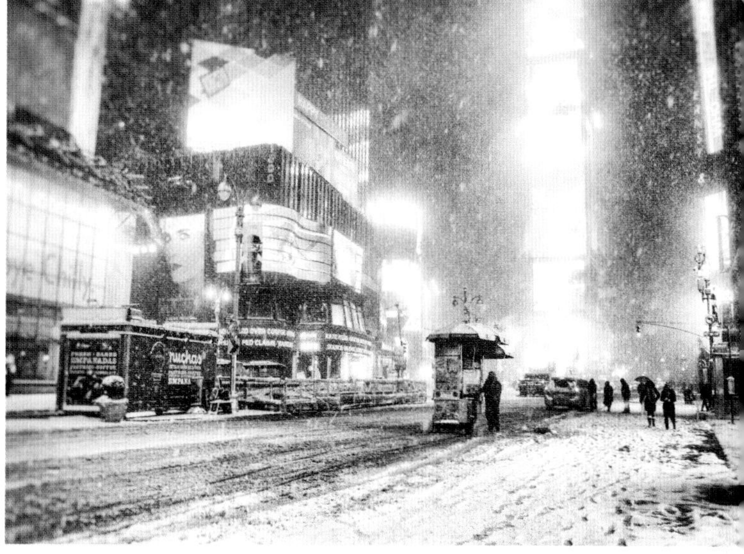

Times Square, Midtown Manhattan
Sony SLT-A99V | *f*/3.2 | 1/40 second | ISO 2000

Times Square, Midtown Manhattan
Sony SLT-A99V | *f*/3.2 | 1/60 second | ISO 2000

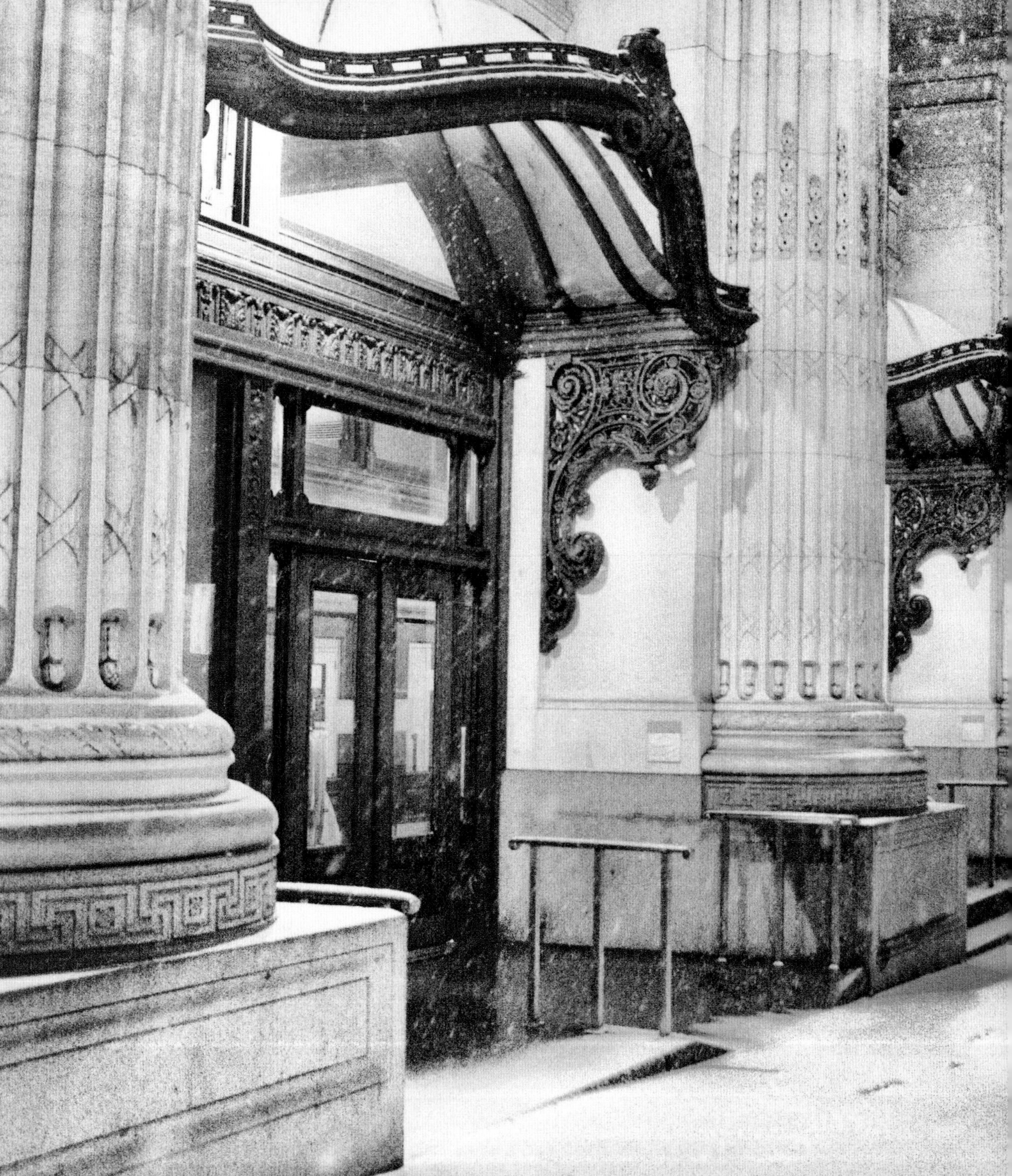

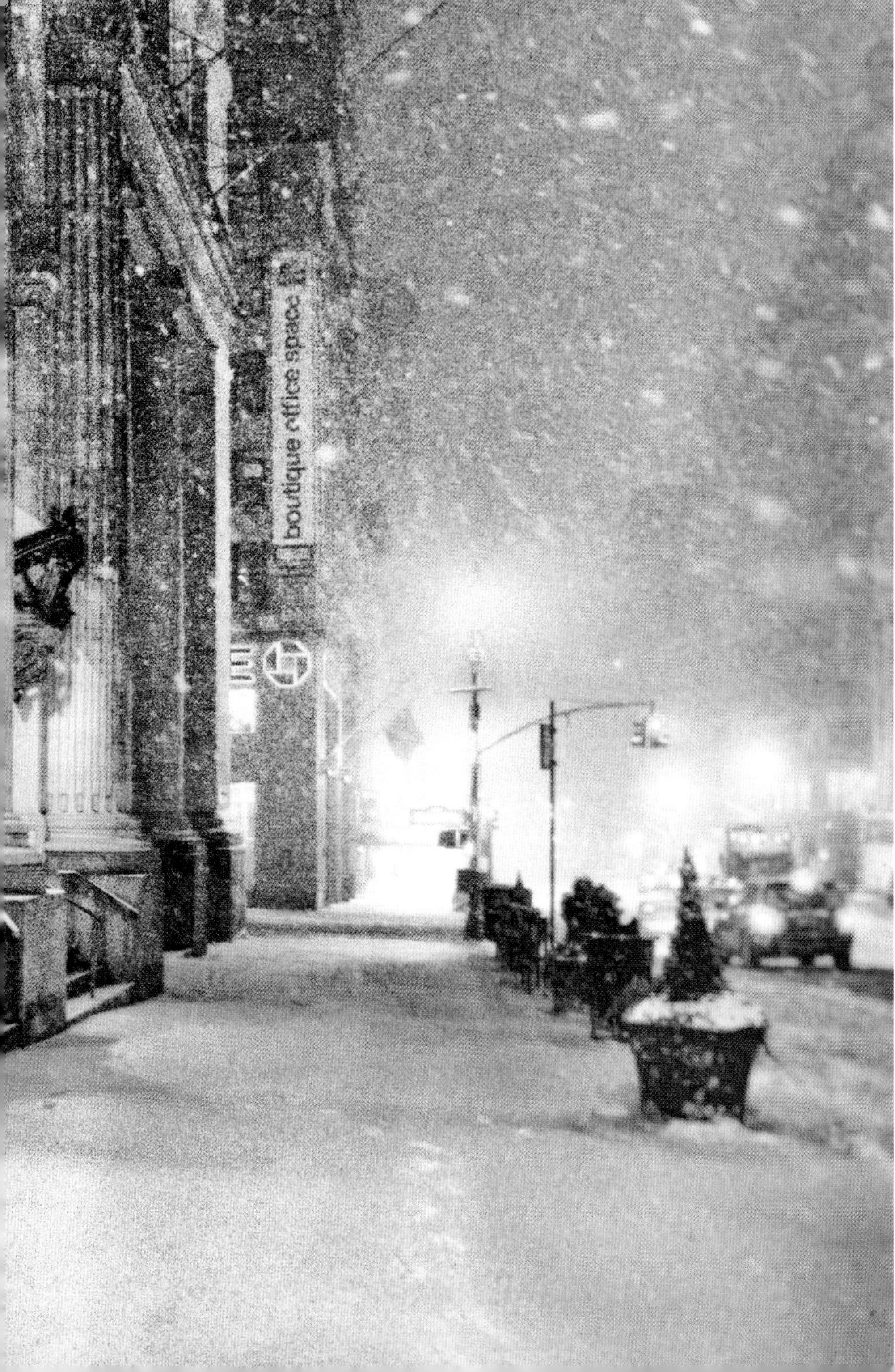

Midtown Manhattan
Sony SLT-A99V | *f*/3.2 | 1/40 second | ISO 4000

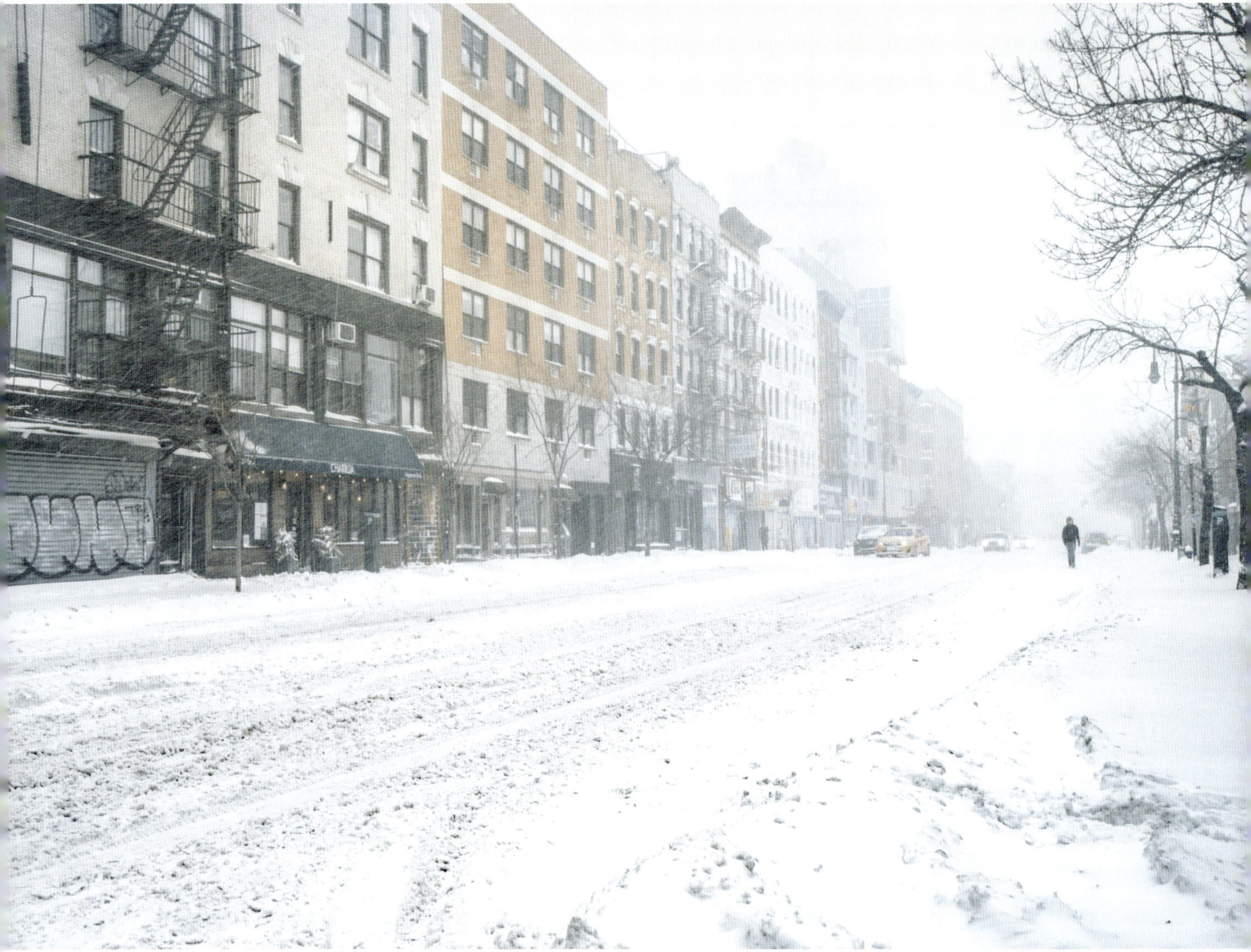

Lower East Side, Manhattan

Sony ILCE-7RM2 | *ƒ*/7 | 1/60 second | ISO 200

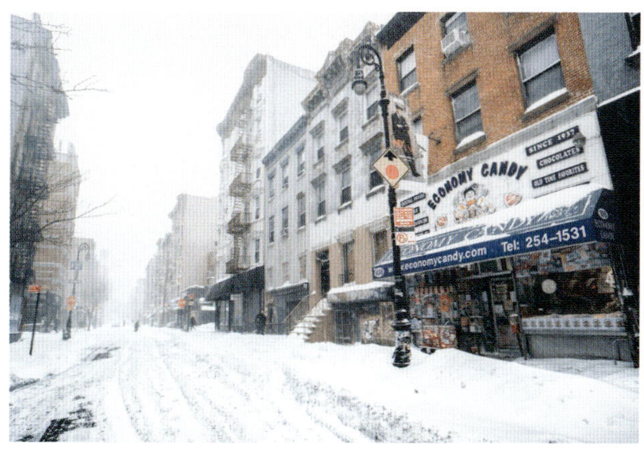

◀ Lower East Side, Manhattan
Sony ILCE-7RM2 | *f*/5 | 1/40 second | ISO 200

▼ Lower East Side, Manhattan
Sony ILCE-7RM2 | *f*/5 | 1/60 second | ISO 200

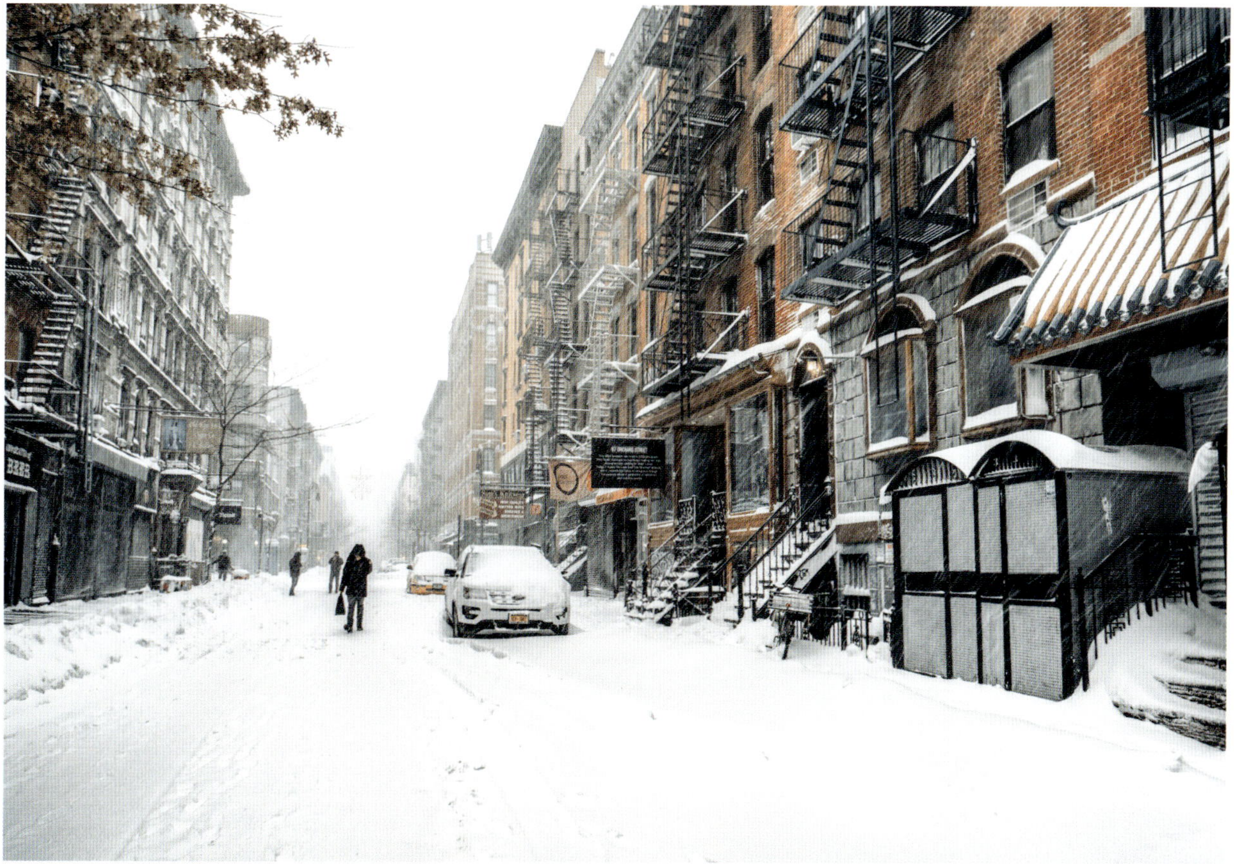

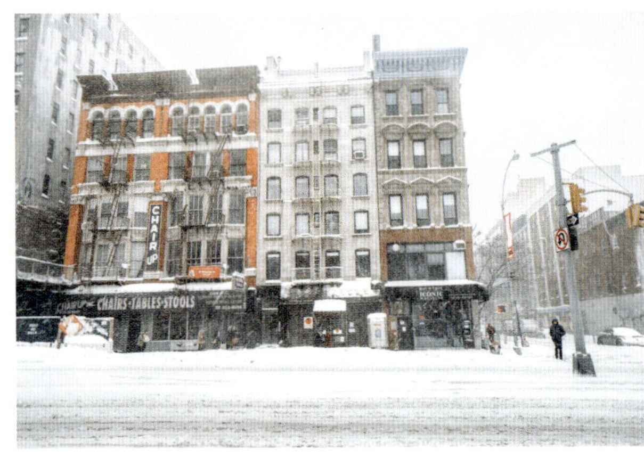

◀ Lower East Side, Manhattan
Sony ILCE-7RM2 | *f*/5 | 1/100 second | ISO 800

▼ Lower East Side, Manhattan
Sony ILCE-7RM2 | *f*/3.2 | 1/20 second | ISO 200

▶ Lower East Side, Manhattan
Sony ILCE-7RM2 | *f*/7 | 1/125 second | ISO 800

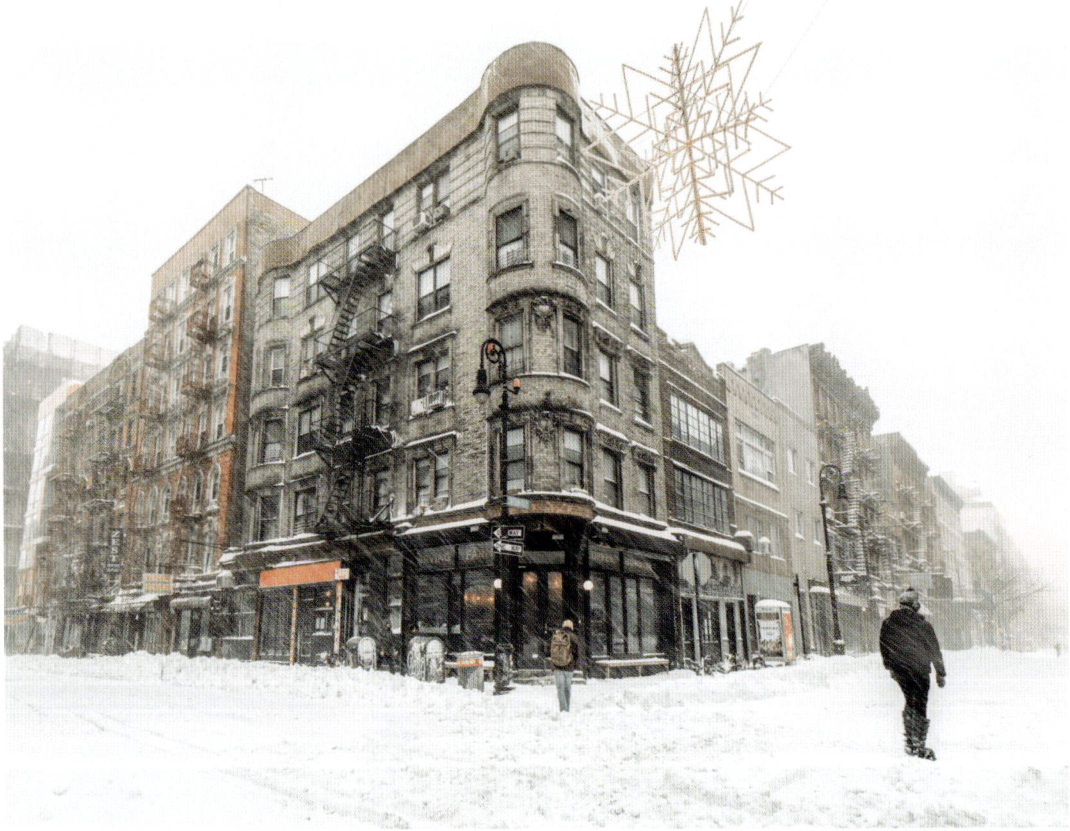

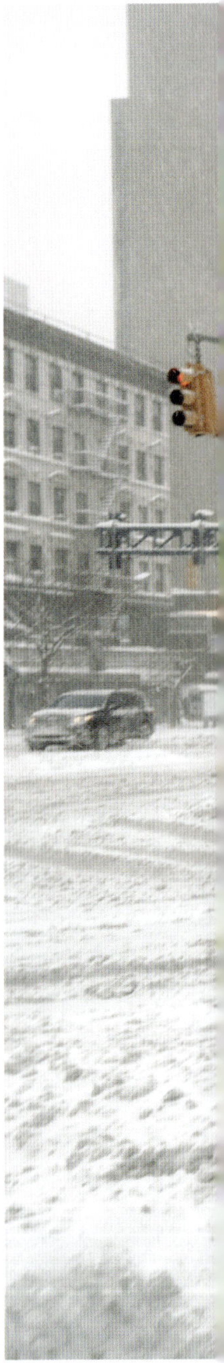

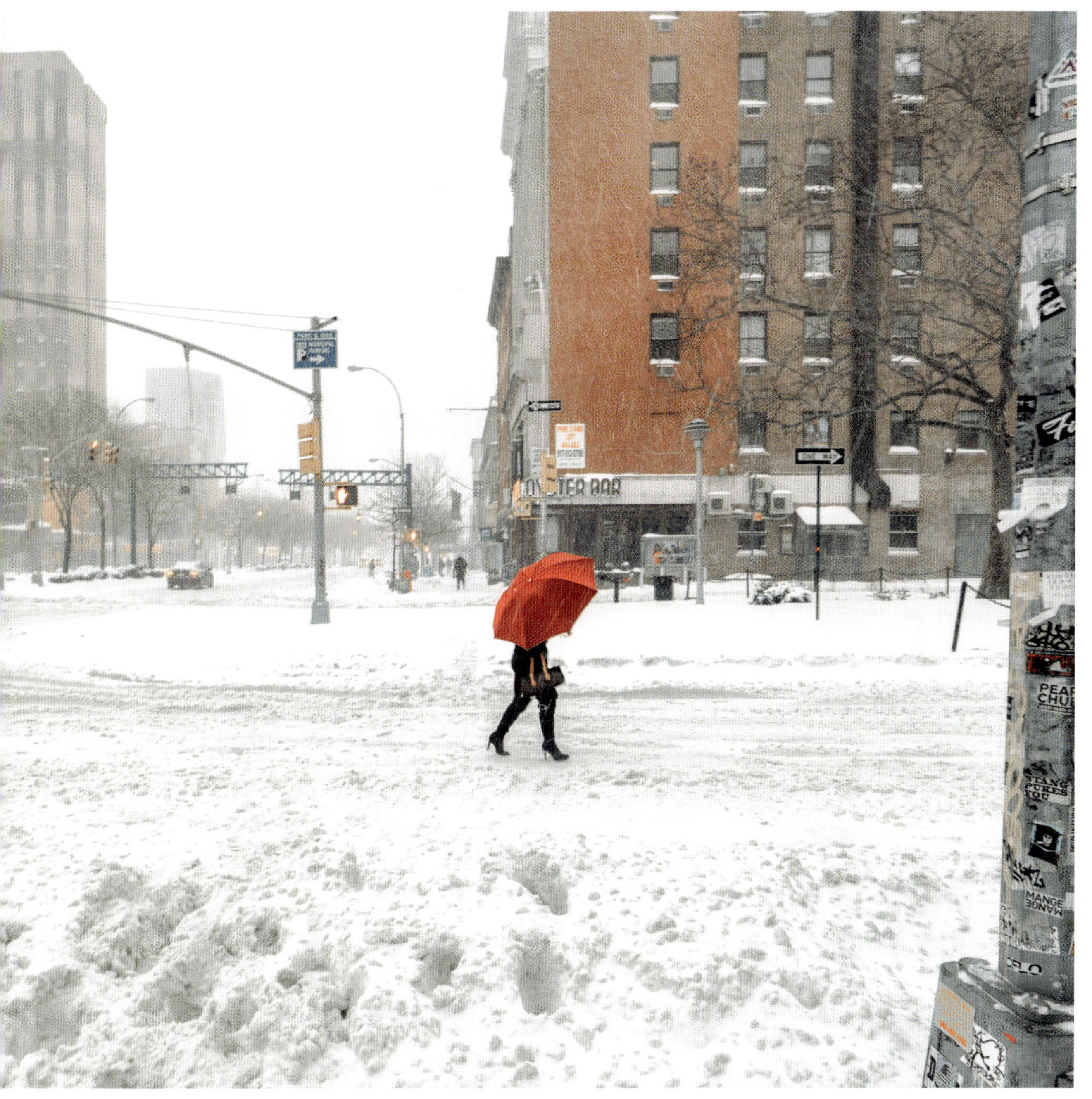
ONE WAY
MANGE

CHAPTER #3 | EMBRACE

"

Covered by a blanket of snow,
the earth stopped spinning.

All was silenced except for the
muffled heartbeat of the city

falling in love with winter
one snowflake at a time.

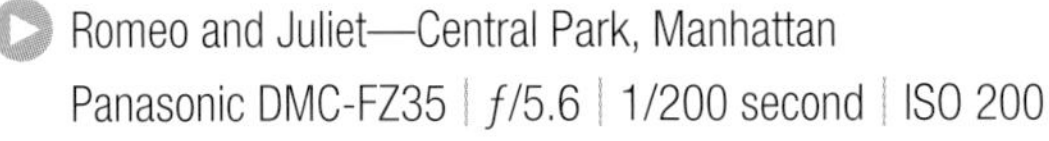
Romeo and Juliet—Central Park, Manhattan
Panasonic DMC-FZ35 | *f*/5.6 | 1/200 second | ISO 200

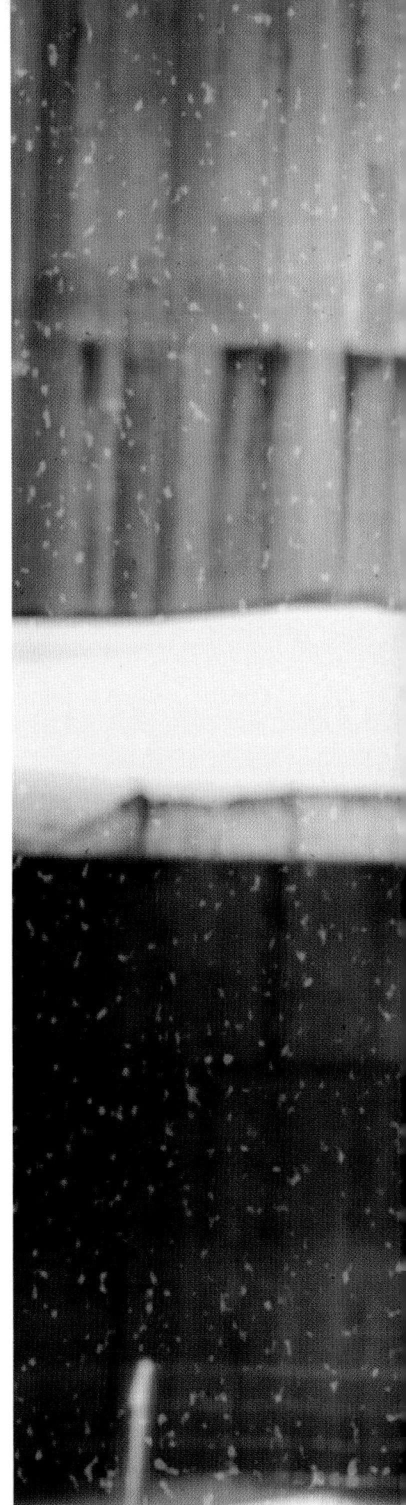

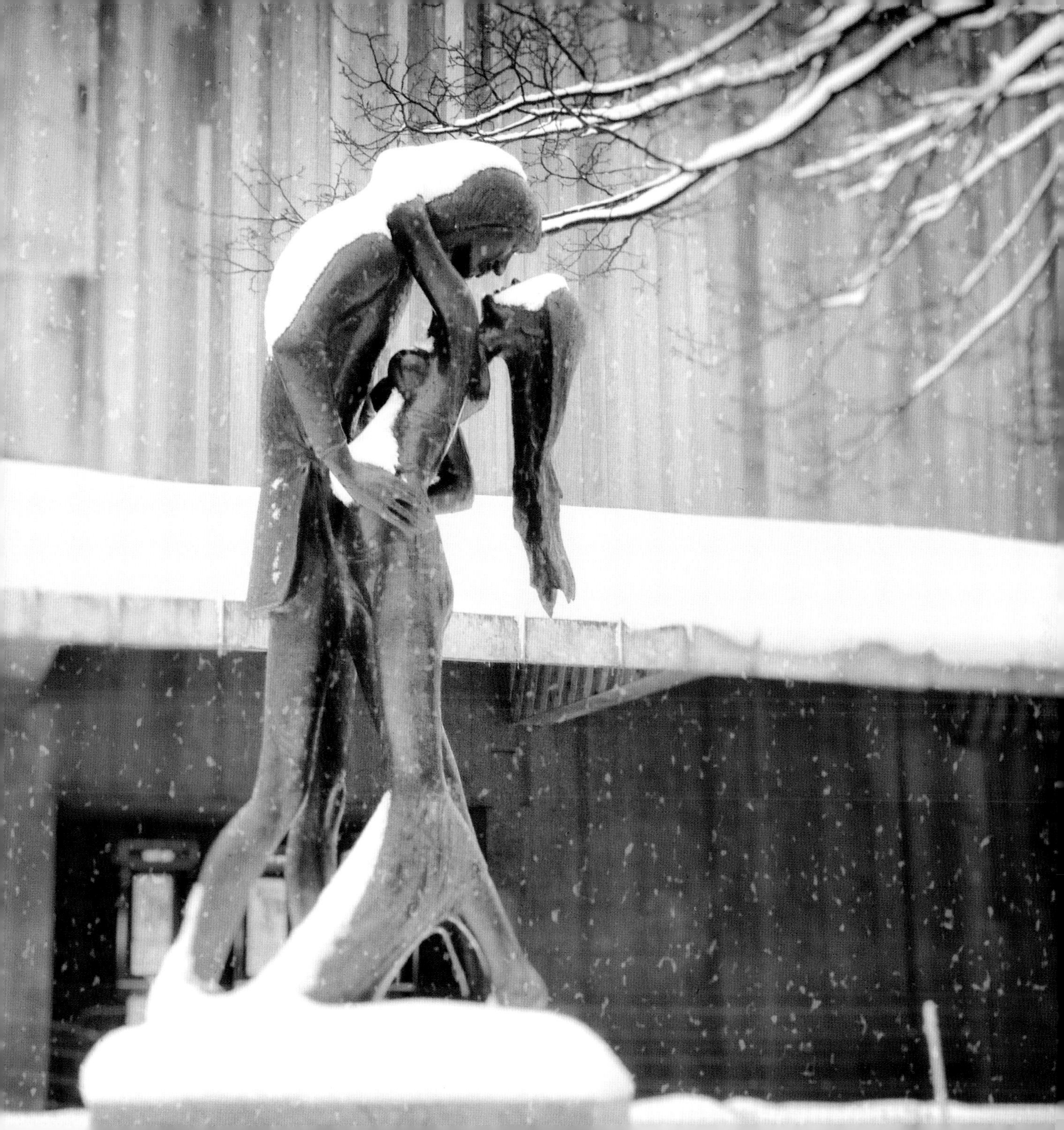

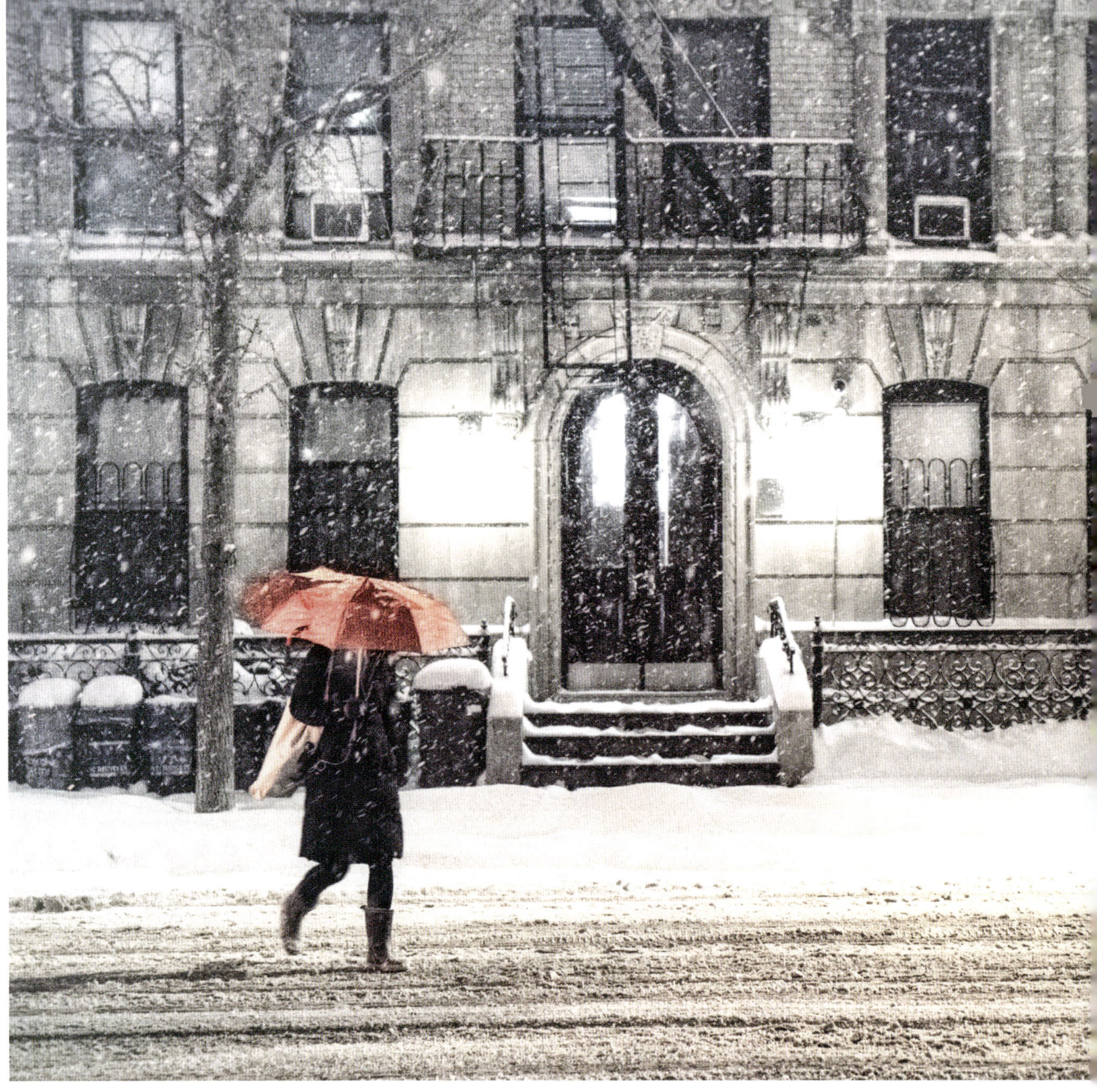

Sutton Place, Midtown Manhattan
Sony SLT-A99V | ƒ/3.5 | 1/80 second | ISO 4000

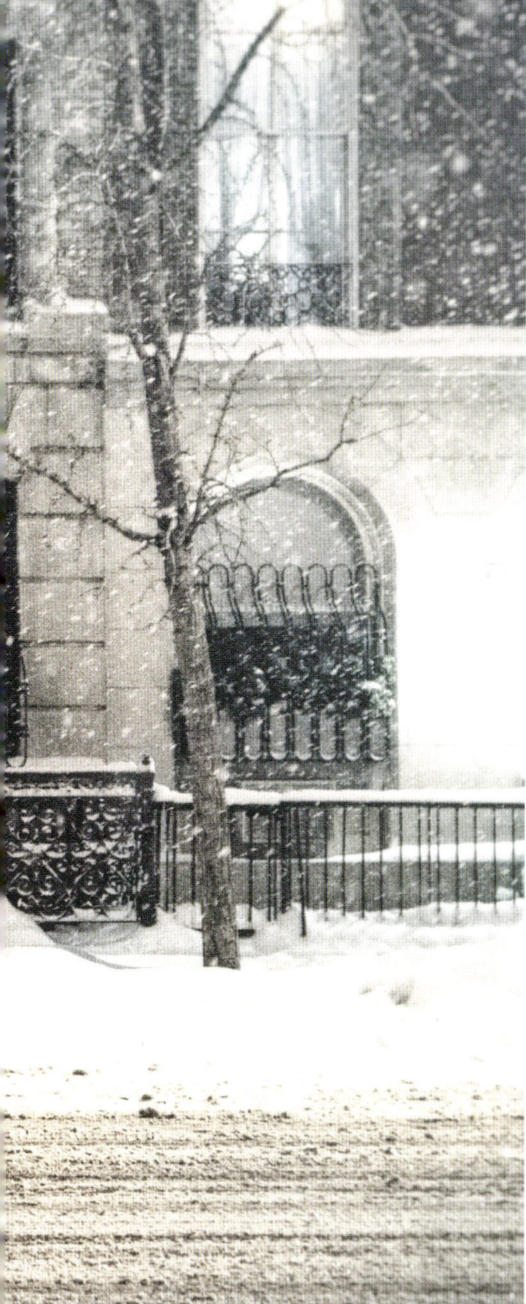

Bryant Park, Midtown Manhattan
Sony SLT-A99V | ƒ/3.2 | 1/20 second | ISO 4000

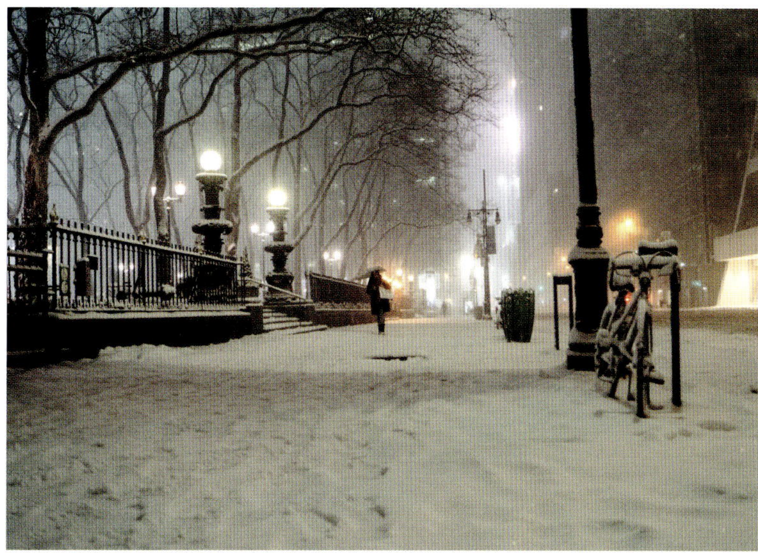

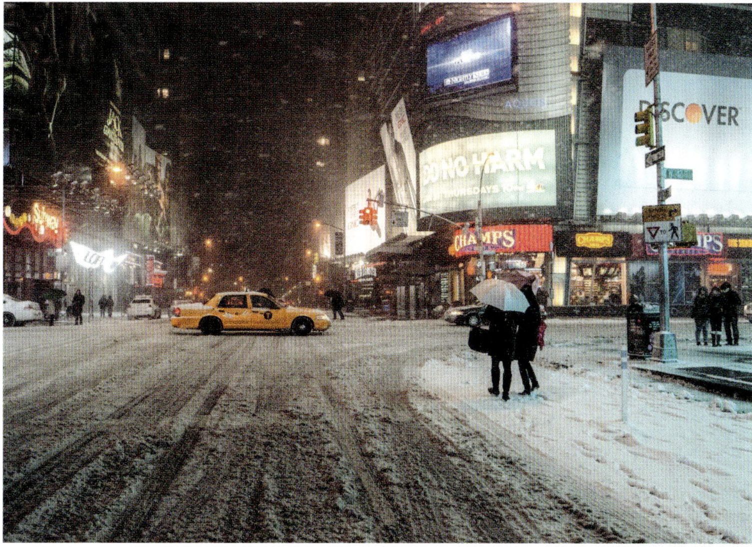

Times Square, Midtown Manhattan
Sony SLT-A99V | ƒ/3.2 | 1/20 second | ISO 4000

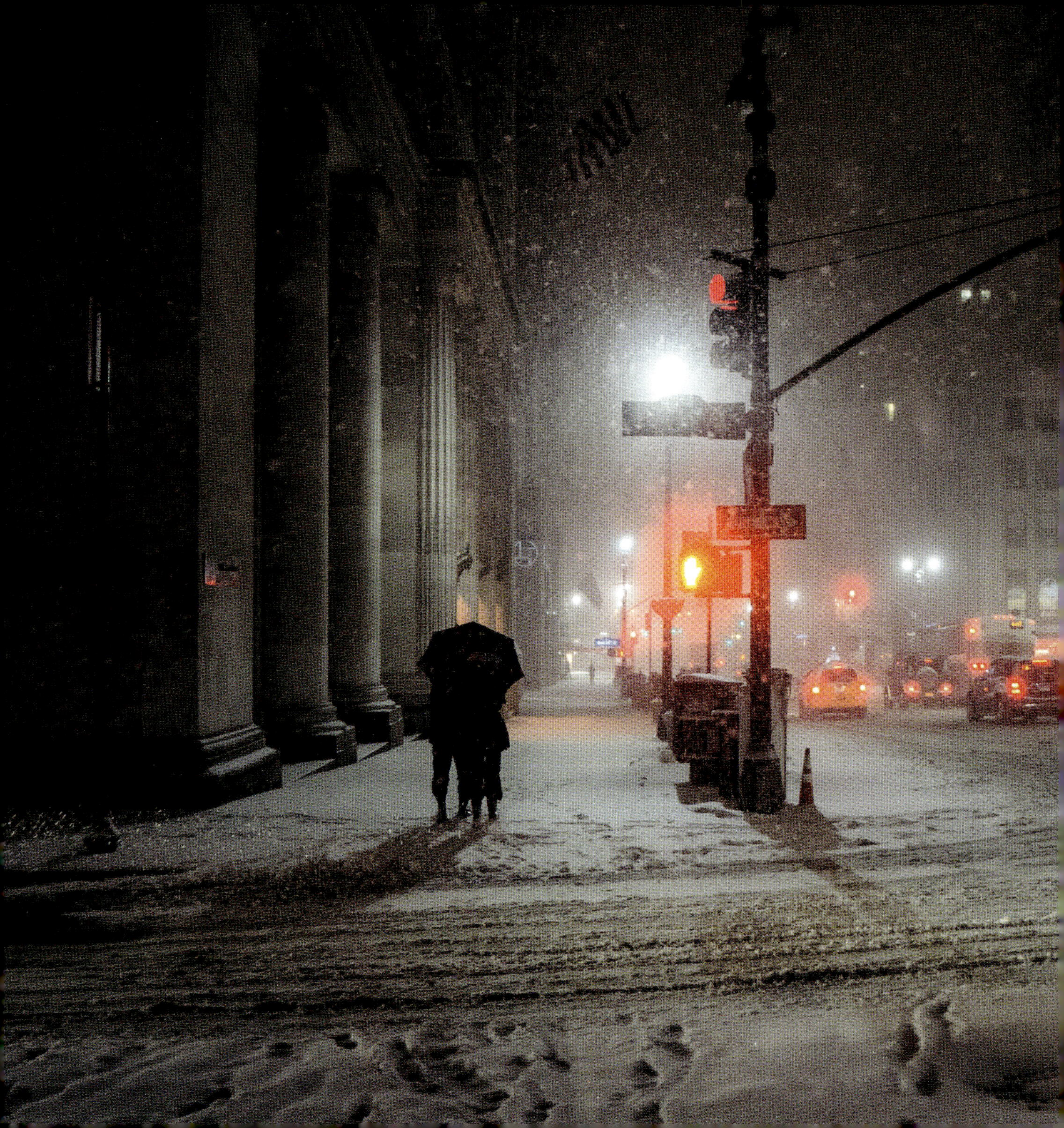

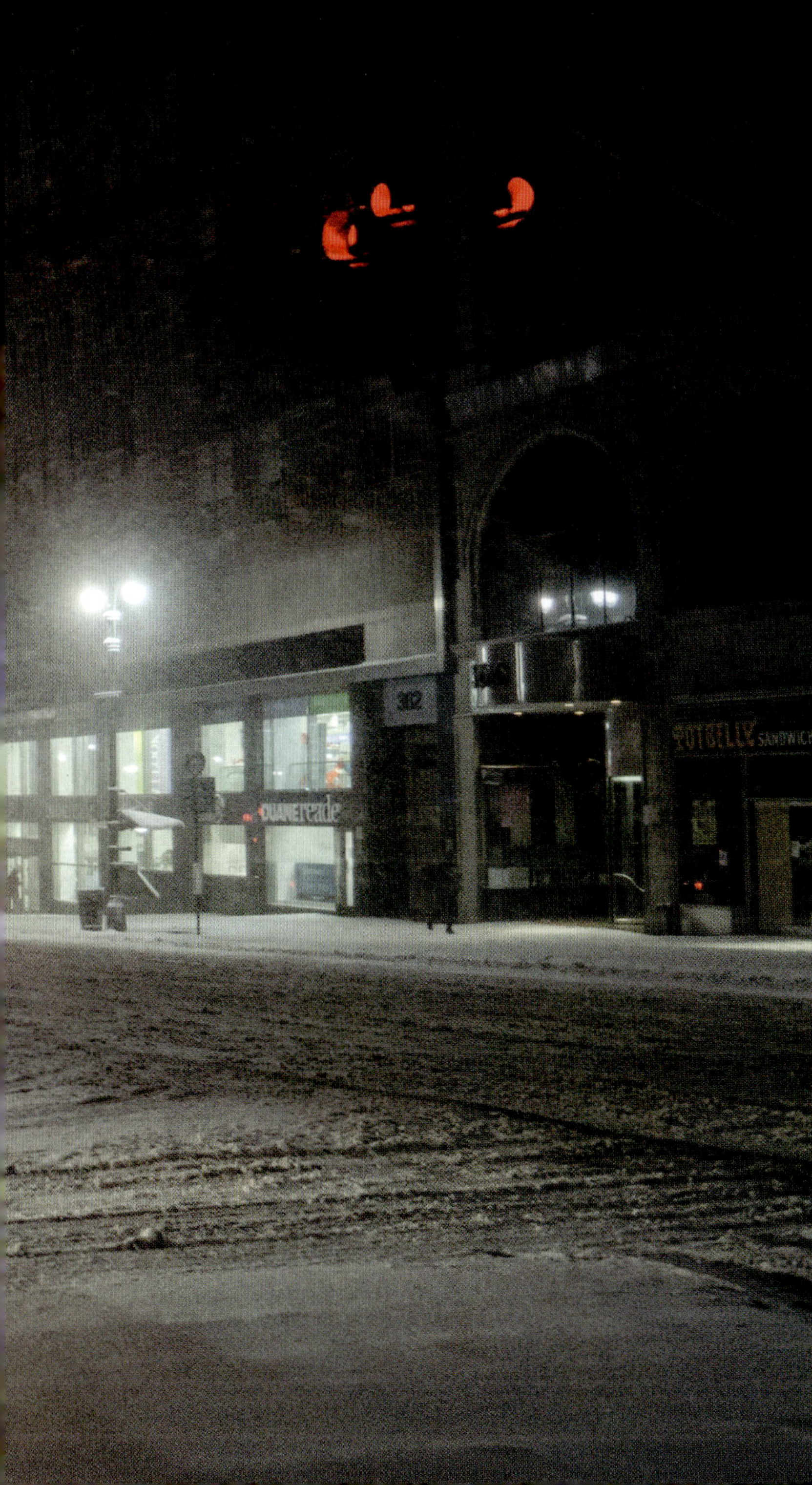

It was a particularly harsh storm that night. The snow was heavy and the wind was whipping through the streets at around 55 miles per hour.

I turned my back to the wind as the eerie silence of the city engulfed me with an existential vastness that made me feel both small and invincible at once.

Something in me made me turn around with my face to the wind and snow, just for a moment. And in that moment a couple stopped on the next corner to embrace in the wind under the shelter of an umbrella for mere seconds.

Maybe they were feeling the same as I was. Maybe we were connected in that moment by the wind rushing into our souls, or by the snow falling from the sky like star matter; glittery white remnants of others who came before us.

> “Or maybe it was just the momentary embrace of chance. Timeless chance as fleeting as snow blowing in the night air.”

Midtown Manhattan
Sony SLT-A99V | *f*/4 | 1/125 second | ISO 4000

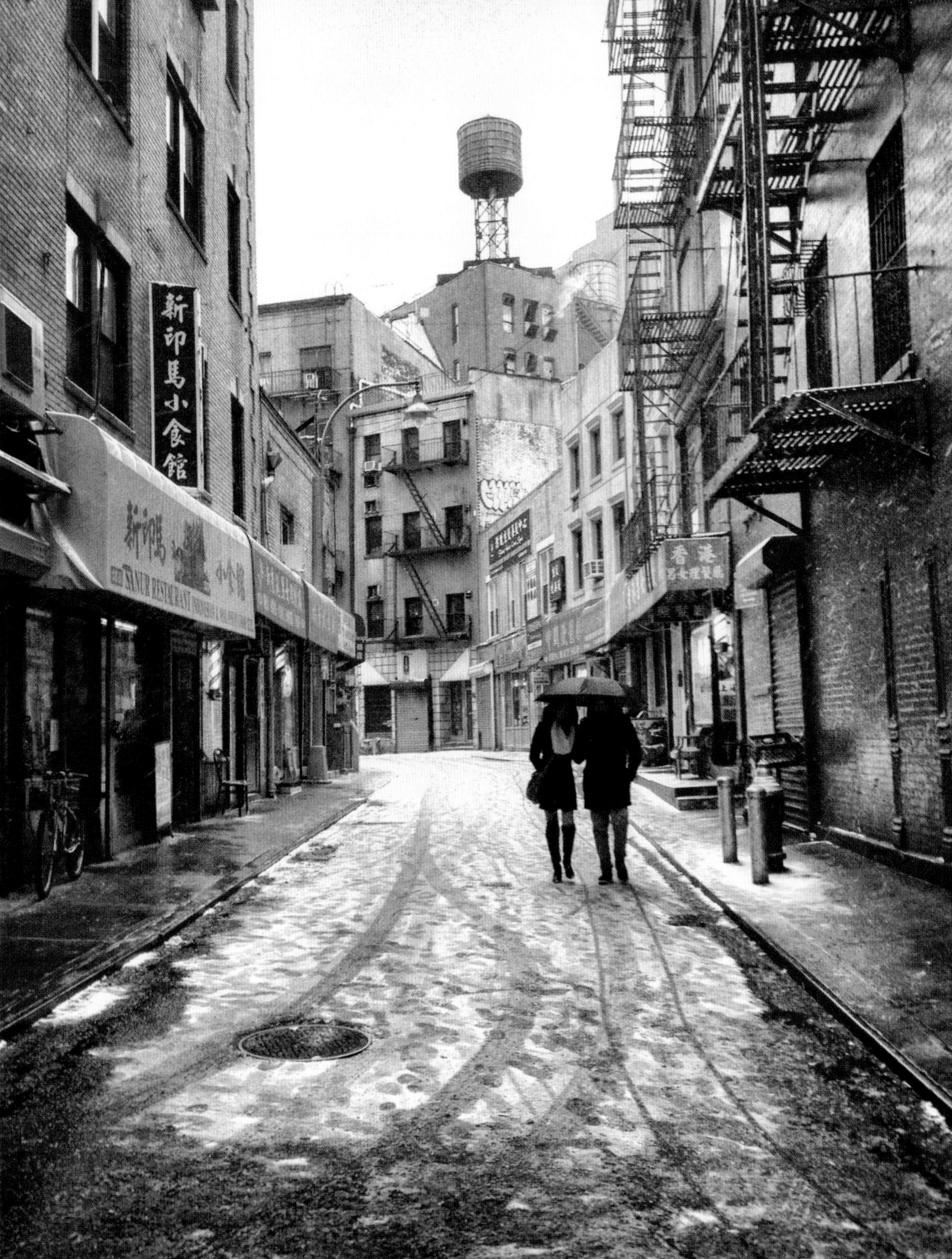
新印馬小食館

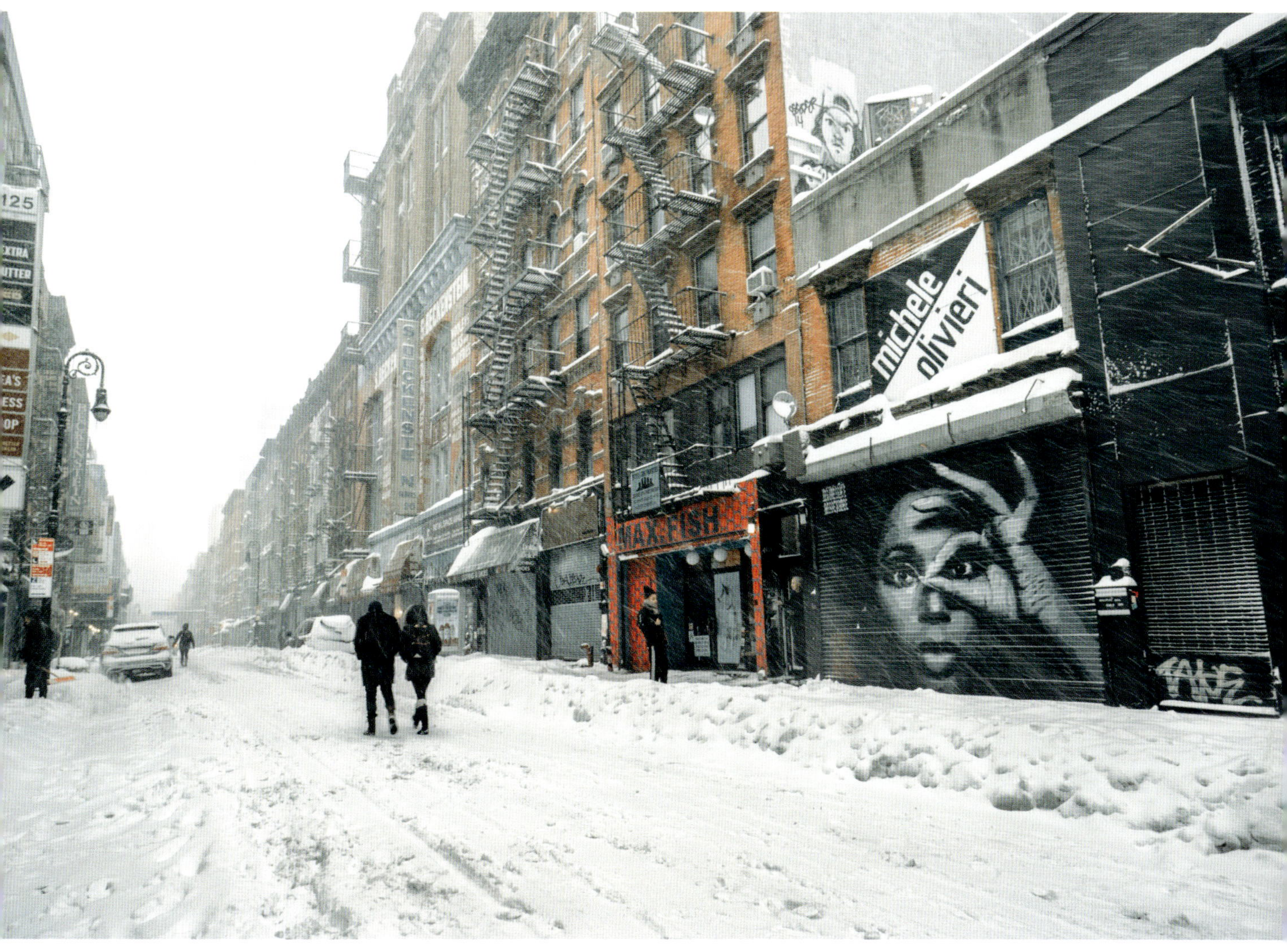

Soho, Lower Manhattan
Sony ILCE-7RM2 | *f*/5 | 1/100 second | ISO 200

Doyers Street, Chinatown, Manhattan
Sony NEX-6 | *f*/3.5 | 1/80 second | ISO 800

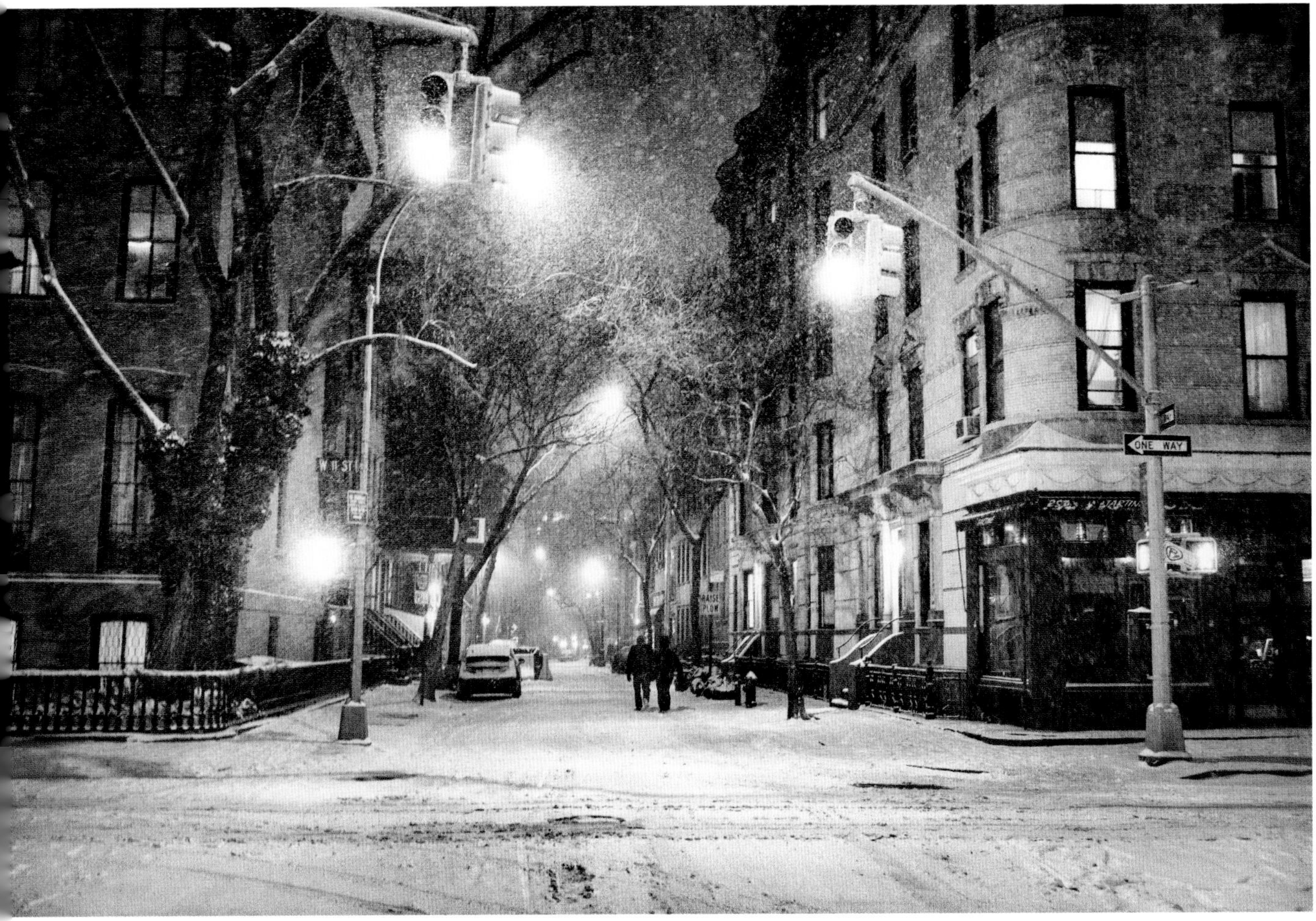

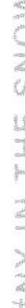

West Village, Lower Manhattan
Sony SLT-A99V | ƒ/3.2 | 1/40 second | ISO 4000

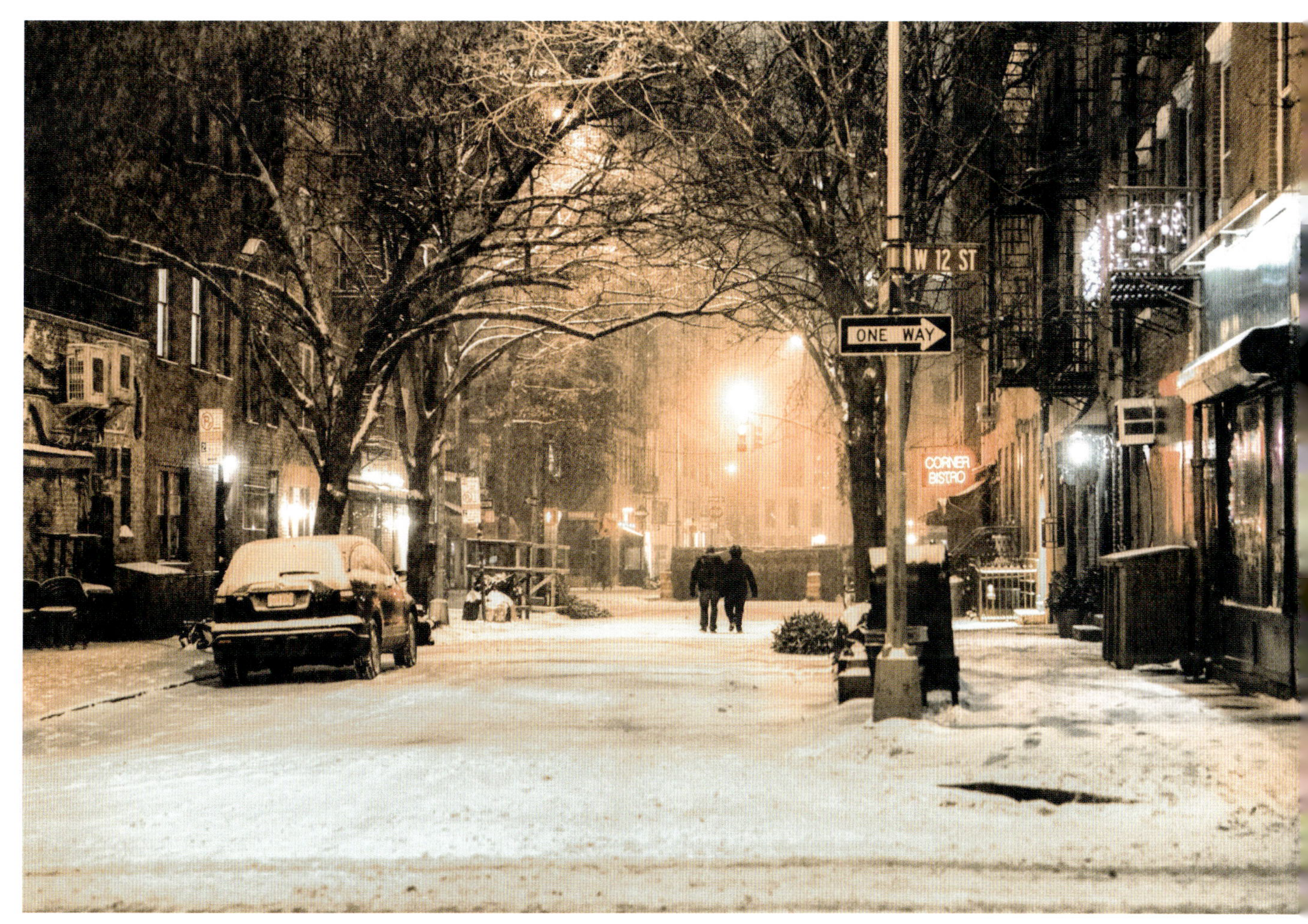

West Village, Lower Manhattan
Sony SLT-A99V | ƒ/3.2 | 1/80 second | ISO 4000

East Village, Lower Manhattan
Sony SLT-A99V | ƒ/3.2 | 1/100 second | ISO 4000

On winter nights
we walk through streets
muffled into silence
by freshly fallen snow
that yields to our
footsteps
eager to record
our passing,
if only for a brief moment.

And as the buildings
rise up like mountains
it's the in-between moments
that stir the hearts
of fellow urban somnambulists.
Held close
under an umbrella
as the city embraces us,
time pauses,
and we huddle in each other's dreams,
the city a glint in our eyes
like every glistening snowflake
that makes its way
to the sidewalk.

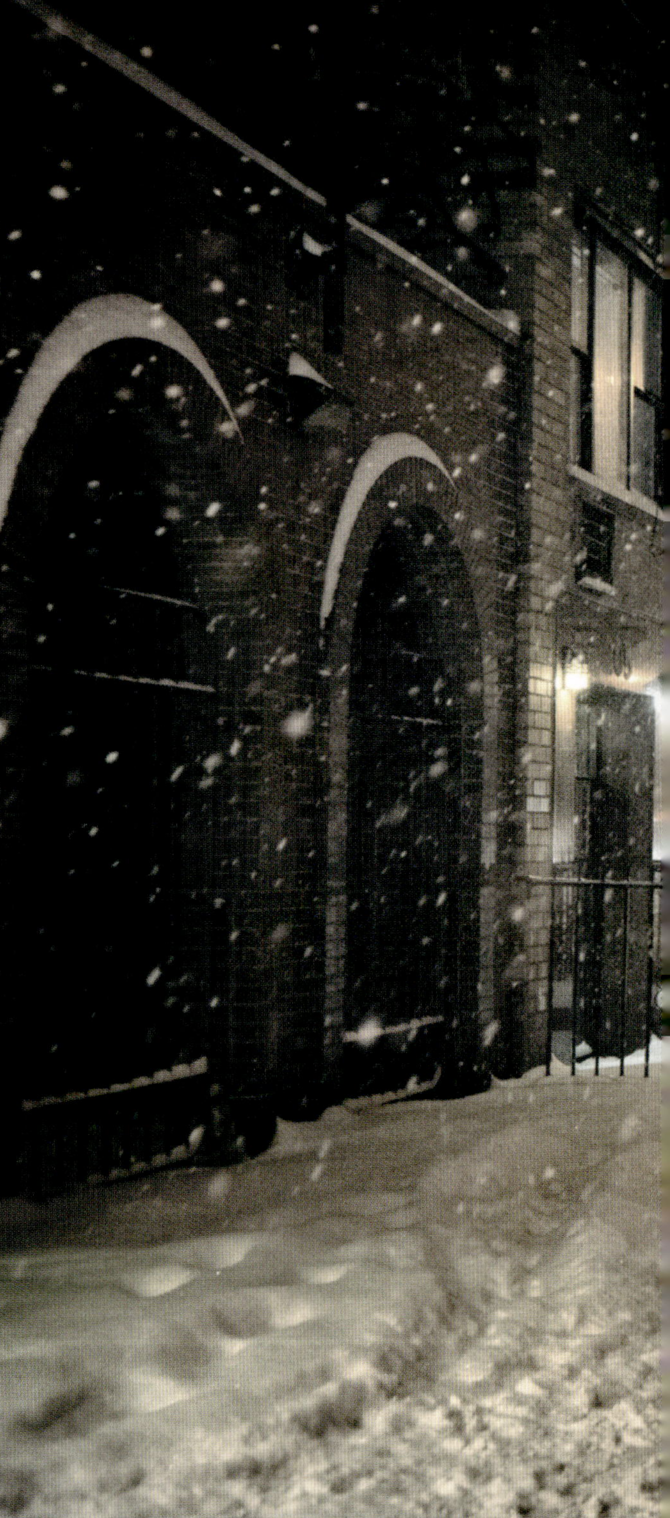

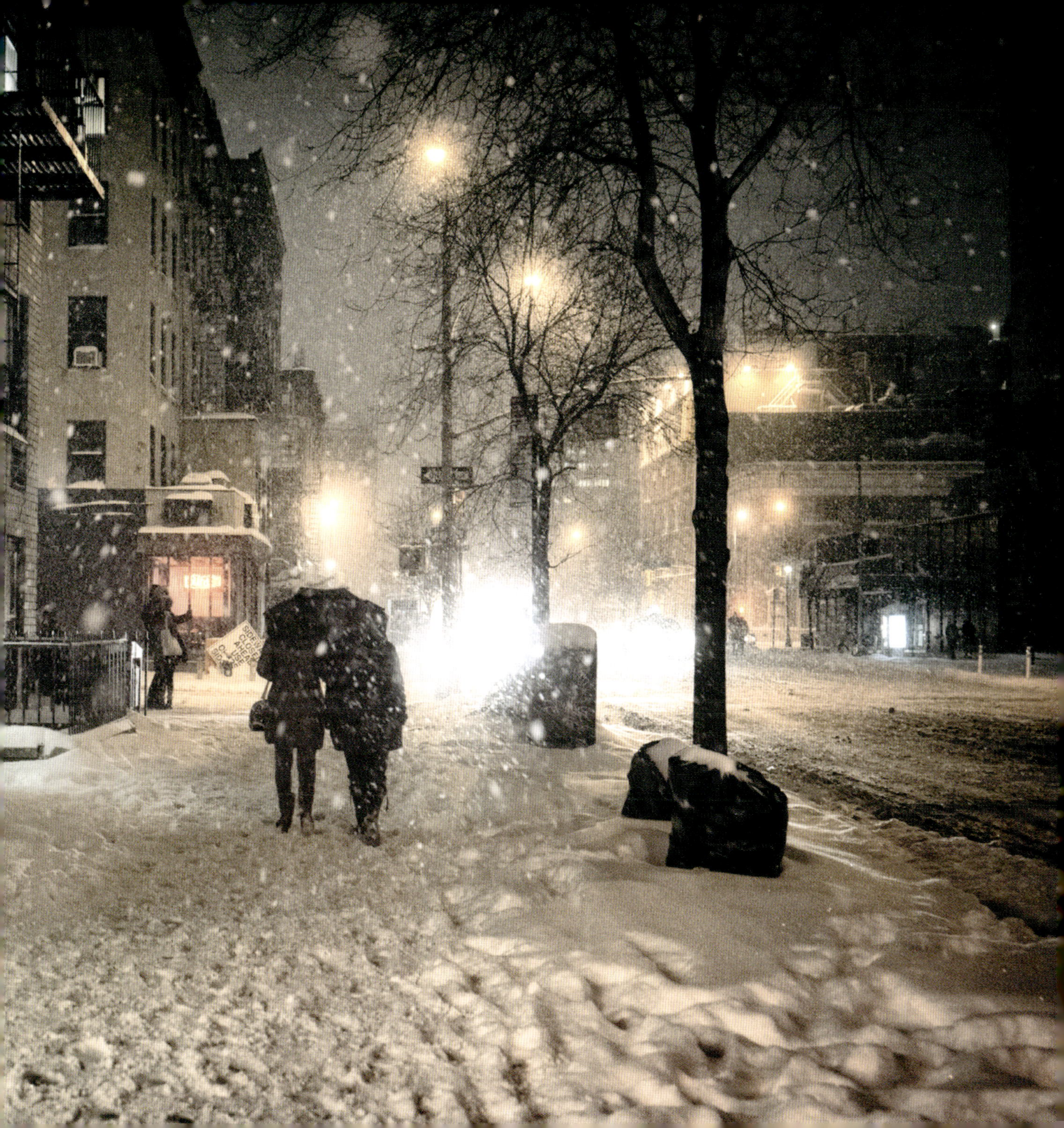

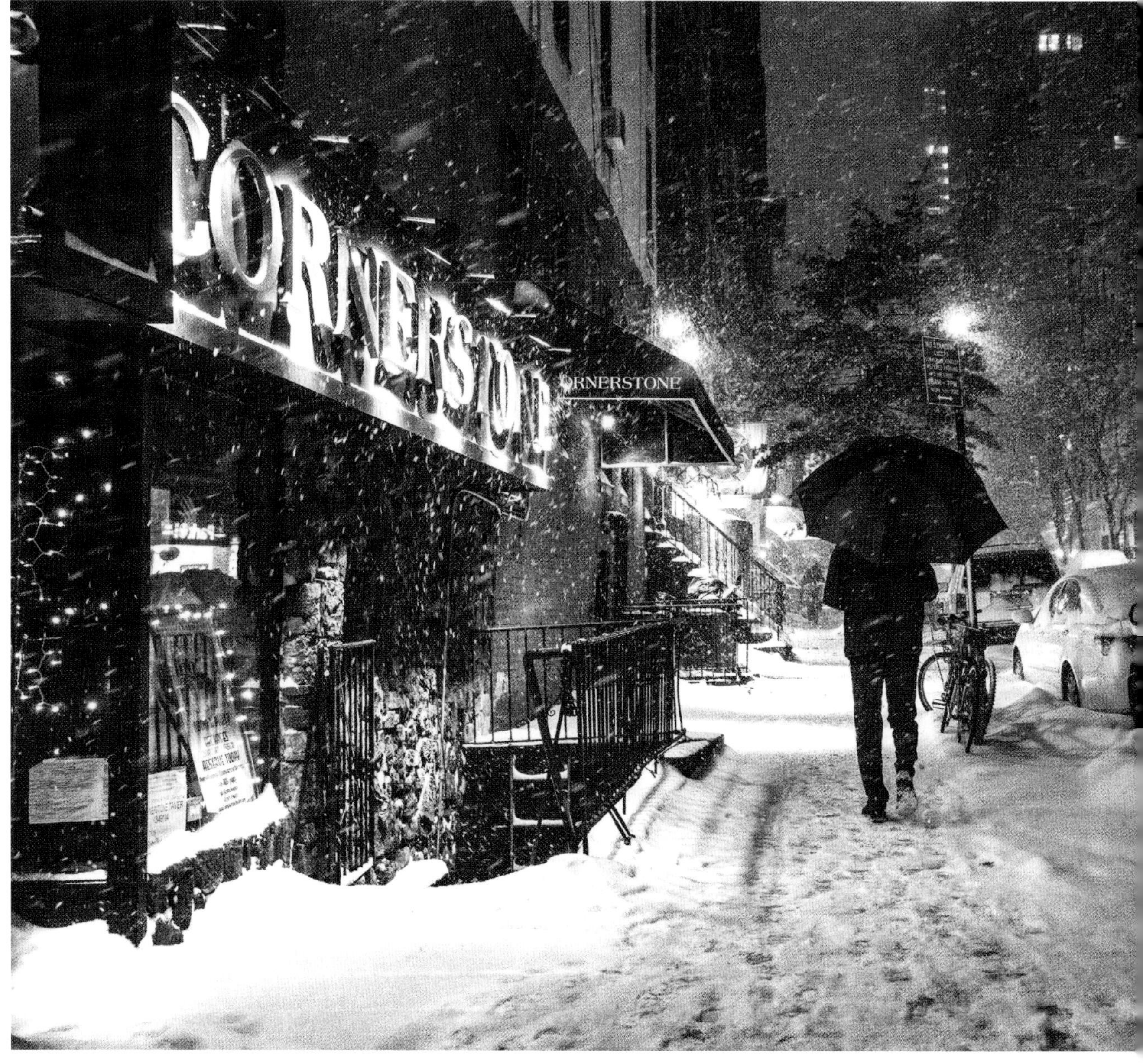

Midtown Manhattan
Sony ILCE-7M2 | *f*/3.2 | 1/100 second | ISO 4000

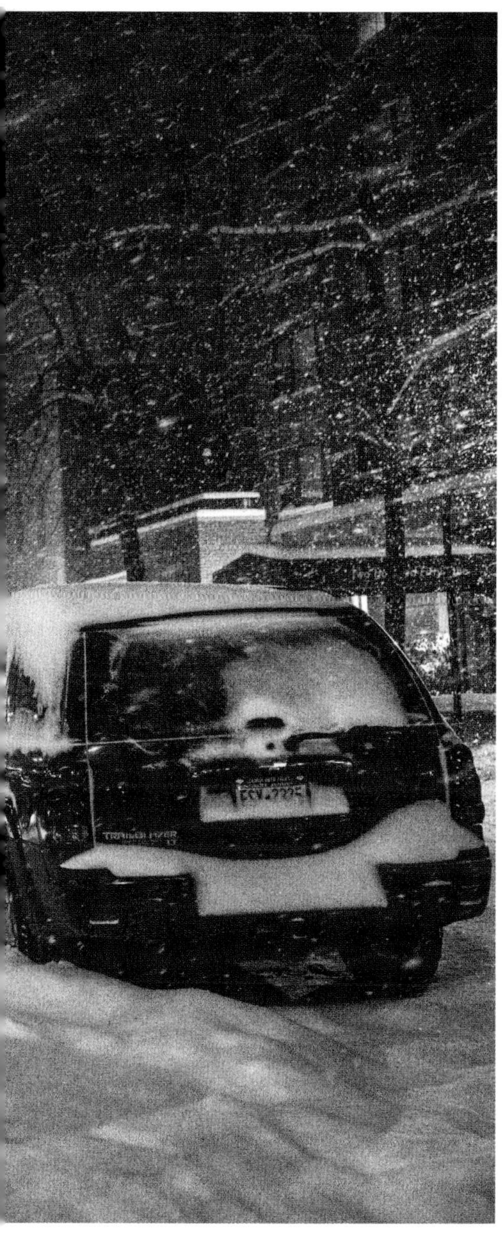

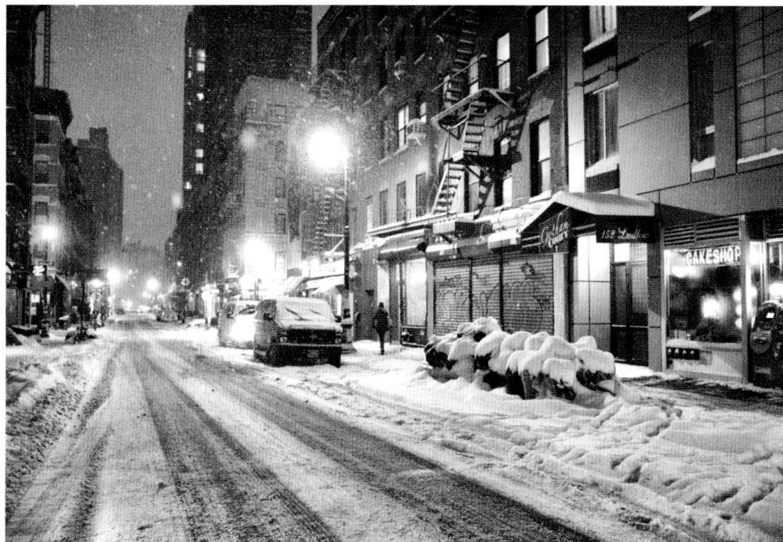

Lower East Side, Manhattan
Sony SLT-A99V | *f*/3.2 | 1/40 second | ISO 4000

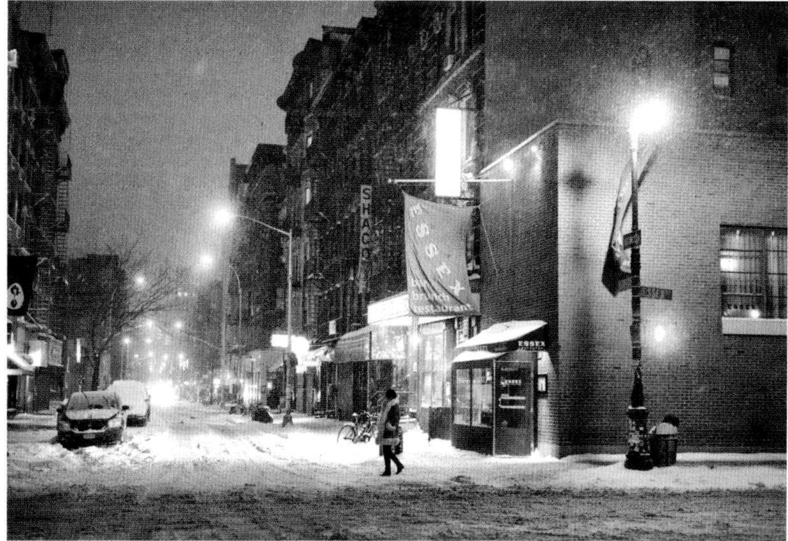

Lower East Side, Manhattan
Sony SLT-A99V | *f*/3.2 | 1/60 second | ISO 4000

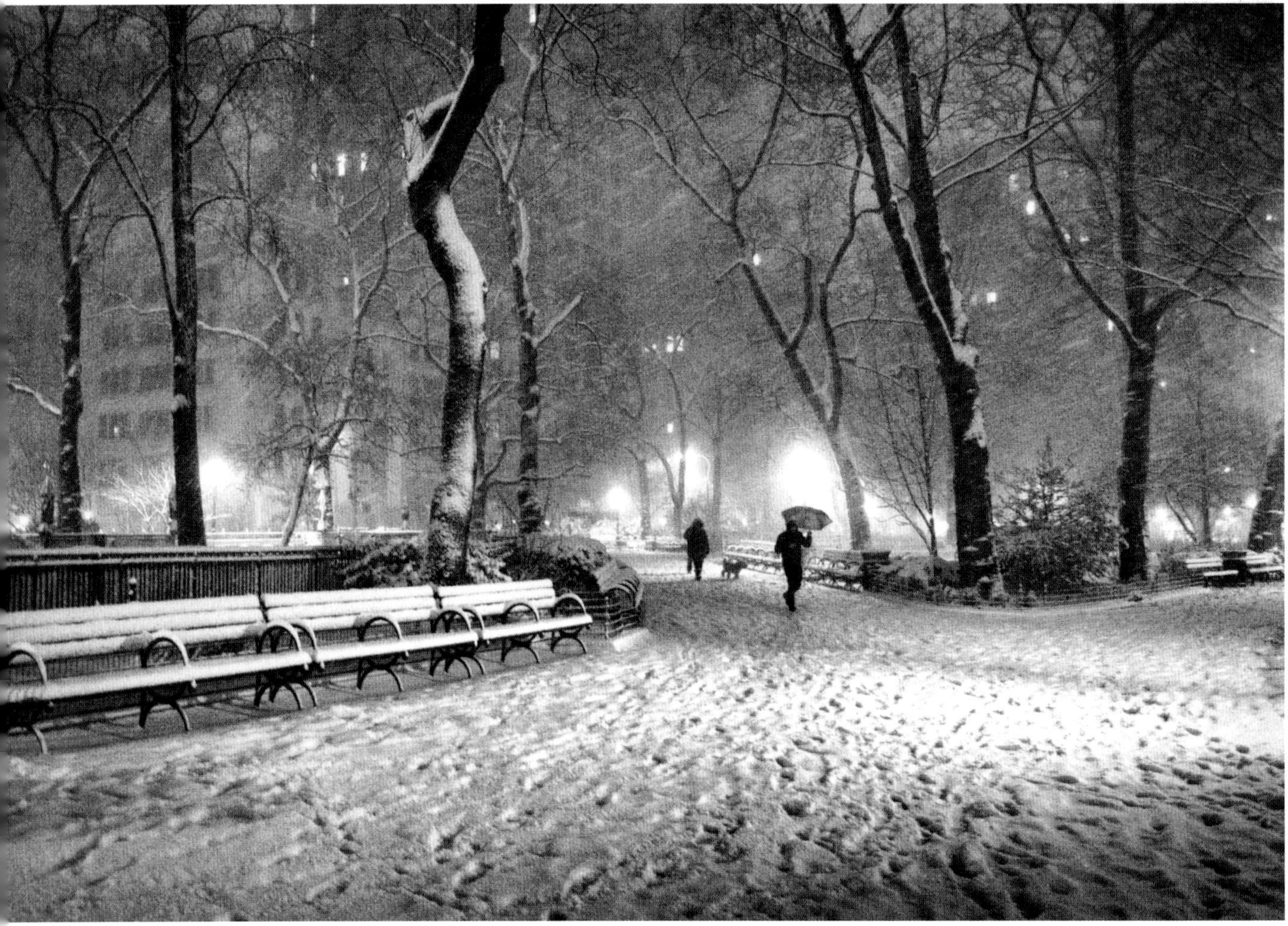

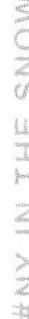

Madison Square Park, Midtown Manhattan
Sony SLT-A99V | $f/2.8$ | 1/40 second | ISO 4000

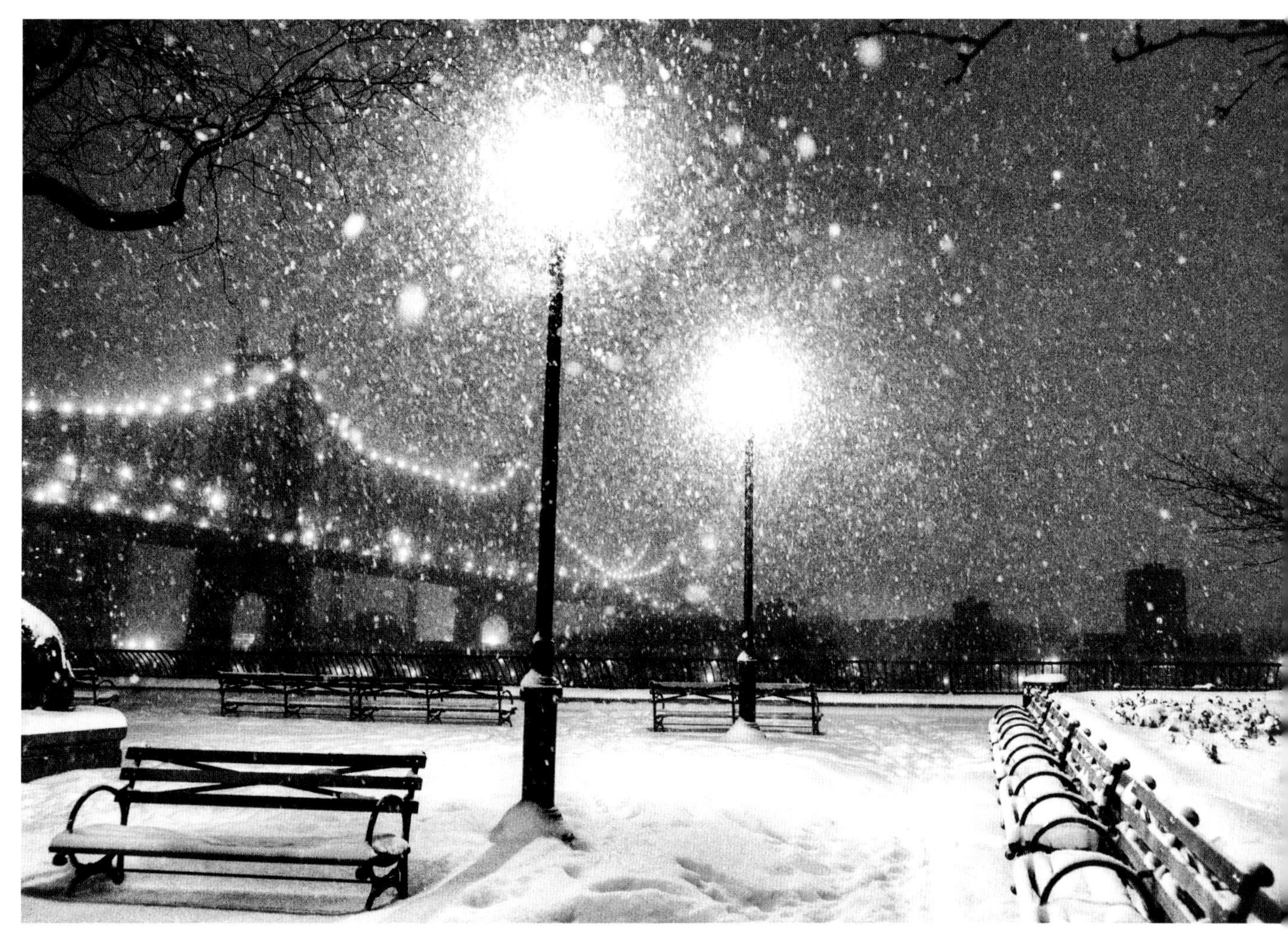

▲ Sutton Place, Midtown Manhattan
Sony ILCE-7M2 | *f*/4 | 1/30 second | ISO 4000

▼ Sutton Place, Midtown Manhattan
Sony ILCE-7M2 | *f*/2.8 | 1/80 second | ISO 4000

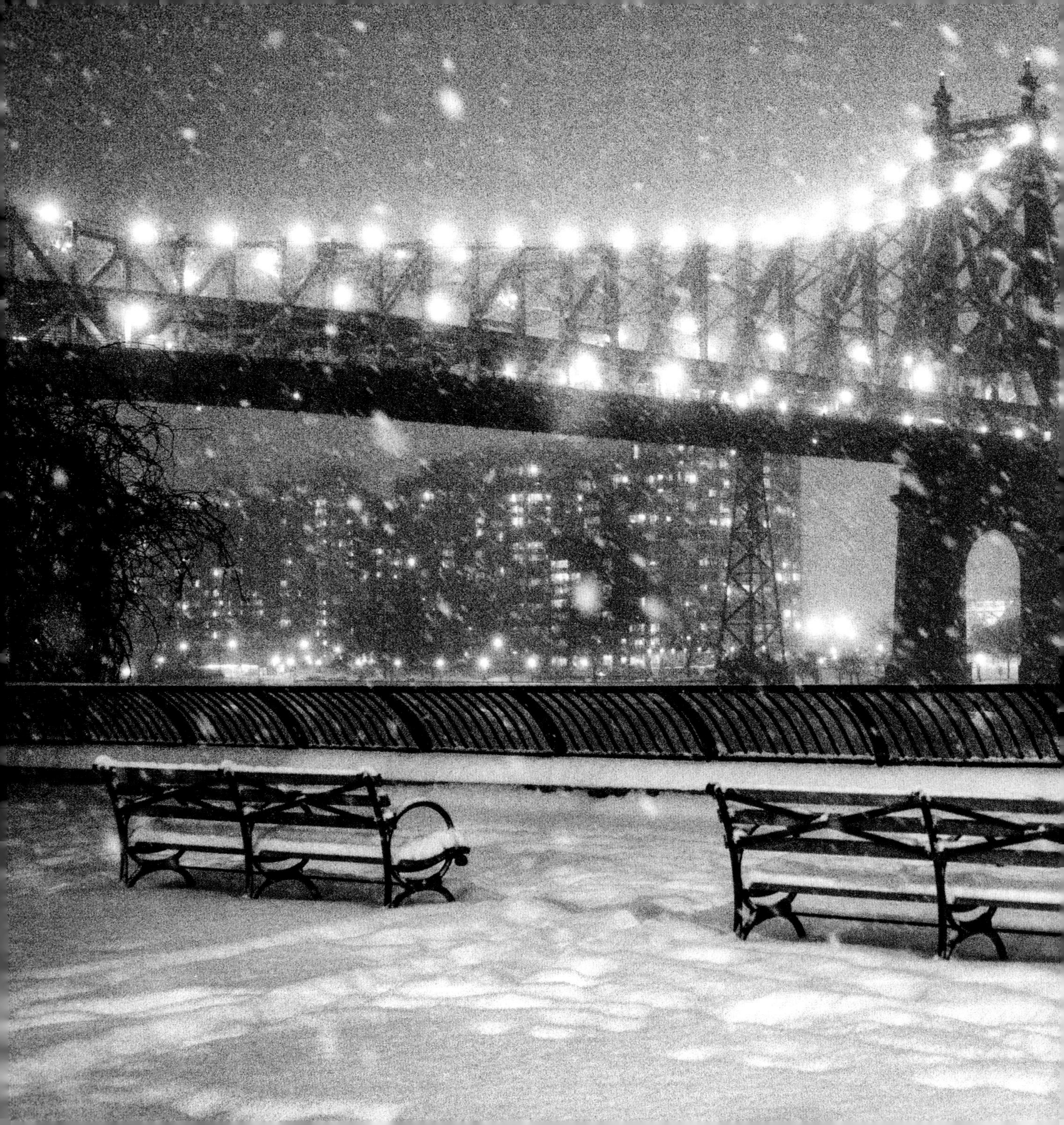

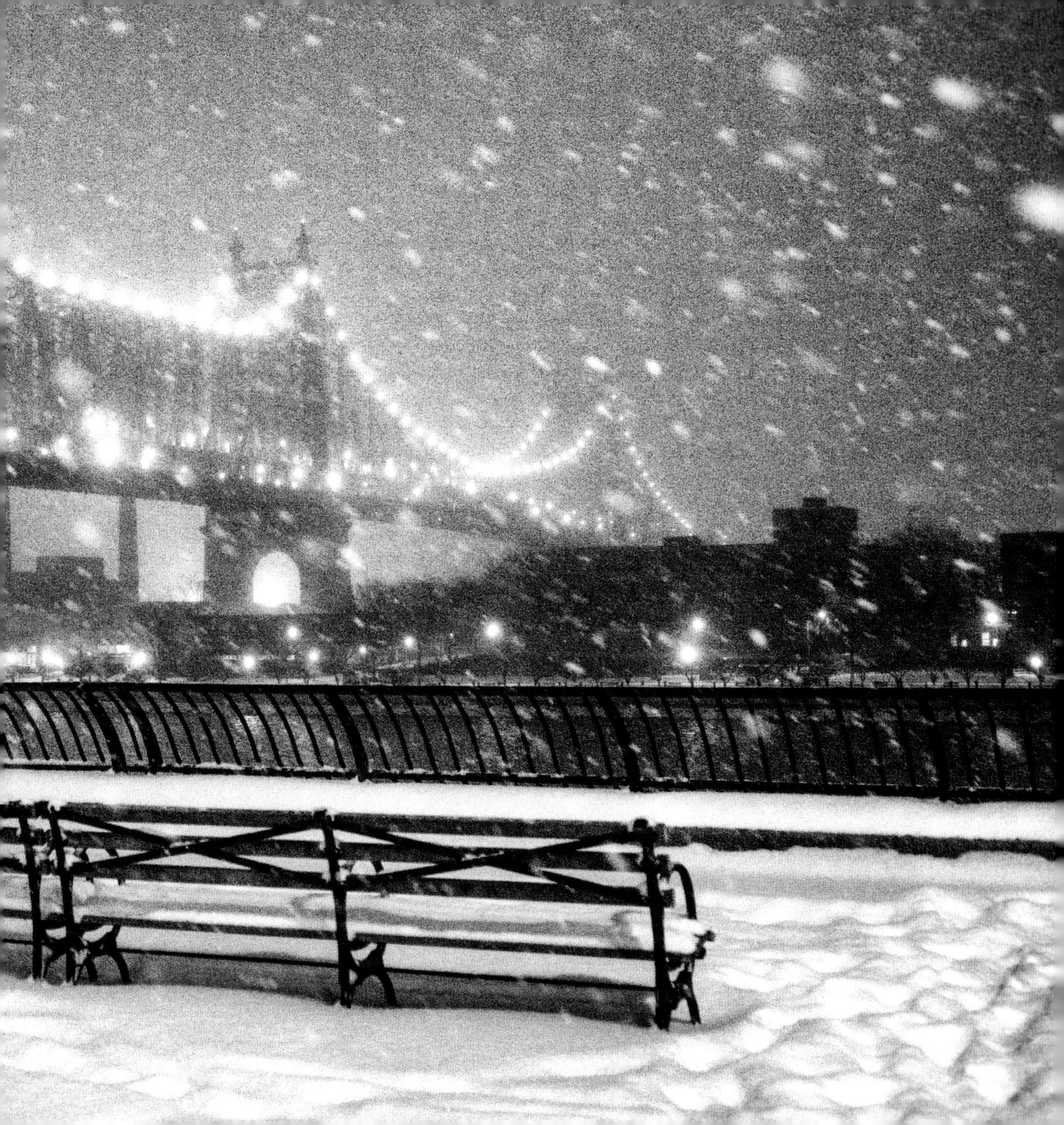

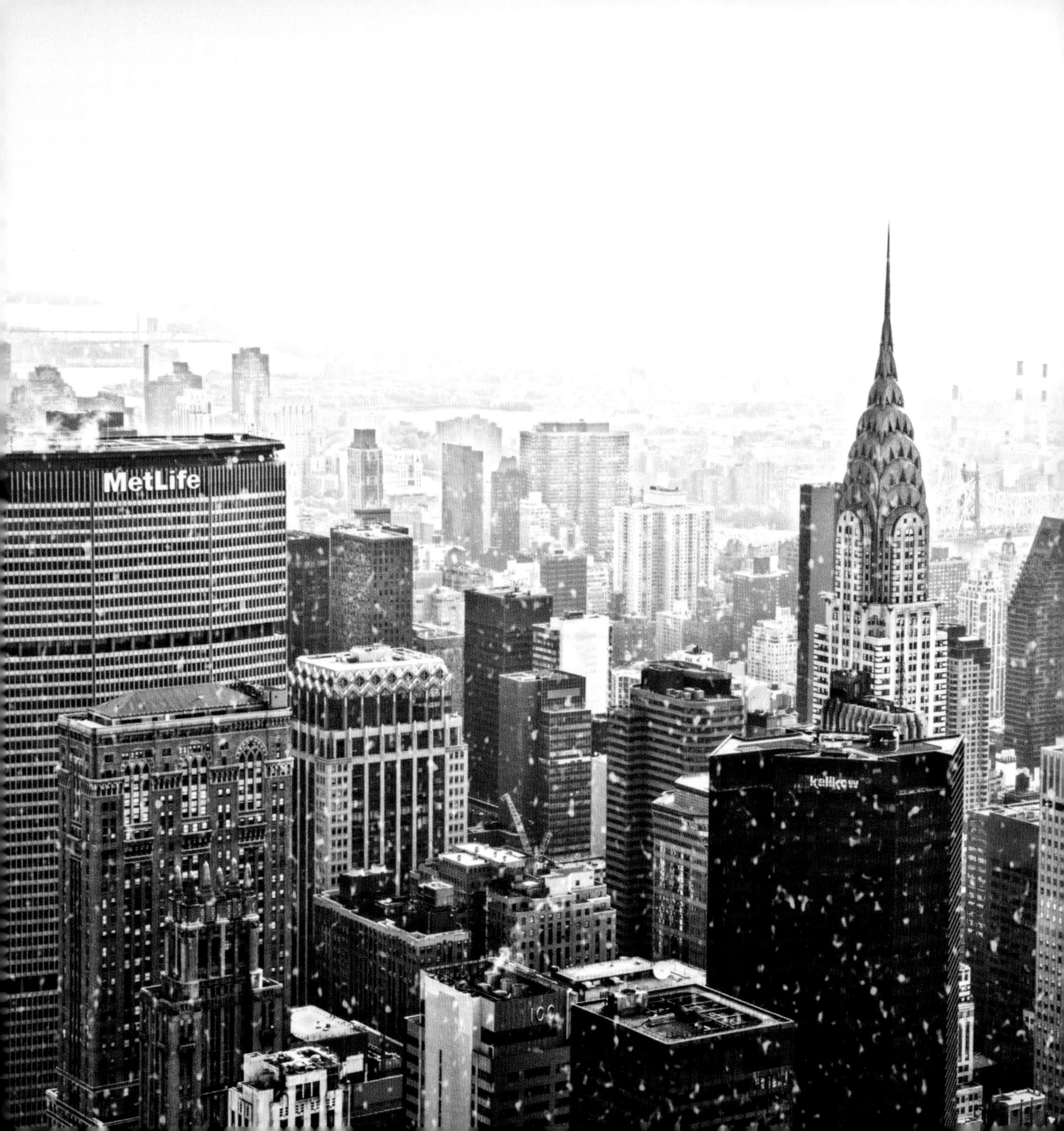
MetLife
kalikow

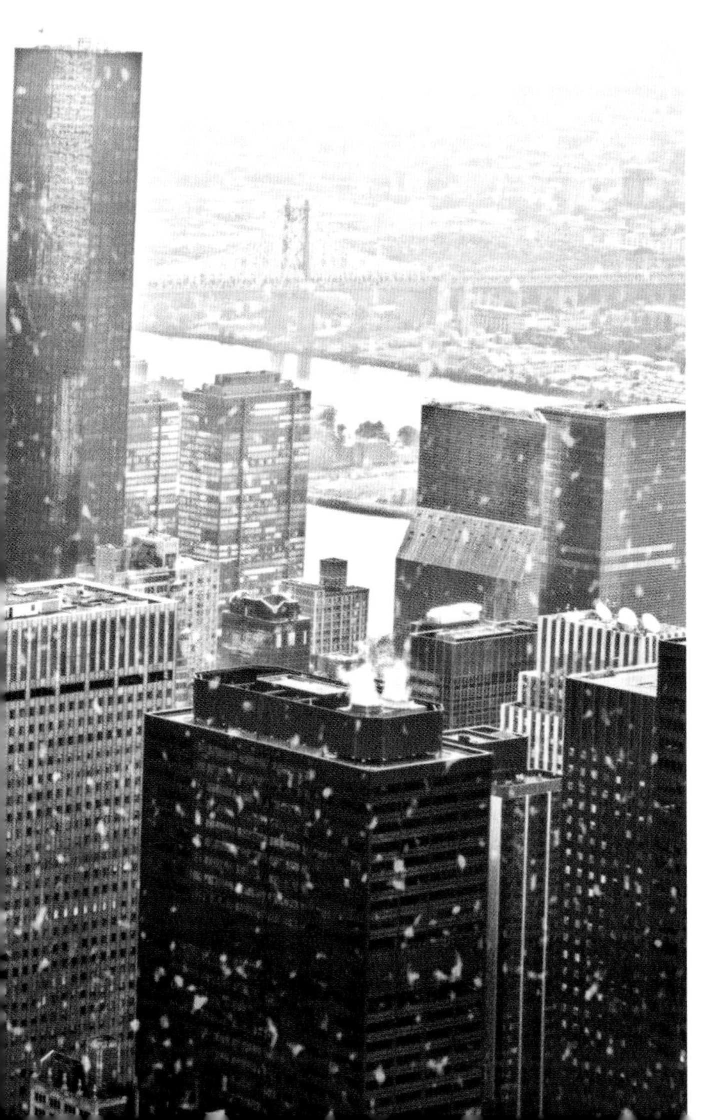

Snowflakes swirl over the skyscrapers and buildings: confetti from the sky blanketing the buildings and streets.

And the world transforms into a snow globe, if only for a brief moment.

Midtown Manhattan
Sony SLT-A99V | *f*/5 | 1/40 second | ISO 200

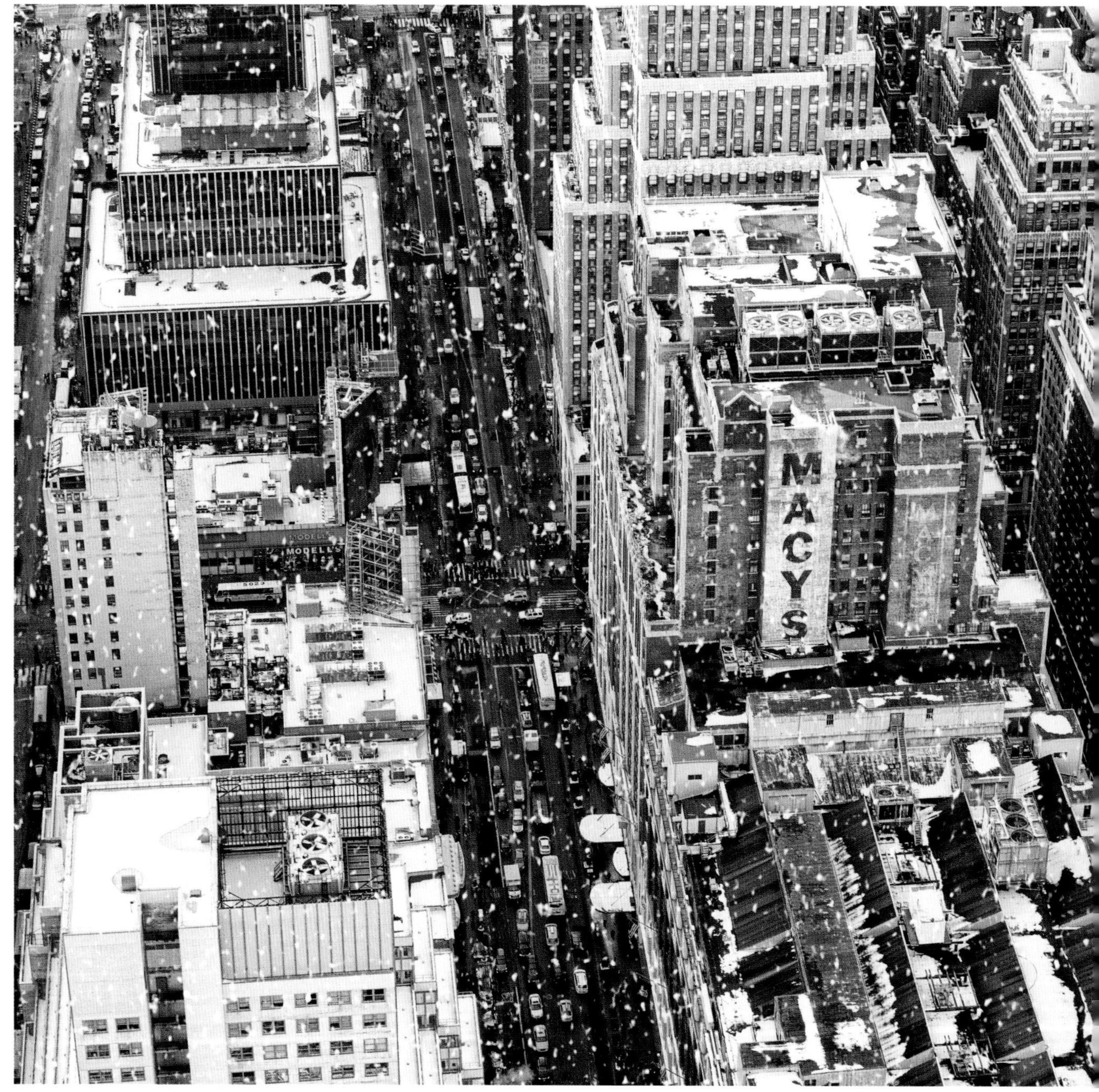
MACYS
MODELL'S

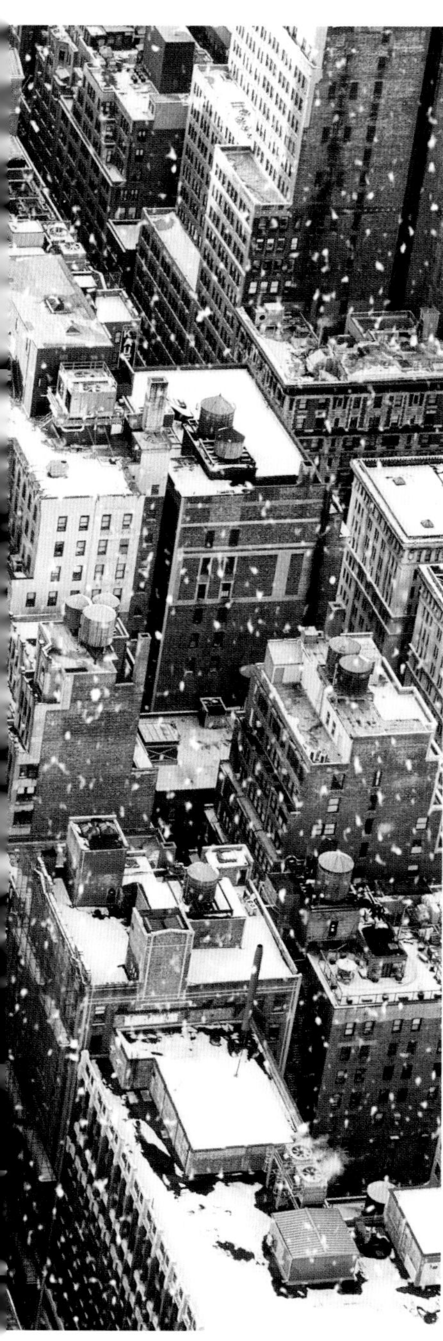

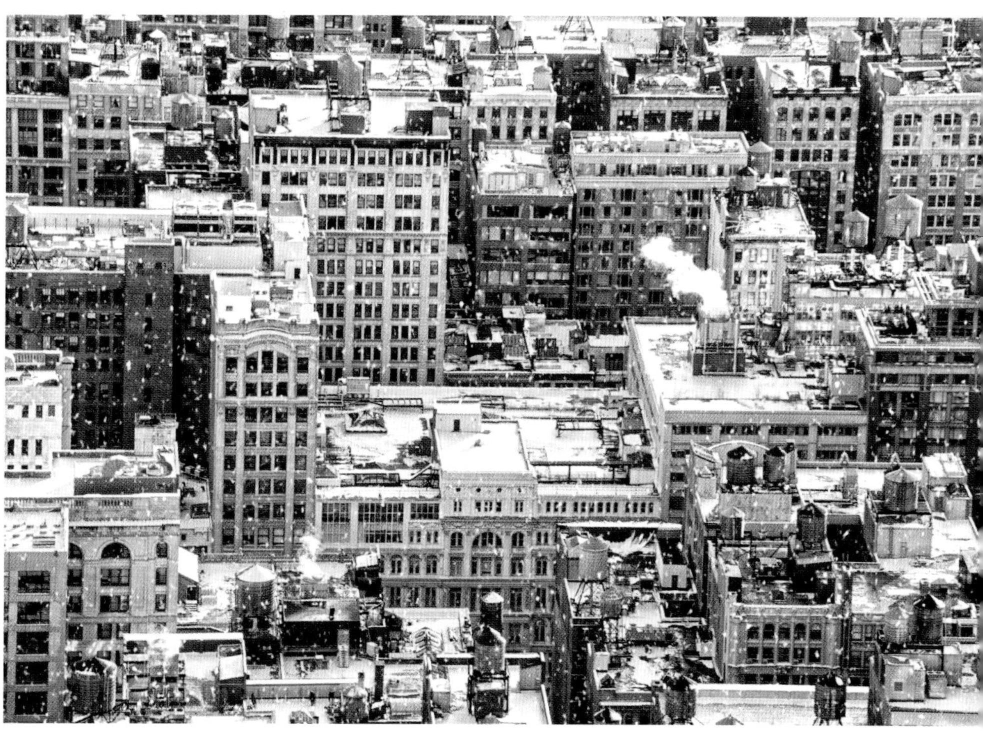

Midtown Manhattan
Sony ILCE-7S | ƒ/9 | 1/160 second | ISO 200

Midtown Manhattan
Sony ILCE-7S | ƒ/9 | 1/160 second | ISO 640

Midtown Manhattan
Sony ILCE-7S | ƒ/9 | 1/160 second | ISO 200

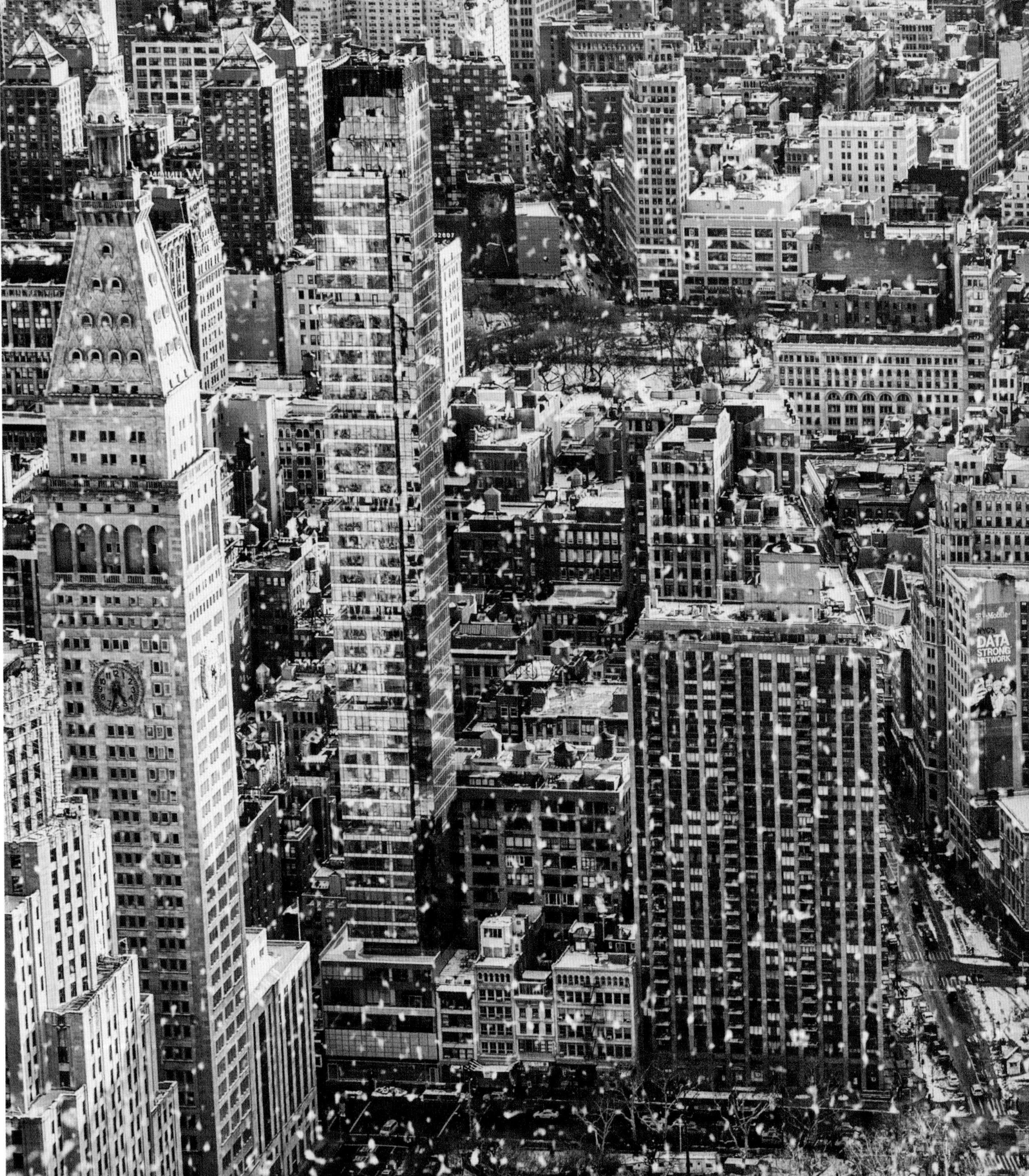
DATA
STRONG
NETWORK

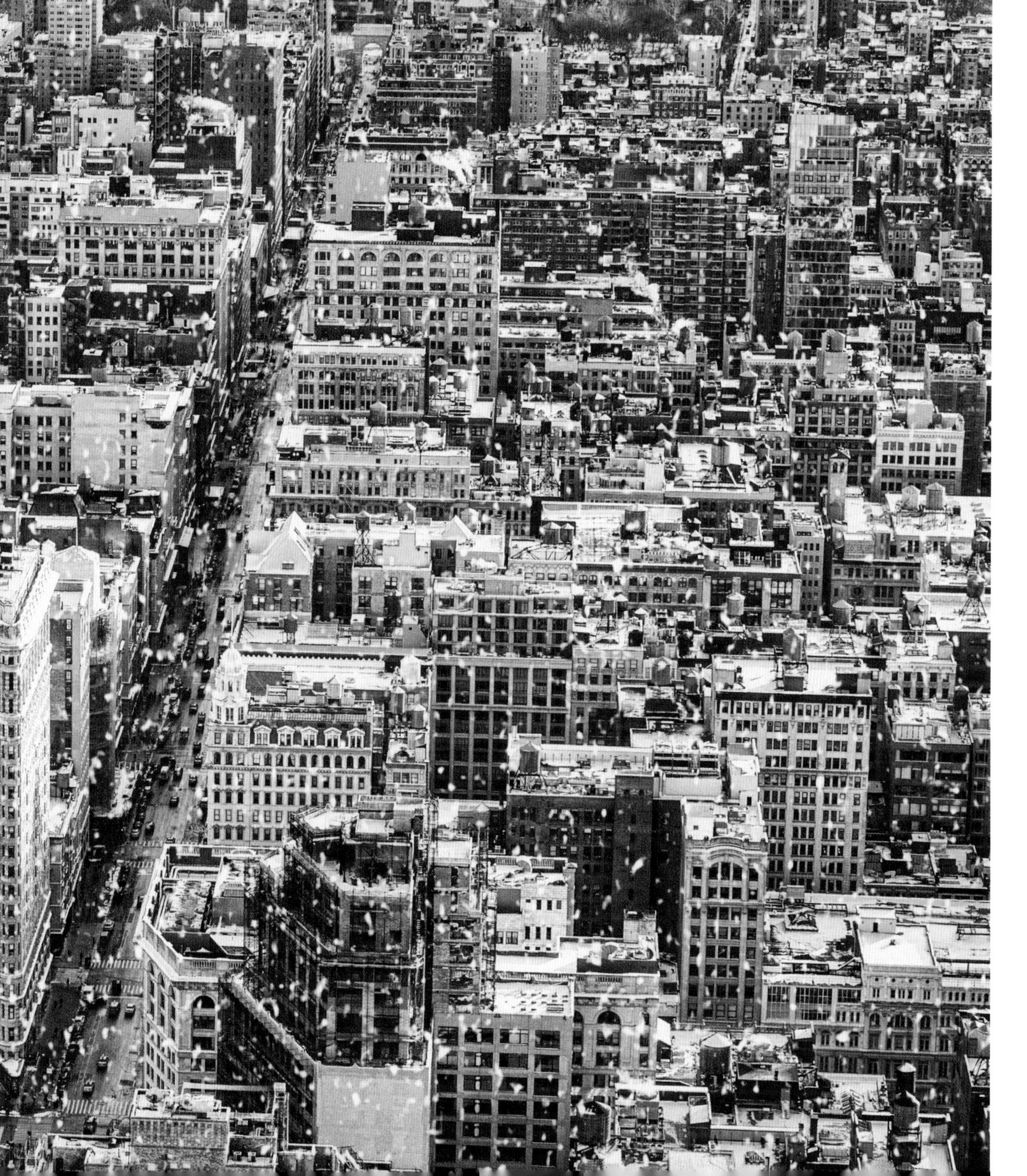

The snow fell
on New York City
like spun sugar,
stretched across
trees and houses
as hearts skipped a beat,
in the pause between moments
while the city streets wound
themselves through the snow
and we climbed right into
winter's dream,
propelling ourselves
into the city's memory,
while distant smokestacks
exhaled into a slumbering sky.
Day melted away
as evening waited patiently
to pull itself like a blanket
over a languid and dreaming afternoon,
and New York City slipped
over glazed rooftops
into the winter night.

Midtown Manhattan
Sony NEX-7 | *f*/5 | 1/80 second | ISO 200

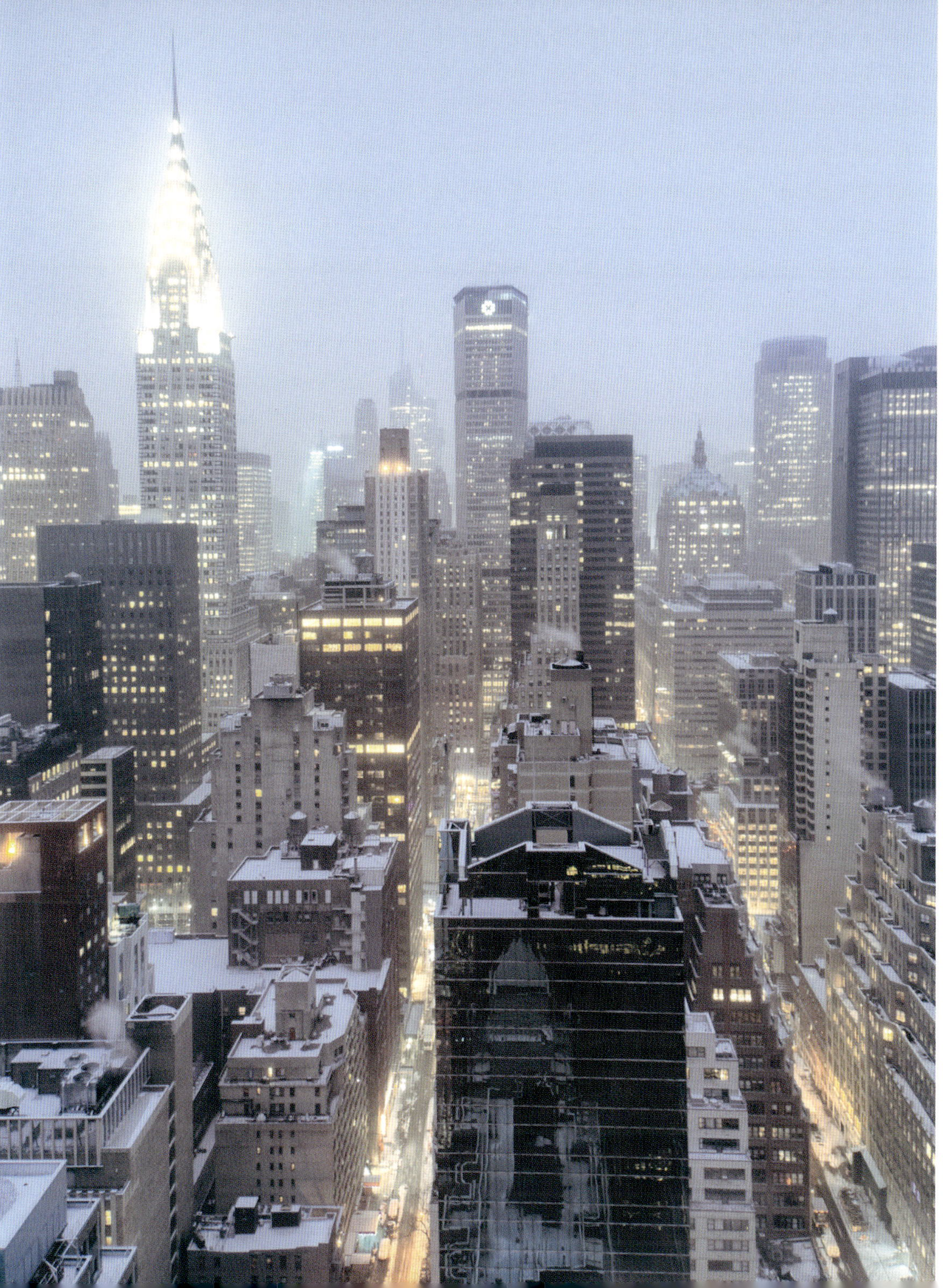

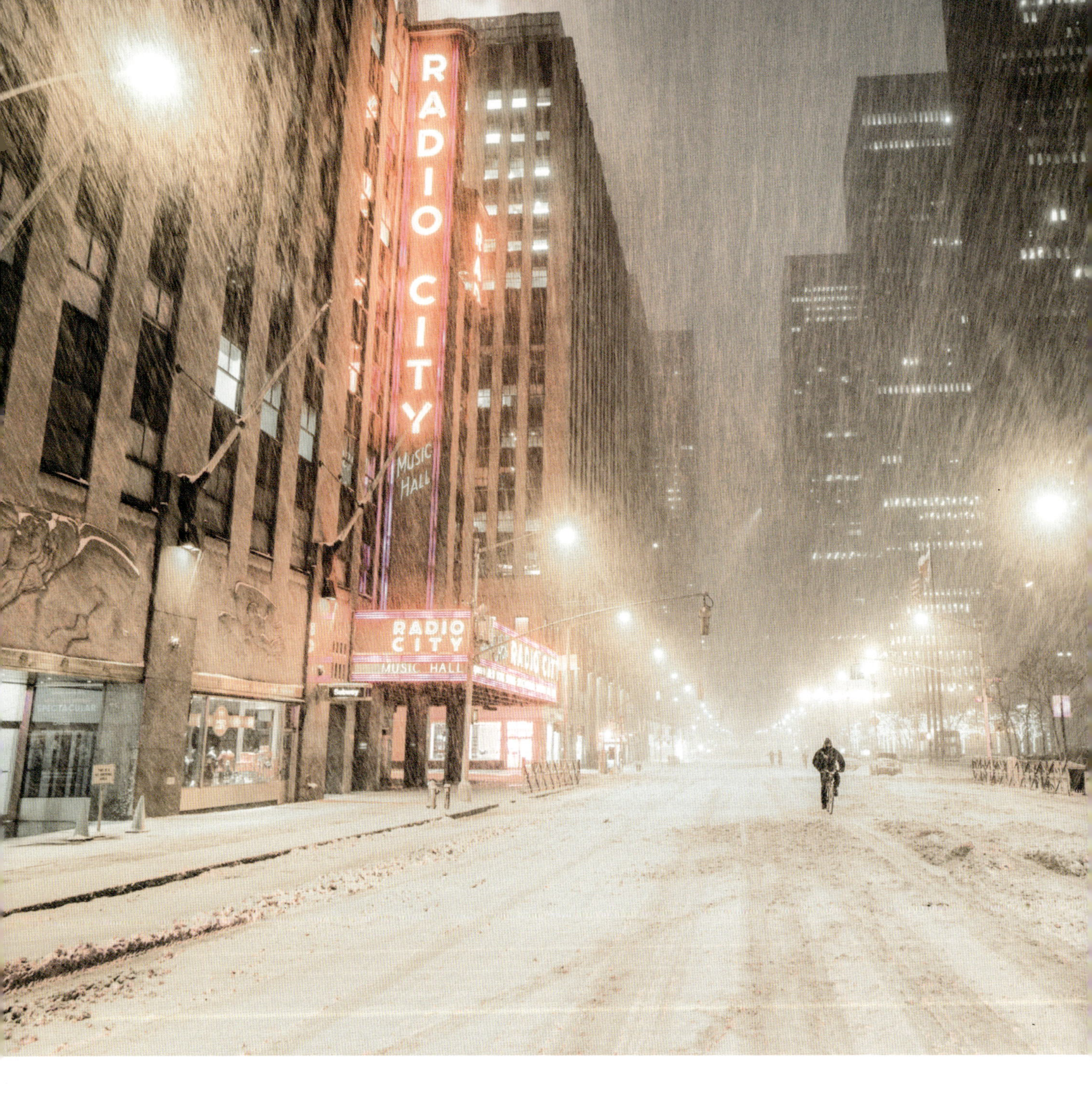
RADIO CITY
MUSIC HALL
RADIO CITY
MUSIC HALL
RADIO CITY
SPECTACULAR

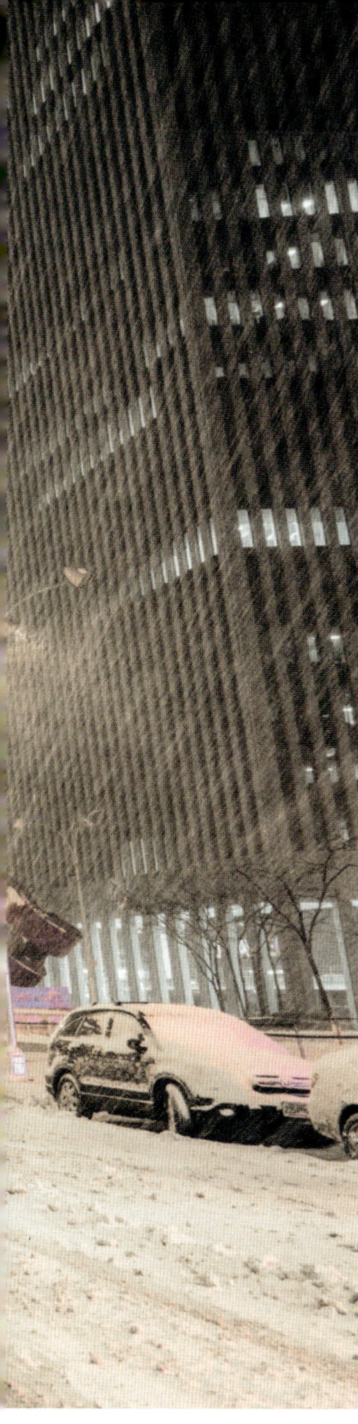

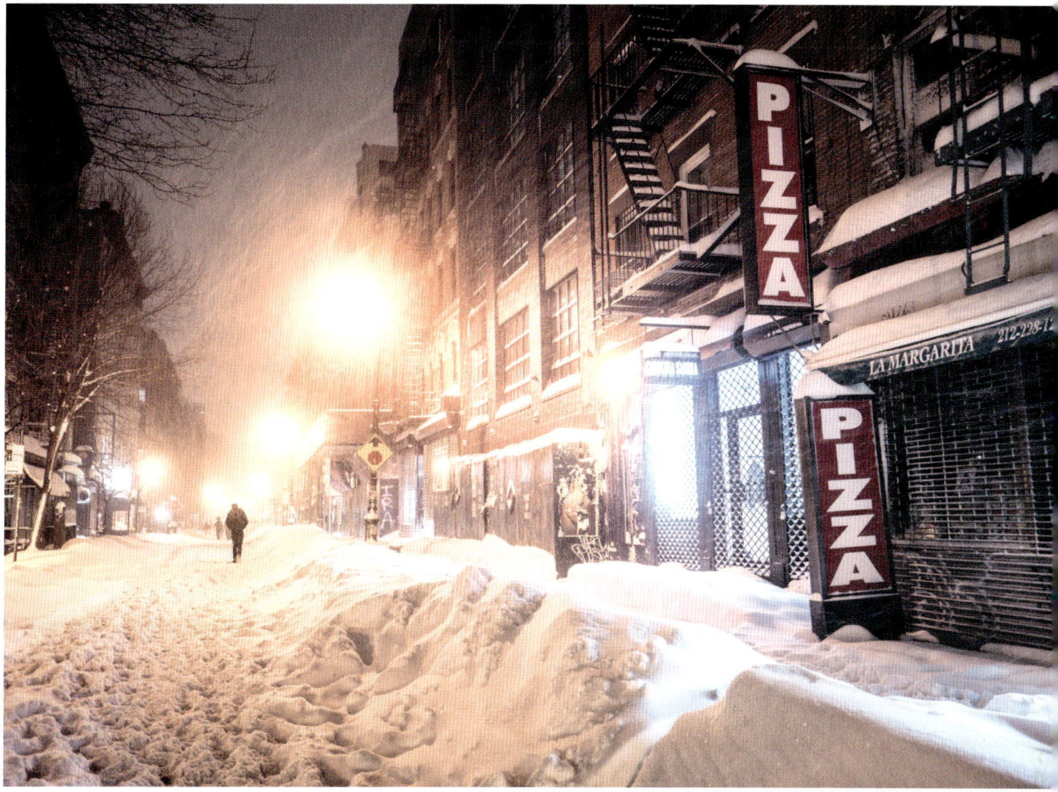

▲ Lower East Side, Manhattan
Sony ILCE-7RM2 | *f*/5 | 1/40 second | ISO 2000

▼ Lower East Side, Manhattan
Sony ILCE-7RM2 | *f*/5 | 1/40 second | ISO 2000

◀ Midtown Manhattan
Sony ILCE-7M2 | *f*/3.2 | 1/60 second | ISO 2000

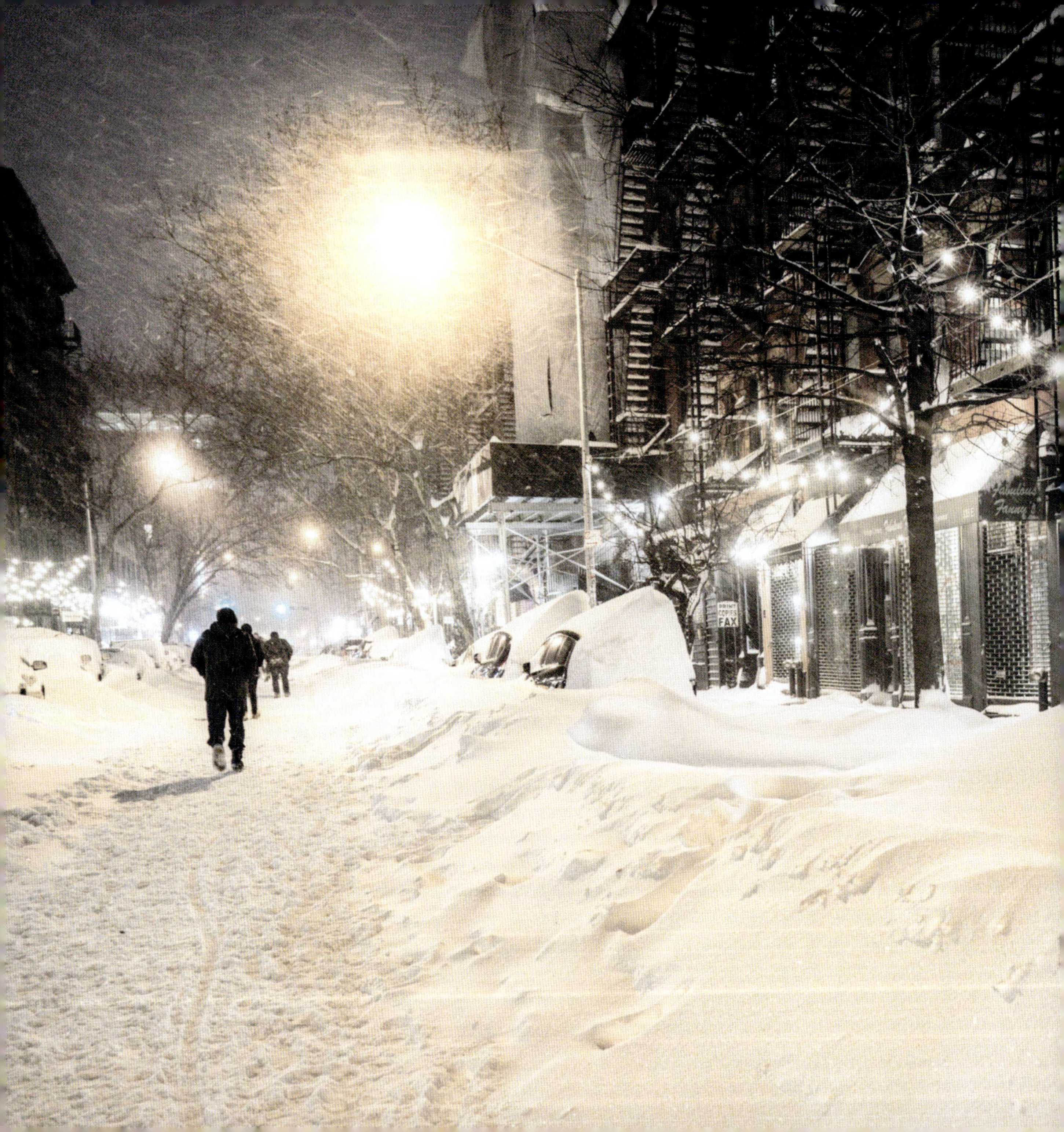
Fabulous Fanny
PRINT
COPIES
FAX

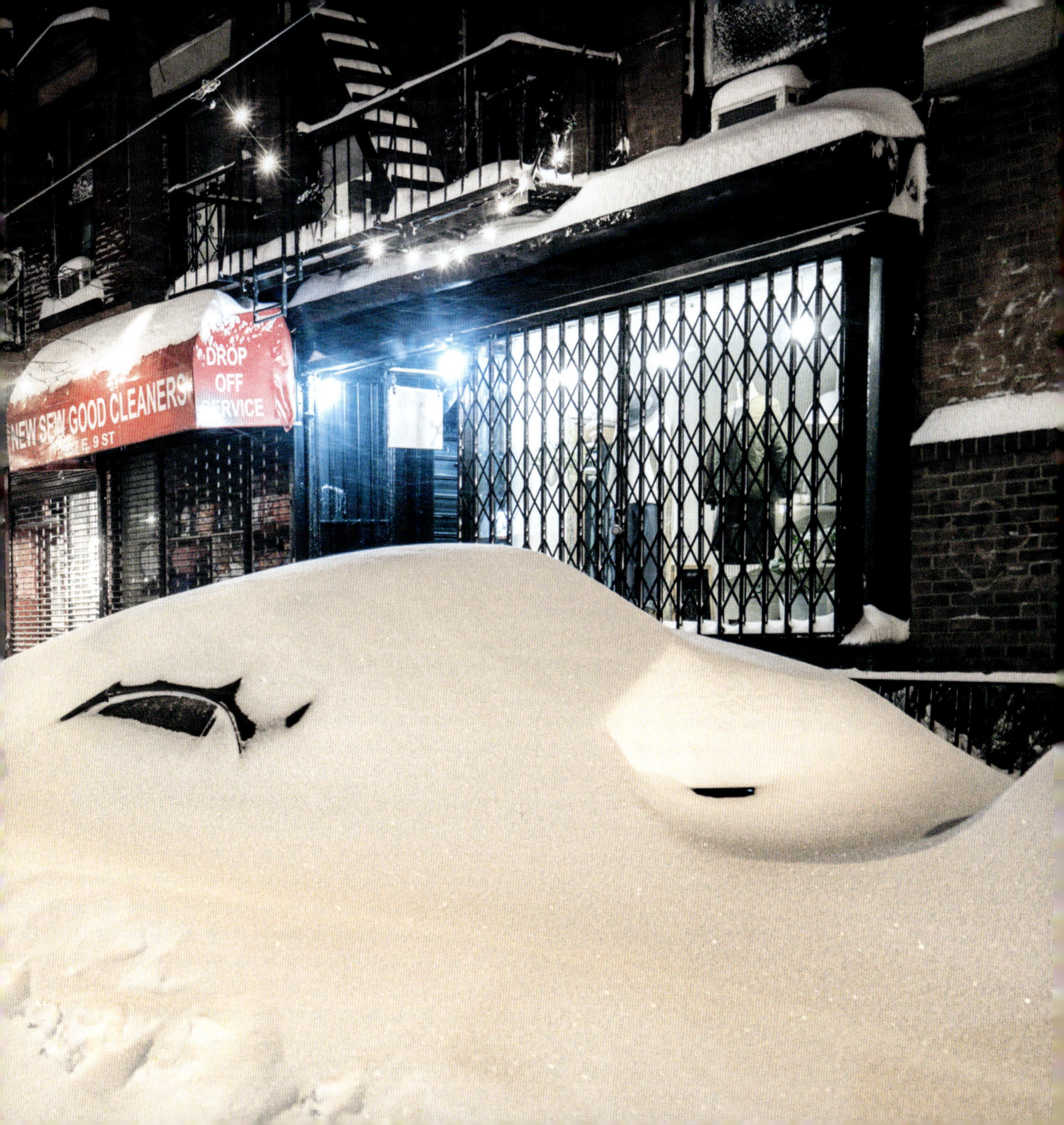
NEW SEW GOOD CLEANERS
DROP
OFF
SERVICE

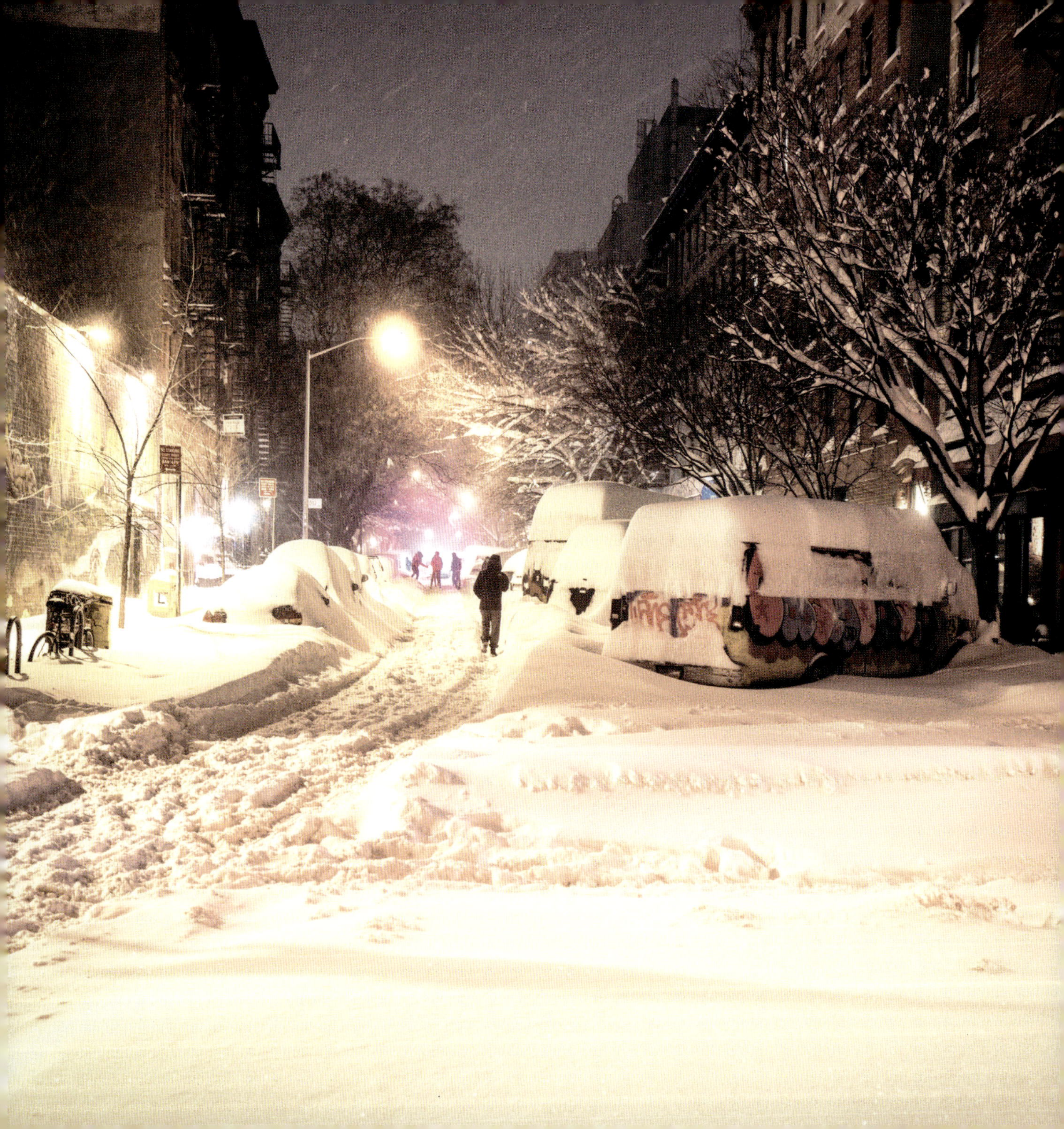

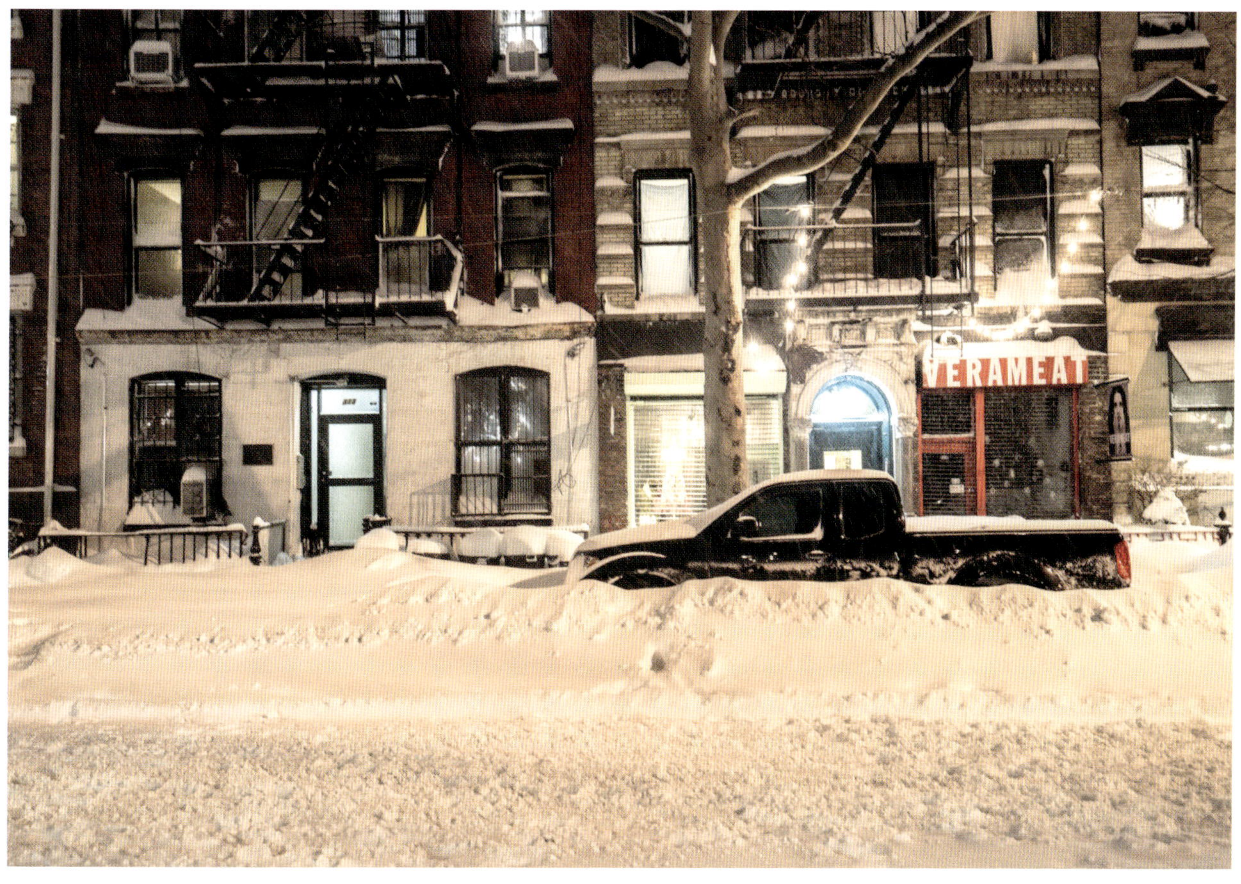

East Village, Lower Manhattan
Sony ILCE-7RM2 | ƒ/5 | 1/40 second | ISO 2000

East Village, Lower Manhattan
Sony ILCE-7RM2 | ƒ/5 | 1/80 second | ISO 2000

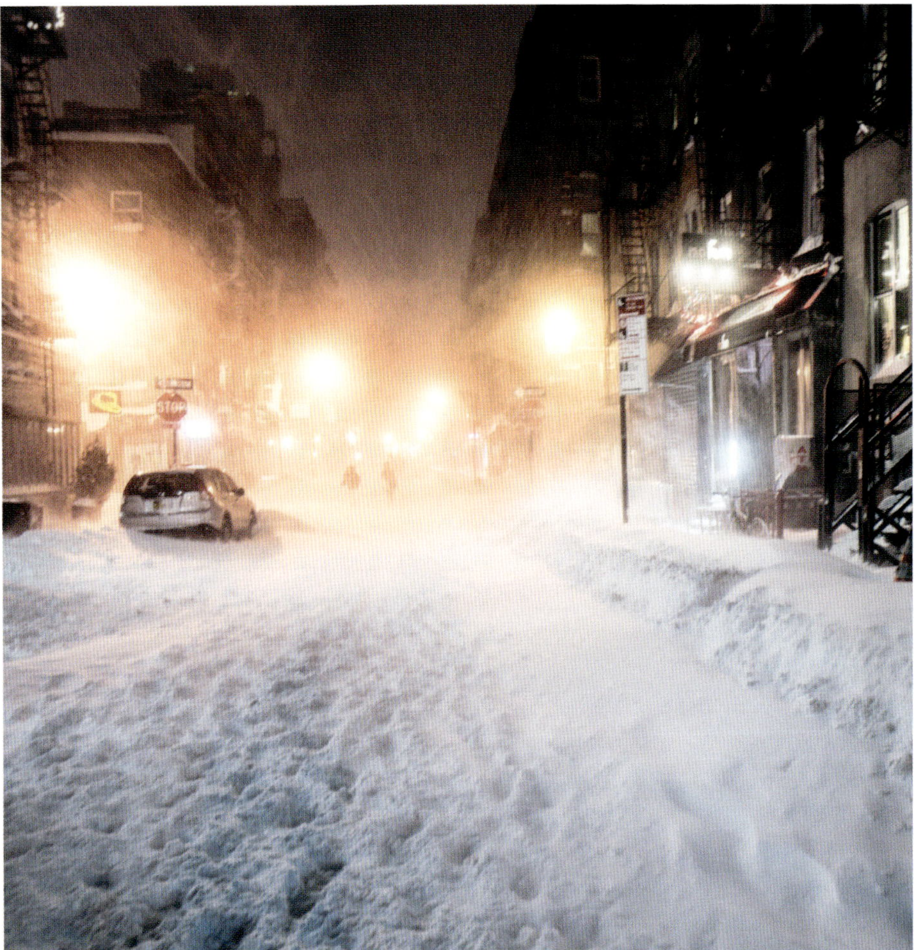

> It was like falling into a cloud. Or at least it is how I imagine a cloud would feel if I had the good fortune of falling into one.

The snow-fog was so dense that it was nearly impossible to see the next block up ahead at points. I fell in the snow for the first time ever during a storm a few minutes later as wind pushed me over and into an enormous snowdrift, which is maybe one of the softest things I have ever fallen into.

East Village, Lower Manhattan
Sony ILCE-7RM2 | *f*/5 | 1/40 second | ISO 2000

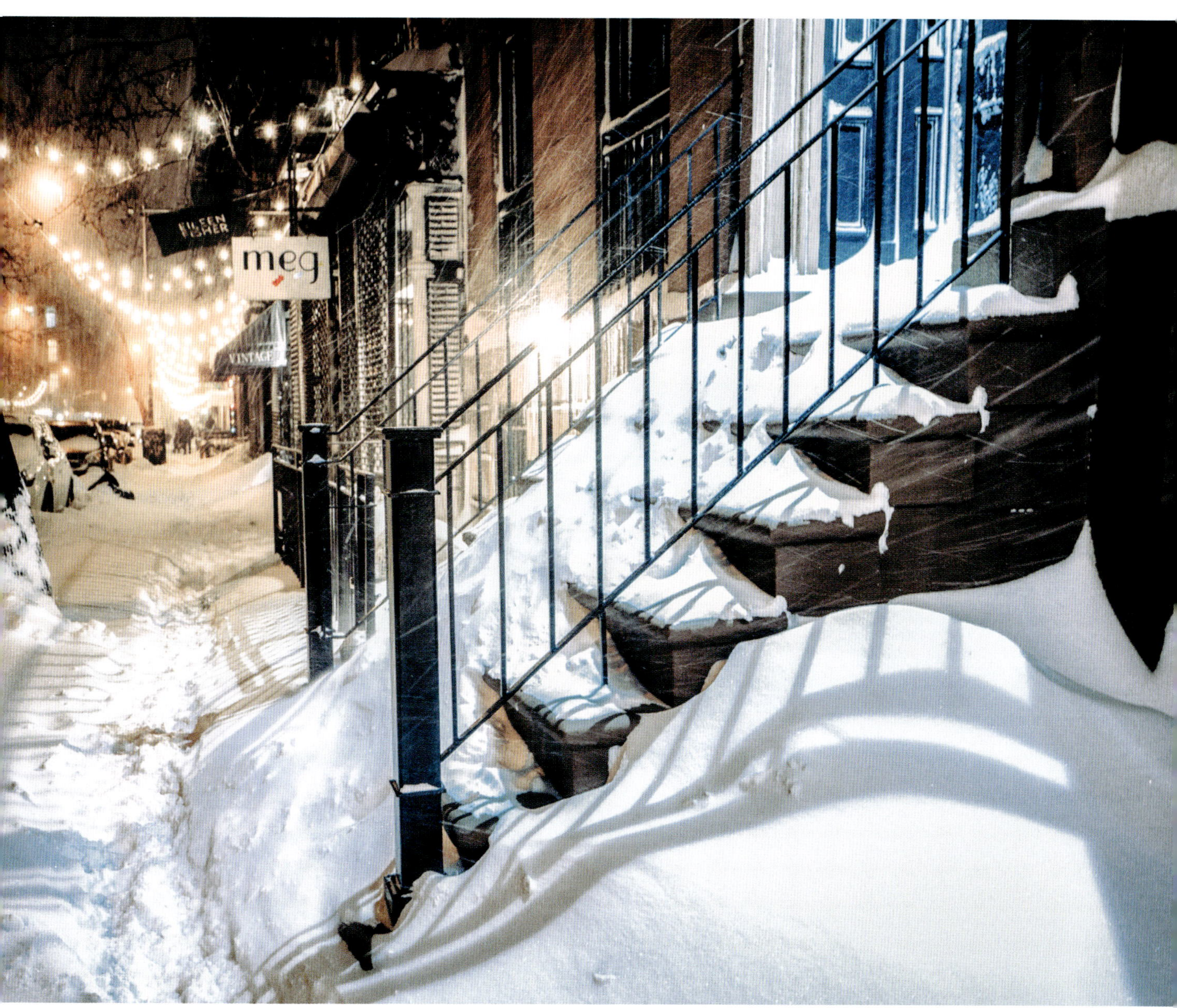

Lower East Side, Manhattan

Sony ILCE-7RM2 | *f*/4 | 1/20 second | ISO 3200

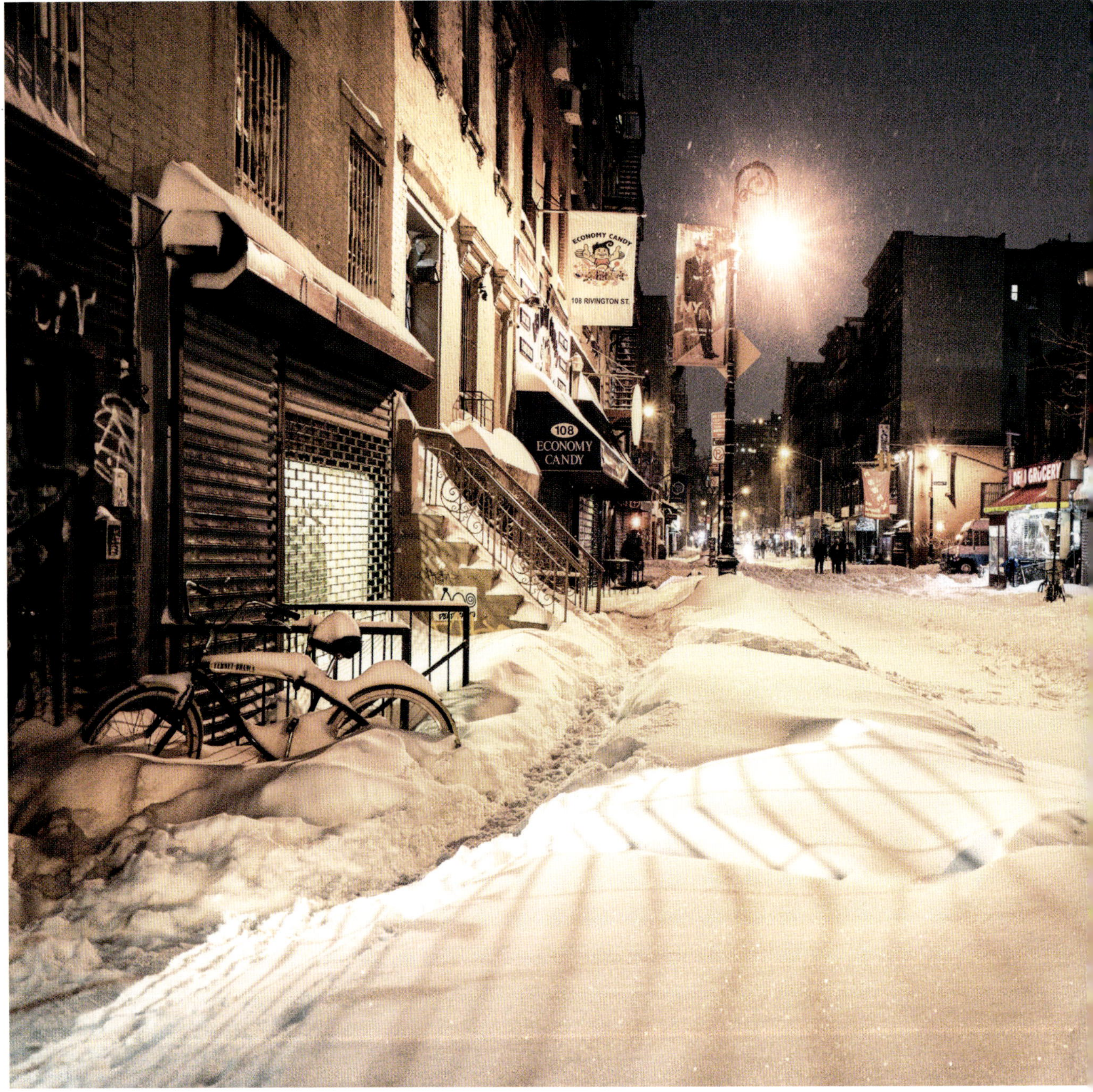
ECONOMY CANDY
108 RIVINGTON ST.
108
ECONOMY
CANDY
DELI GROCERY

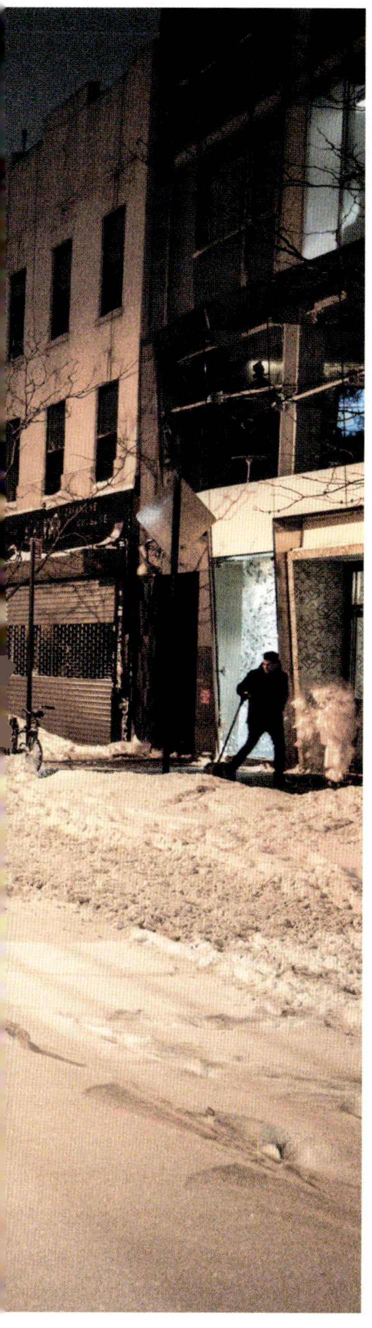

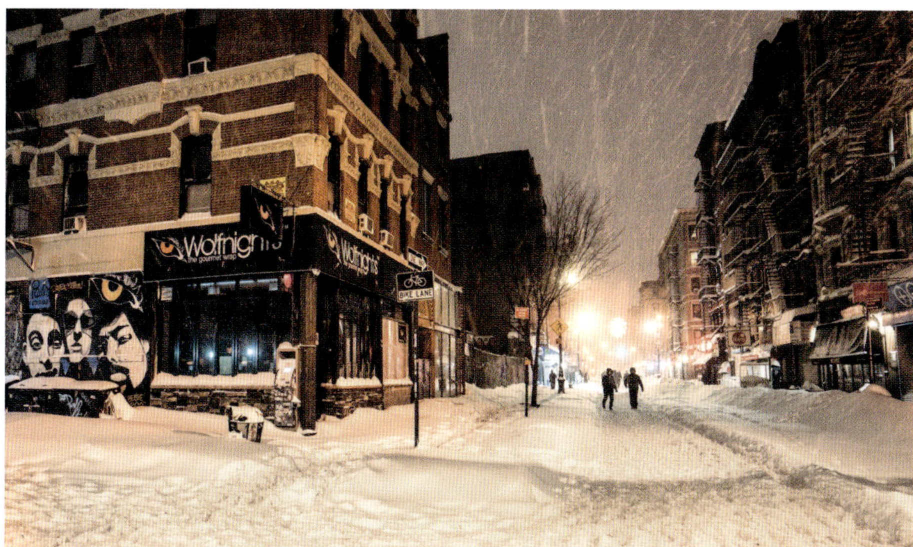

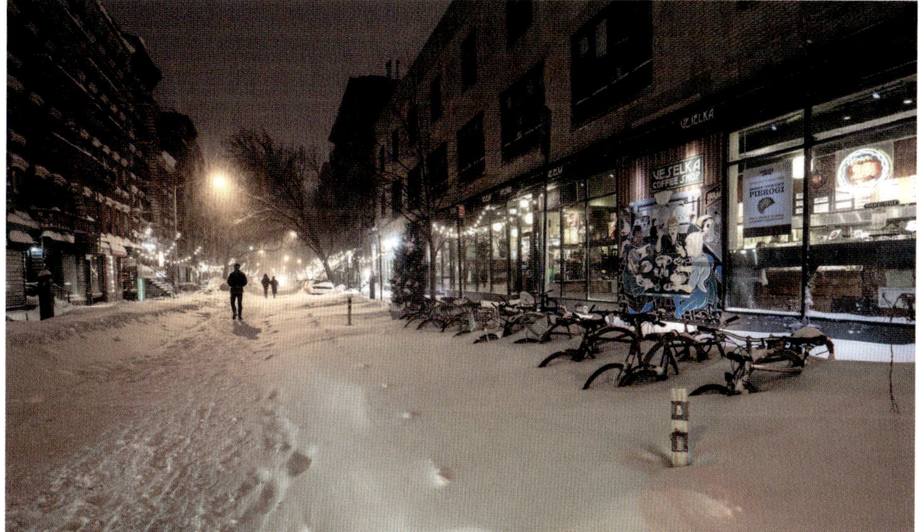

▲ Lower East Side, Manhattan
Sony ILCE-7RM2 | *f*/4 | 1/20 second | ISO 3200

◀ Midtown Manhattan
Sony ILCE-7M2 | *f*/4 | 1/30 second | ISO 4000

▼ Midtown Manhattan
Sony ILCE-7RM2 | *f*/4 | 1/20 second | ISO 3200

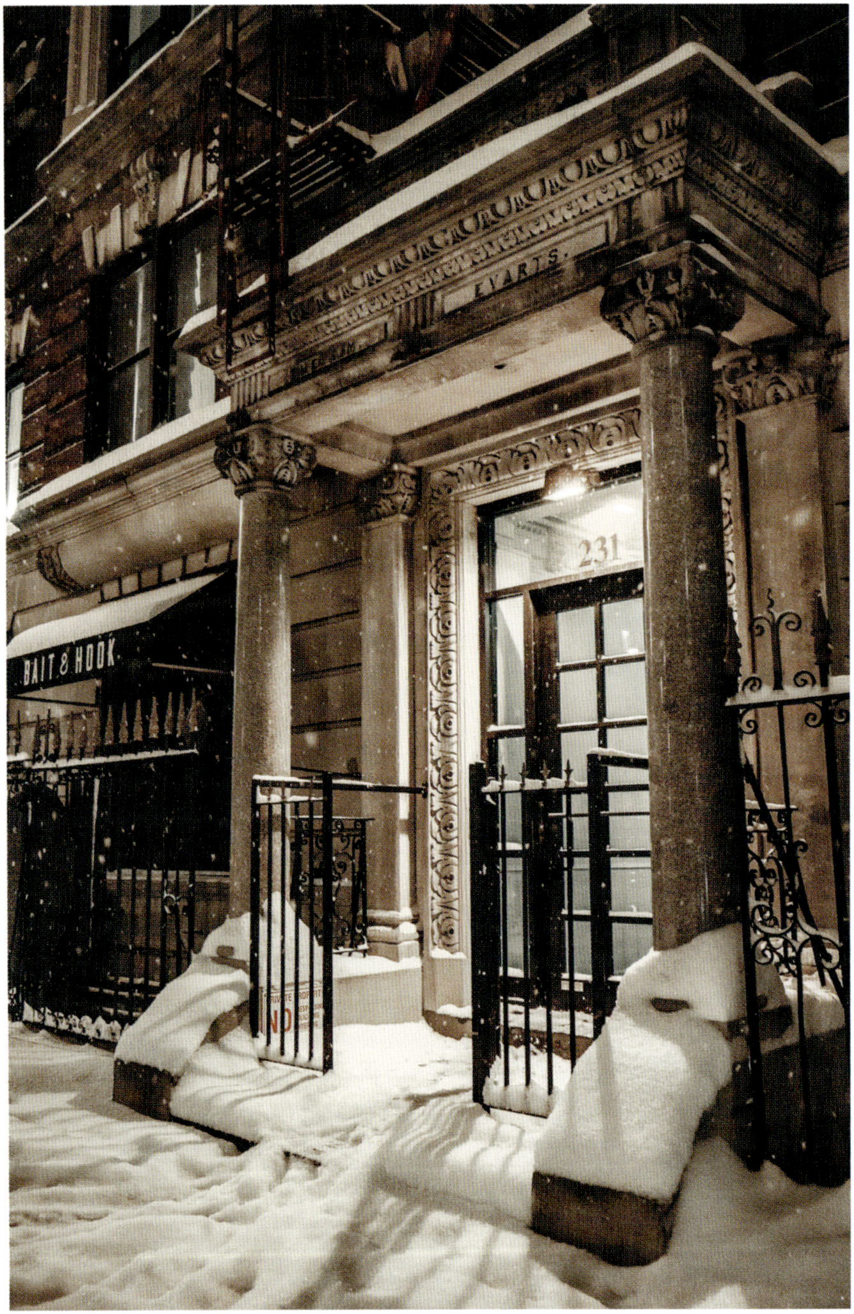

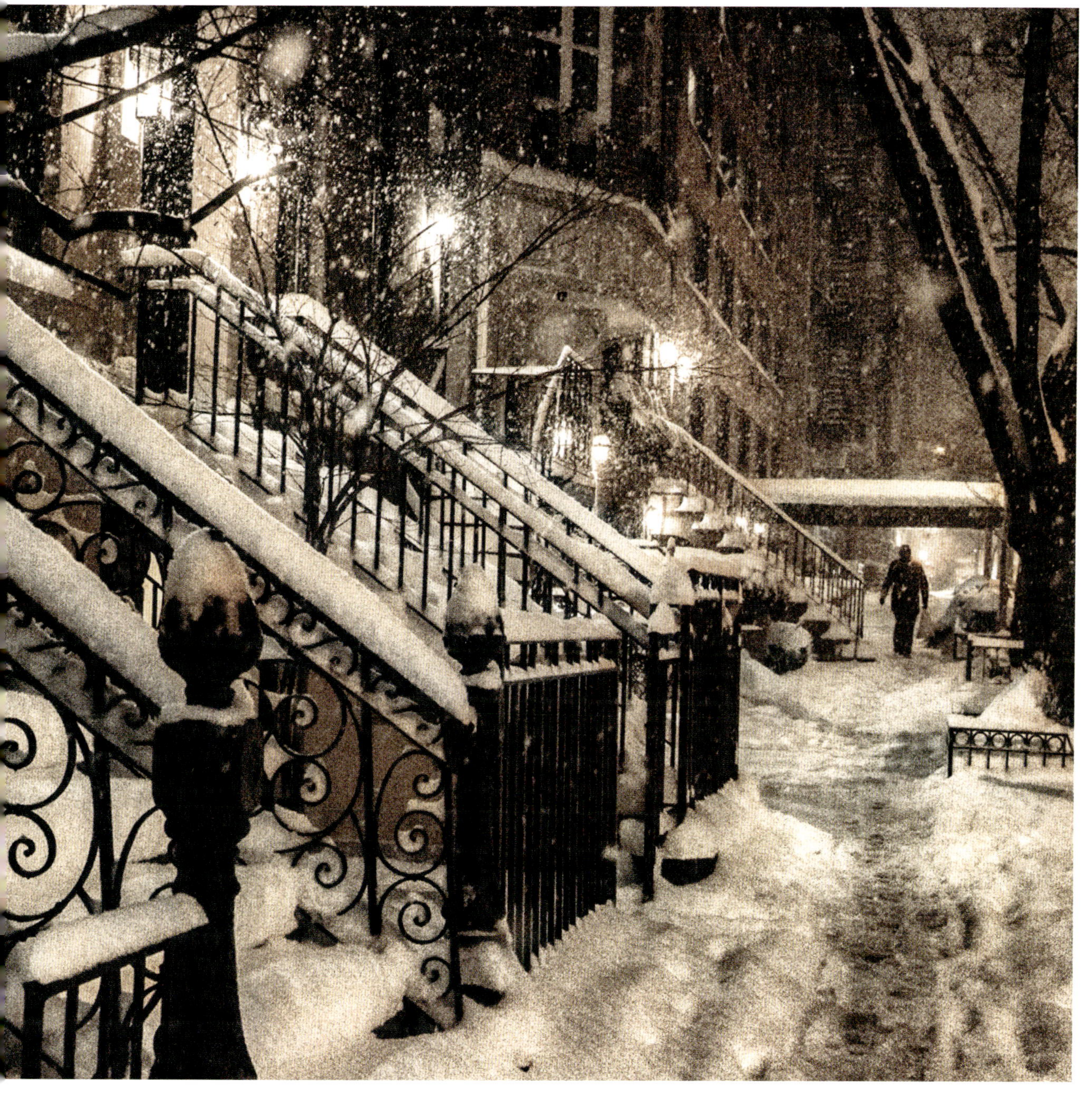

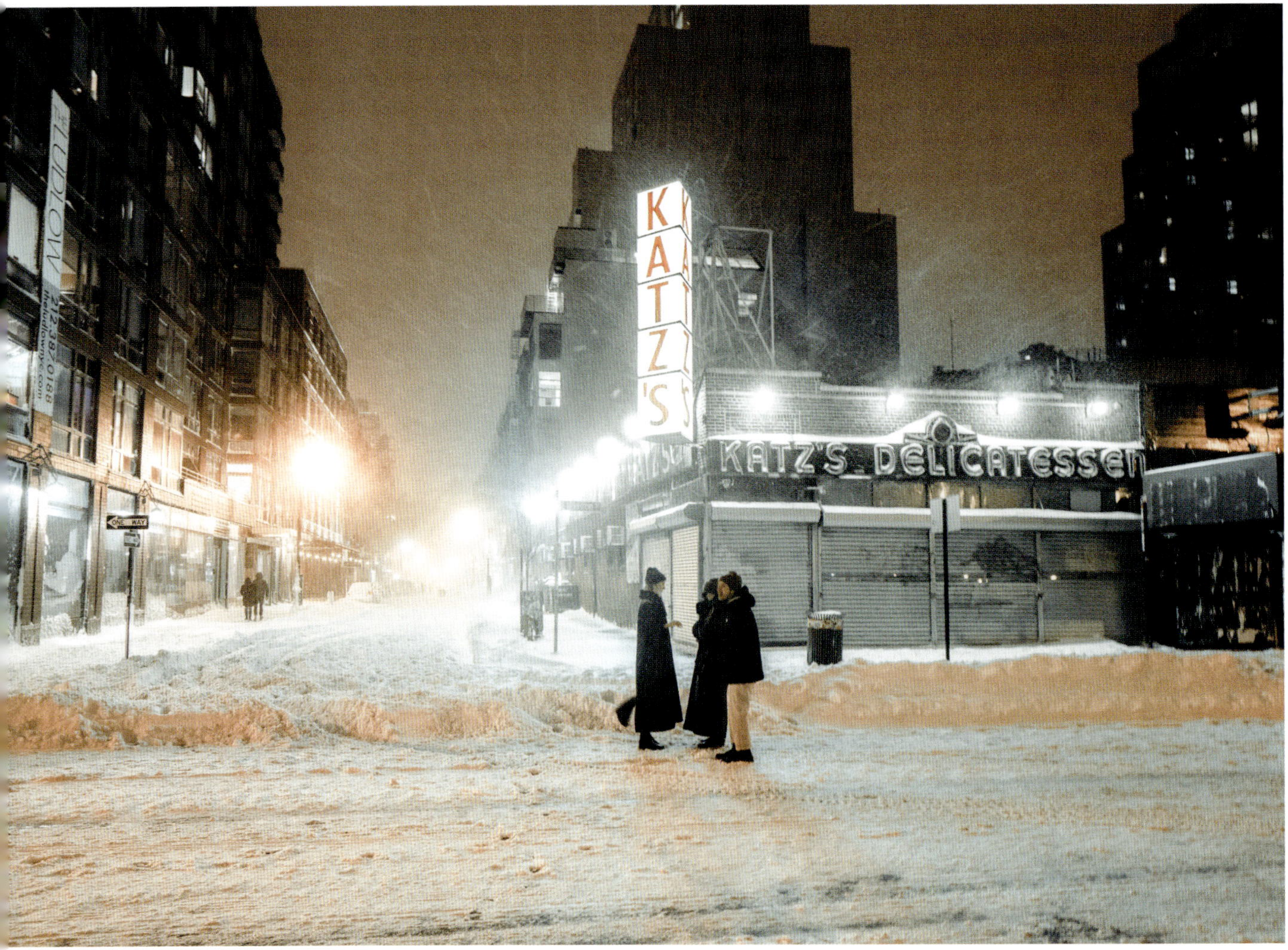

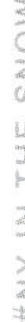

Lower East Side, Manhattan
Sony ILCE-7RM2 | ƒ/4 | 1/20 second | ISO 3200

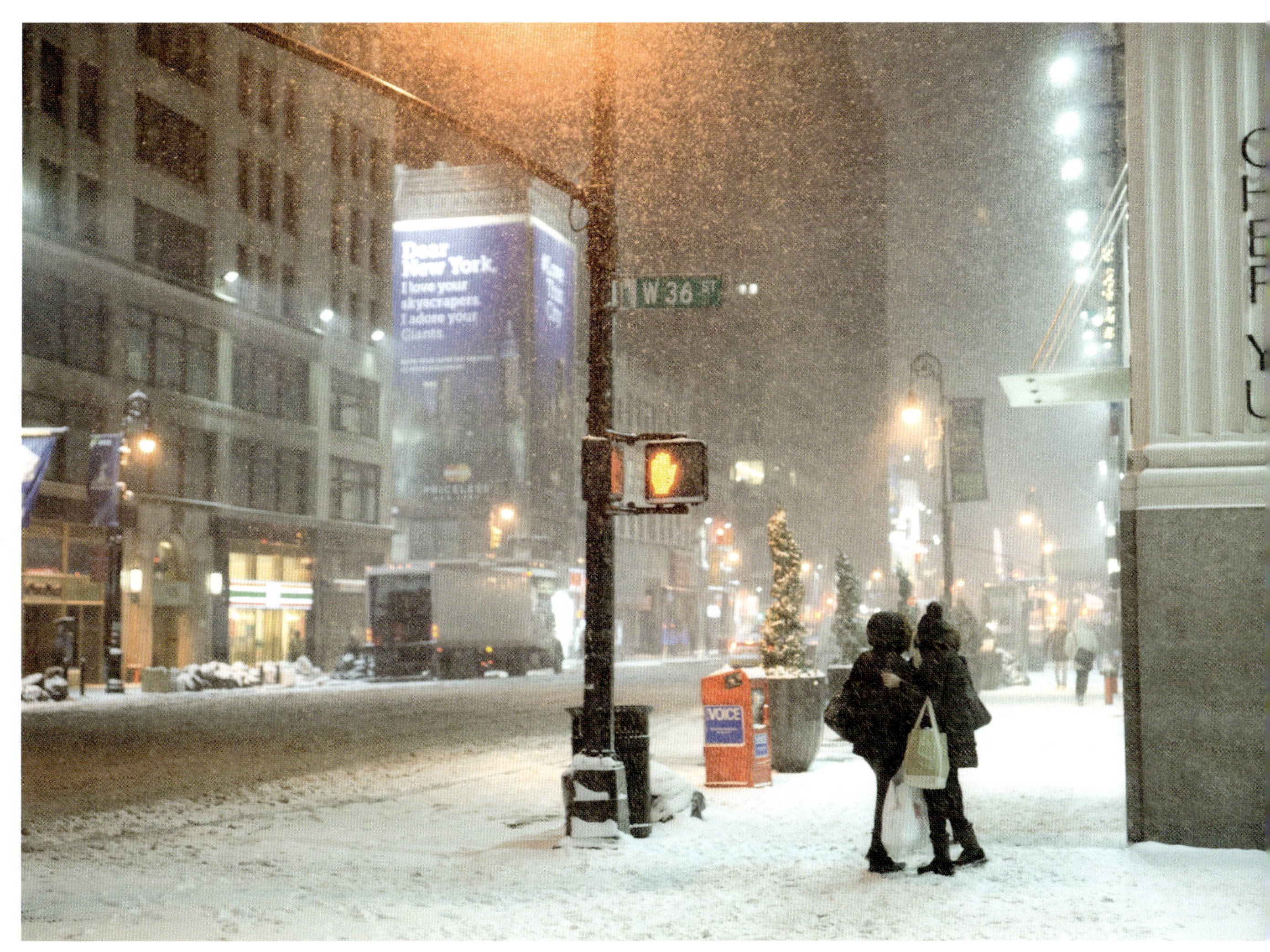

Times Square, Midtown Manhattan
Sony ILCE-7M2 | ƒ/4 | 1/30 second | ISO 4000

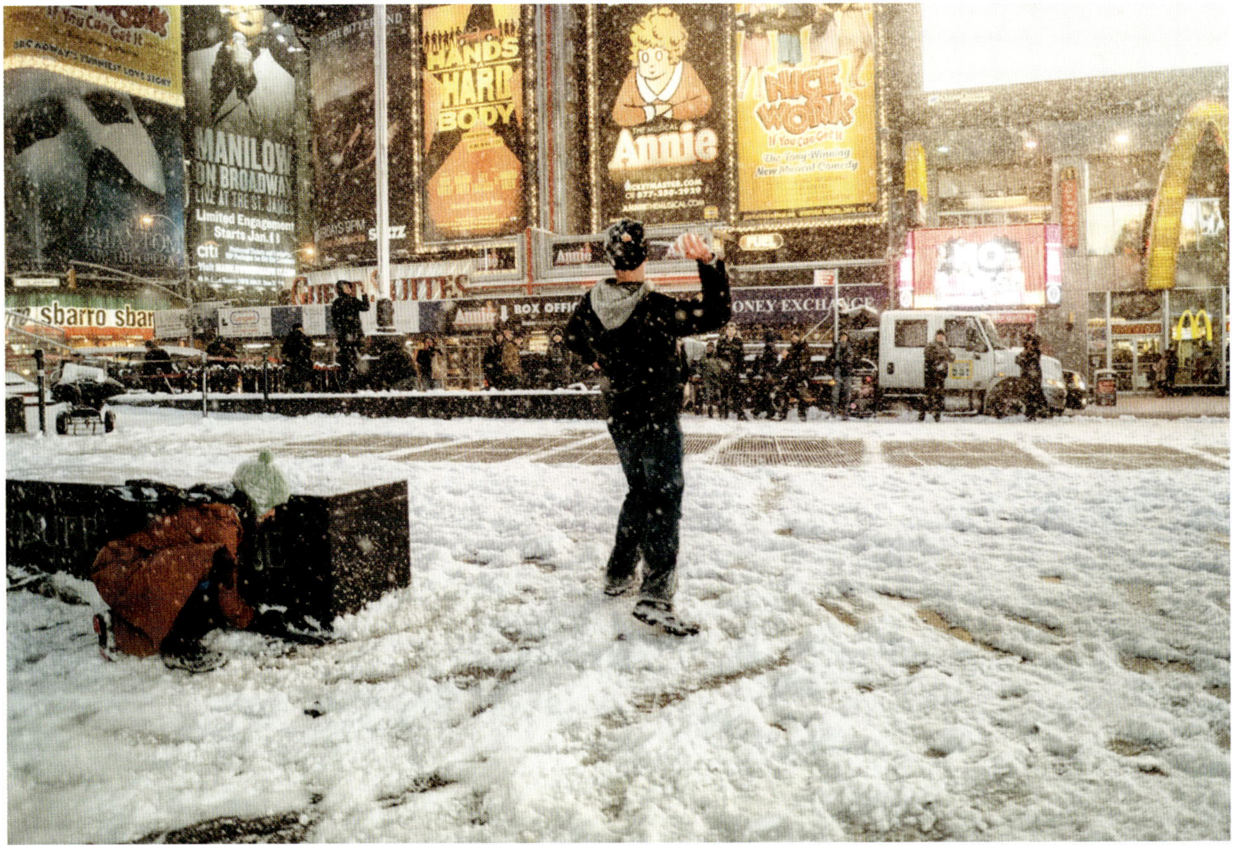

There was a brief period of time when people would get together on Reddit to organize snowball fights in Times Square. And so I would make Times Square my goal destination during my walks around Manhattan in various stages of snowstorms.

This series was taken during one of my favorite Times Square snowball fights. A large group of adults had gathered and it was heartwarming to watch people forget the troubles of the day and revert back to childhood as snow fell on one of the most iconic locations in the world.

The backdrop here is one of my favorites due to the Broadway shows that were popular at the time, and lends an almost surreal feel to this series.

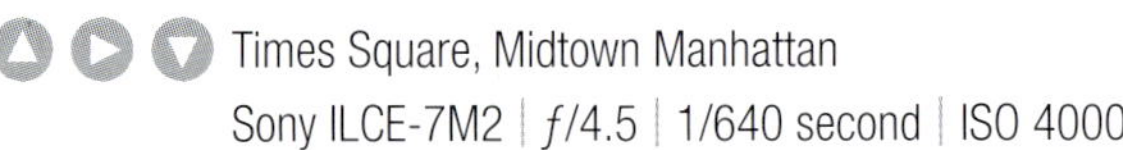

Times Square, Midtown Manhattan
Sony ILCE-7M2 | ƒ/4.5 | 1/640 second | ISO 4000

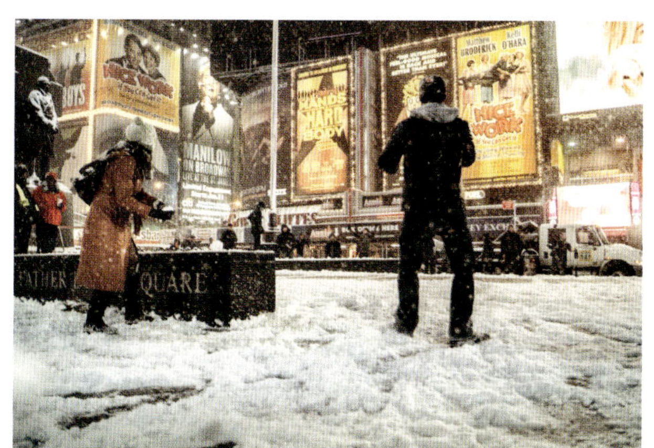

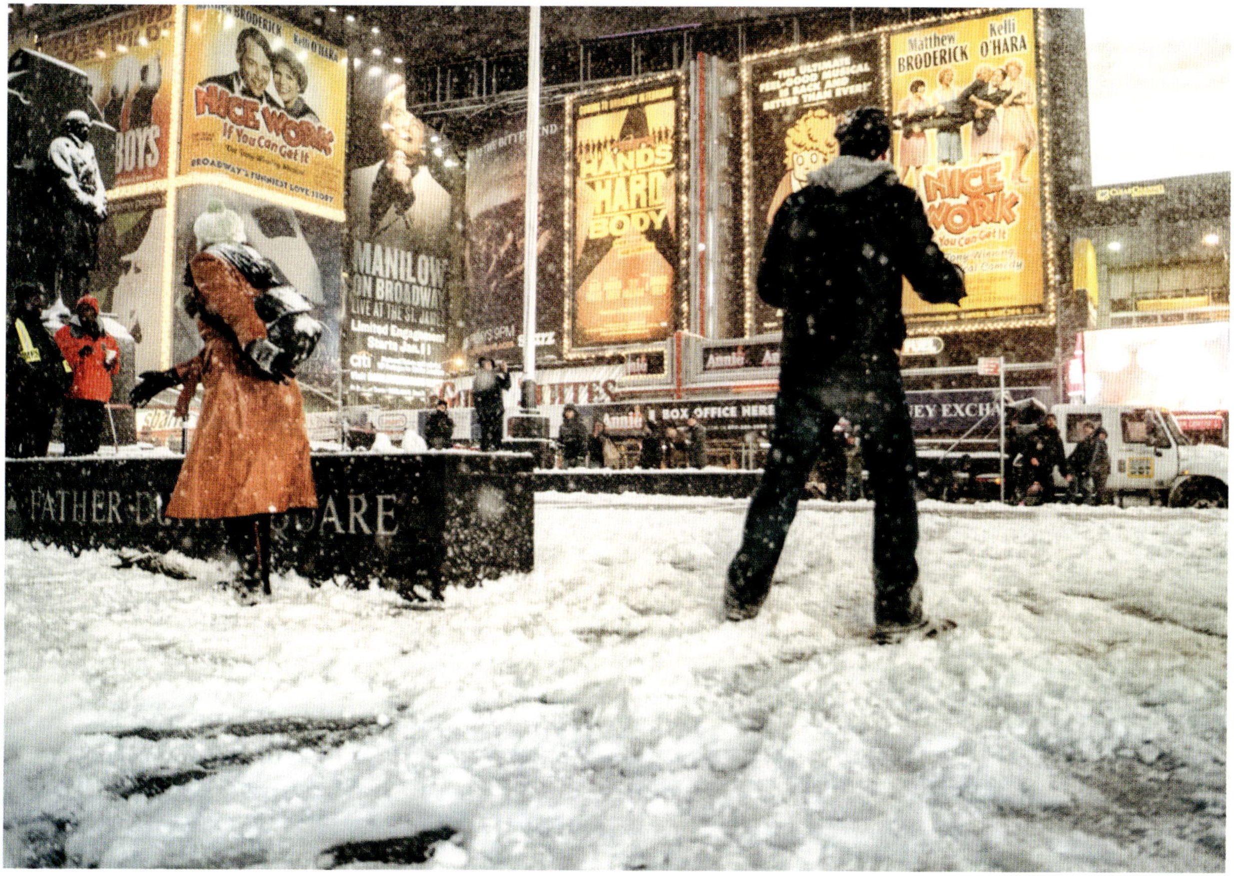

Matthew BRODERICK
Kelli O'HARA
NICE WORK
MANILOW ON BROADWAY

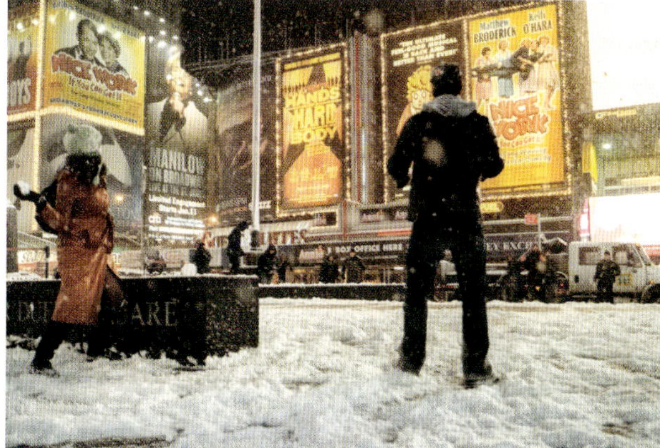

Matthew BRODERICK
Kelli O'HARA
NICE WORK
MANILOW

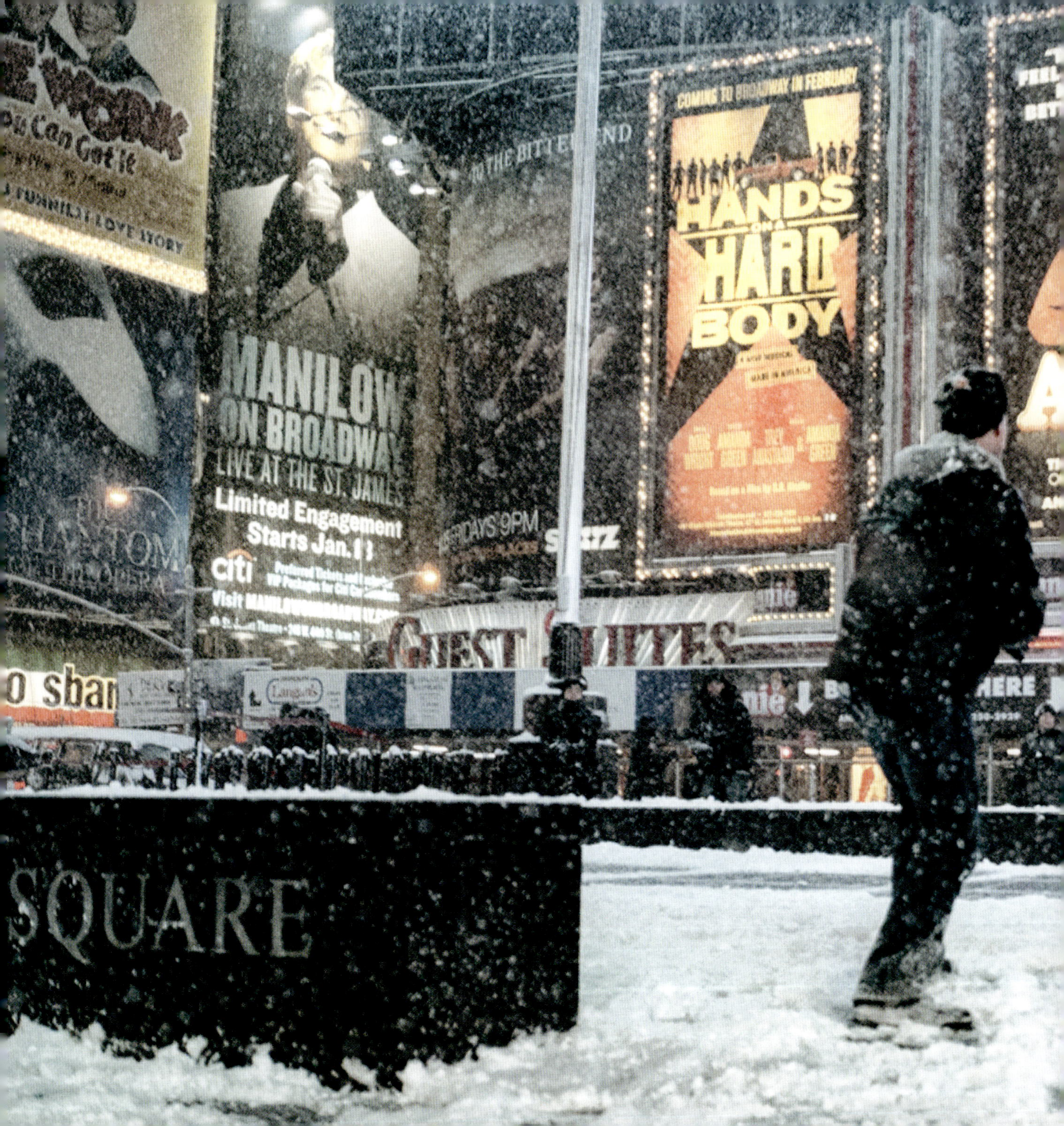
MANILOW
ON BROADWAY
LIVE AT THE ST. JAMES
Limited Engagement
COMING TO BROADWAY IN FEBRUARY
HANDS ON A HARD BODY
SQUARE

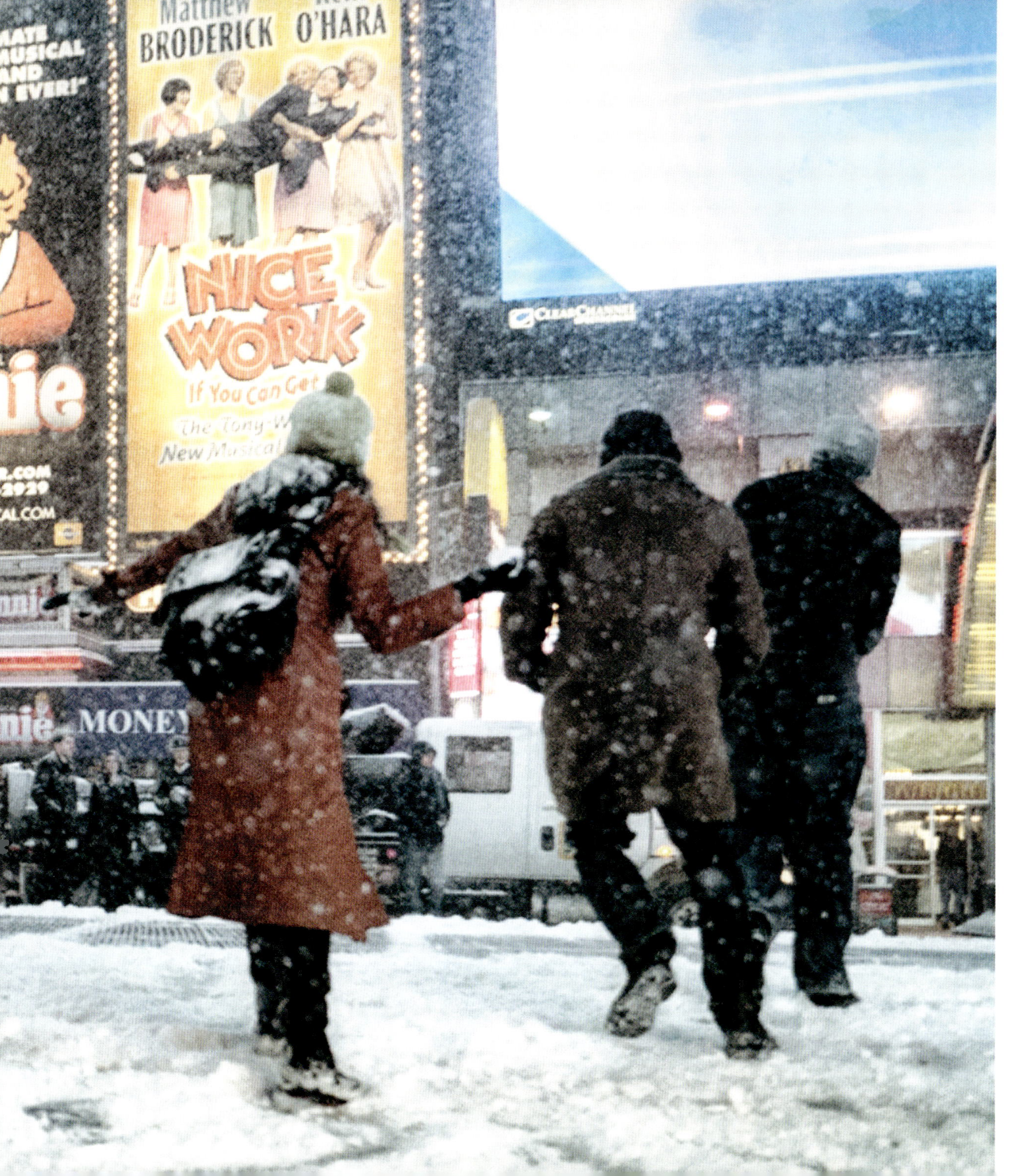
Matthew
BRODERICK
O'HARA
NICE WORK
If You Can Get

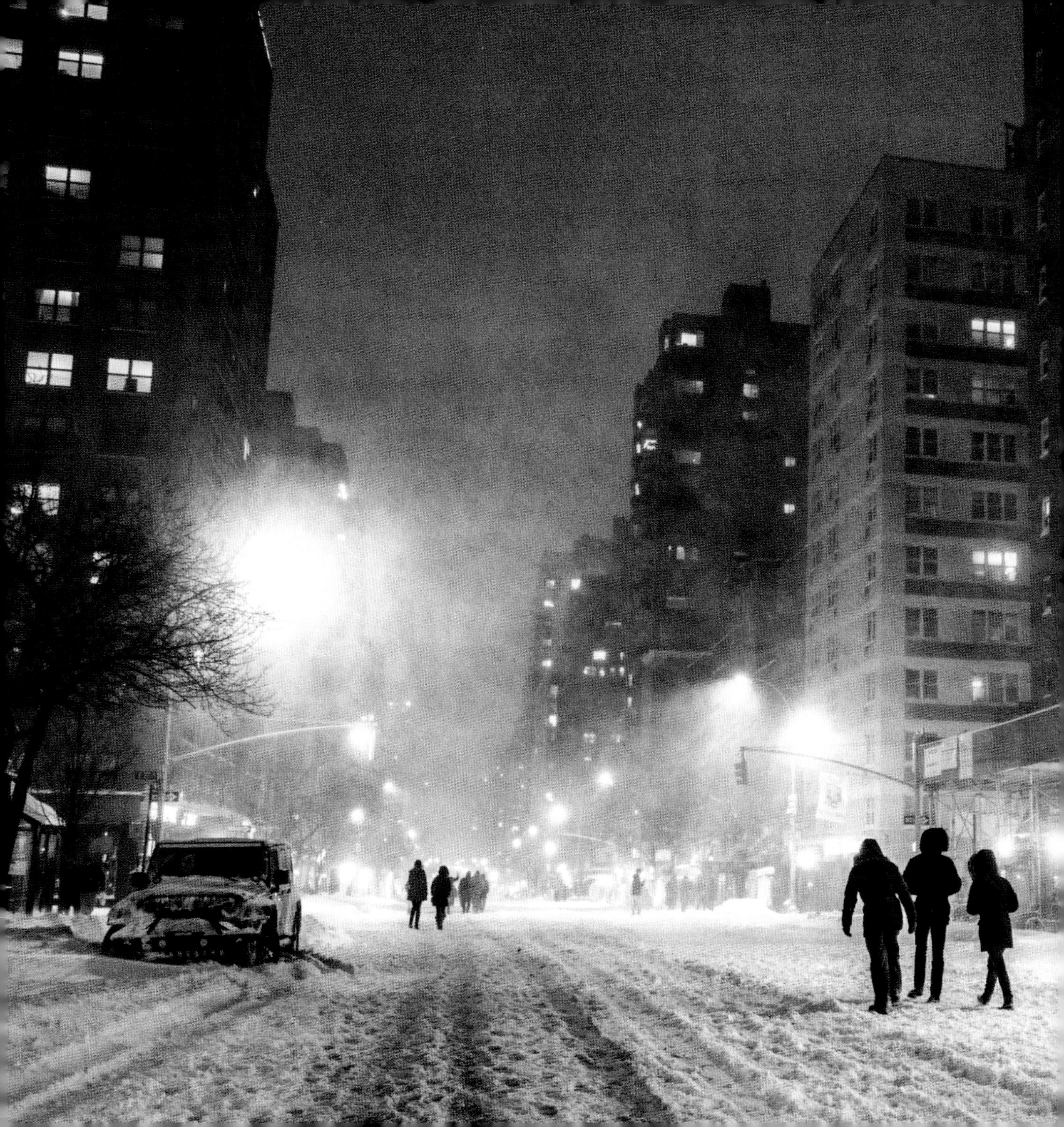

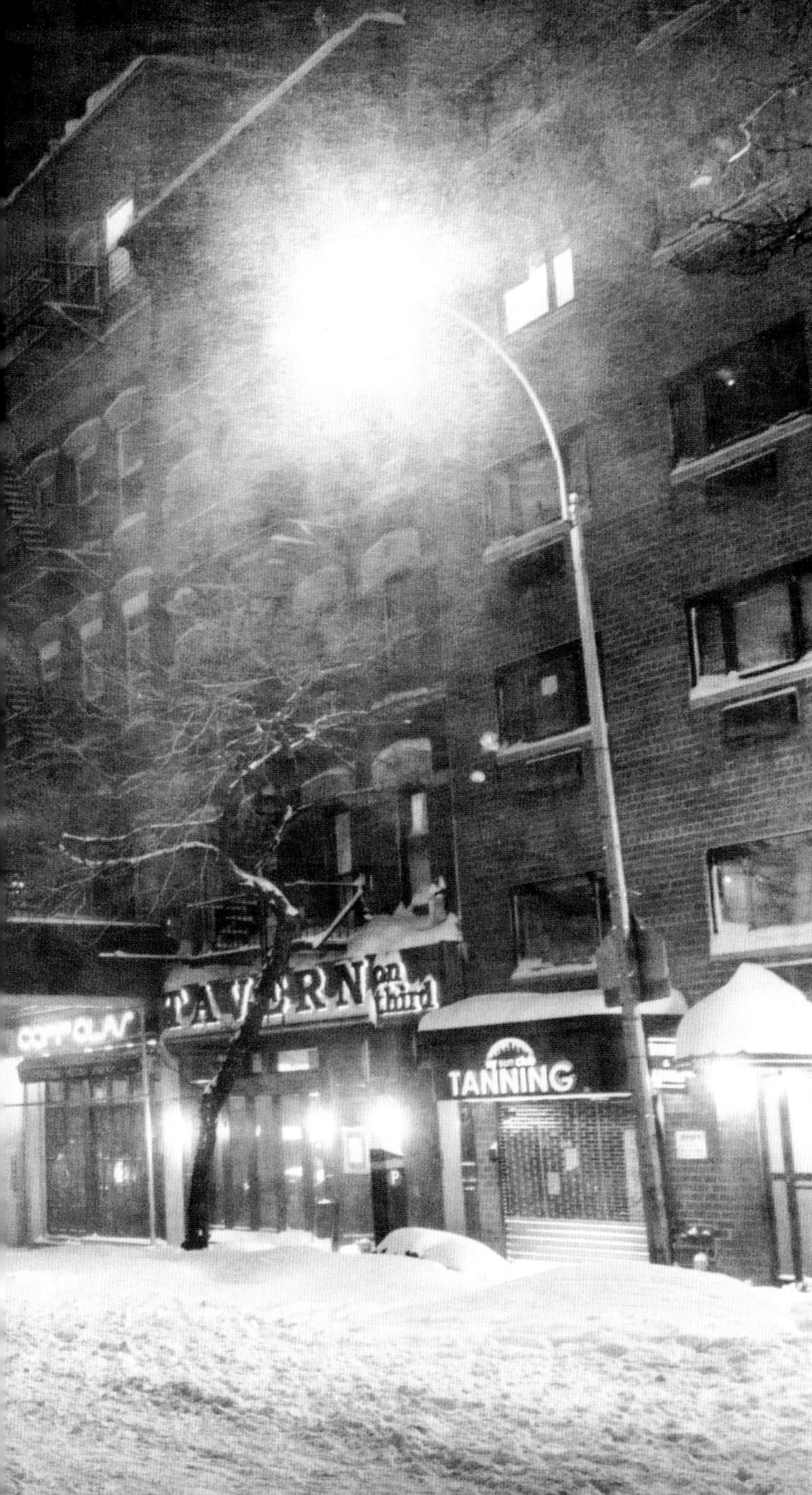

This was taken at the end of a blizzard while wind whipped through the streets in Midtown Manhattan. The wind was so strong that its rushing whistle could be heard before it descended down to where I was standing.

During this moment, everyone had heard the whistle and turned their backs to the wind because the icy gusts were so incredibly painful (thankfully I had face protection on!).

A rare choreographed moment in New York City.

Midtown Manhattan
Sony ILCE-7RM2 | *ƒ*/4 | 1/20 second | ISO 3200

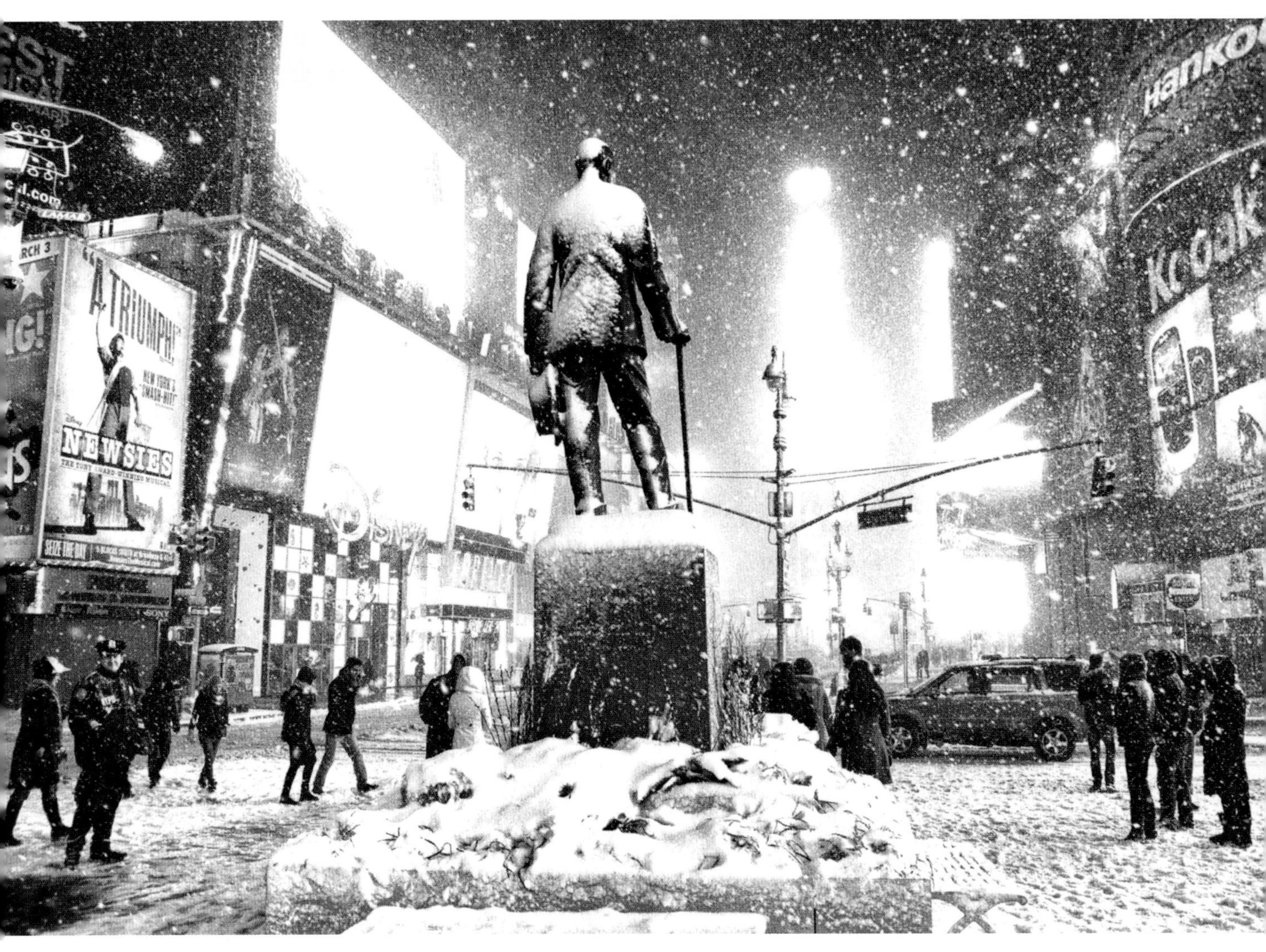

Times Square, Midtown Manhattan
Sony SLT-A99V | $f/3.2$ | 1/100 second | ISO 4000

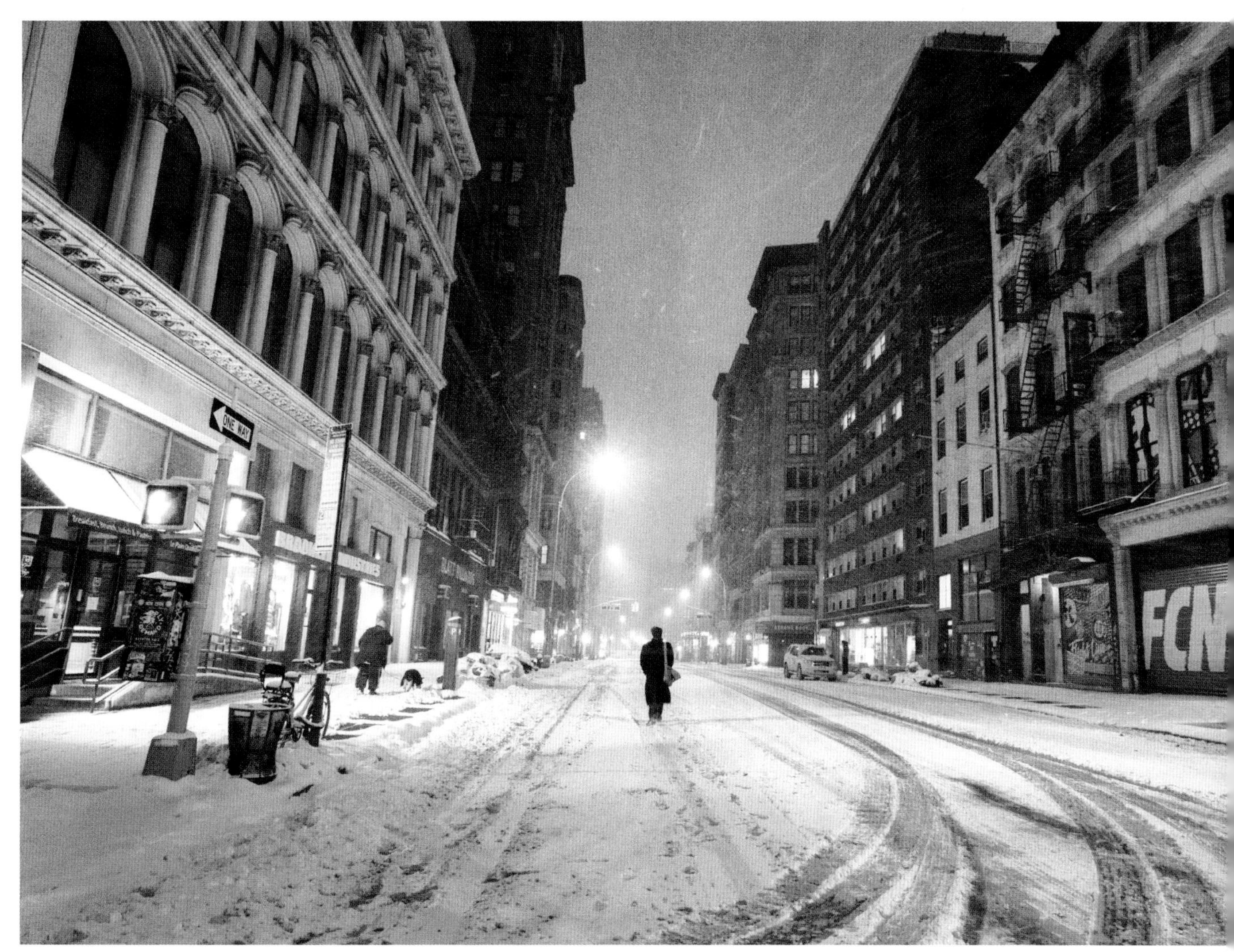

Greenwich Village, Midtown Manhattan
Sony ILCE-7M2 | $f/5$ | 1/20 second | ISO 4000

Snow is a blanket of stars
that stretches across
the urban universe:
a patchwork of dreams
that casts its
glistening dust
from the skies
to enchant
dreamers who
venture
into the city streets
in search of
the glittery manifestations
of inspired utterances
that once escaped
on the ends
of impassioned tongues
into the night air.

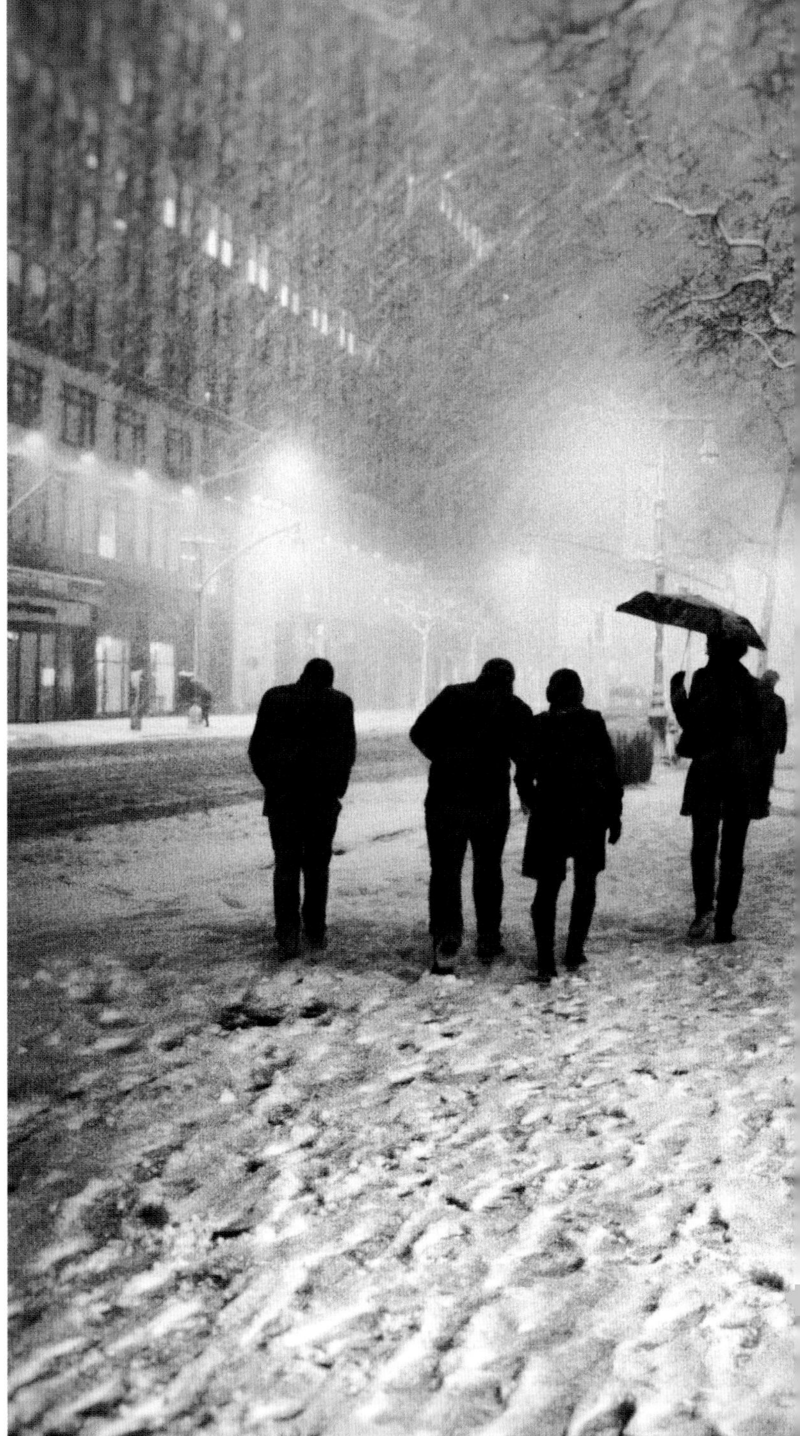

Bryant Park, Midtown Manhattan
Sony SLT-A99V | *f*/3.2 | 1/125 second | ISO 4000

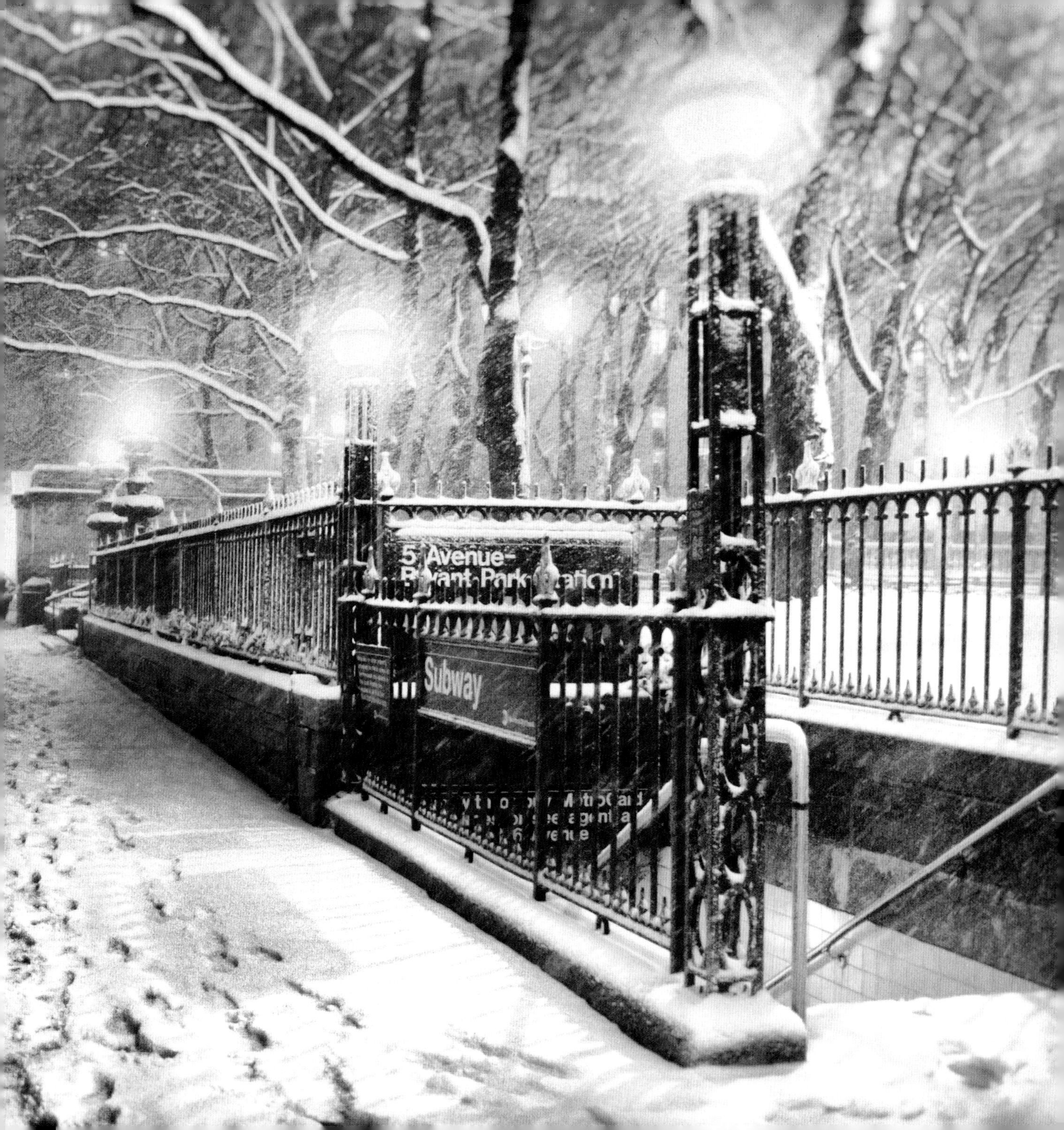

5 Avenue–
Subway
MetroCard

CHAPTER #4 | MEMORY

"We walk through snow as if we are walking through clouds: immortal cloud-walkers drifting into memory-strewn webs spun with the sparkling condensation of nostalgia."

Flatiron District, Manhattan
Sony SLT-A99V | ƒ/3.2 | 1/100 second | ISO 2500

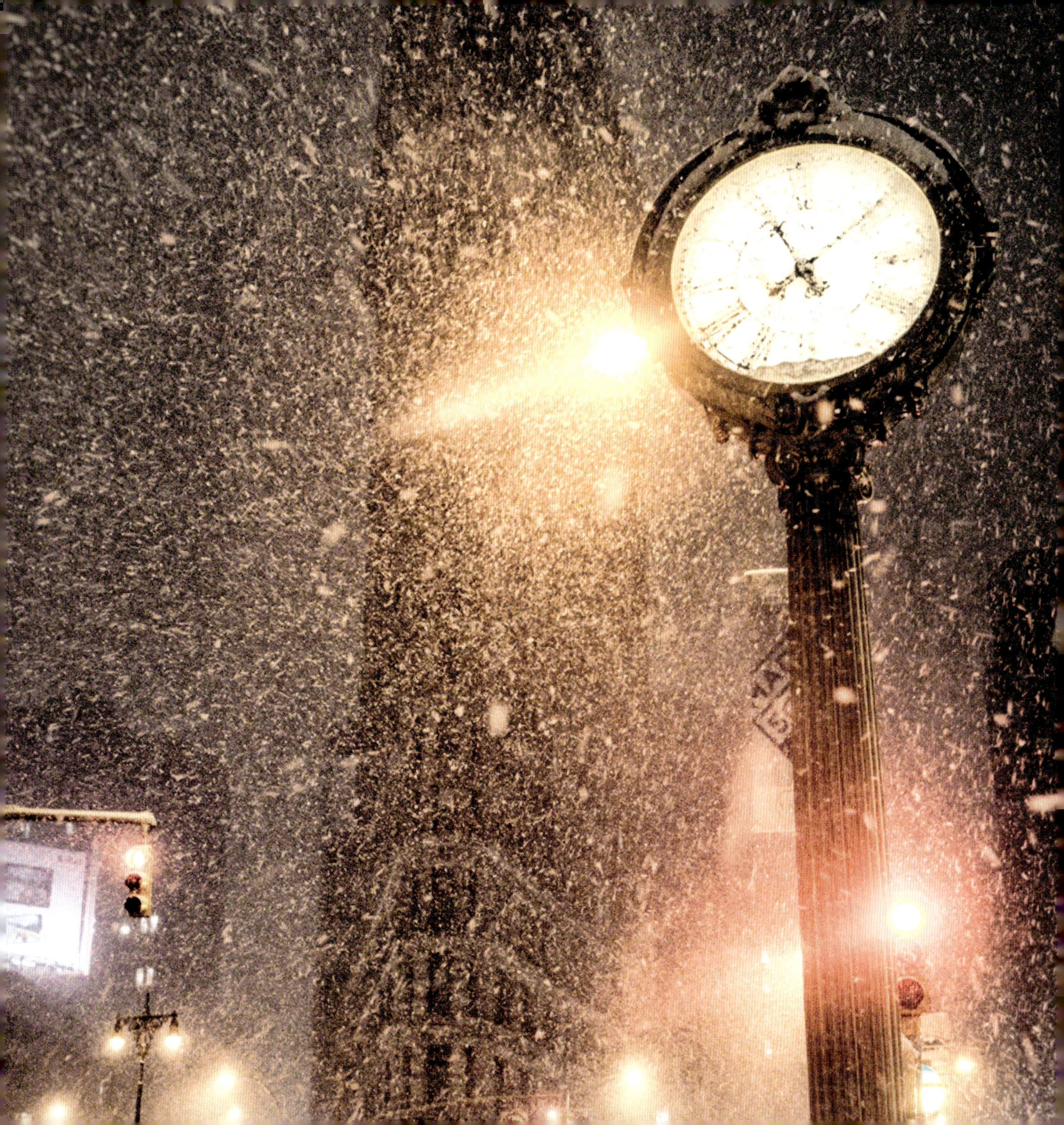

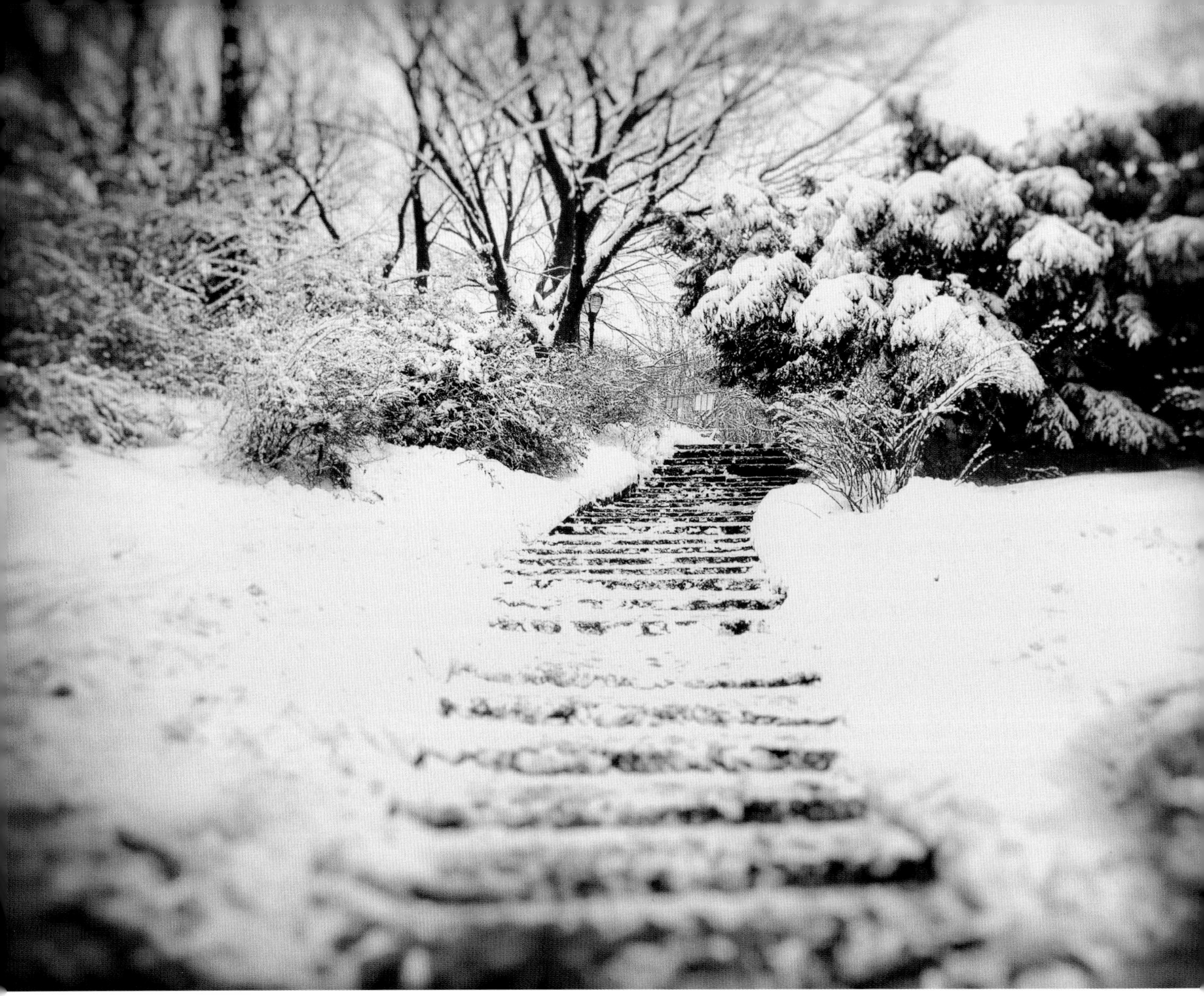

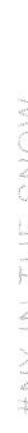

It's on days like this, when the sun rests longer
than usual and winter's essence seeps through
every crack and crevice, that the earth quivers
a ghost shiver that rests in summer's memory.

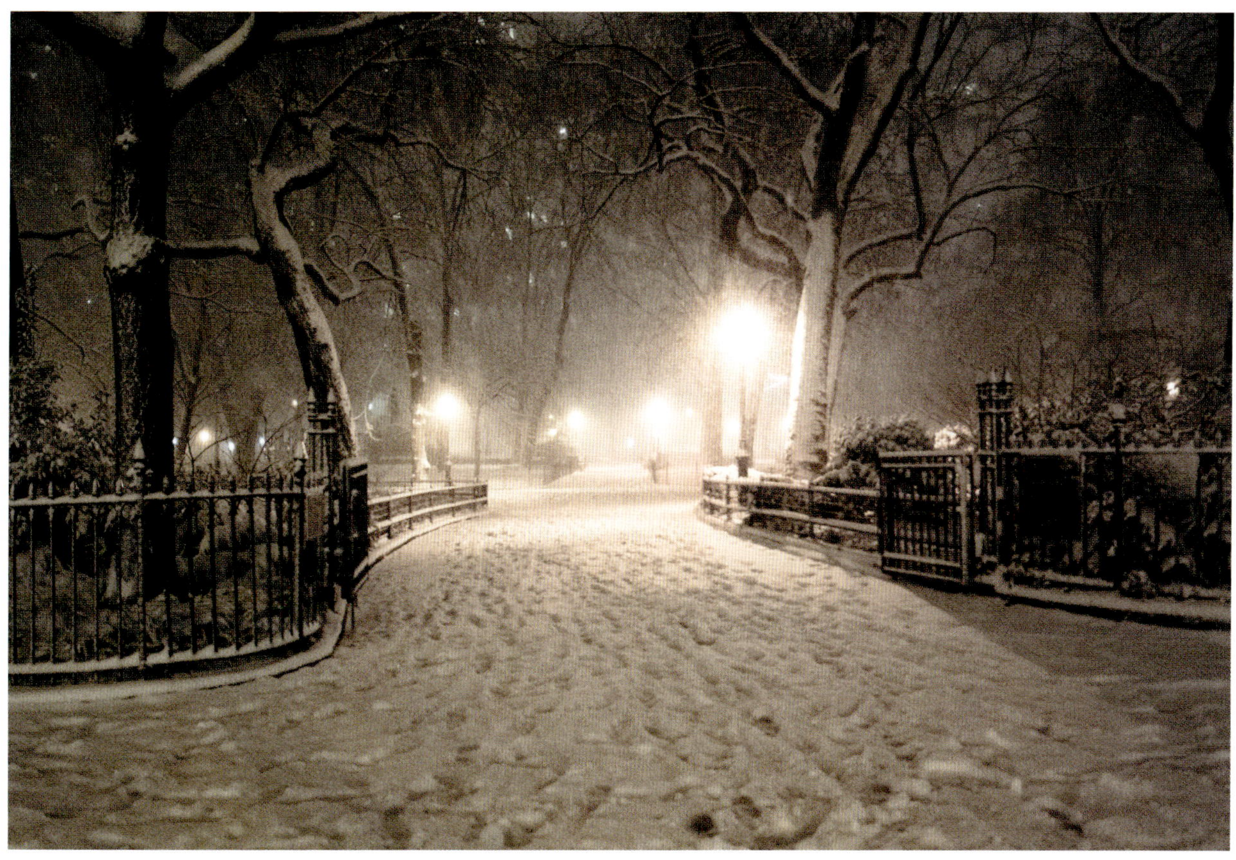

Central Park, Manhattan
Sony SLT-A99V | *f*/4.5 | 1/80 second | ISO 400

Madison Square Park, Midtown Manhattan
Sony SLT-A99V | *f*/2.8 | 1/30 second | ISO 4000

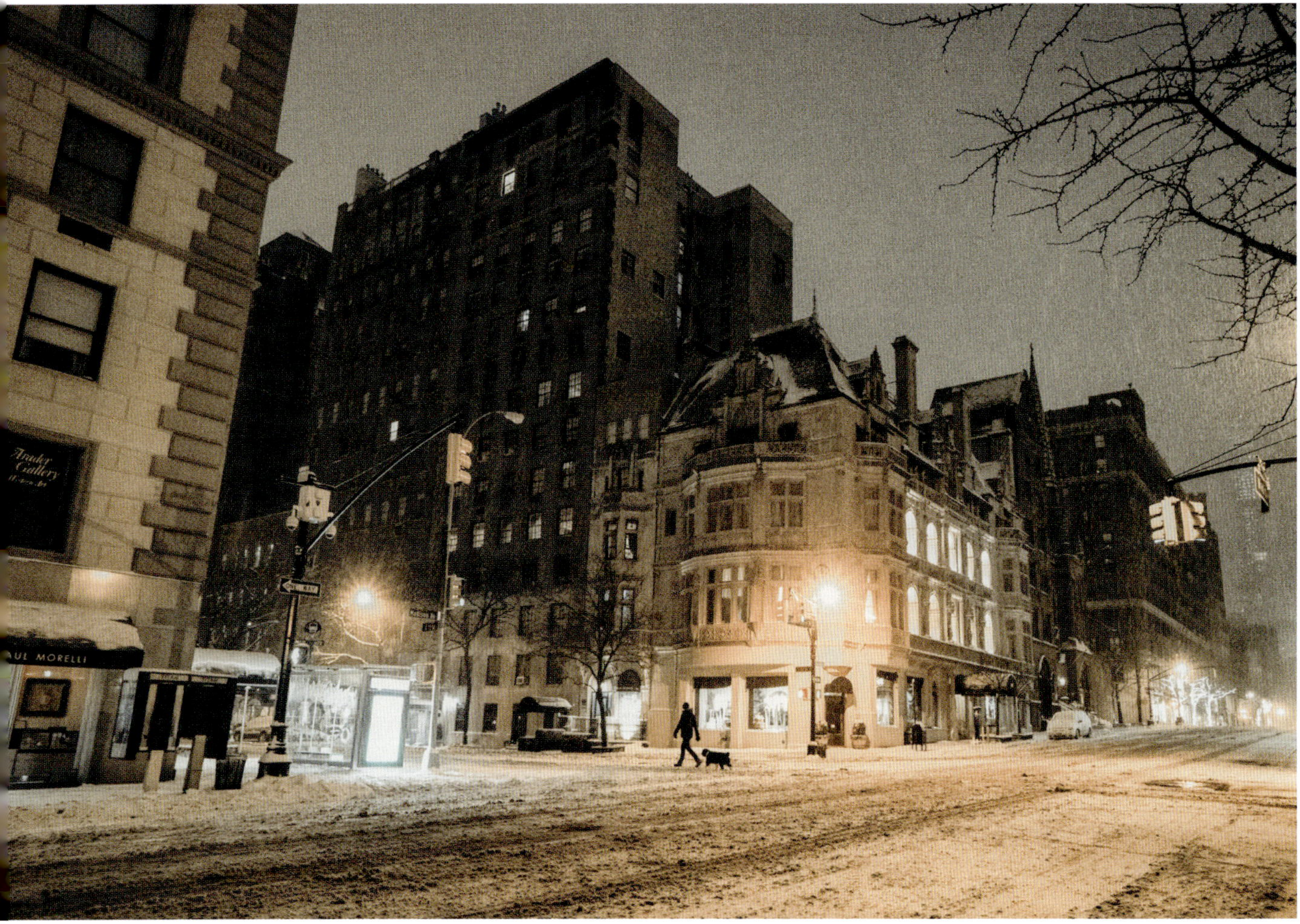

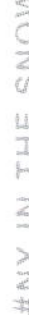

Upper East Side, Manhattan
Sony ILCE-7M2 | ƒ/2.8 | 1/60 second | ISO 2000

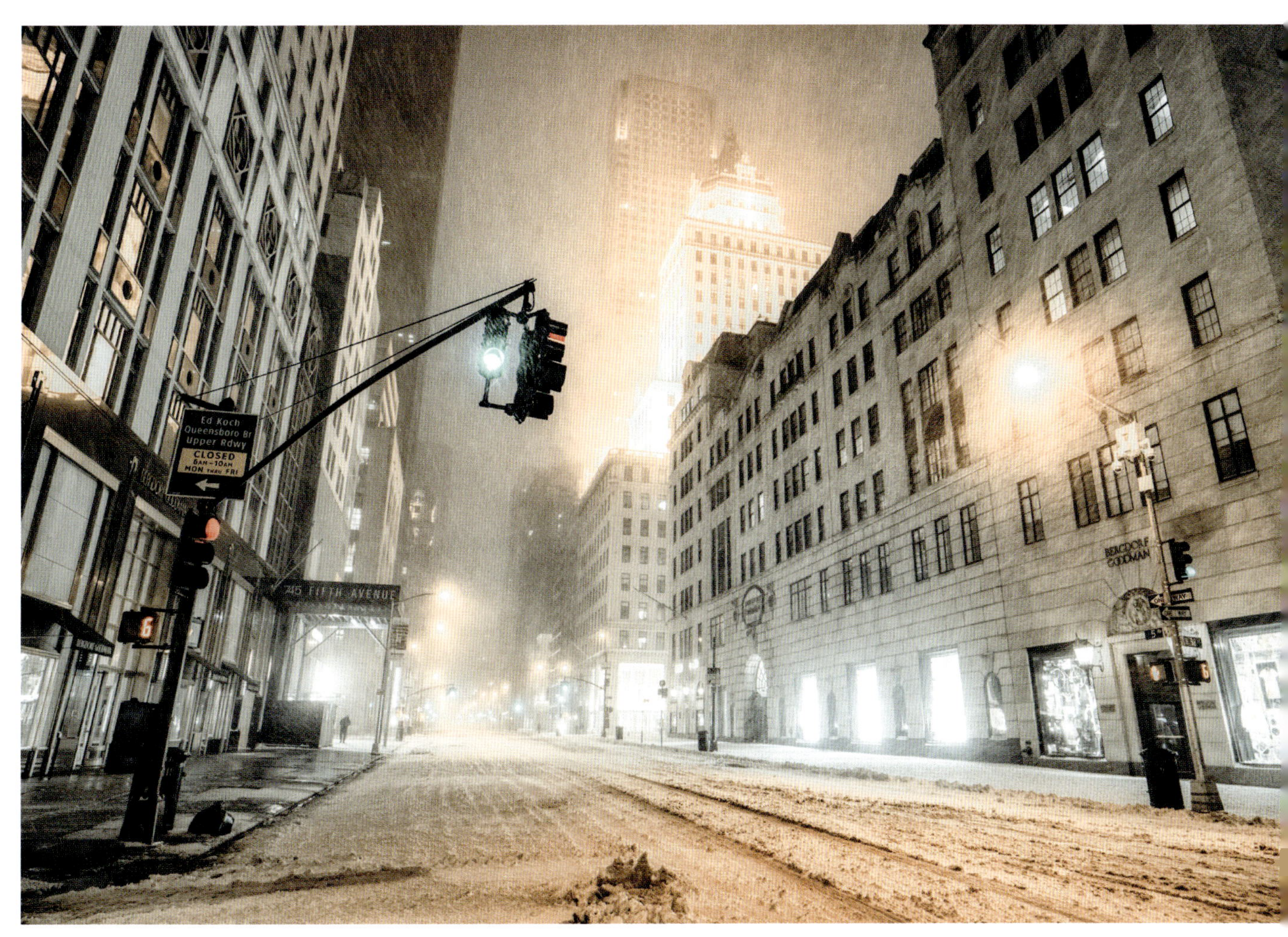

Midtown Manhattan

Sony ILCE-7M2 | *f*/3.2 | 1/40 second | ISO 2000

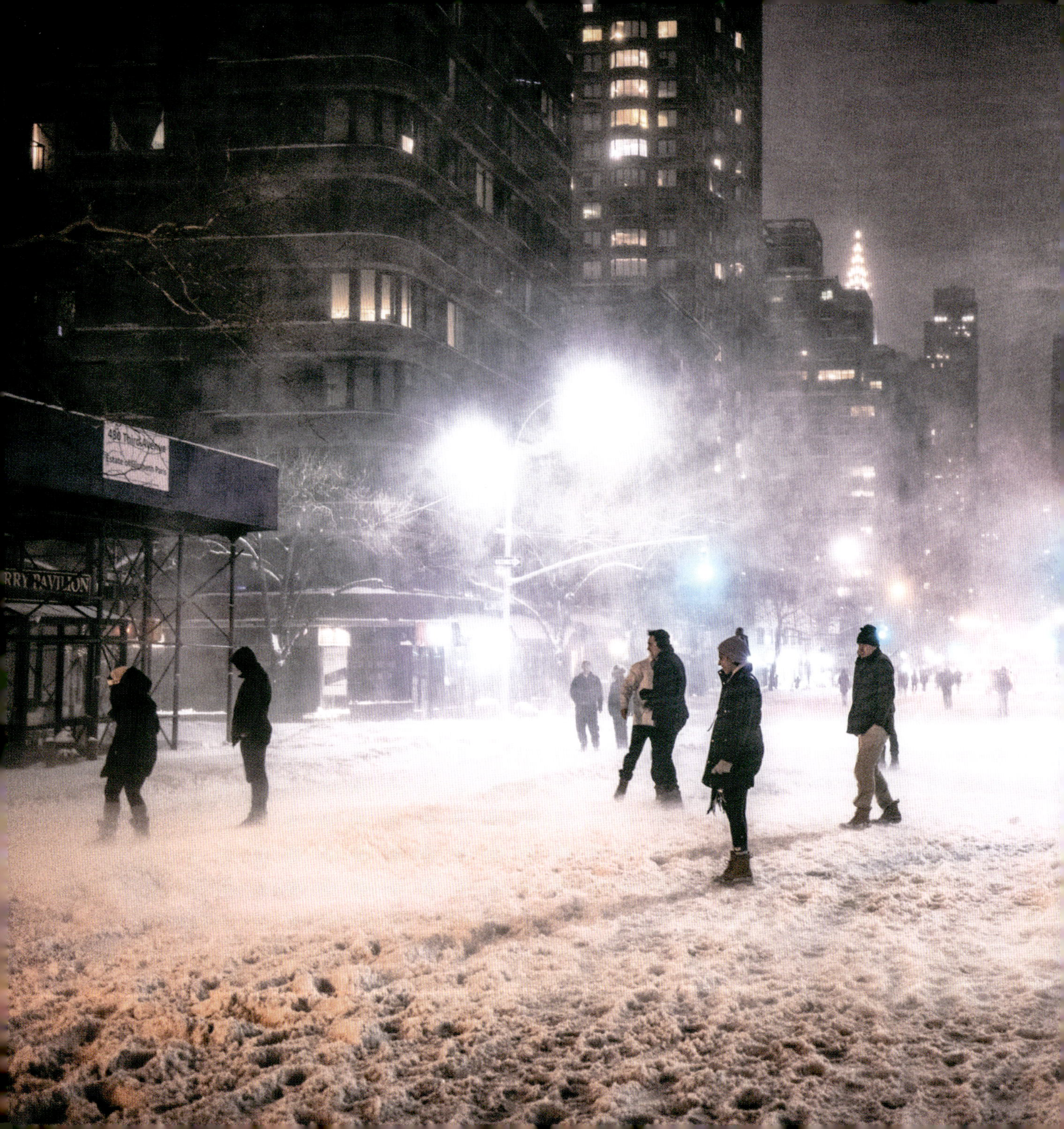
RRY PAVILION

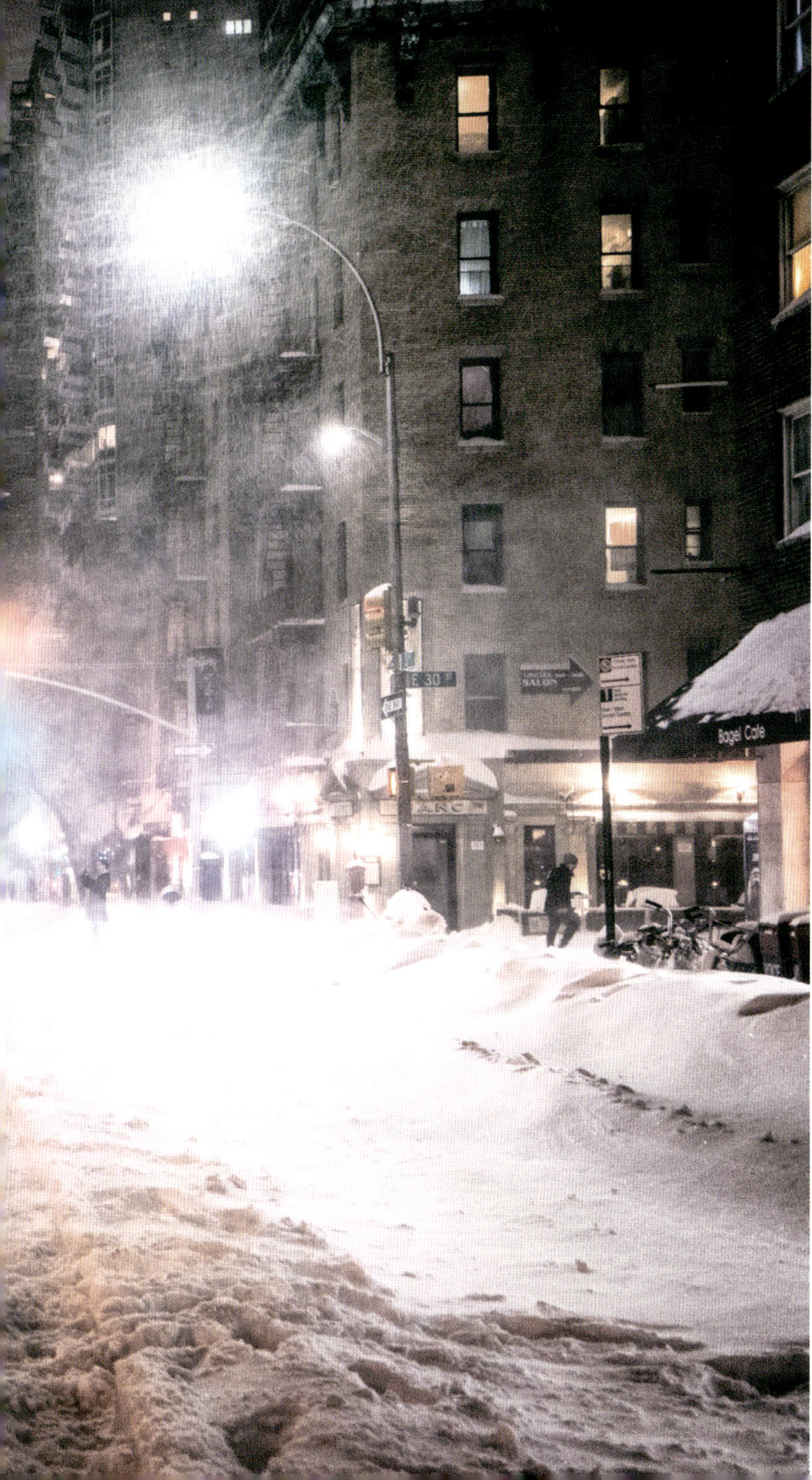

Soho, Lower Manhattan
Sony ILCE-7RM2 | f/3.2 | 1/20 second | ISO 2000

> There is something undeniably magical that occurs as snow falls, swirling and twirling in the air until it hits the ground, heavy with the weight of a thousand promises, as the street lights render each flake immortal.

Times Square, Midtown Manhattan
Sony SLT-A99V | ƒ/3.2 | 1/100 second | ISO 4000

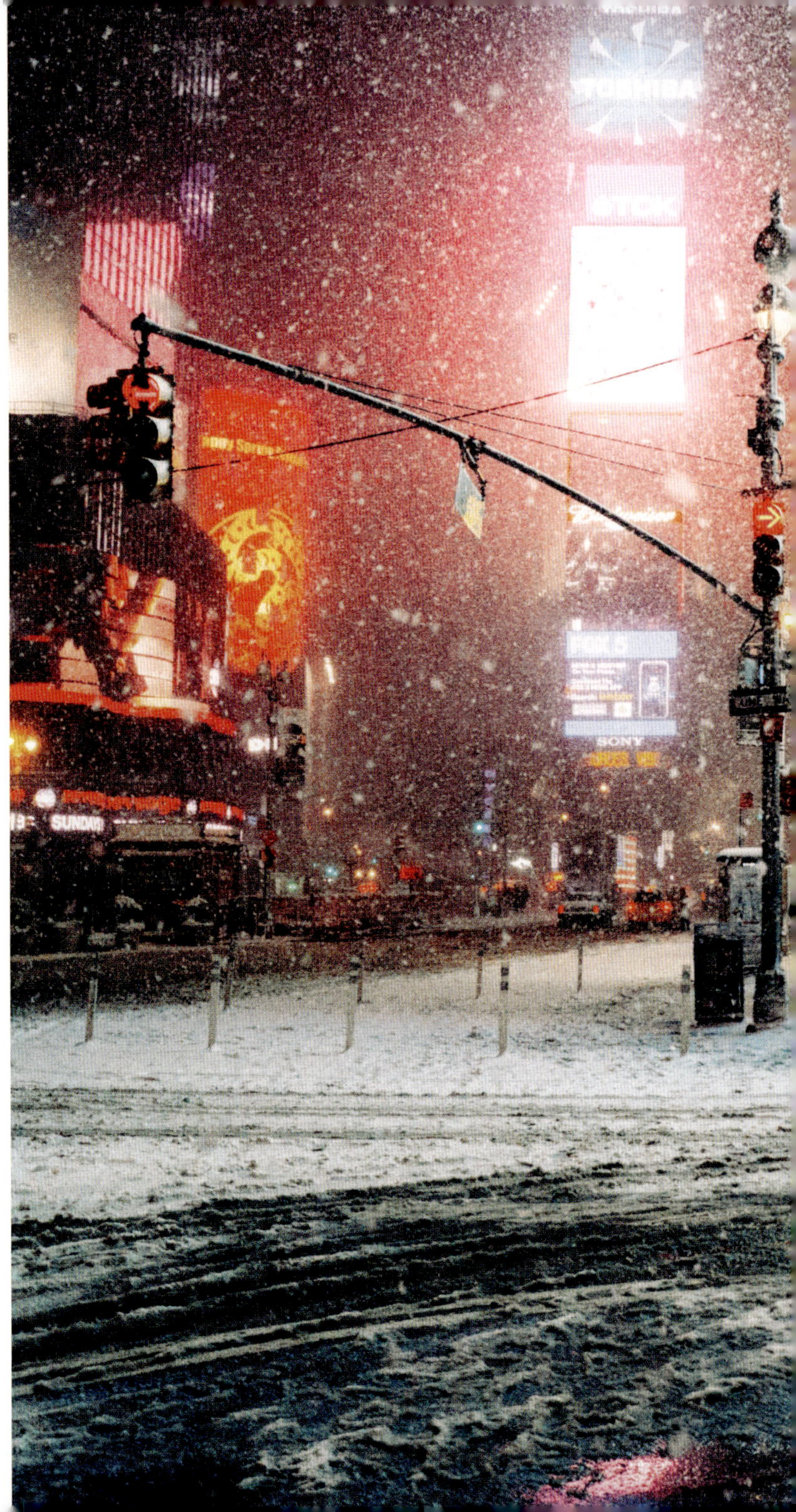

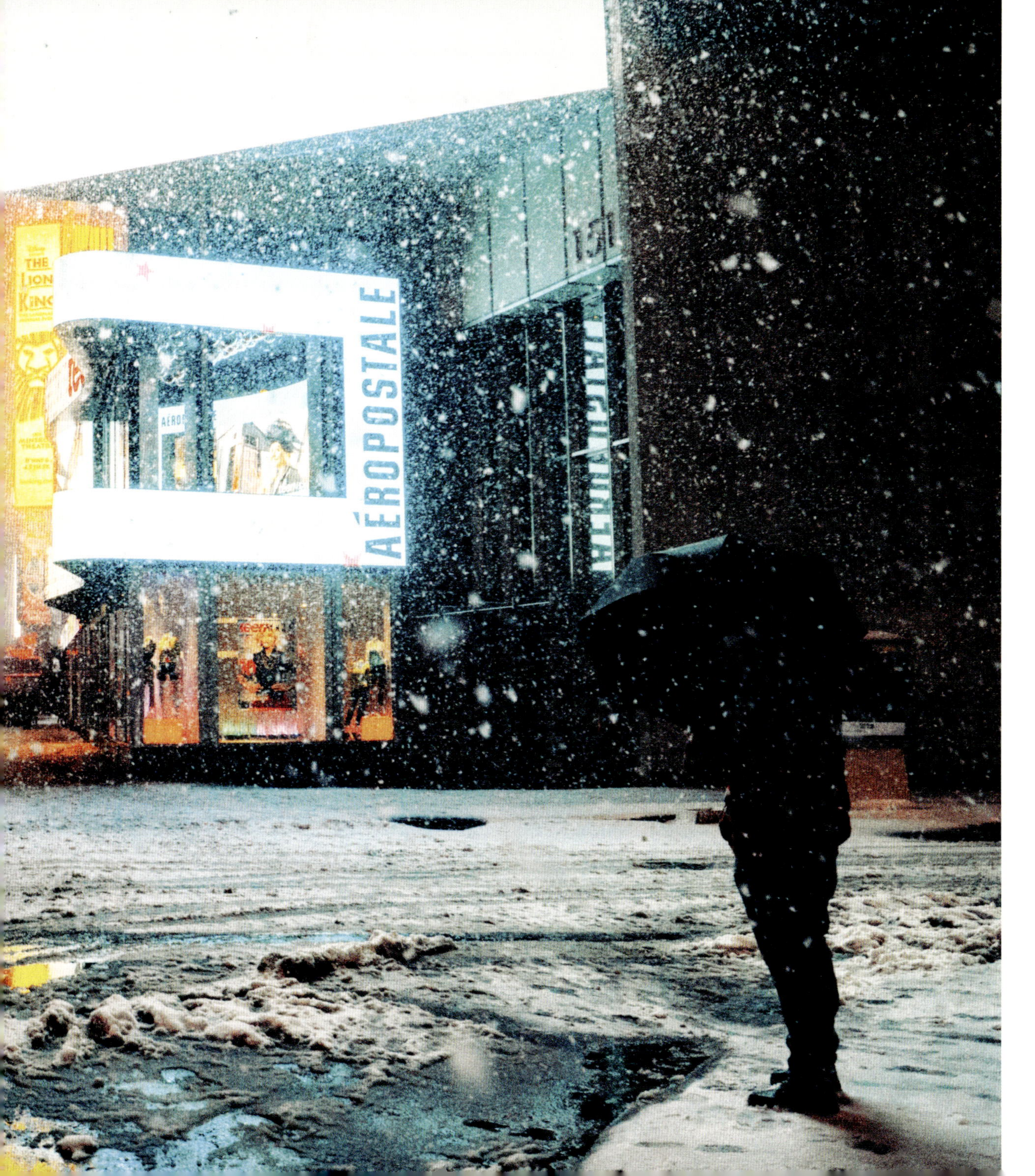
THE
LION
KING
AÉROPOSTALE

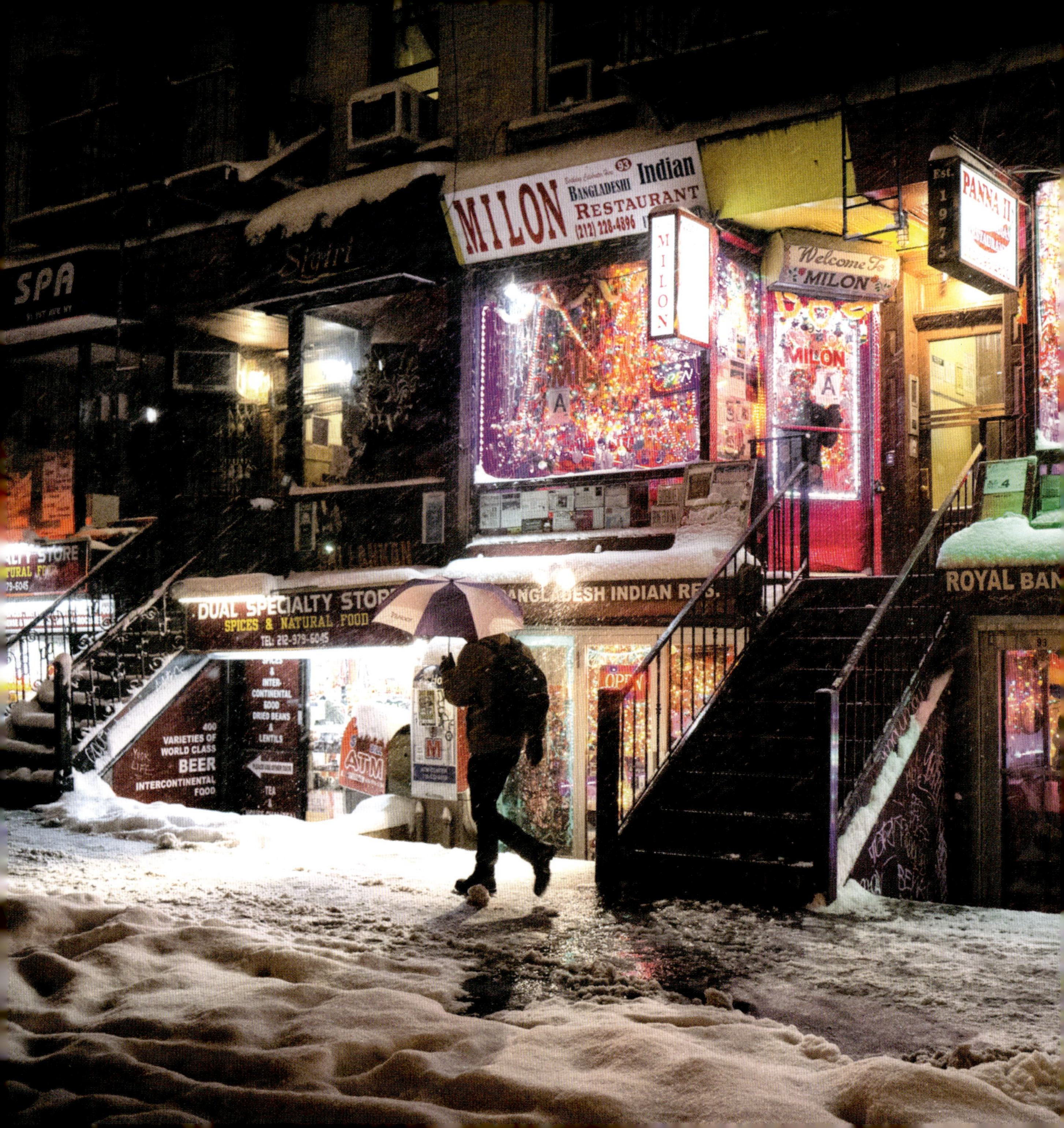

MILON
BANGLADESHI Indian
RESTAURANT
(212) 228-4896
MILON
Welcome To MILON
MILON
Est. 1975
PANNA II
SPA
DUAL SPECIALTY STORE
SPICES & NATURAL FOOD
TEL: 212-979-6045
BANGLADESH INDIAN RES.
ROYAL BAN
400 VARIETIES OF WORLD CLASS BEER
INTERCONTINENTAL FOOD
SPICES & INTER-CONTINENTAL FOOD DRIED BEANS & LENTILS
ATM
OPEN

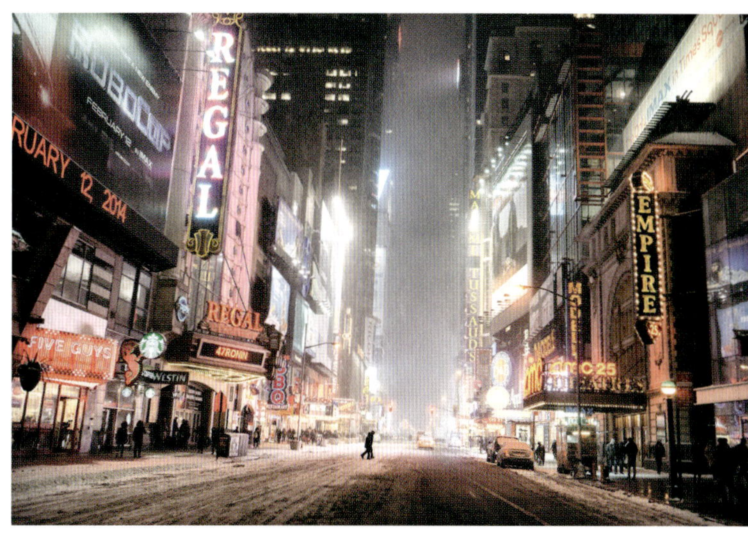

Times Square, Midtown Manhattan
Sony SLT-A99V | ƒ/3.2 | 1/40 second | ISO 2000

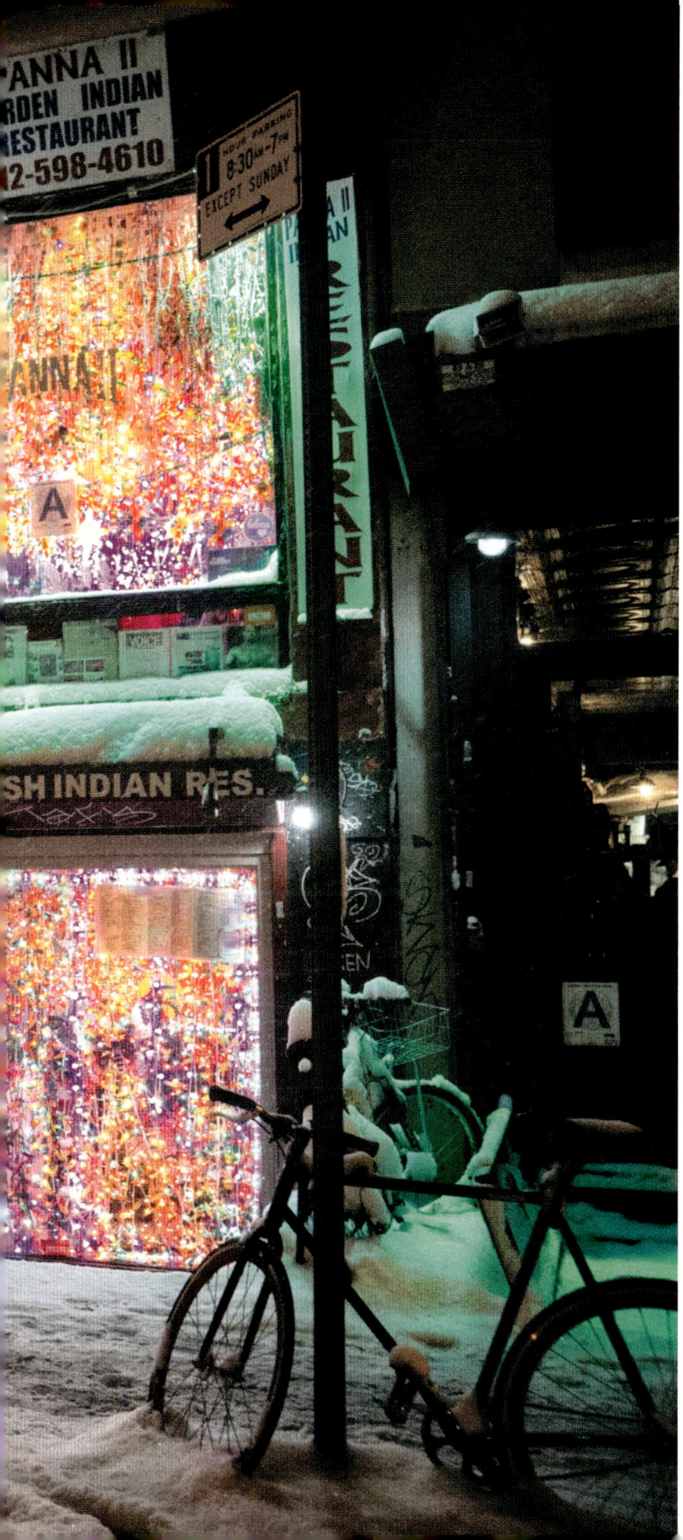

East Village, Lower Manhattan
Sony SLT-A99V | ƒ/3.5 | 1/80 second | ISO 4000

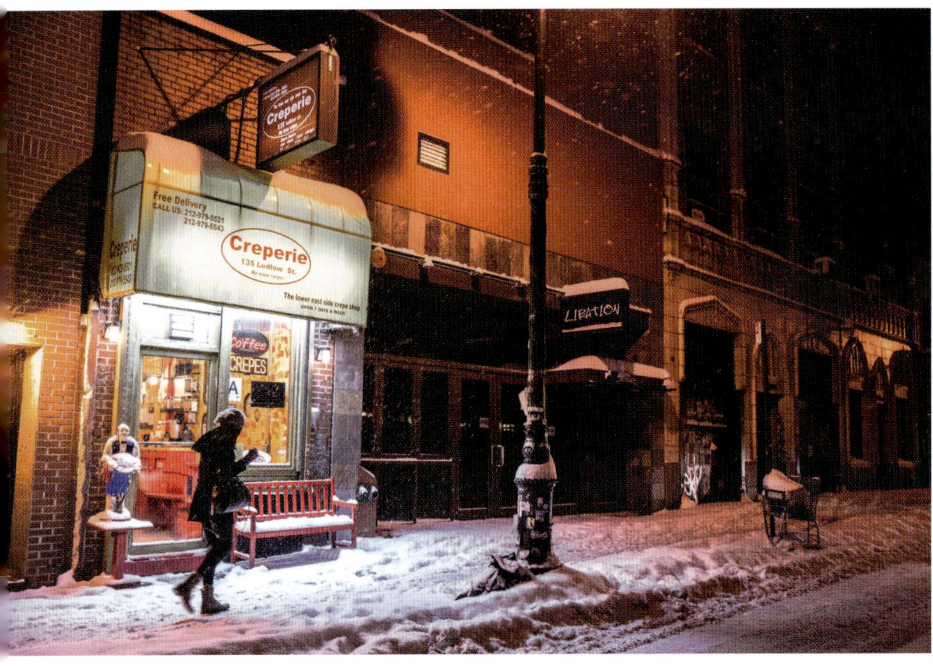

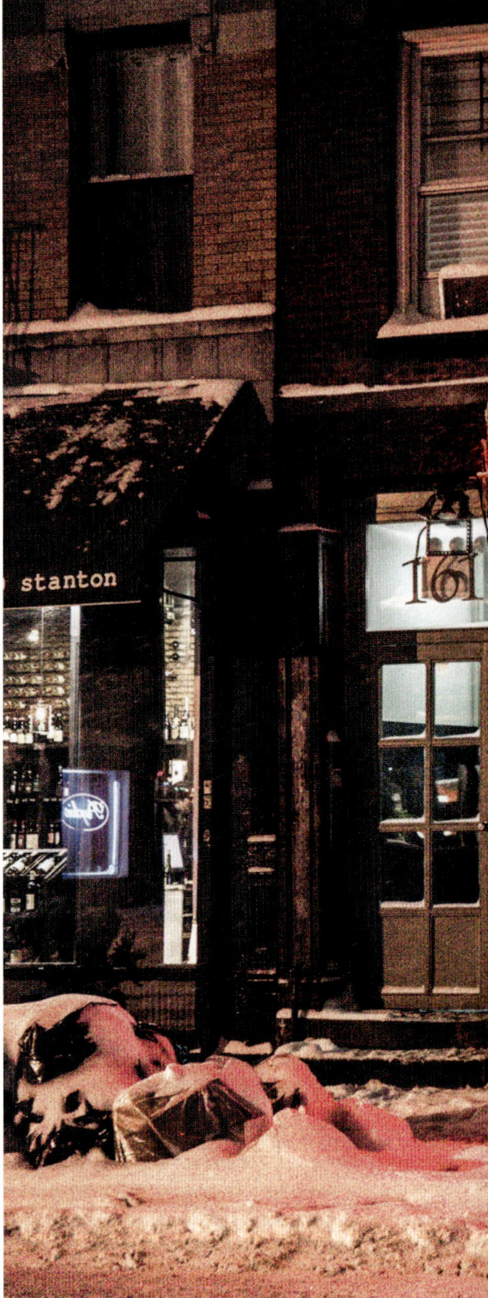

Lower East Side, Manhattan
Sony SLT-A99V | *f*/4 | 1/80 second | ISO 4000

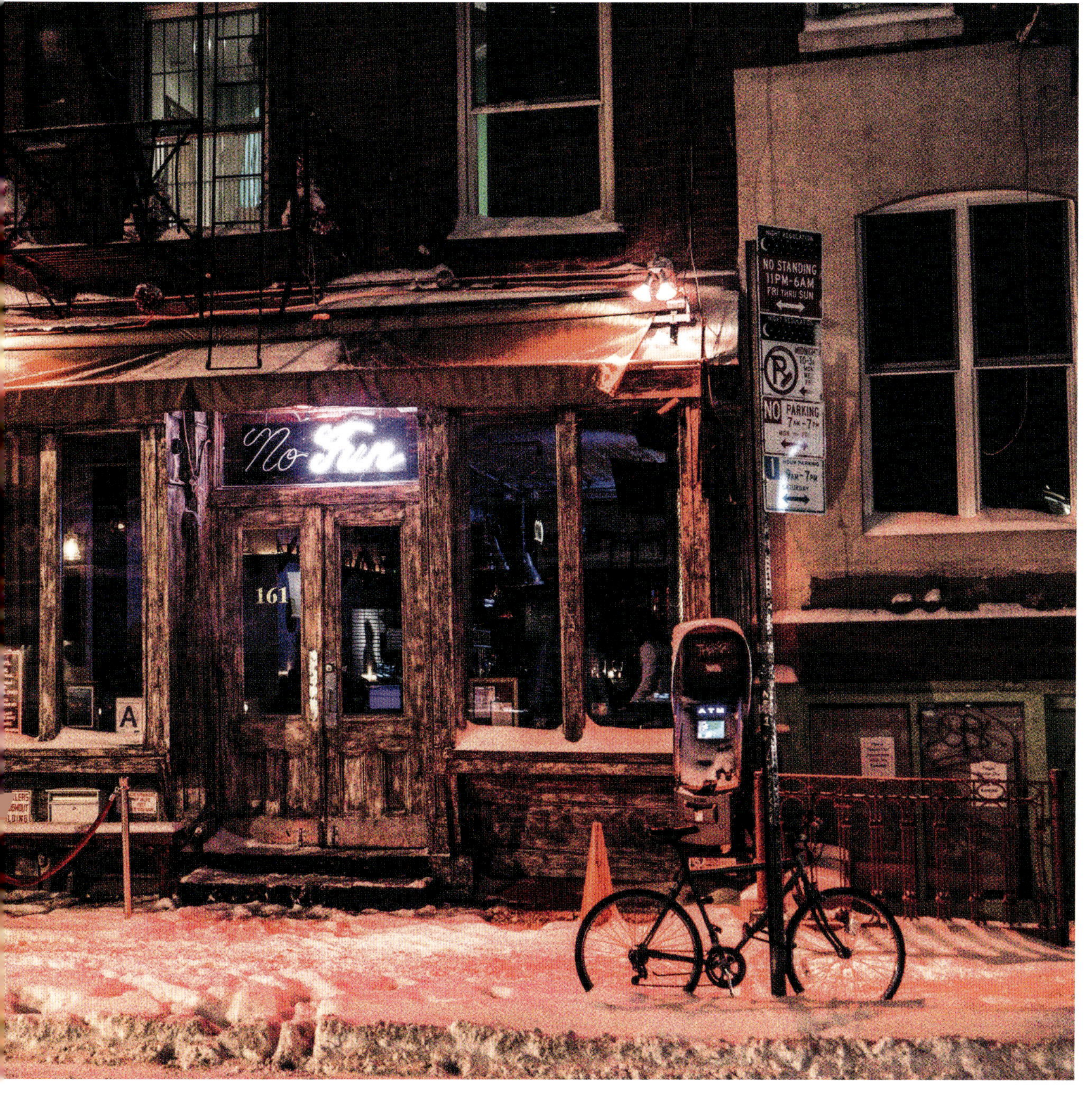
No Fun
161
NO STANDING
11PM-6AM
FRI THRU SUN
NO PARKING
7AM-7PM
9AM-7PM
ATM
A

The first few snowstorms I ever photographed were also the harshest snowstorms I ever dealt with physically. I barely had enough money for proper gloves and layered up with many cotton layers, which is not the best fabric to use to avoid hypothermia. Some of the photos I took remain some of my favorites, like this one, but it's a bittersweet feeling because I can vividly recall how intensely the cold hit my naked fingers and how drenched and cold I was while I walked through the East Village. I would duck into random bodegas and McDonalds to try to recuperate but it was not the most pleasant experience. However, it was such a beautiful night, complete with thundersnow and driving blizzard winds.

The photograph on this page was one of the first of my snow images to be used commercially—by the popular musician Ryan Adams on the cover of his single "Lucky Now." I remember being flabbergasted that anyone would want to use this photo for anything because all I remember about taking it was feeling so woefully unprepared for the storm—and a few brief moments of awe and wonder.

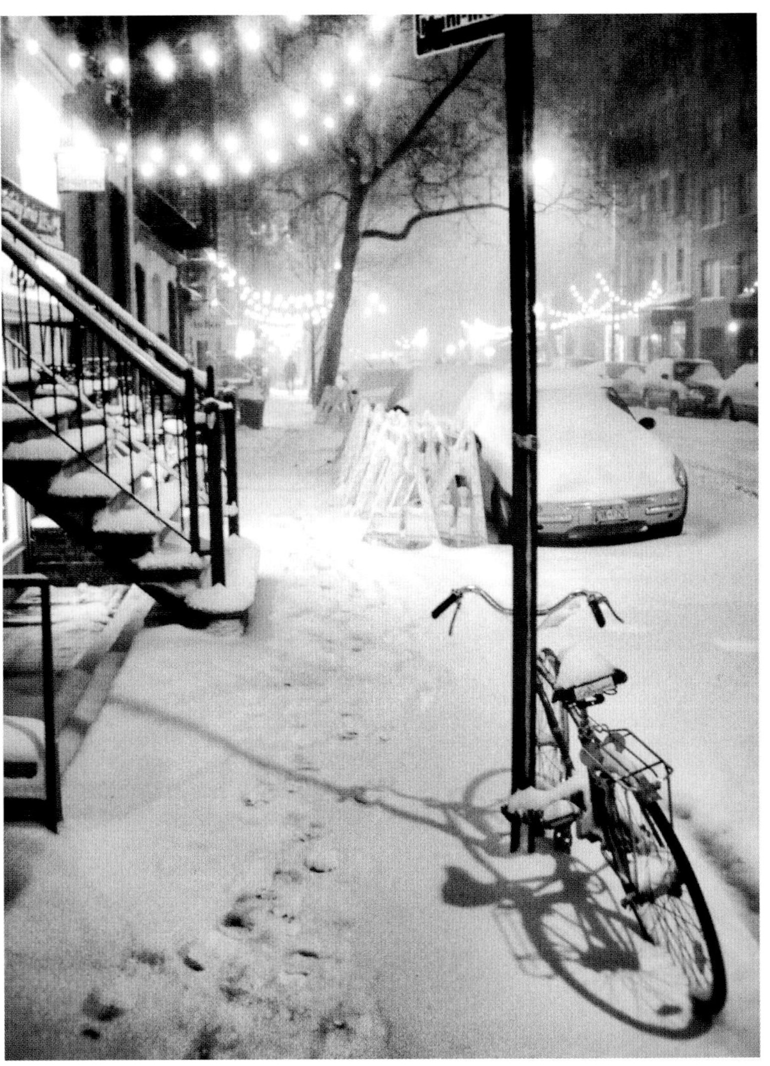

East Village, Lower Manhattan
Sony SLT-A99V | *f*/3.2 | 1/40 second | ISO 2000

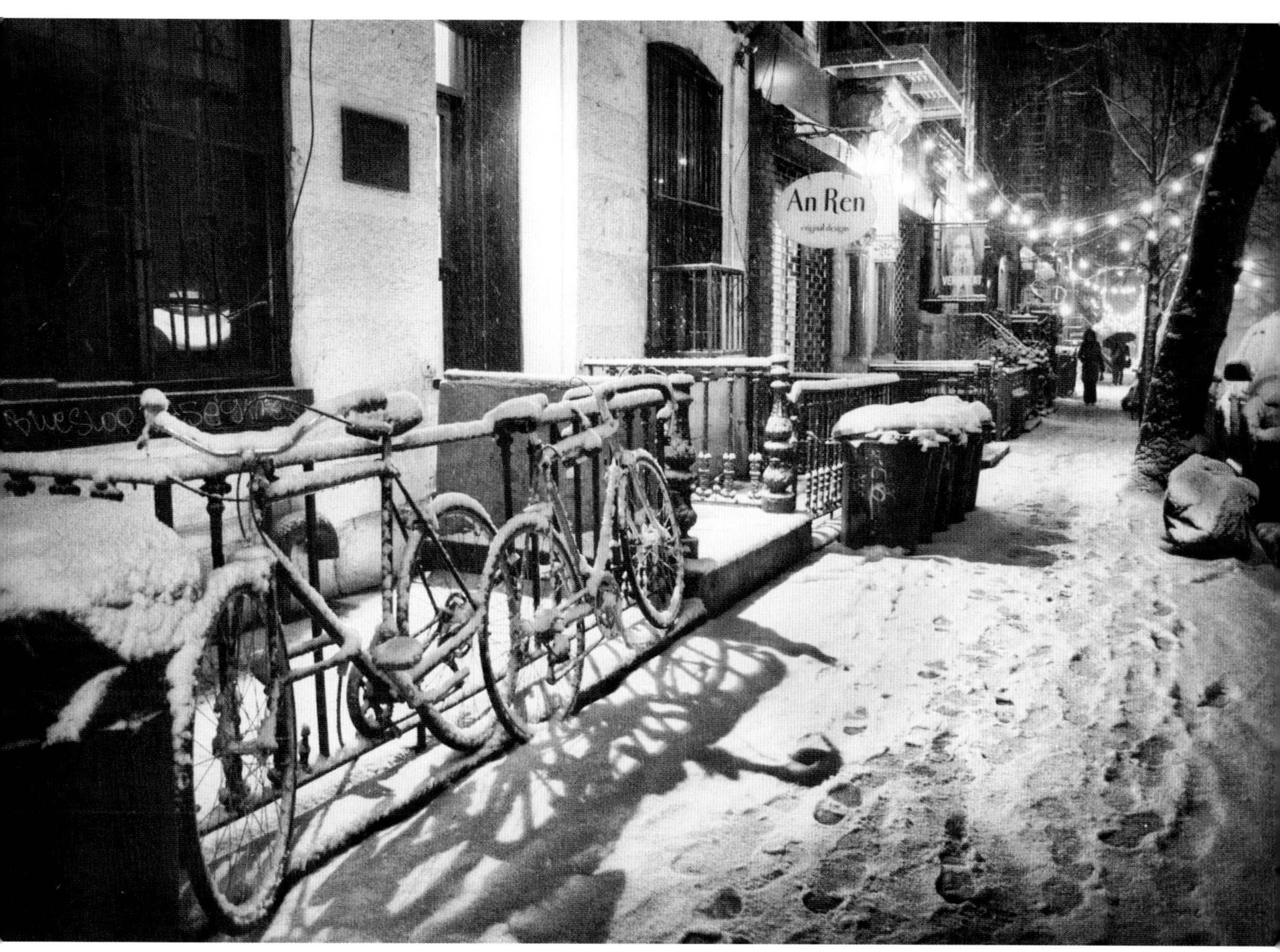

East Village, Manhattan
Panasonic DMC-FZ35 | *f*/5 | 1/60 second | ISO 800

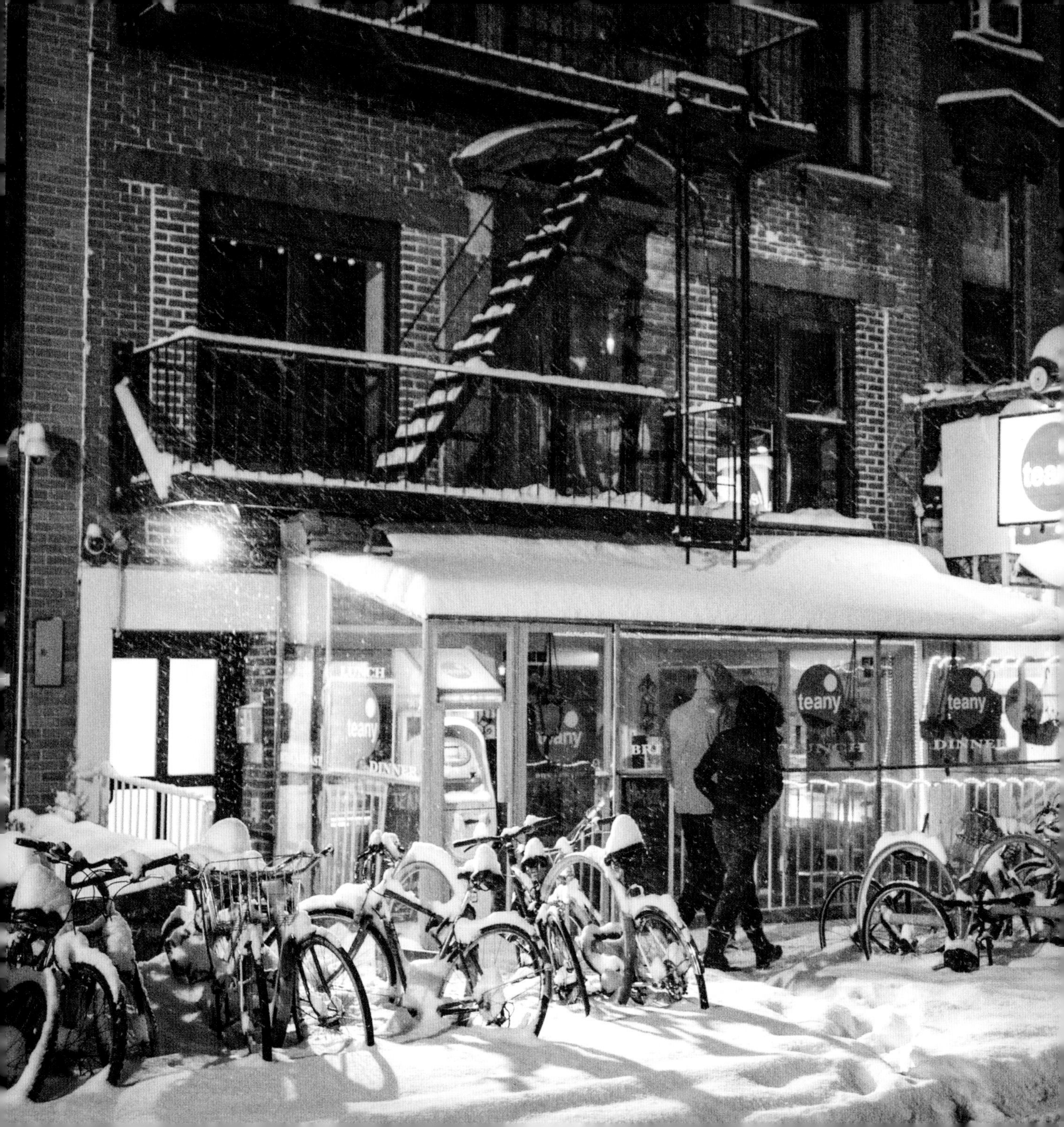

LUNCH
teany
DINNER
teany
teany
DINNER

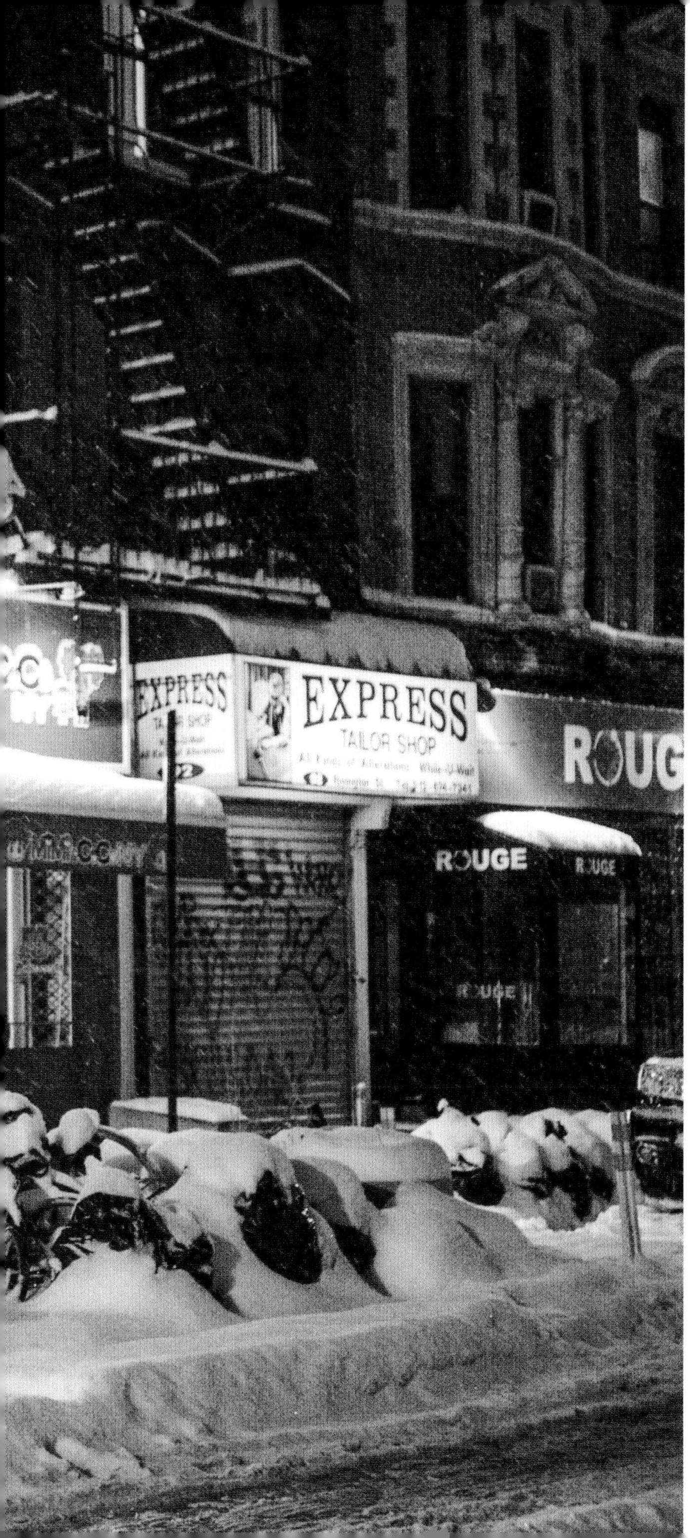

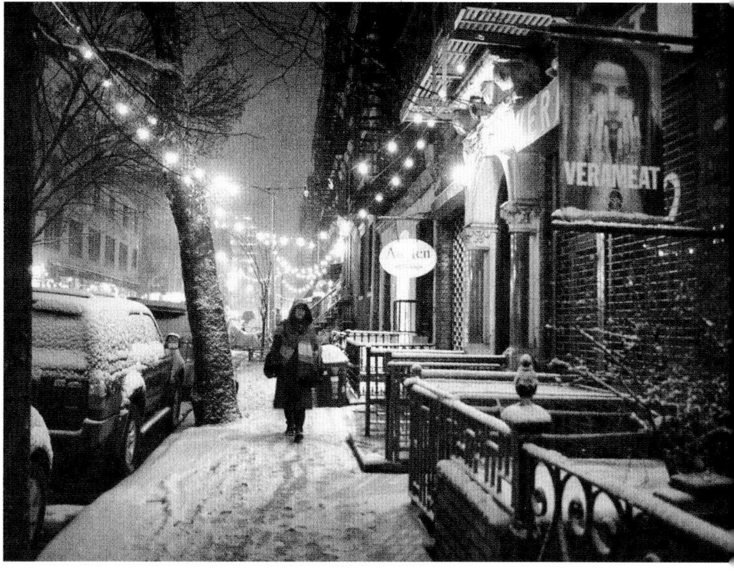

East Village, Lower Manhattan
Sony SLT-A99V | ƒ/3.2 | 1/125 second | ISO 4000

Lower East Side, Manhattan
Sony SLT-A99V | ƒ/4 | 1/80 second | ISO 4000

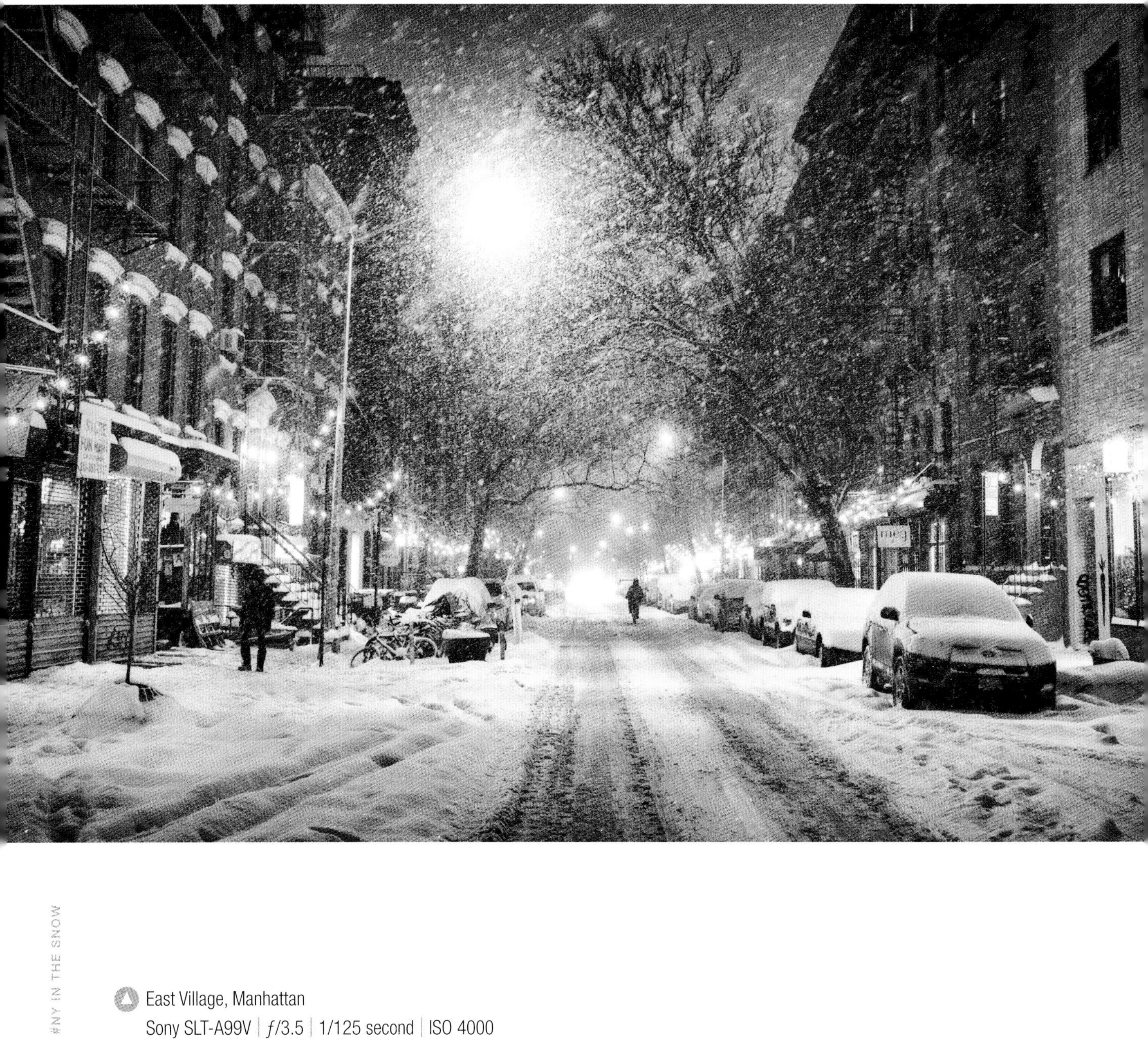

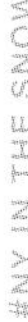

East Village, Manhattan
Sony SLT-A99V | *f*/3.5 | 1/125 second | ISO 4000

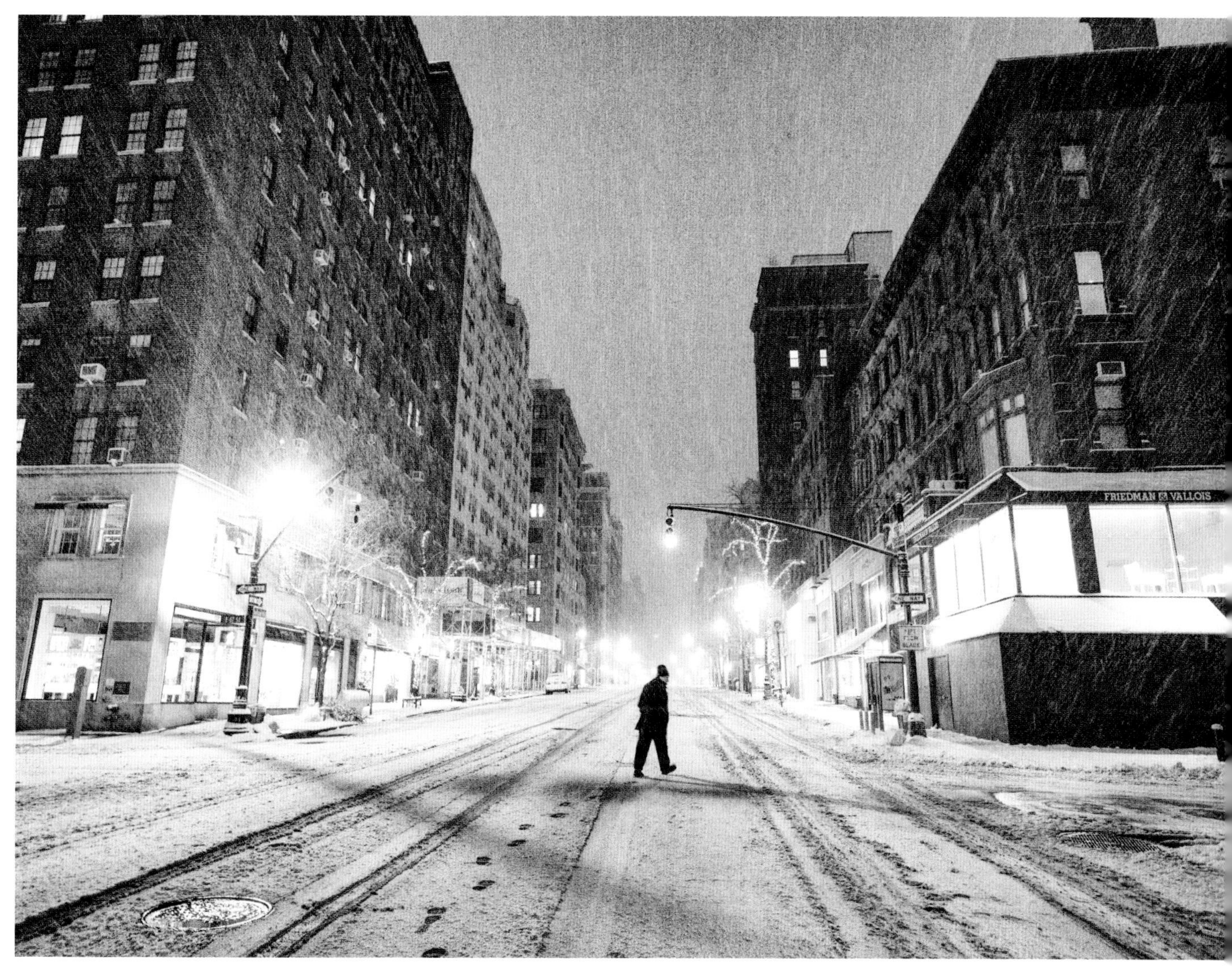

Greenwich Village, Manhattan
Sony ILCE-7M2 | *f*/5 | 1/20 second | ISO 4000

> "The silence of winter nights while tiny lights twinkle, diffused by the falling snow, is maybe one of the most intensely magical feelings I can possibly think of and attempt to capture with my photography."

This photo has almost taken on a life of its own over the years as it has been shared millions of times online, over and over again, every year without fail. It's one of my favorite photos that I have ever taken.

I remember specifically walking to this street to capture this scene on this night. This scene tells a story I felt compelled to tell, and evokes everything I try to capture with my snow photography. I waited for the right person to walk into the scene and the signs were as much a part of the story for me as the lights. When I was younger, this is how the East Village looked in my imagination when I would think about it late at night before drifting off to sleep.

East Village, Lower Manhattan
Sony SLT-A99V | *f*/3.2 | 1/100 second | ISO 4000

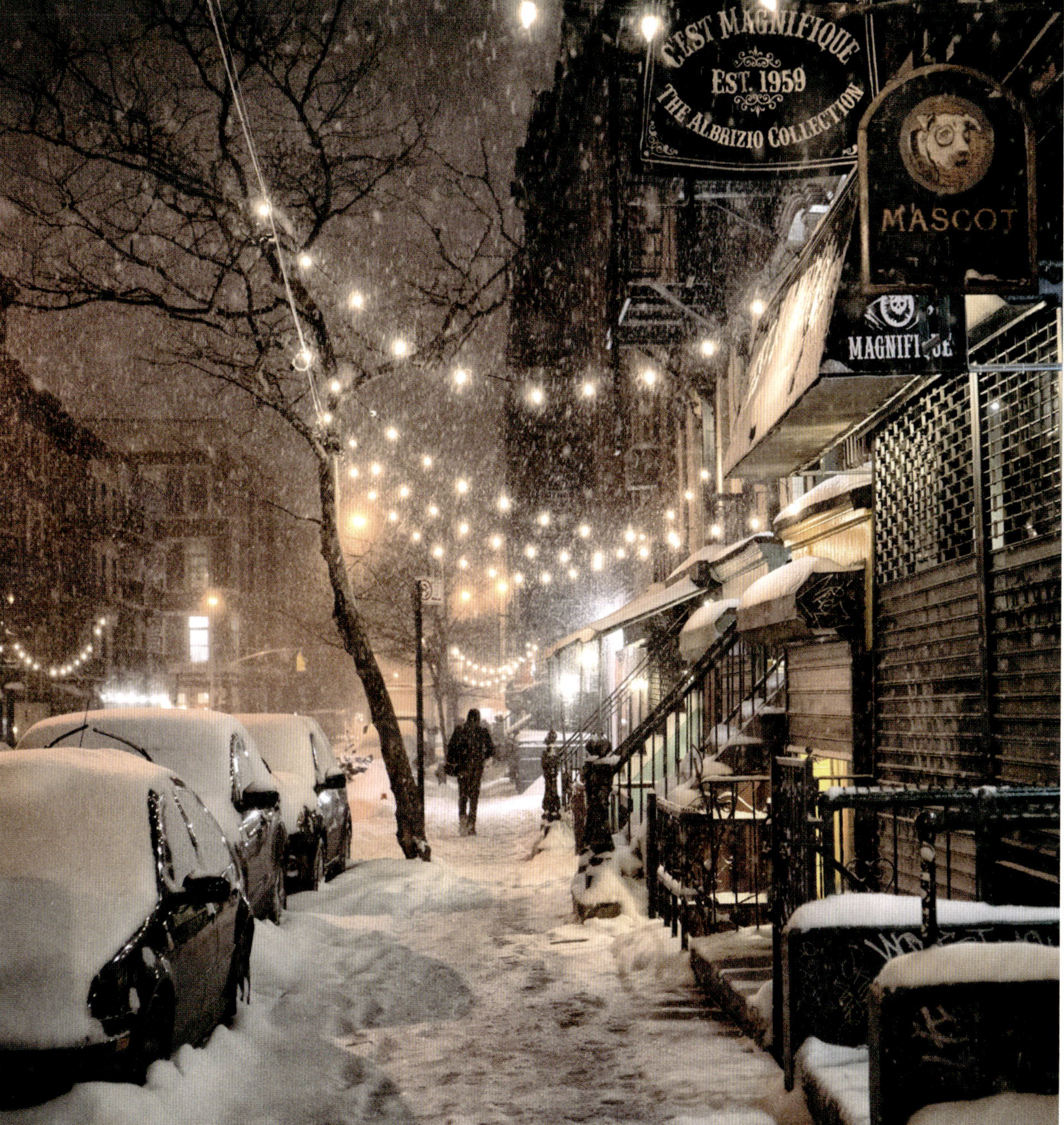
C'EST MAGNIFIQUE
EST. 1959
THE ALBRIZIO COLLECTION
MASCOT
MAGNIFIQUE

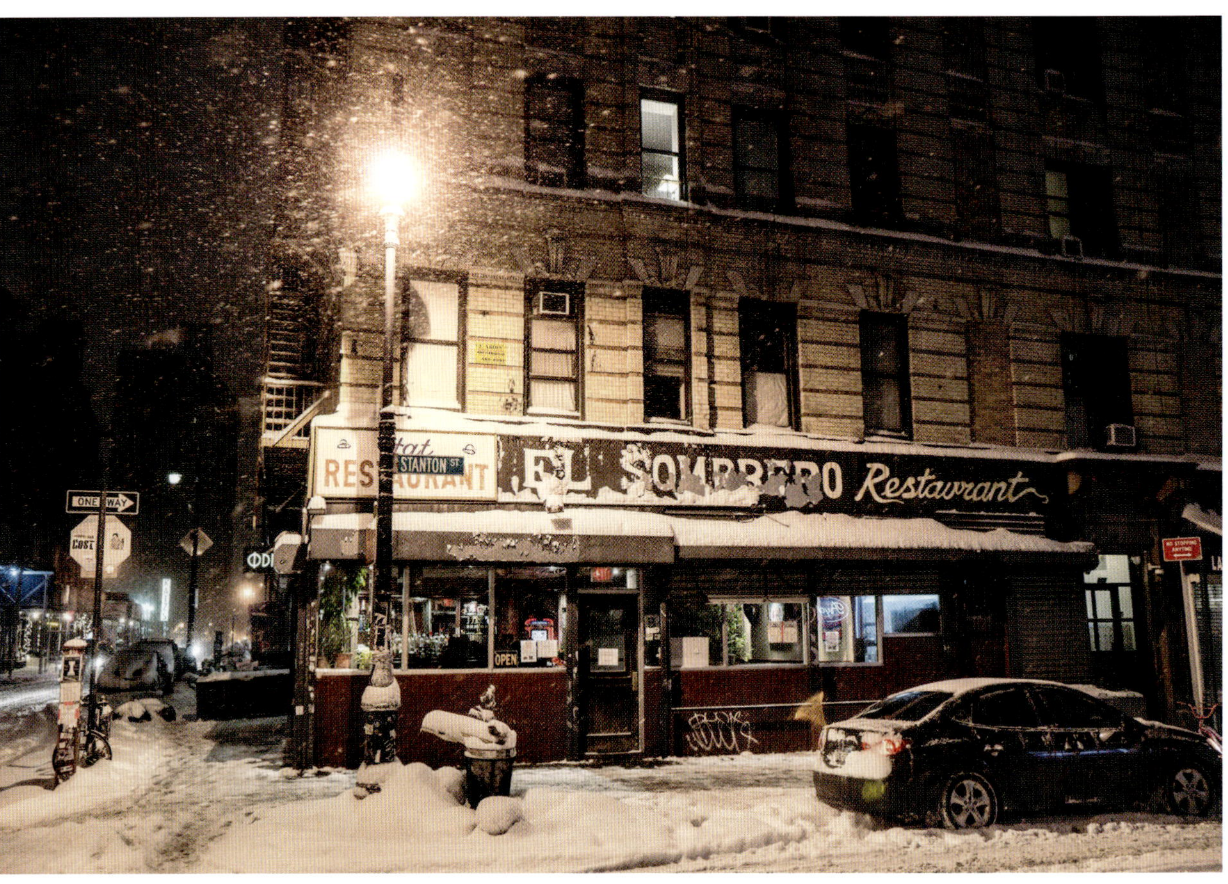

Lower East Side, Manhattan
Sony ILCE-7M2 | ƒ/4 | 1/80 second | ISO 4000

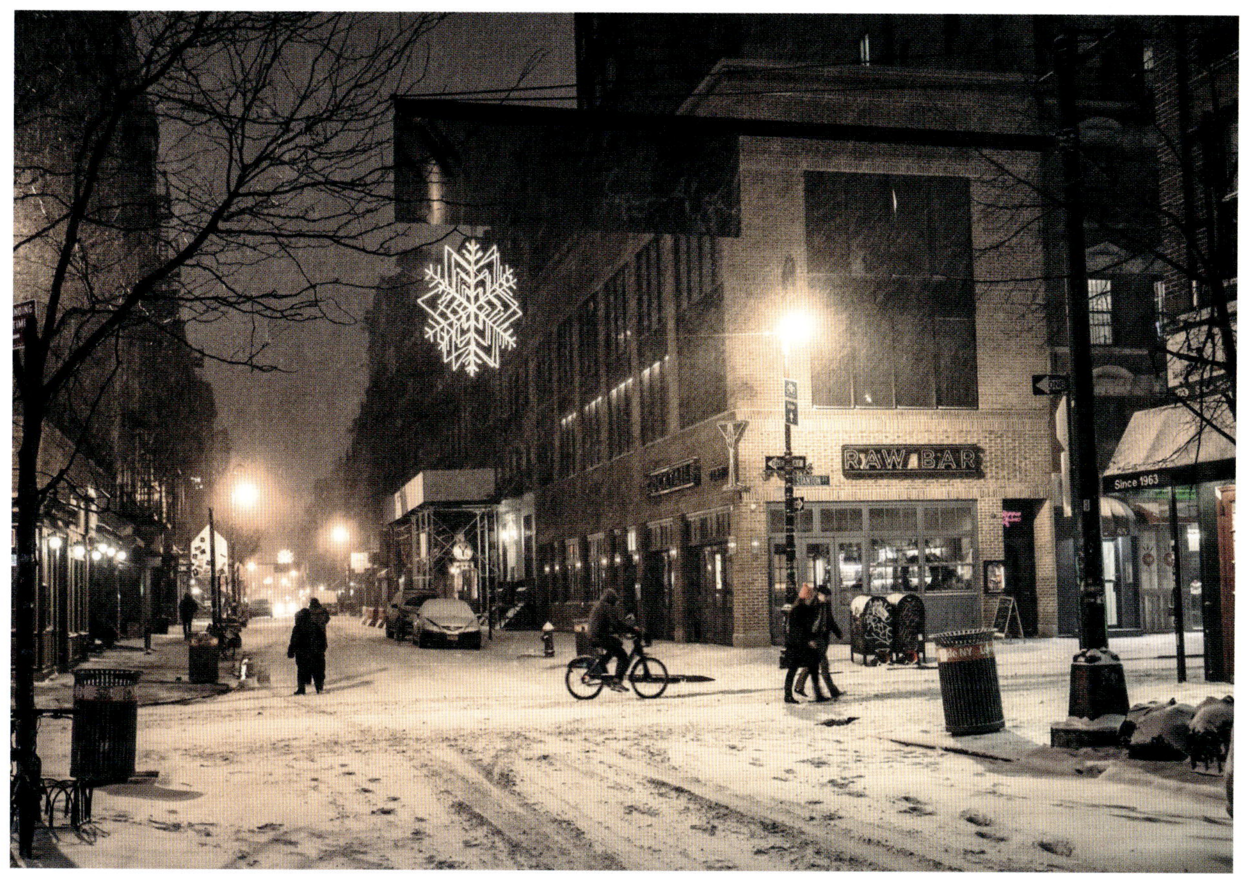

Lower East Side, Manhattan
Sony ILCE-7M2 | *f*/3.2 | 1/80 second | ISO 4000

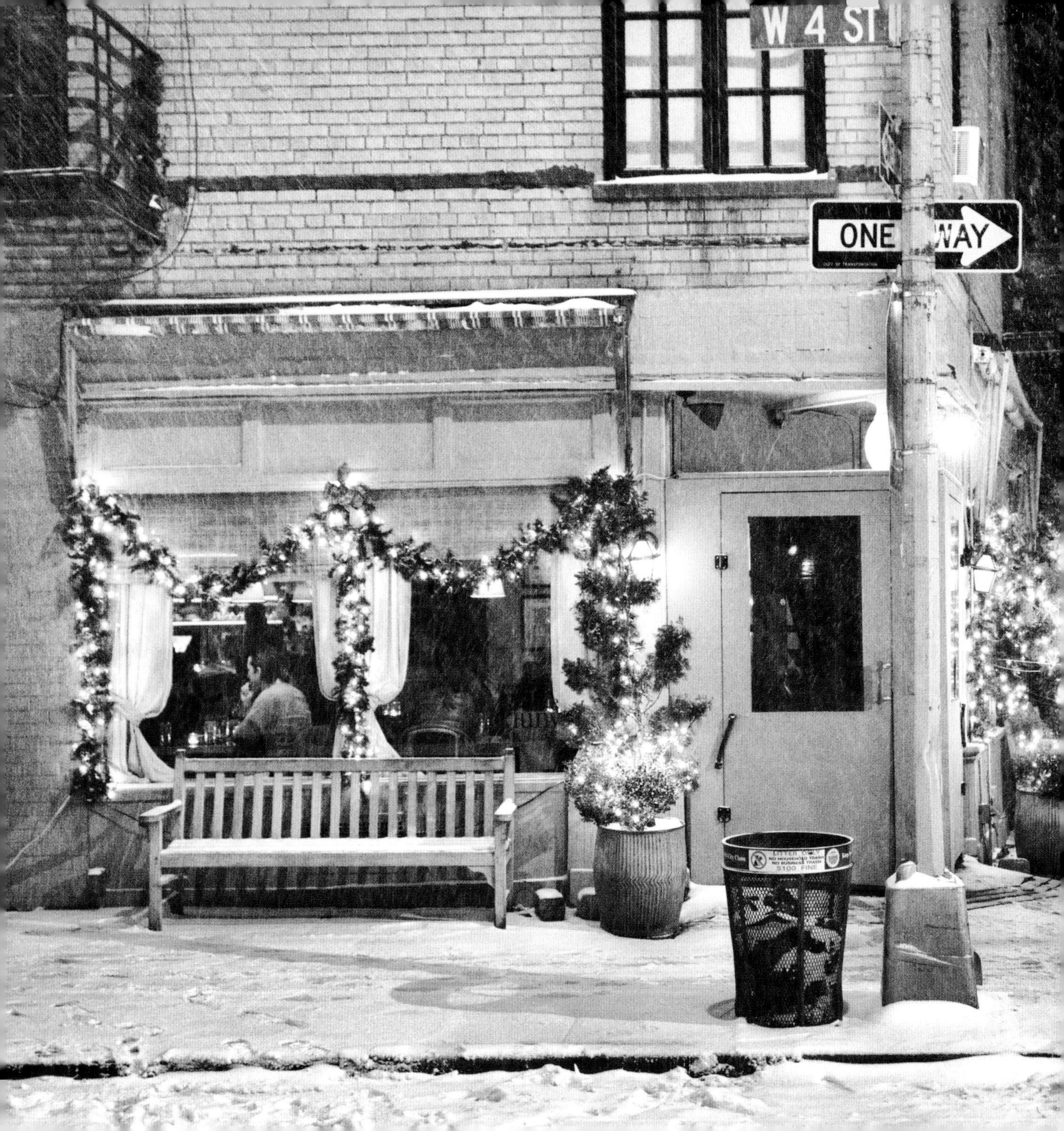
W 4 ST
ONE WAY
NO HOUSEHOLD TRASH
NO BUSINESS TRASH
$100 FINE

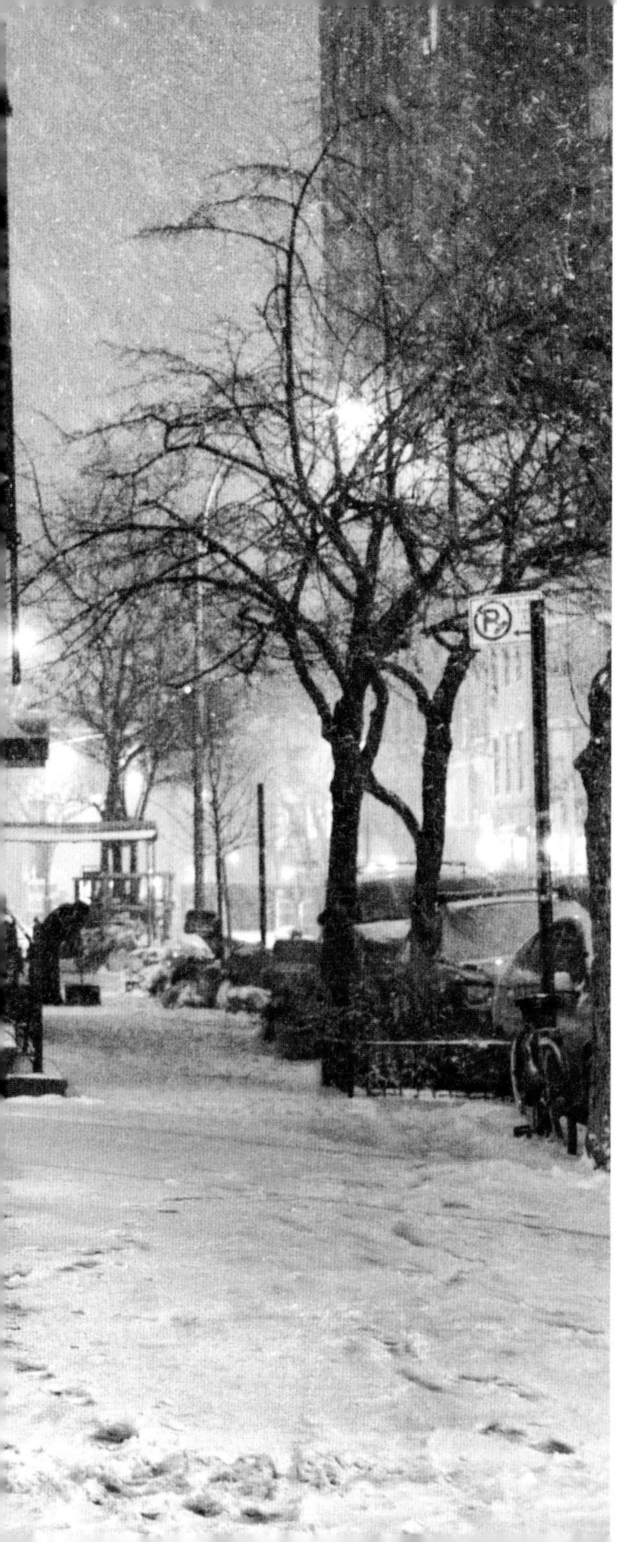

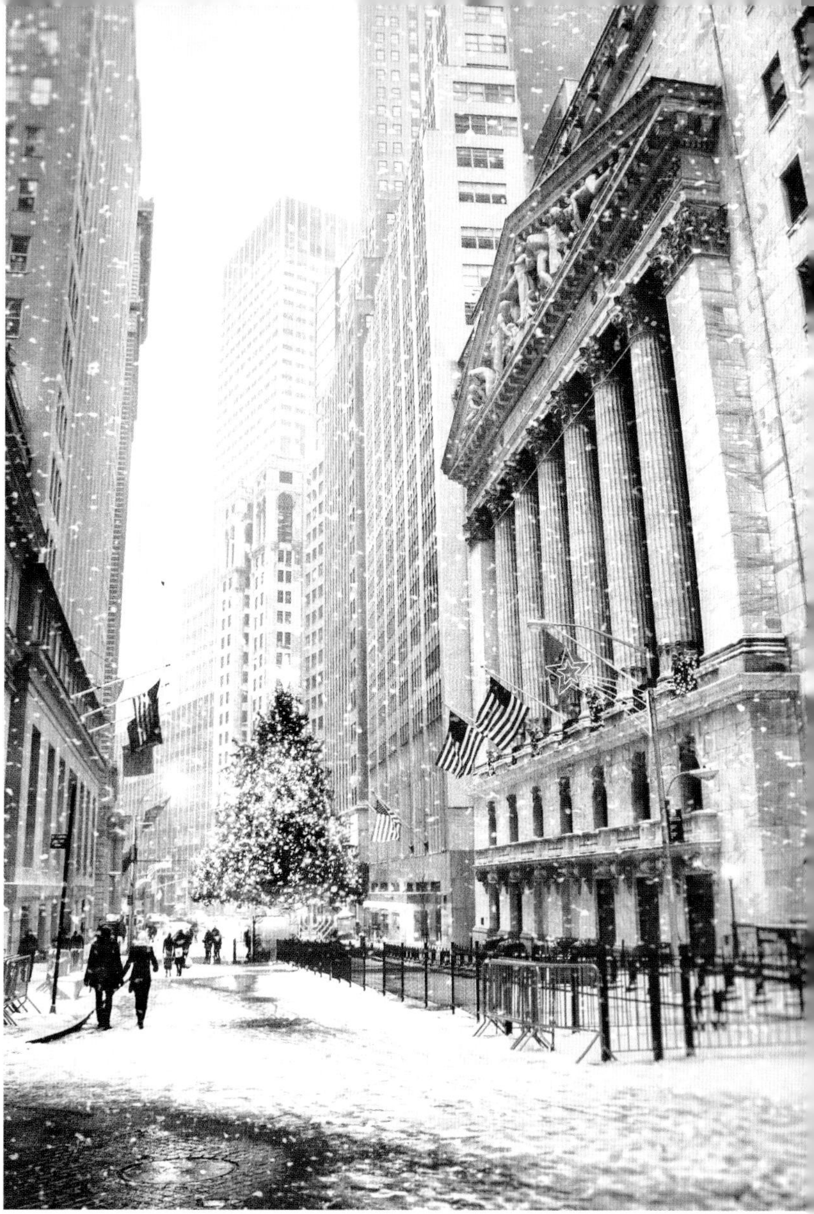

▲ New York City Stock Exchange, Financial District, Lower Manhattan
Sony NEX-6 | *ƒ*/3.2 | 1/80 second | ISO 4000

◀ West Village, Lower Manhattan
Sony ILCE-7M2 | *ƒ*/3.5 | 1/60 second | ISO 4000

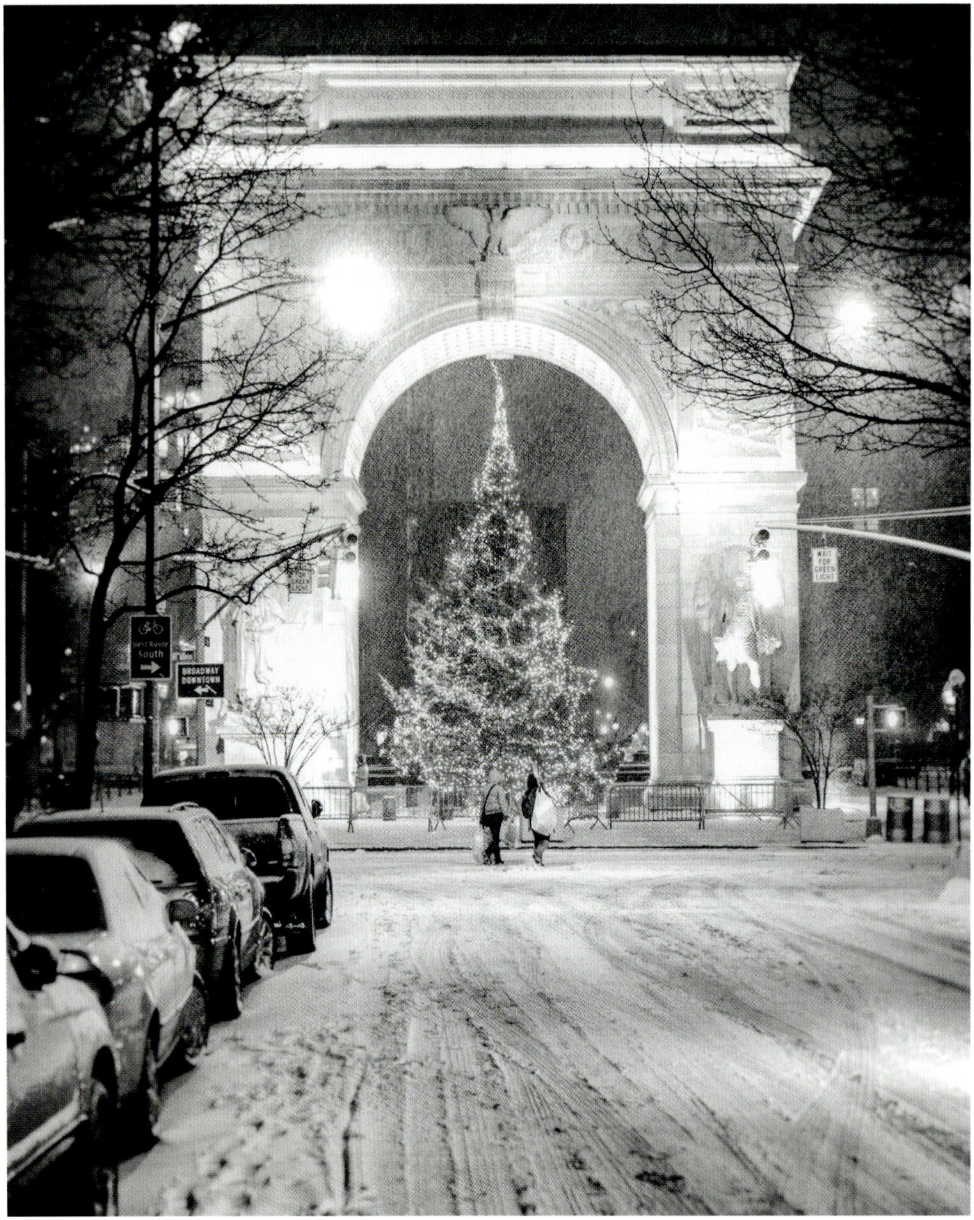

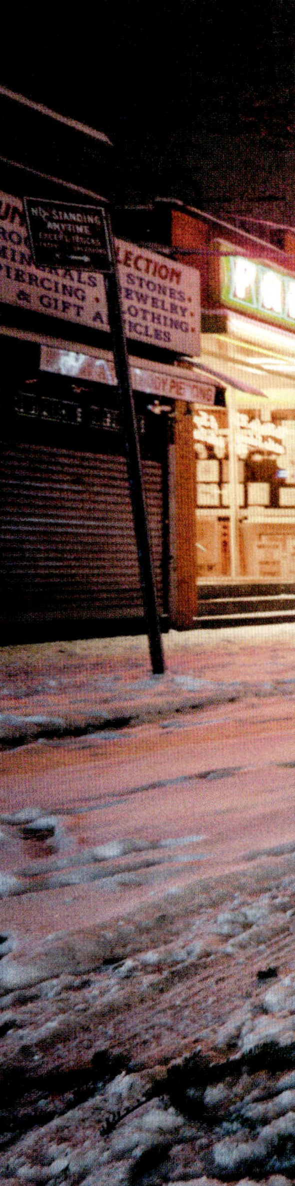

West Village, Lower Manhattan
Sony ILCE-7M2 | f/2.8 | 1/30 second | ISO 4000

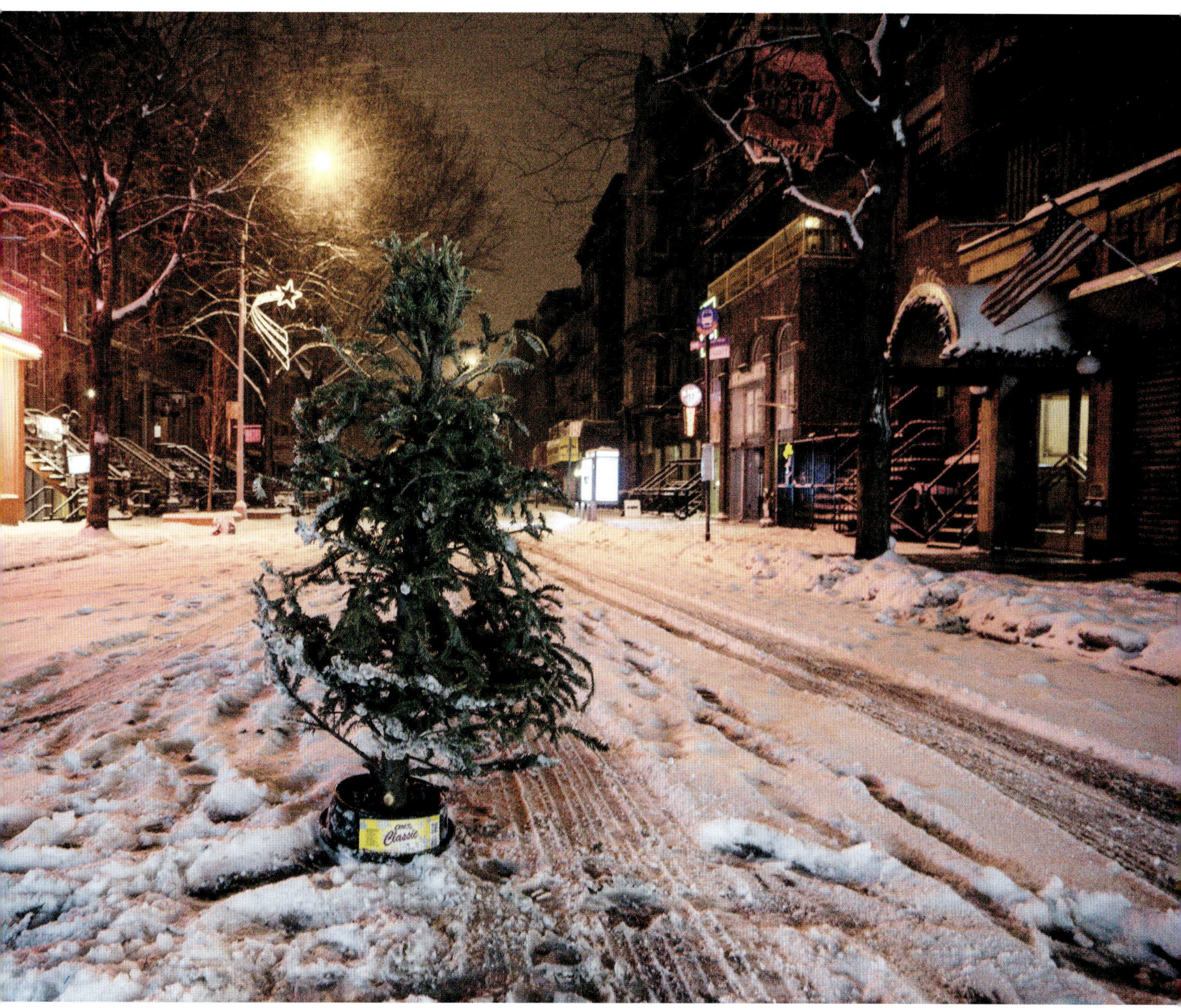

East Village, Lower Manhattan
Sony SLT-A99V | *f*/4 | 1/80 second | ISO 4000

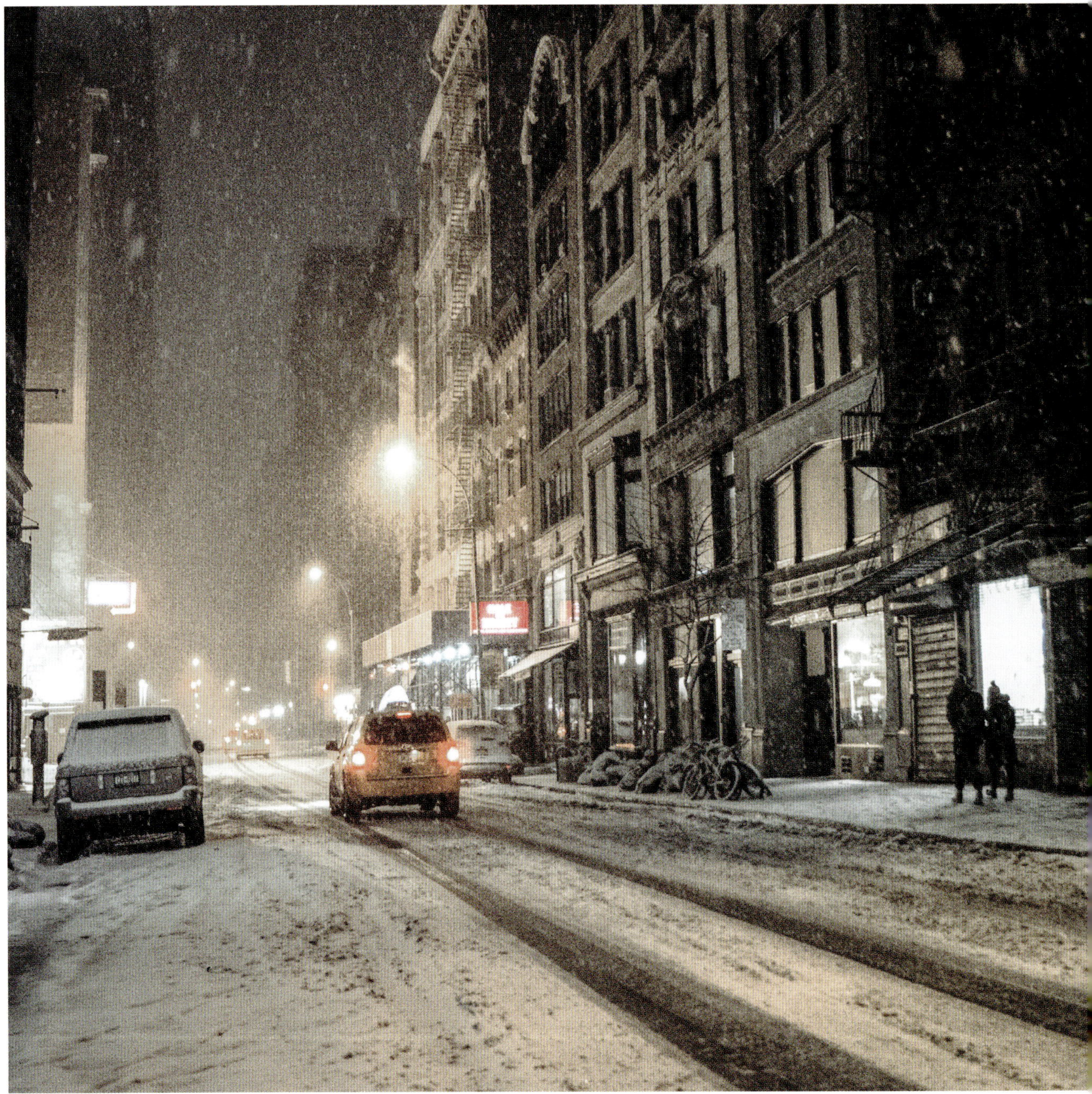

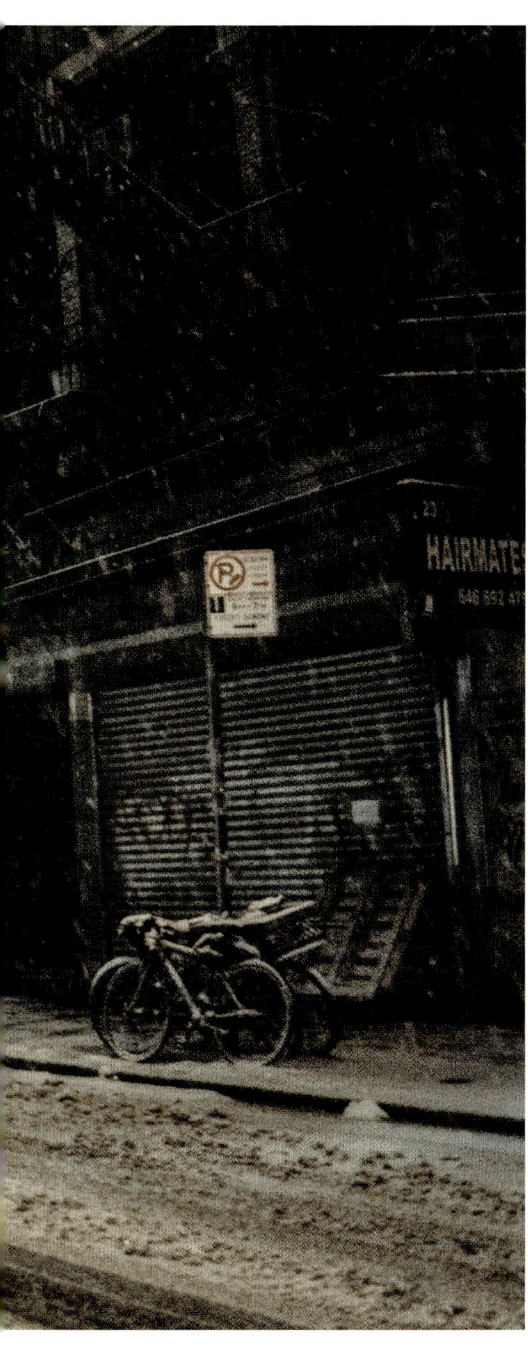

Financial District, Lower Manhattan
Sony SLT-A99V | *ƒ*/3.2 | 1/60 second | ISO 400

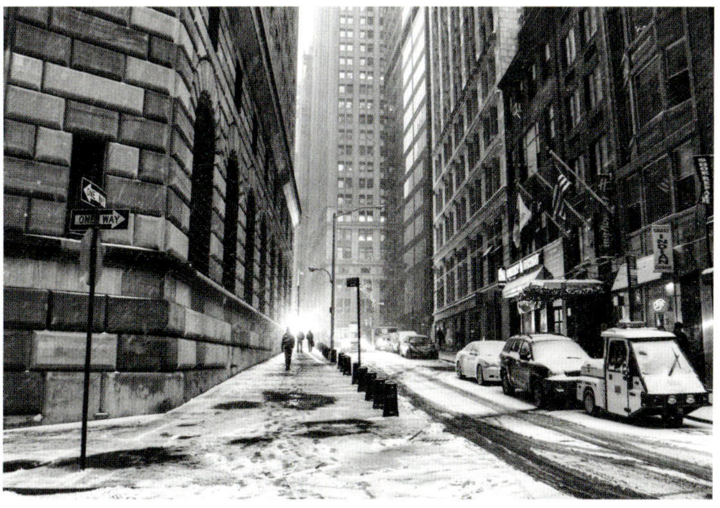

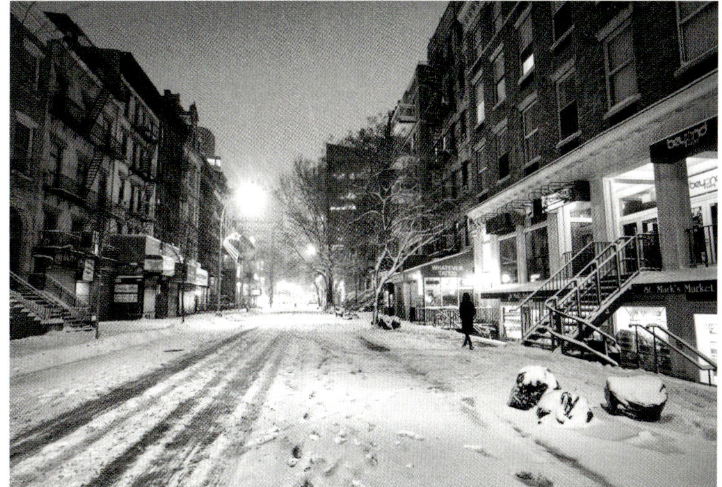

West Village, Lower Manhattan
Sony ILCE-7M2 | *ƒ*/5 | 1/60 second | ISO 4000

Greenwich Village, Lower Manhattan
Sony SLT-A99V | *ƒ*/3.5 | 1/80 second | ISO 4000

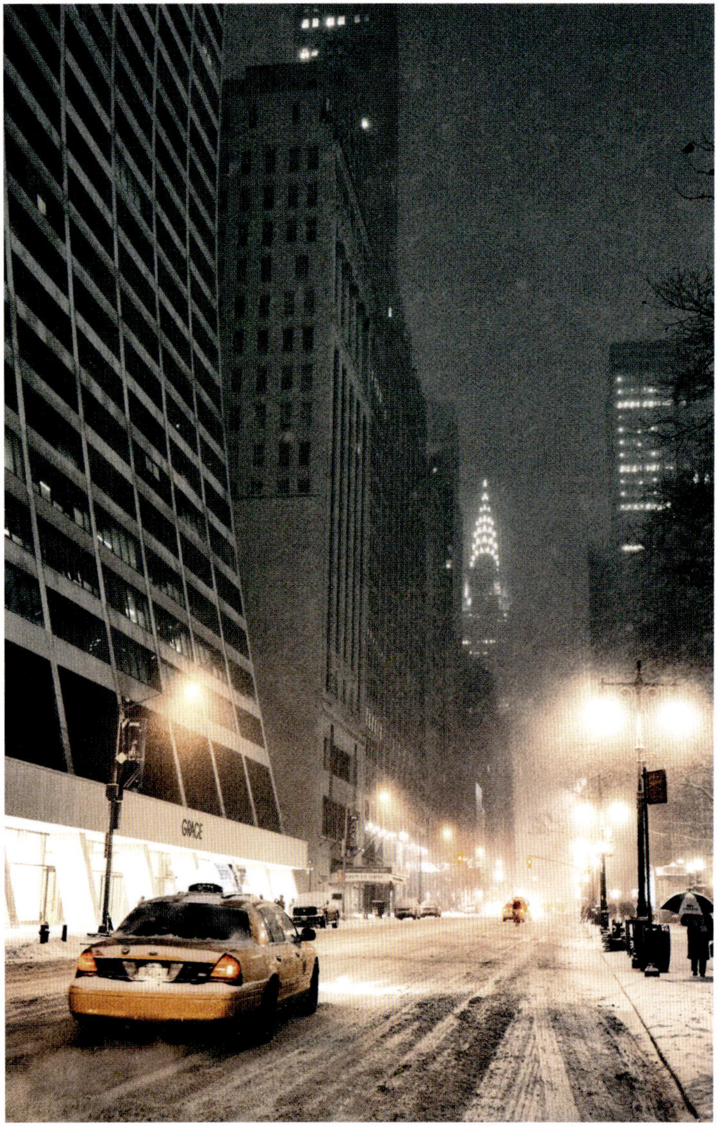

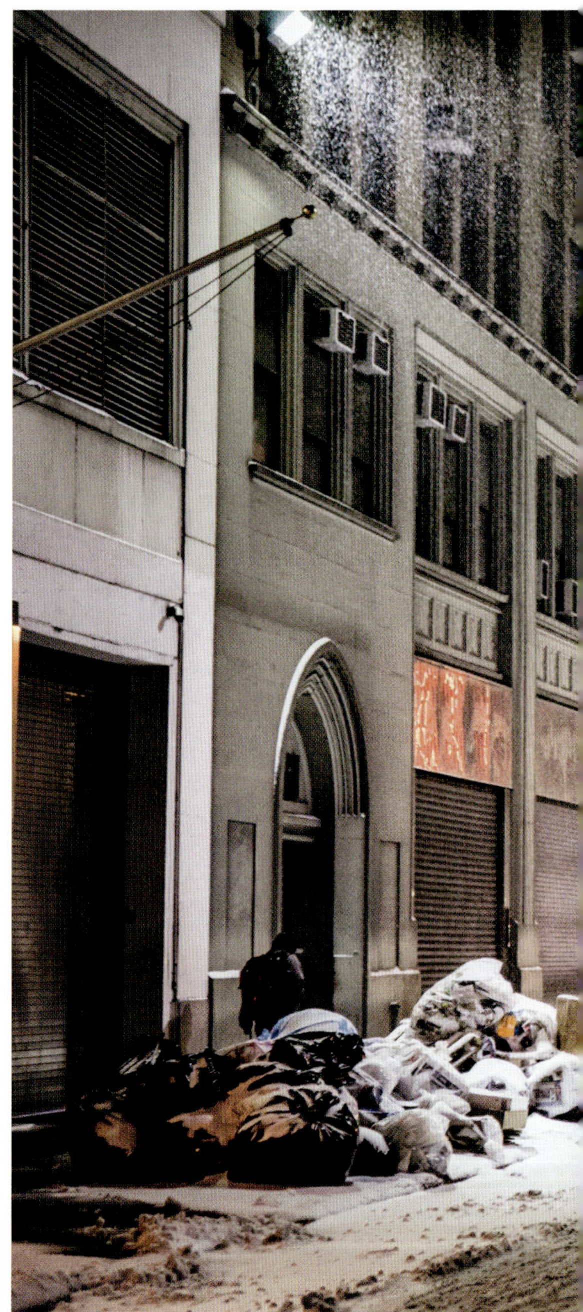

By Bryant Park, Midtown Manhattan
Sony SLT-A99V | ƒ/3.2 | 1/80 second | ISO 4000

Midtown Manhattan
Sony SLT-A99V | ƒ/3.2 | 1/80 second | ISO 4000

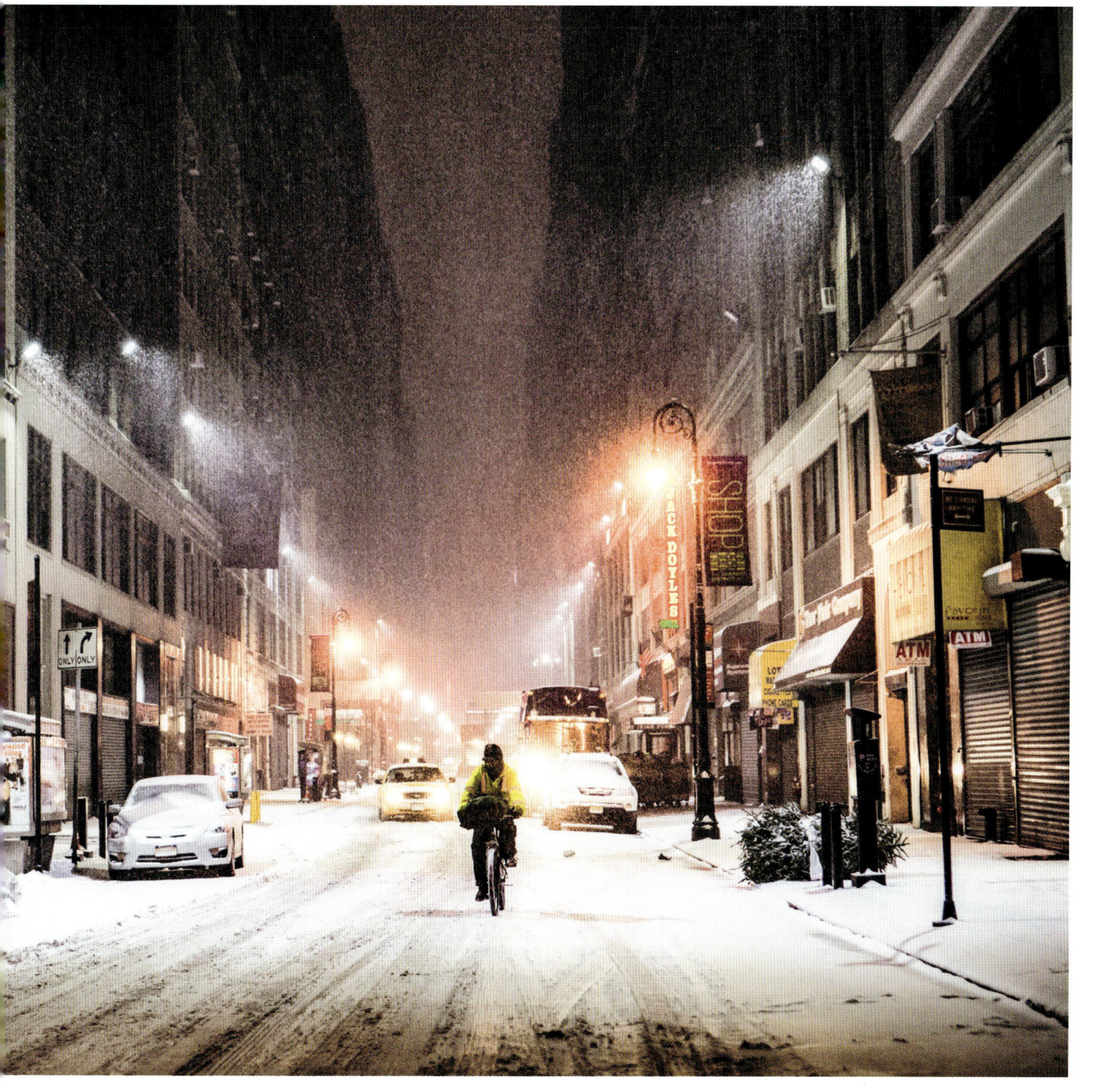
ONLY
ONLY
SHOP
ATM
ATM

Each snowstorm I photograph takes on its own personality. I tend to walk around seven to eight miles each snowstorm, and it's often toward the end of each walk that I find the moments that resonate the most. During this snowstorm I had already walked quite a way and the wind was picking up. I was close to my apartment on the Lower East Side when I passed this theater which is City Cinemas Village East Cinema on 2nd Avenue in the East Village.

I stopped when I passed the theater because it provoked a very visceral reaction. It reminded me of childhood, nostalgia, blissful naiveté of the hard edges of the world. Cinemas are the vehicle where dreams ride alongside imagination. They are where we escape to feel that sense of wonder we exude during childhood.

I knew that I wanted the right person to walk into the scene and in my mind I really wanted someone to cross the street in the distance to add a bit more to the story. I waited about 30 minutes in the driving wind as a handful of people passed by. And then, this person passed with a guitar on their back and I knew they were everything I was looking for: a weaver of stories passing under the marquee of the ultimate imagination vehicle. The bonus was the person crossing the street in the distance.

East Village, Lower Manhattan
Sony SLT-A99V | *f*/3.2 | 1/100 second | ISO 4000

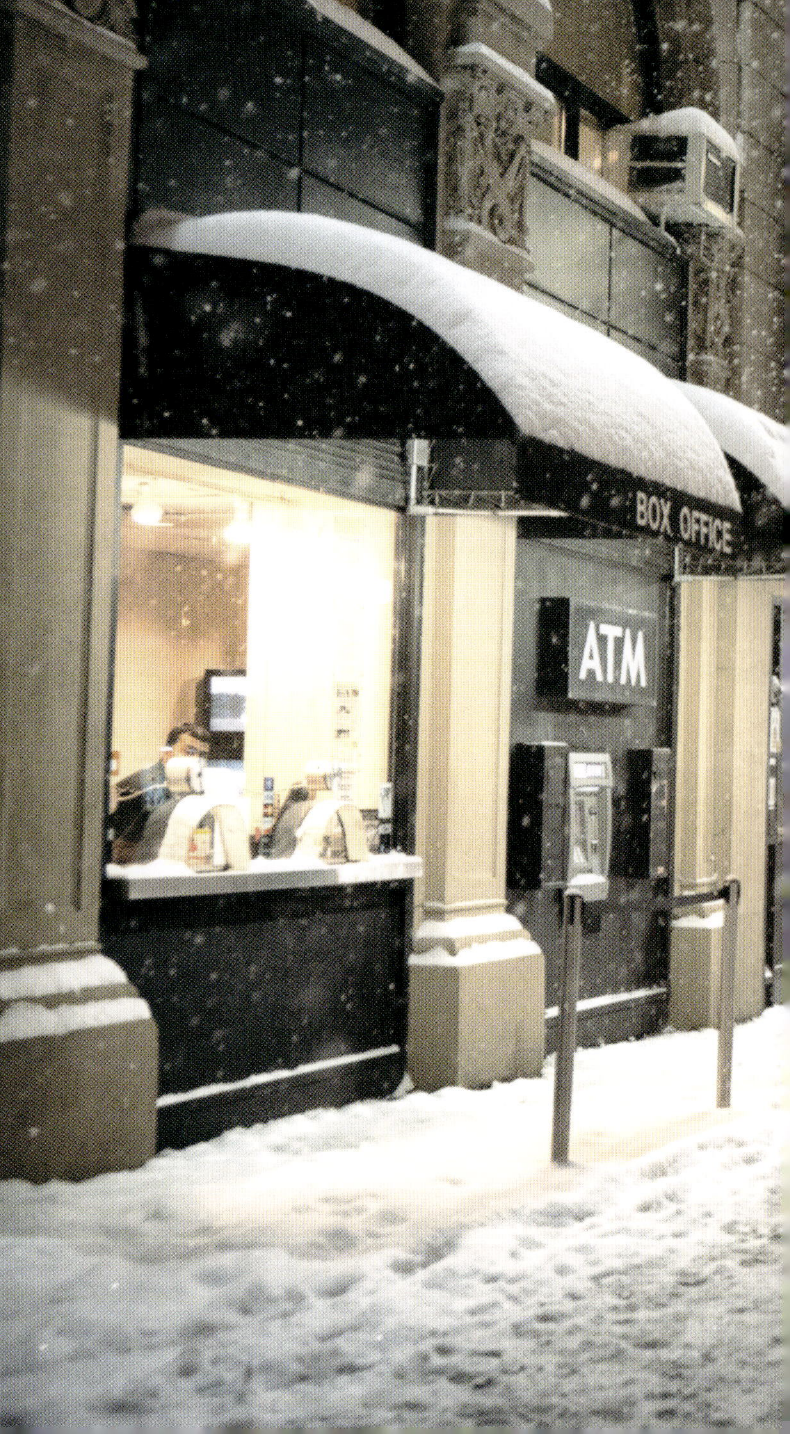

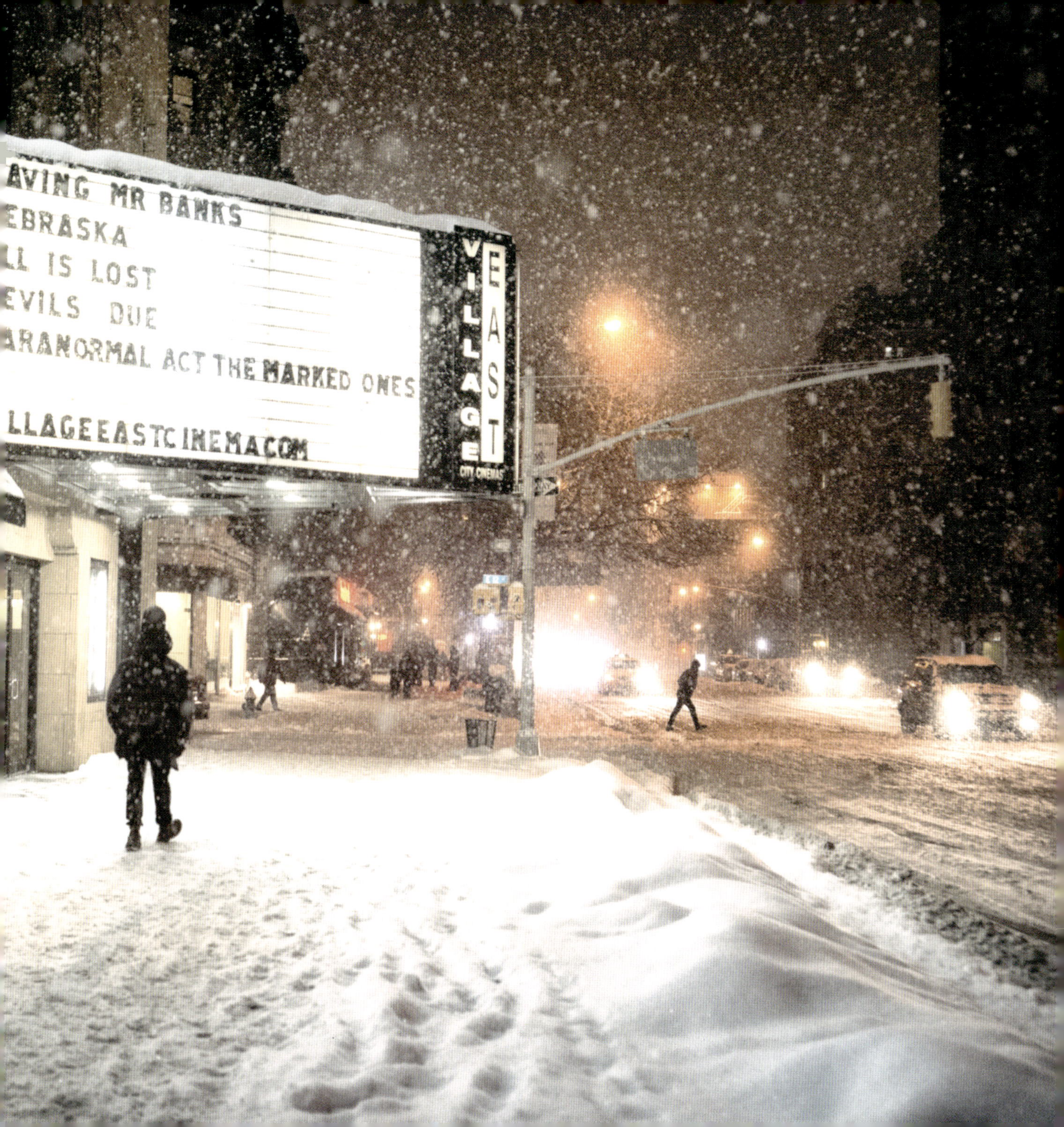
AVING MR BANKS
EBRASKA
LL IS LOST
EVILS DUE
ARANORMAL ACT THE MARKED ONES
LLAGEEASTCINEMACOM
VILLAGE EAST
CITY CINEMAS

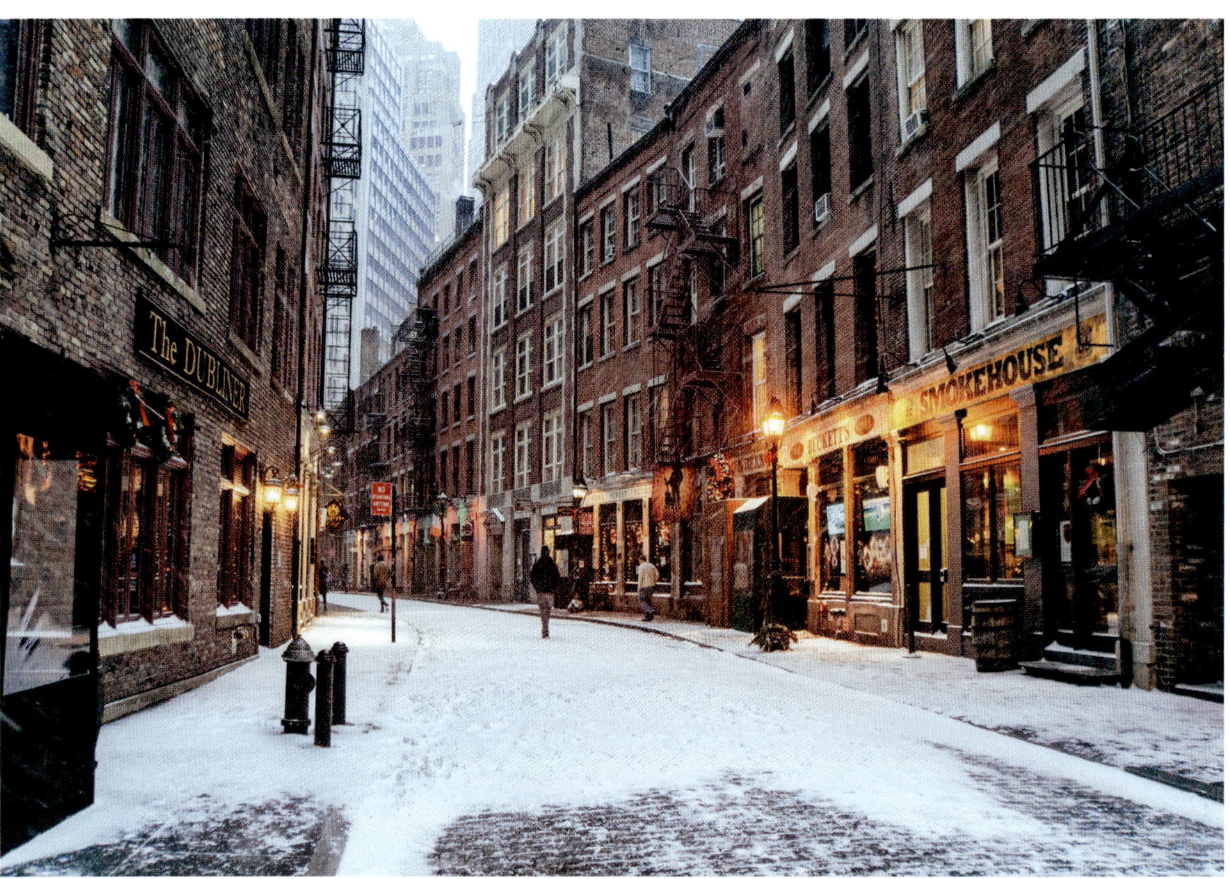

Financial District, Lower Manhattan
Sony NEX-6 | ƒ/5 | 1/60 second | ISO 8400

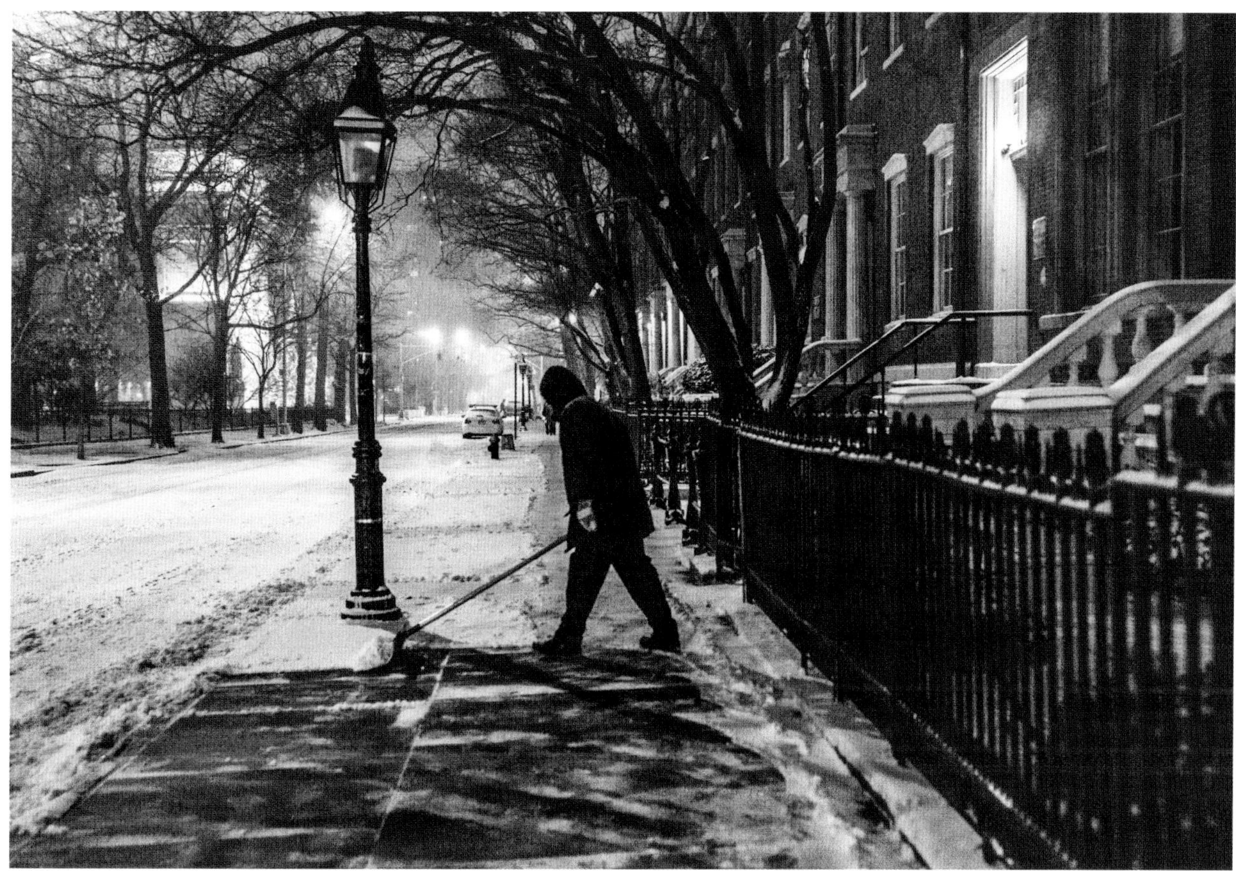

▲ Greenwich Village, Lower Manhattan
Sony SLT-A99V | *f*/3.2 | 1/80 second | ISO 4000

▼ Midtown Manhattan
Sony NEX-7 | *f*/5 | 1/60 second | ISO 200

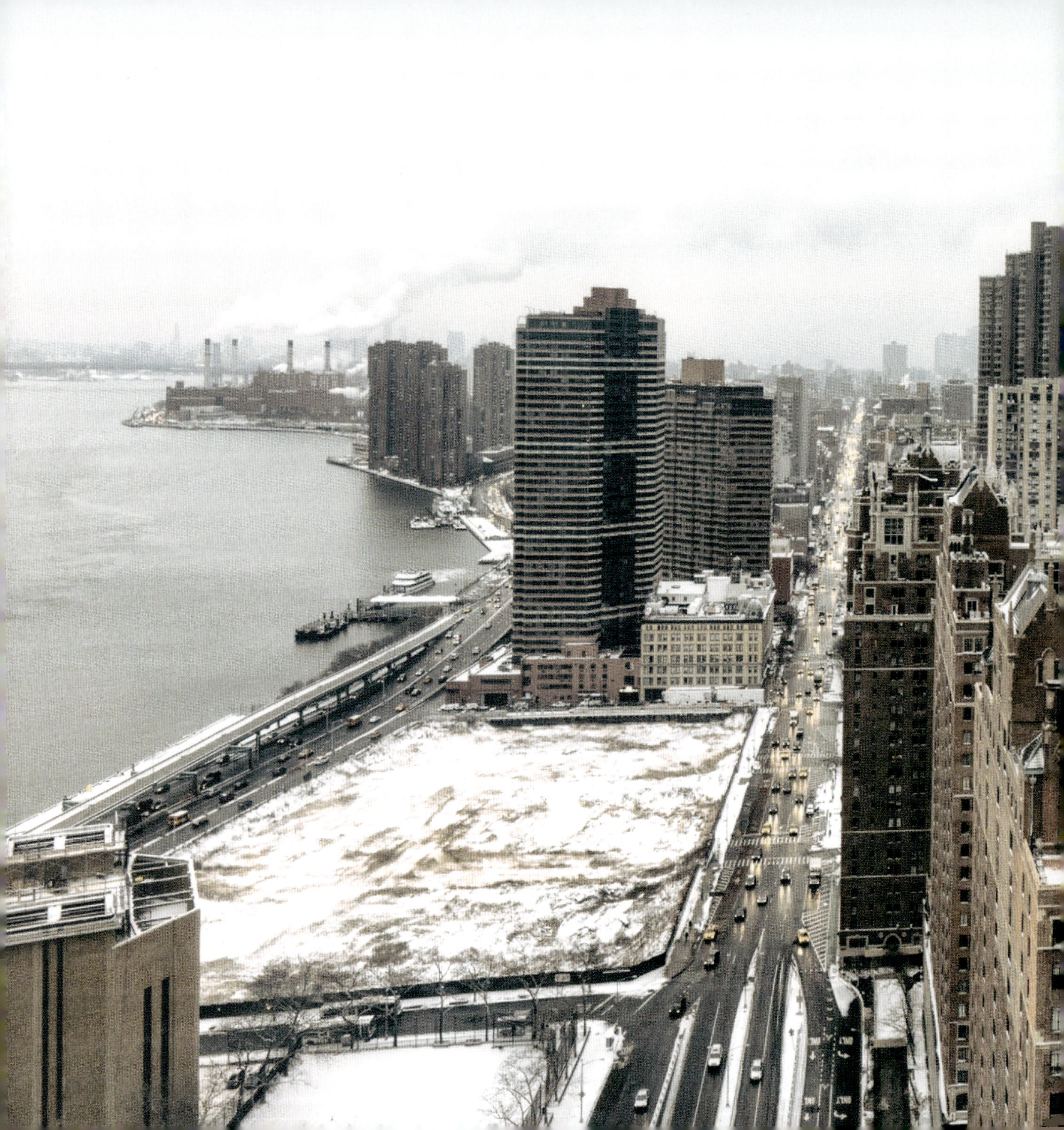

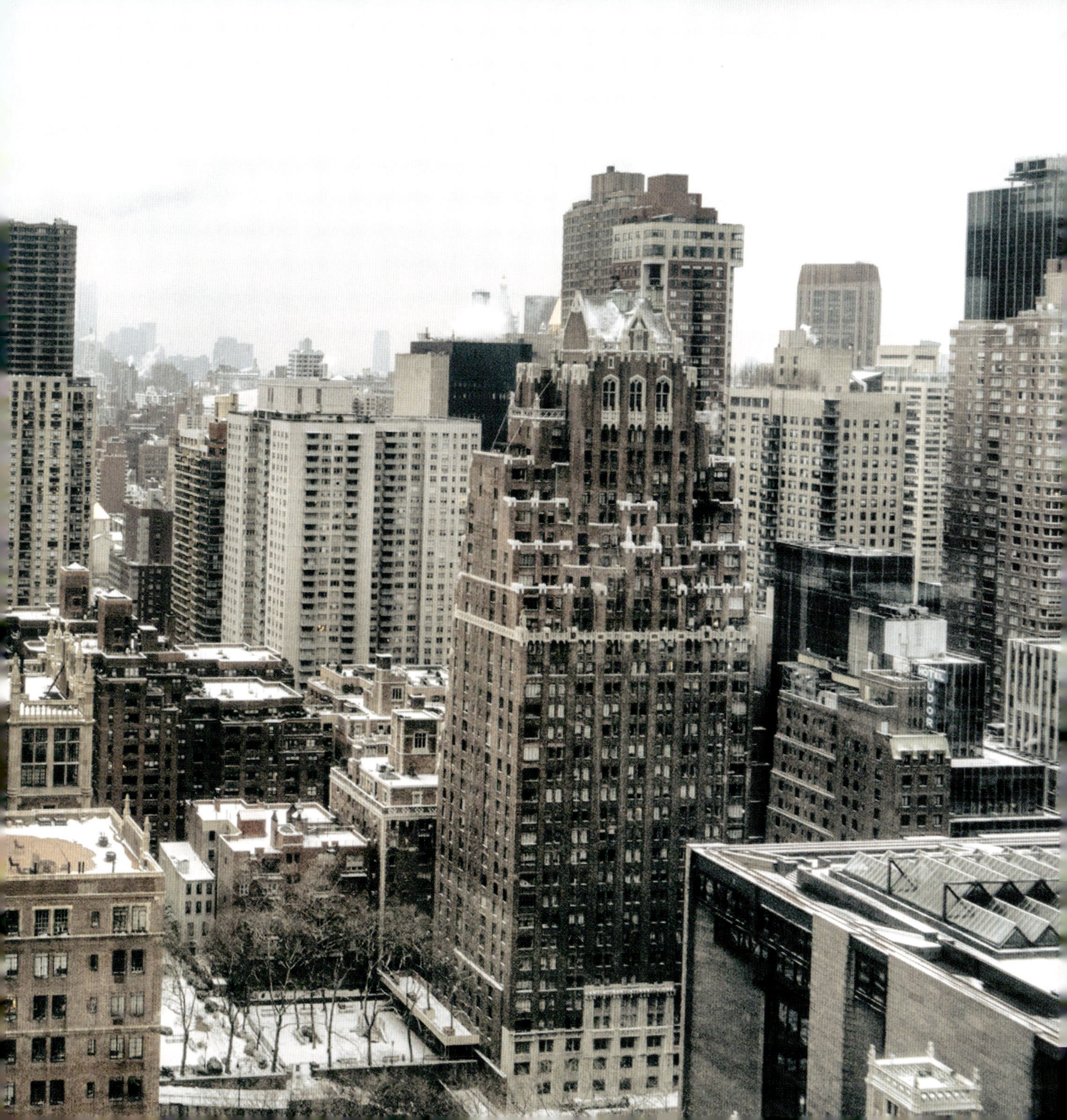
HOTEL
UDOR

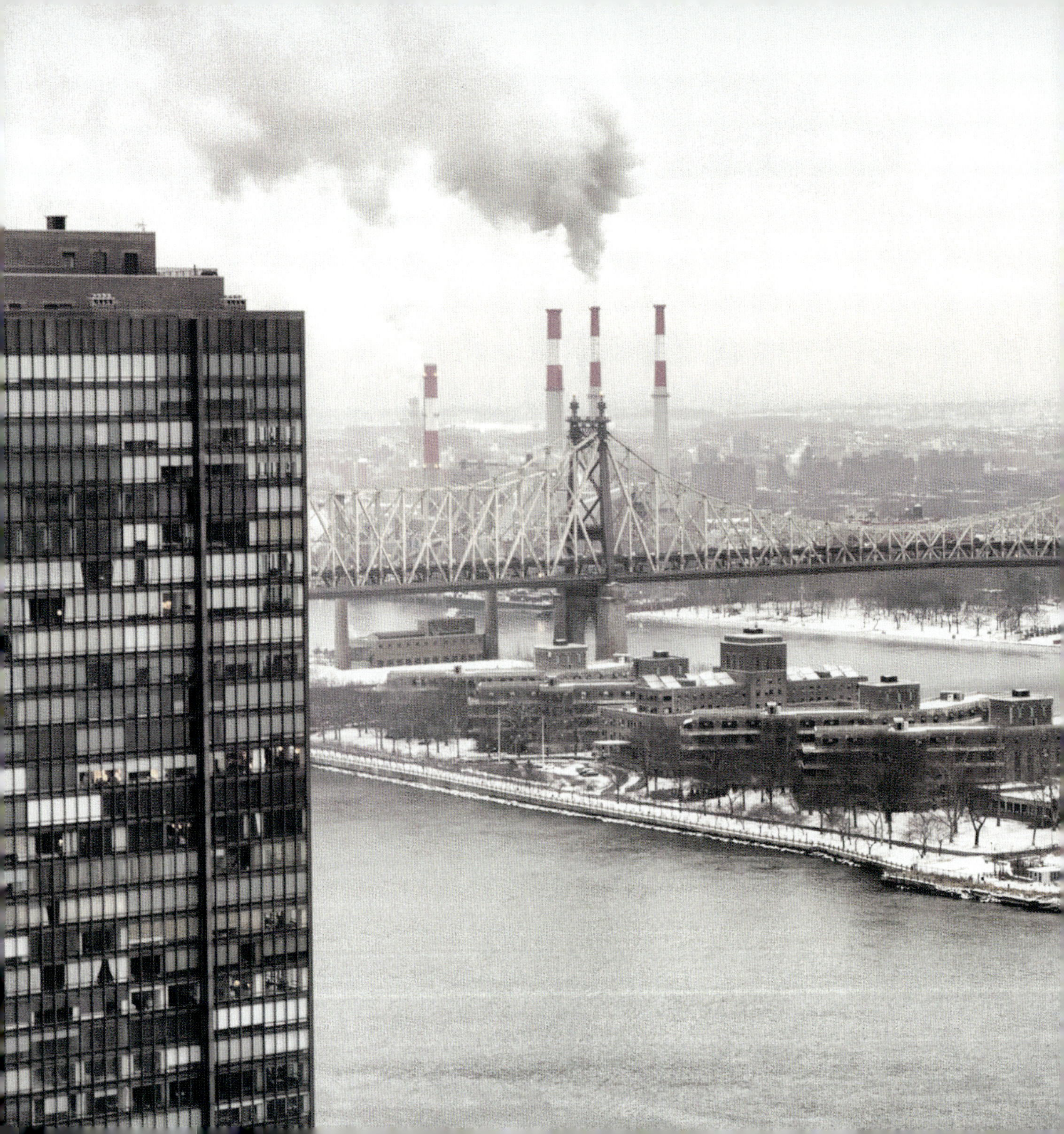

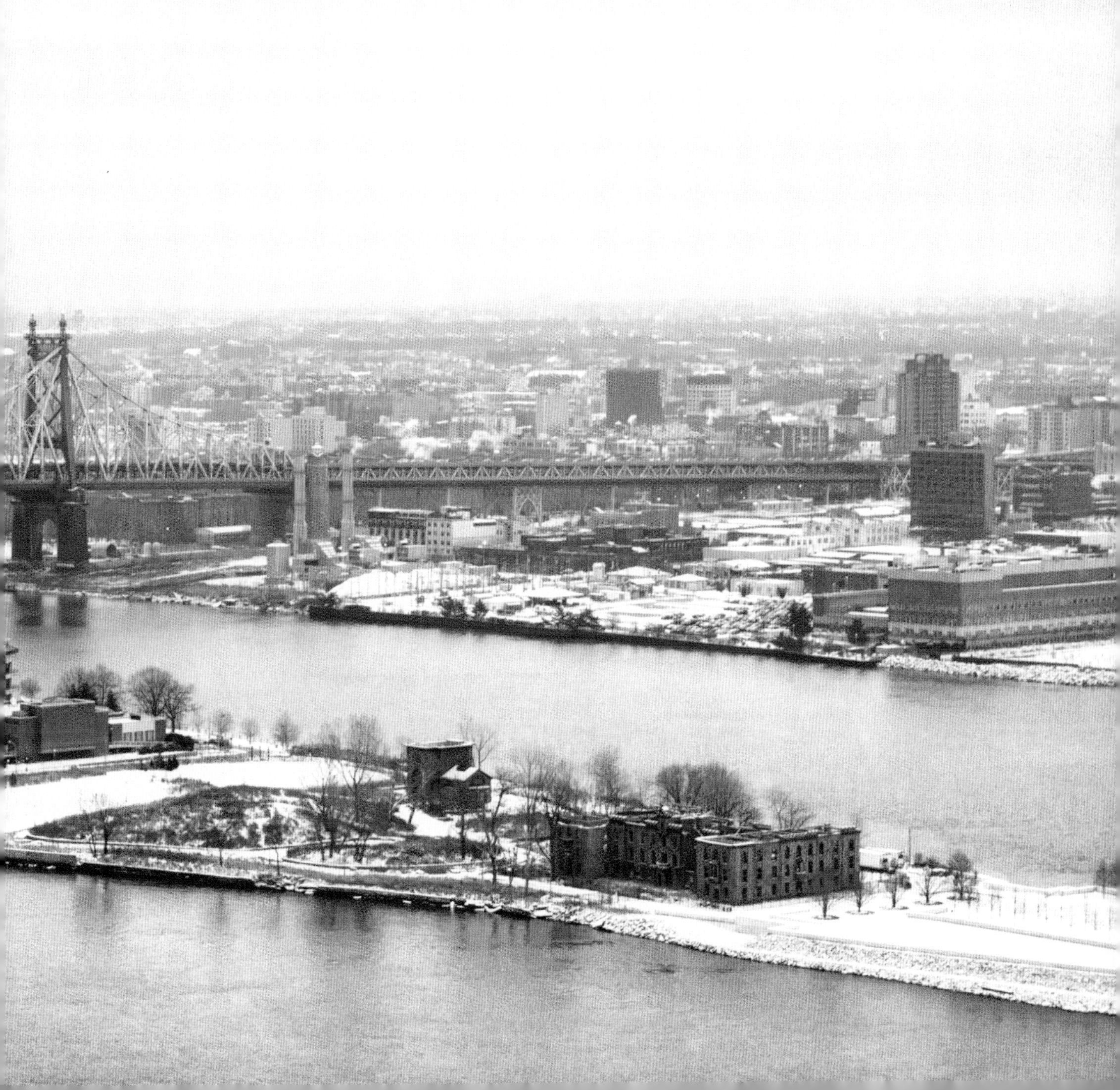

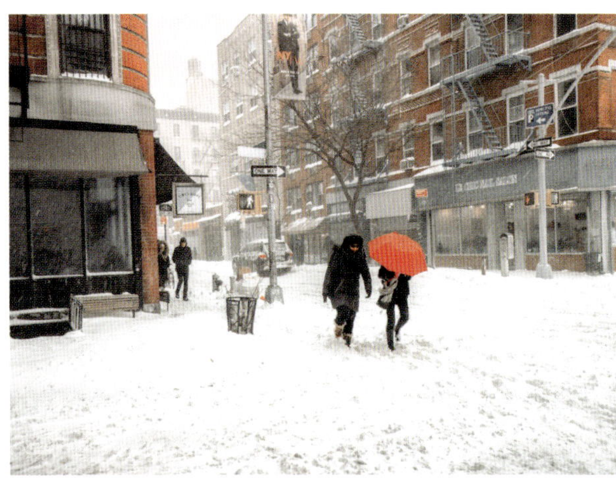

▲ Midtown Manhattan
Sony NEX-7 | ƒ/5 | 1/60 second | ISO 200

◀ Soho, Lower Manhattan
Sony SLT-A99V | ƒ/4.5 | 1/80 second | ISO 400

▼ Lower East Side, Manhattan
Sony ILCE-7RM2 | ƒ/5 | 1/100 second | ISO 200

▶ Upper East Side, Manhattan
Sony SLT-A99V | ƒ/4.5 | 1/80 second | ISO 400

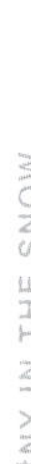

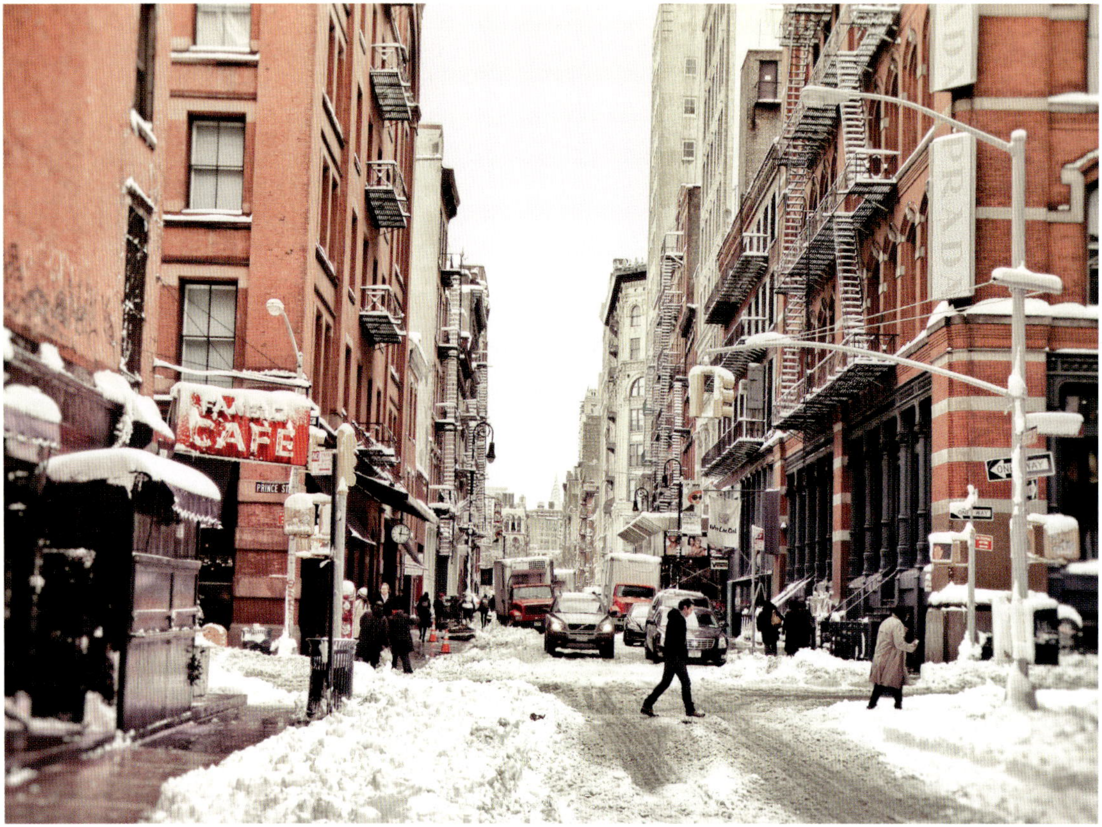

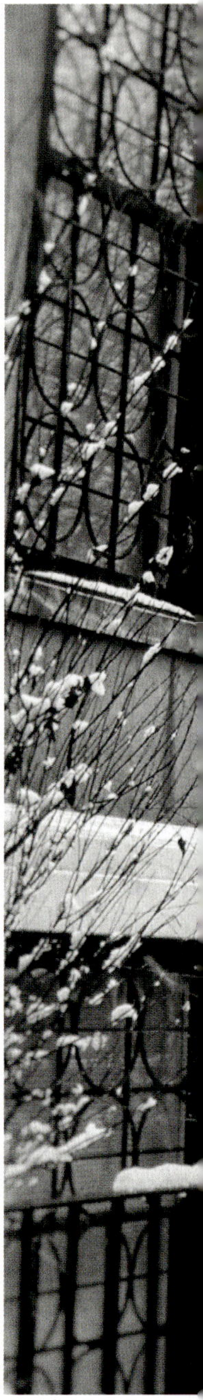

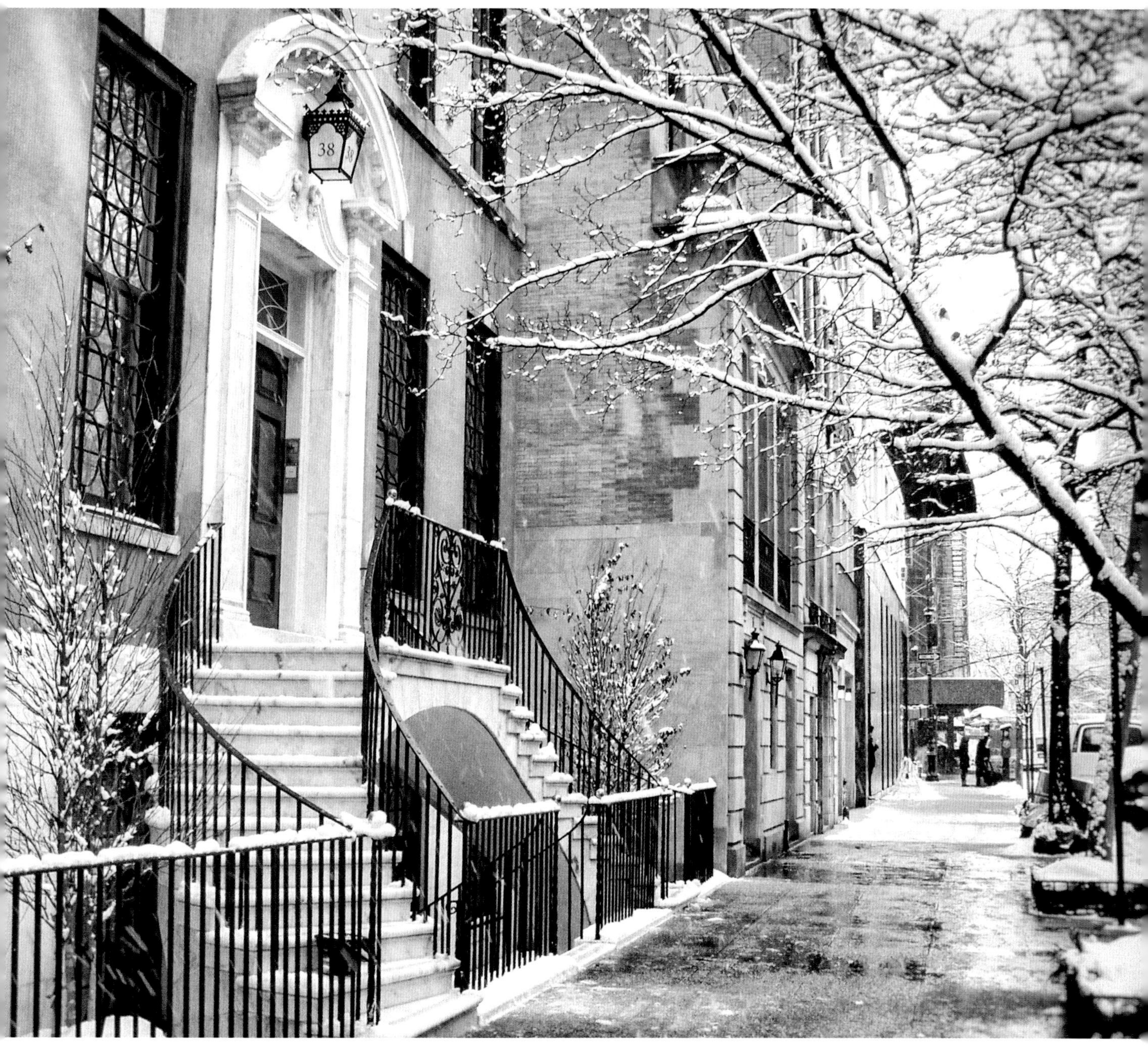
38

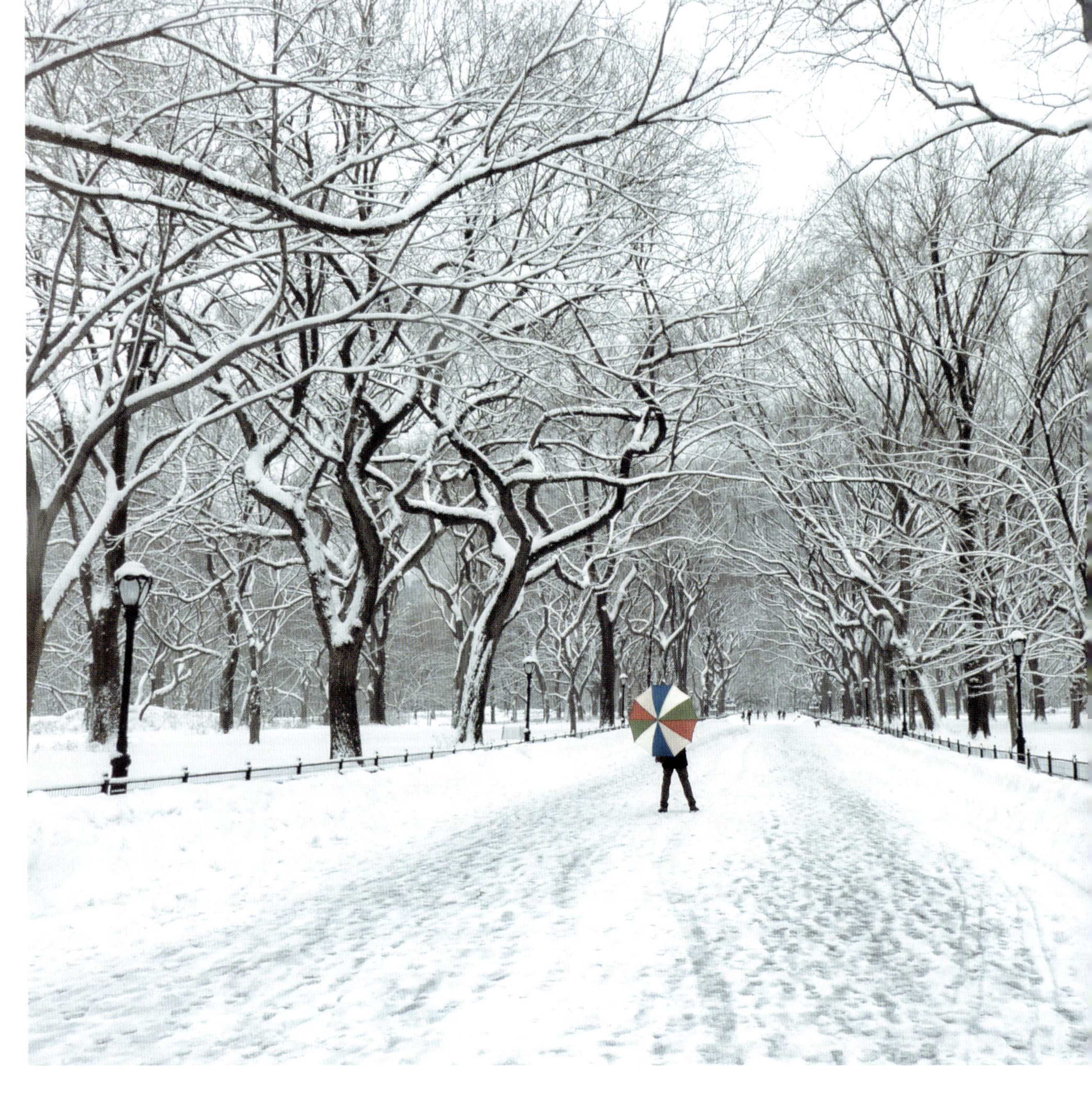

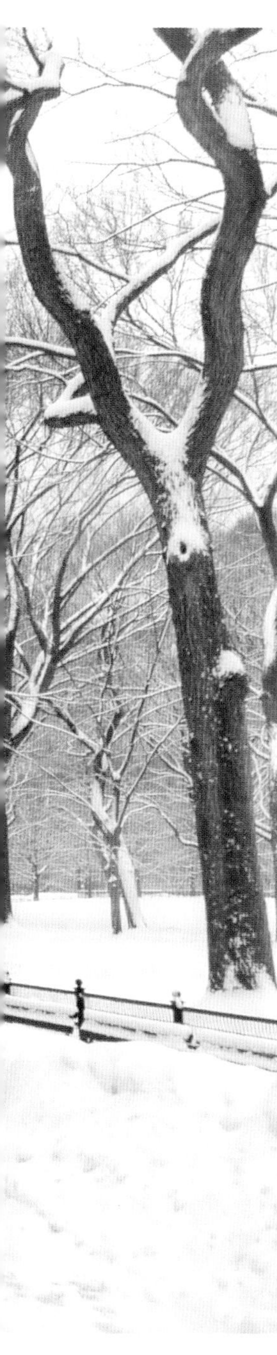

It was the first blizzard I ever photographed, back in 2010–2011. I had no idea what I was doing with my camera and I was underdressed for the storm, but I was having the time of my life climbing around Central Park in winds that were rushing past at 65 miles per hour, and snow that was blowing relentlessly toward me.

I started to get disoriented toward the end of my exploration and stumbled into this (famous) area of the park.

There were barely any people in the park and those who were there were either snow-lovers or curious about storms of such magnitude.

And this man just took a look at me standing there looking wild-eyed and wild-haired, dressed poorly for the weather, and then smiled and took his umbrella, turned around, and proceeded to pose like that for what seemed like an eternity.

I thought he wanted a photo of himself. So, I walked up to him after the photo was taken and asked if he wanted me to email him the photo. He smiled and took a bow without saying anything, and then proceeded to walk off into the storm.

Central Park, Manhattan
Sony SLT-A99V | *f*/5 | 1/60 second | ISO 400

CONCLUSION

Snow is a dream that wraps itself around you.

Winter nights open up their arms to those who walk through city streets strewn with glinting white embers: alabaster sparks left over from clenched-fist hopes that burst from eager palms onward and upward into the sky.

Winter nights are like the feeling you get when you are wrapped in a blanket as memories and scenes from all the other lives you will live and have lived play on the back of your eyelids like a fever-dream cinematic sequence.

Winter nights in New York City wrap themselves around you like a cocoon surrounding you with the sweetest of silences as trees spin their branches like webs over streets held down by the barest hint of gravity.

And we walk through the city like somnambulists moving through an otherworldly landscape: gliding slowly through the white remnants of dream-laden clouds, with our eyes drawn to lights that hang over streets like stars leading the way back to the places we rest our heads.

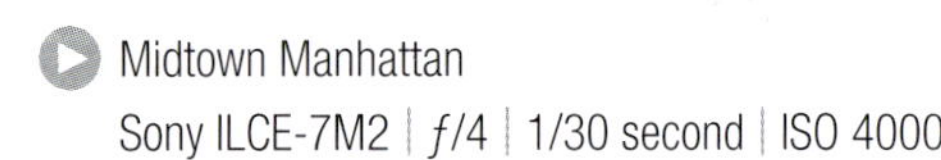

Midtown Manhattan
Sony ILCE-7M2 | f/4 | 1/30 second | ISO 4000

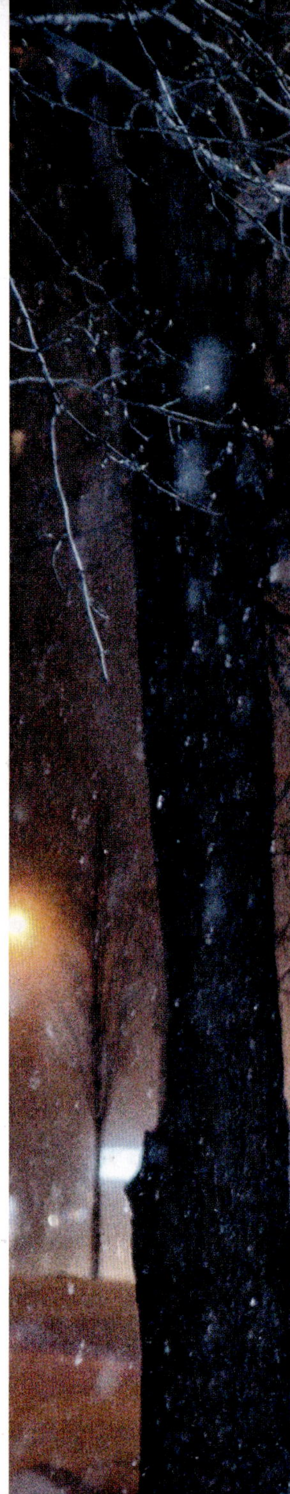

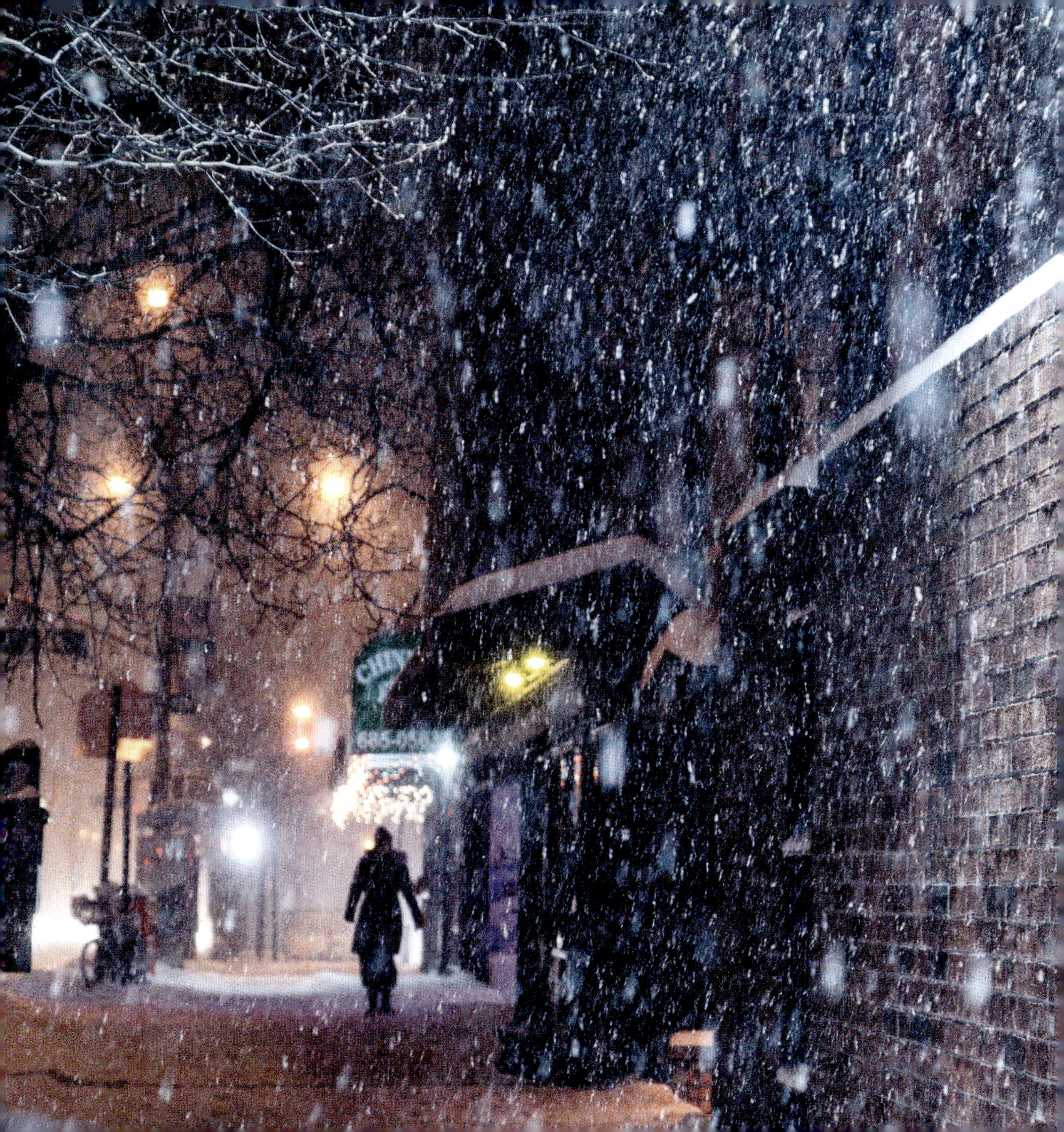

ACKNOWLEDGMENTS

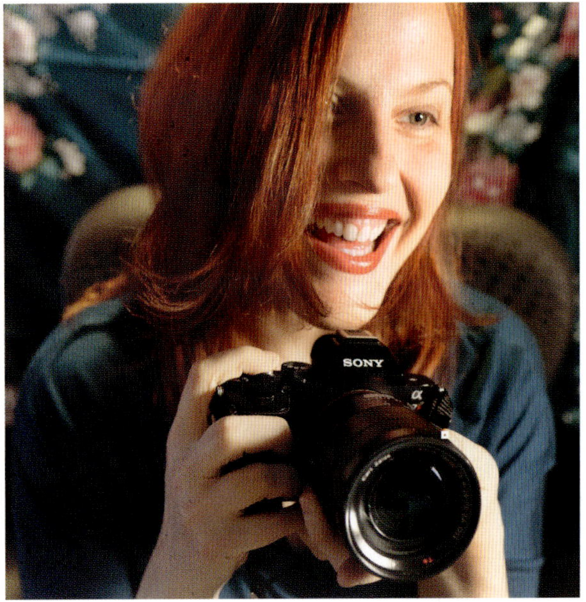

Dedicated to:
Every dreamer out there. Keep dreaming.
Dreams are what make life rich and beautiful.

Thanks to:
Sony for enabling the capturing of my own snowy dream-walking experiences.

Octopus for breathing life into these dream-walks in the form of this book.

And a very special thanks to:
Spencer and Tallulah—My endless gratitude to both of you for your forever support (and endless purrs). Without you both, all of these snow-filled nights would have not been nearly as profound or beautiful.

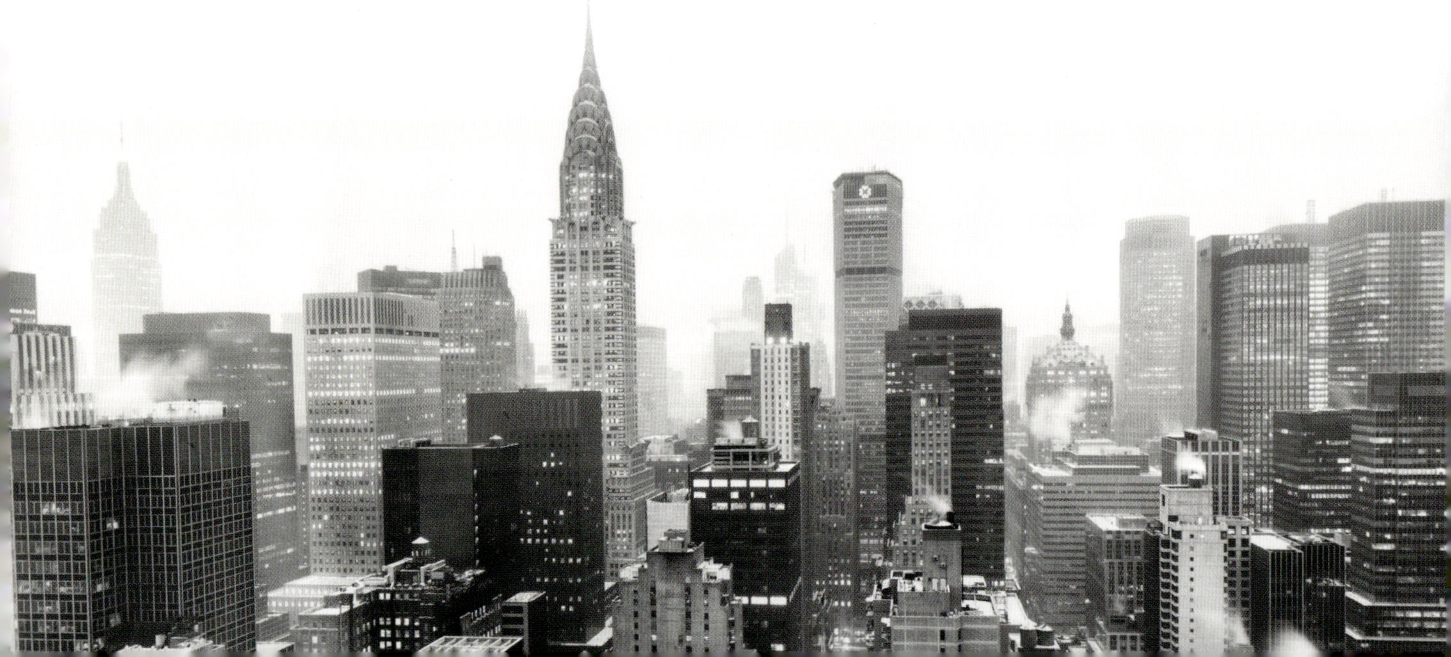